Getting Started With Sage ACT! Pro 2013

By Indera E. Murphy

Tolana Publishing
Teaneck, New Jersey

Getting Started With Sage ACT! Pro 2013

Published By
Tolana Publishing
PO Box 719
Teaneck, NJ 07666 USA

Find us online at www.tolanapublishing.com
Inquiries may be sent to the publisher: tolanapub@yahoo.com

Our books are available online at www.barnesandnoble.com. They can also be ordered from Ingram and Baker & Taylor.

Quantity discounts are available for corporations, non-profit organizations and educational institutions for educational purposes, fundraising or resale. www.tolana.com/wholesale.html

Copyright © 2012 Dr. Indera E. Murphy

All rights reserved. No part of this book may be reproduced or transmitted in any form or by any means, electronic or mechanical, including photocopying, recording, storage in an information retrieval system, or otherwise, without prior written permission from the publisher.

ISBN-13: 978-1-935208-22-8
ISBN-10: 1-935208-22-5

Library of Congress Control Number: 2012950533

Printed and bound in the United States Of America

Notice of Liability
Every effort has been made to ensure that this book contains accurate and current information. However, the publisher and author shall not be liable to any person or entity with respect to any loss or damage caused or alleged to be caused directly or indirectly, as a result of any information contained herein or by the computer software and hardware products described in it.

Trademarks
All companies and product names are trademarks or registered trademarks of their respective companies. They are used in this book in an editorial fashion only. No use of any trademark is intended to convey endorsement or other affiliation with this book.

Cover by Mary Kramer, owner of Milkweed Graphics, www.milkweedgraphics.com

v1.0

Who The Book Is For

This book is for everyone that wants to learn Sage ACT! Pro 2013. People that are upgrading from a previous version of the software will have a refresher of the basics and then learn about the features and options that are new in this version of ACT!.

About The Series

Getting Started With Sage ACT! Pro 2013, is part of the growing series of computer software books that are designed to be used as a self-paced learning tool, in a classroom setting or in an online class. The books in this series contain an abundance of step-by-step instructions and screen shots to help reduce the "stress" often associated with learning new software.

Titles In The Series

Title	ISBN
ACT! 2007	978-0-9773912-5-7
ACT! 2009	978-1-935208-07-5
ACT! 2010	978-1-935208-09-9
ACT! Pro 2011	978-1-935208-13-6
ACT! Pro 2012	978-1-935208-17-4
Sage ACT! Pro 2013	978-1-935208-22-8
Using Crystal Reports 2008 With ACT! 2010 Databases	978-1-935208-10-5
Crystal Reports XI For Beginners (2nd Edition)	978-1-935208-00-6
What's New In Crystal Reports 2008	978-1-935208-01-3
Crystal Reports 2008 For Beginners	978-0-9773912-9-5
Crystal Reports 2011 For Beginners	978-1-935208-15-0
Crystal Reports Beyond The Basics	978-1-935208-18-1
Crystal Reports For Visual Studio 2005	978-0-9773912-6-4
Crystal Reports Basic For Visual Studio 2008	978-0-9773912-8-8
Crystal Reports For Visual Studio 2010	978-1-935208-12-9
Crystal Xcelsius 4.5	978-1-935208-02-0
Xcelsius 2008	978-1-935208-05-1
SAP Crystal Dashboard Design 2011 For Beginners	978-1-935208-11-2
OpenOffice.org 2 Writer	978-0-9773912-4-0
OpenOffice.org 3 Writer	978-1-935208-08-2
Microsoft Office Starter 2010 (Word & Excel)	978-1-935208-14-3
Microsoft PowerPivot For Excel 2010	978-1-935208-16-7
Microsoft Works 7	978-0-9773912-2-6
Microsoft Works 8 & 8.5	978-0-9773912-1-9
Microsoft Works 9	978-0-9773912-7-1
Windows XP	978-0-9773912-0-2

Coming Soon

Crystal Reports For Sage Peachtree Accounting	978-1-935208-19-8
Alpha Five Desktop Applications	978-1-935208-23-5

About The Author

Dr. Indera E. Murphy is an author, educator and IT professional that has over 20 years of experience in the Information Technology field. She has held a variety of positions including technical writer, programmer, consultant, web designer, course developer and project leader. Indera has designed and developed software applications and web sites, as well as, manage technology driven projects in several industries. In addition to being an Executive Director and consultant, as an online adjunct professor, she has taught courses in a variety of areas including project management, technical writing, information processing, Access, HTML, Windows, Excel, Dreamweaver and critical thinking.

Why A Book On Sage ACT! Pro 2013

After reading the brief Users Guide that comes with ACT!, I felt that users, especially new users, would prefer to have more assistance in learning how to get the most out of ACT!. The Users Guide provides a starting point of reference, but often the Users Guide refers you to the Help system to get more information. As a professor and author, I do not feel that flipping through the Help system is the most ideal way to learn how to use a software package.

I know that many books claim to have "step-by-step instructions". If you have tried to follow books that make this claim and you got lost or could not complete a task as instructed, it may not have been your fault. When I decided to write computer books, I vowed to really have step-by-step instructions that actually included every step. This includes steps like which file to open, which menu option to select, when to save a file and more. In my opinion, it is this level of detail that makes a computer book easy to follow.

CONTENTS

GETTING STARTED WITH SAGE ACT! PRO 2013 .... **1-1**
   What Is ACT! And What Can It Do For Me? 1-2
   What Is A Database? 1-6
   Exercise 1.1: First Time Opening ACT! 1-6
   Welcome View 1-6
   ACT! Demo Database 1-7
   Getting Help 1-8
      Feature Tours 1-8
      Online Manuals 1-8
      Request A Feature 1-9
      Setup Assistant Wizard 1-9
   Exercise 1.2: Create A Folder For Your Files 1-10
   What Is The "My Record"? 1-10
   Database Naming Conventions 1-11
   Exercise 1.3: Create A Database 1-11
   Password Protected Databases 1-13
   Open/Share Database Dialog Box 1-15
   Exercise 1.4: How To Make A Copy Of A Database 1-15

ACT! WORKSPACE **2-1**
   Workspace Overview 2-2
      Menu Bar 2-3
      Global Toolbar 2-4
      Navigation Pane 2-4
   Resizing The Top And Bottom Sections Of Detail Views 2-9
   Detail View Tabs 2-10
   Exercise 2.1: View And Modify The Preferences 2-12
      General Tab Preferences 2-12
      Colors & Fonts Tab Preferences 2-13
      Themes 2-14
      Calendar & Scheduling Tab Preferences 2-14
      E-mail & Outlook Sync Tab Preferences 2-15
      ACT! E-mail Editor Tab Preferences 2-16
      Communication Tab Preferences 2-17
      Startup Tab Preferences 2-19
   Exercise 2.2: Select A Database And View To Automatically Open With ACT! 2-20
      Admin Tab Preferences 2-20
      Using The Duplicate Checking Options 2-21
   Exercise 2.3: Viewing Layouts 2-22
   The Views In ACT! 2-22

CREATING AND EDITING CONTACT RECORDS **3-1**
   What Is A Contact? 3-2
   Contact Detail View Toolbar 3-2
   Contact List View Toolbar 3-3
   Difference Between The Enter And Tab Keys 3-3
   Exercise 3.1: Creating A New Contact Record 3-3
   The Notes Tab 3-6

How To Attach A File To A Contact Record 3-9
Attaching Files On The Documents Tab 3-11
Relationships 3-11
Entering Information On The Personal Info Tab 3-13
Contact Access Tab 3-14
Latest Activities Tab 3-15
User Fields Tab 3-15
Exercise 3.2: Duplicating Contact Information 3-15
    Creating A New Contact Based On The Primary Fields 3-16

FINDING CONTACTS IN A DATABASE 4-1
Finding Records 4-2
Exercise 4.1: Using The Lookup Options On The Navigation Pane 4-2
Exercise 4.2: Using The Lookup Command 4-3
Exercise 4.3: Using Keyword Search Lookups 4-4
Exercise 4.4: How To Create A Lookup Using Multiple Fields 4-6
Exercise 4.5: Using The Add To Lookup Option 4-7
Universal Search 4-8
Exercise 4.6: Find Contacts Without An Email Address 4-8
Exercise 4.7: Finding Contacts That You Added To The Database 4-9
Exercise 4.8: Lookup Annual Events 4-10
Contact Activity Lookup 4-11
Exercise 4.9: Find Contacts That Have Not Been Updated 4-11
Exercise 4.10: How To Modify Several Records At The Same Time 4-13
Exercise 4.11: How To Delete Data From Several Records At The Same Time 4-14
Using The Contact List View 4-14
    Sorting By Columns In The Contact List View 4-15
    View Detail Information From The Contact List View 4-15
    How To Select And View Specific Records 4-15
Exercise 4.12: Sorting Records 4-16
Exercise 4.13: How To Delete Contacts From The Database 4-17
View The My Record 4-18

CREATING COMPANY AND DIVISION RECORDS 5-1
Company And Division Records Overview 5-2
Company vs Group Records 5-3
Company Detail View Toolbar 5-3
Companies Tree 5-4
Exercise 5.1: Create New Contact Records 5-4
Exercise 5.2: Create A Company Record 5-5
Exercise 5.3: Create Divisions For A Company 5-5
Exercise 5.4: Associate A Contact To A Company Record 5-6
Exercise 5.5: Create A Company Record From A Contact Record 5-8
Exercise 5.6: Create A Contact Record From A Company Record 5-9
Refreshing Linked Data In Contact Records 5-9
Linking Company And Contact Records 5-9
Associate vs Linking 5-10
Associating Companies And Groups 5-11
Exercise 5.7: Creating Manual Links Between Contacts And Companies 5-11
Exercise 5.8: Link Multiple Contact Records To A Company Record 5-12
Exercise 5.9: Understanding The Power Of Linking 5-12
Linking And Unlinking Contact And Company Fields 5-12
Exercise 5.10: Create A Linked Billing Address Field 5-13

Billing And Shipping Tab	5-14
Updating Contact Address Fields From The Linked Company Record	5-14
Exercise 5.11: Test The Linked Field That You Created	5-15
Company Profile Tab	5-15
Company Access Tab	5-16
Unlink A Company Record Field	5-16
Adding Contacts To Divisions	5-16
Exercise 5.12: Using The Companies Tree To Move A Division	5-17
Exercise 5.13: Duplicating Company And Division Records	5-17
Exercise 5.14: Finding Companies	5-18
Create A Company Note And Attachment	5-18
Viewing Company Notes	5-18
Moving Companies And Divisions	5-19
Removing Links Between Contact And Company Records	5-19
Using The Company List View	5-21

GROUPING CONTACTS 6-1

Groups Overview	6-2
Group Detail View Toolbar	6-2
Groups Tree	6-3
Exercise 6.1: How To Create A Group	6-4
Exercise 6.2: How To Add Contacts One By One To A Group	6-5
Exercise 6.3: Finding Group Records	6-6
Exercise 6.4: How To Rename A Group	6-6
Exercise 6.5: Add Contacts To An Existing Group	6-7
Exercise 6.6: Use The Lookup Command To Add Contacts To A Group	6-8
Exercise 6.7: How To Manage Group Notes And Attachments	6-9
How To Create A Group Note And Attach A File To The Group Note	6-9
Exercise 6.8: Assign A Contact Note To A Group And Individual Contacts	6-10
Exercise 6.9: How To Save The Result Of A Lookup As A Group Or Company	6-13
Subgroups	6-14
Exercise 6.10: Creating Subgroups	6-14
Exercise 6.11: Moving Contact Records Between Groups And Subgroups	6-15
Deleting Groups Or Subgroups	6-17
Removing Contacts That Are Not Linked From Companies Or Groups	6-17
Exercise 6.12: Using The Convert Groups To Companies Wizard	6-18
Group Address Tab	6-20
Group Access Tab	6-20
Group List View	6-21

SCHEDULING ACTIVITIES 7-1

Activities Overview	7-2
Activity Types	7-5
Timeless Activities	7-5
Public Or Private Activities	7-5
Exercise 7.1: How To Schedule A To-Do Activity	7-6
How To Schedule An Activity For A New Contact	7-7
How To Add A New Contact To An Activity From The Schedule Activity Dialog Box	7-7
How To Select Multiple Contacts	7-7
Send Invitation E-Mail Option	7-9
Viewing An Activity With Multiple Contacts	7-9
Exercise 7.2: Scheduling Activities For Other Users	7-10

Exercise 7.3: Using The Alarm 7-10
Exercise 7.4: Rescheduling An Activity 7-12
Exercise 7.5: Handling Activity Conflicts 7-13
Exercise 7.6: Group Activities 7-14
Recurring Activities 7-15
Exercise 7.7: How To Schedule Recurring Activities 7-16
Exercise 7.8: How To Schedule Random Activities 7-17
Scheduling An Activity For The Last Workday Of The Month 7-18
Deleting Recurring Activities 7-19
Exercise 7.9: How To Clear All Future Recurring Activities 7-19
Exercise 7.10: How To Clear A Single Recurring Activity 7-19
Clearing Activities 7-20
Exercise 7.11: Clear An Activity For A Contact 7-20
Exercise 7.12: Clear An Activity For A Group 7-21
Exercise 7.13: How To Filter Activities 7-22
Exercise 7.14: How To Delete An Activity 7-22
Activity Series 7-22
Exercise 7.15: Create An Activity Series 7-23
Exercise 7.16: How To Edit An Activity Series 7-26

RUNNING REPORTS 8-1
Reports Overview 8-2
Define Filters Dialog Box 8-2
Exercise 8.1: The Contact Report 8-3
Report Print Preview Toolbar 8-5
The Contact Directory Report 8-7
Exercise 8.2: The Phone List Report 8-7
Exercise 8.3: The Activities Report 8-8
How To Create A Custom Date Range 8-8
Exercise 8.4: The Group Membership Report 8-9
Exercise 8.5: The Company Comprehensive Report 8-10
Other Reports 8-10
Source Of Referrals Report 8-11
Notes/History Report 8-11
Reports View 8-11
Reports View Toolbar 8-12
Printing In ACT! 8-12
Exercise 8.6: How To Print Labels 8-12
Exercise 8.7: How To Print Envelopes 8-14
Exercise 8.8: How To Create And Print An Address Book 8-15
Exercise 8.9: Using The Quick Print Options 8-17

WRAP UP OF THE BASICS 9-1
Wrap Up Overview 9-2
Understanding The ID/Status And Referred By Fields 9-2
Why Are Drop-Down Lists Important? 9-3
Exercise 9.1: Tagging Contacts 9-3
Using The Omit Selected Option 9-5
Copying Data From One Field To Another 9-5
Exercise 9.2: How To Copy Data 9-5
Exercise 9.3: How To Swap Data 9-6
What Are Supplemental Files? 9-7
What Are Secondary Contacts And Why Should I Use Them? 9-7

Exercise 9.4: Entering Information On The Secondary Contacts Tab 9-7
Exercise 9.5: Promoting A Secondary Contact 9-8
Deleting A Secondary Contact 9-9
Notes Tab 9-9
    Attaching A Document To An Existing Note 9-10
    How To Copy A Note From One Contact Record To Another 9-10
Editing A Shared Note 9-10
Filtering Notes 9-10
History Tab 9-11
    Automatic Additions To The History Tab 9-11
    Finding Records On The History Tab 9-12
    The Dates Field 9-12
    History Record Types 9-12
    Select Users Button 9-13
Using The New History Tool 9-13
    How To Create A History Record For Multiple Contacts 9-13
    How To Edit History Records 9-13
    How To Edit A History Record Associated With Multiple Contacts 9-14
Preventing History Records From Being Deleted 9-14
Documents Tab 9-14
Record Creation Options 9-16
Web Info Tab 9-16
Marketing Results Tab 9-17
Exercise 9.6: Export Contact Data To Excel 9-17
Adding Graphics To ACT! Notes 9-18
How To Edit Attachments 9-18
Using The Scratchpad 9-18

OPPORTUNITIES 10-1
What Is An Opportunity? 10-2
Opportunity Detail View 10-2
    Opportunity Detail View Tabs 10-2
    Opportunity Detail View Toolbar 10-4
Opportunity List View 10-4
    Opportunity List View Toolbar 10-4
    Using The Opportunity List Filters 10-5
    Status Bar 10-6
    Opportunity List View Shortcut Menu 10-6
Exercise 10.1: Create An Opportunity 10-7
What Is A Process List? 10-9
Select The Products And Services For The Opportunity 10-10
Exercise 10.2: Schedule A Follow Up Activity For The Opportunity 10-12
Exercise 10.3: Edit The Product List 10-12
Exercise 10.4: How To Associate An Opportunity To A Company 10-13
Exercise 10.5: Lookup Opportunities 10-13
How To Close An Opportunity 10-15
Exercise 10.6: Export Opportunities To Excel 10-16
Crash Course In Pivot Table Data 10-17
Generating Quotes 10-18
Exercise 10.7: Create A Quote 10-19
Exercise 10.8: How To Change The Status Of An Opportunity 10-20
Viewing Opportunities From The Opportunities Tab 10-20

Opportunity Reports 10-20
   Exercise 10.9: Sales Analysis By Record Manager Report 10-21
   Exercise 10.10: Opportunities Adjusted For Probability Report 10-21
Opportunity Graphs And Pipelines 10-22
   Exercise 10.11: Creating Graphs 10-22
      Create A Bar Graph 10-22
      Create A Line Graph 10-24
Pipelines 10-25
   Exercise 10.12: Create A Pipeline Graph 10-25
How To Create And Customize Product And Process Lists 10-26
   Exercise 10.13: Creating Process Lists And Stages 10-27
   Exercise 10.14: Importing Stages 10-27
   Exercise 10.15: Exporting Stages 10-28
   Exercise 10.16: Importing Products 10-28
   Exercise 10.17: Exporting Products 10-30

USING THE TASK LIST AND CALENDAR 11-1
Task List View 11-2
   Toolbar 11-2
   Status Bar 11-2
   Filter Options 11-3
   Options Button 11-3
Exercise 11.1: Create A Task List Lookup Using Filters 11-3
Exercise 11.2: Clearing Tasks From The Task List View 11-4
How To Print The Task List 11-5
Looking Up Records On The Task List 11-5
Customizing The Task List View 11-6
Calendar Preferences 11-7
Calendar Views 11-7
   Calendar Toolbar 11-7
   Mini-Calendar 11-7
   Daily Calendar 11-9
   Calendar Pop-Ups 11-10
   Today (Calendar) Button 11-10
   Work Week Calendar 11-10
   Weekly Calendar 11-10
   Monthly Calendar 11-11
   Status Bar 11-12
   Filtering Activities In A Calendar View 11-12
Using The Calendar To Schedule Activities 11-12
Exercise 11.3: Granting Calendar Access 11-13
Viewing Other Users Calendars 11-14
Exercise 11.4: Printing Calendars 11-14

DASHBOARDS 12-1
What Is A Dashboard? 12-2
Dashboard Layouts 12-2
Dashboard Toolbar 12-4
Exercise 12.1: Selecting A Dashboard Layout 12-5
Dashboard Components 12-5
   Activity Components 12-5
   Opportunity Components 12-5
Activity Component Shortcut Menu Options 12-6

Opportunity Component Shortcut Menu Options..12-6
Filtering Data In A Dashboard 12-7
Exercise 12.2: Filtering Activity Component Data..12-7
    My Schedule At-A-Glance Filter Component Options..12-7
    Activities By Type Filter Component Options..12-8
Activity List Filter Options 12-8
Exercise 12.3: Filtering Opportunity Component Data..12-8
Administrative Dashboard 12-9
Dashboard Designer 12-9
Exercise 12.4: Modify The ACT! Activities Dashboard Layout..12-12
Exercise 12.5: Modify The ACT! Default Dashboard Layout 12-13
Component Configuration Wizard 12-14
    Step 1: Select Display Type 12-14
    Step 2: Edit Default Filters..12-14
    Step 3: Edit Header/Footer 12-15
    Step 4: Change Legend 12-16
    Step 5: Change Totals..12-16
    Step 6: Specify Targets 12-16
    Step 7: Scale/Limits 12-17
Top Opportunities Component 12-18
Exercise 12.6: Modify The Components Of The My Default Dashboard 12-18
    Modify The My Activities Component Filter Options 12-18
    Modify The Closed Sales To Date Component Filter Options 12-19
Create A New Dashboard 12-20
Data Chart Component 12-20

CREATING QUERIES 13-1
Queries Overview..13-2
Exercise 13.1: Creating Queries Using The Lookup By Example Tool 13-2
Saving Lookup By Example Queries 13-3
Wildcards 13-4
Exercise 13.2: How To Run A Saved Query 13-4
    How To Run A Query From The Advanced Query Window 13-5
Advanced Queries 13-5
Exercise 13.3: How To Create An Advanced Query 13-7
Exercise 13.4: Find Records Created In The Last 30 Days Query 13-9
Exercise 13.5: Find Contacts In CA With Open Opportunities 13-10
How To Edit A Query 13-10
Exercise 13.6: Sorting Records Retrieved From A Query 13-11
Dynamically Linking Contacts To Companies 13-11
Exercise 13.7: Find Prospects Query...13-11
Exercise 13.8: How To Create A Dynamic Group 13-12

USING SMART TASKS 14-1
Smart Tasks Overview..14-2
Managing Smart Tasks 14-2
    Workflow...14-2
    Available Steps 14-3
Exercise 14.1: Duplicate And Modify A Smart Task Template 14-4
    Step 1: Duplicate The Template...14-4
    Step 2: Modify The Template...14-4
    Step 3: Modify The Filter Criteria 14-5

Step 4: Add, Edit And Delete Steps	14-6
Step 5: Enable Auto-Run	14-7
Running A Smart Task Manually	14-7
Viewing And Editing Pending Smart Tasks	14-8
Exercise 14.2: Create A Smart Task Template	14-9

CUSTOMIZING ACT! 15-1

Why Waiting To Customize ACT! Is A Good Idea	15-2
Modifying Preferences	15-2
Name And Salutation Preferences	15-2
Exercise 15.1: Calendar Preferences	15-3
Exercise 15.2: Scheduling Preferences	15-4
Exercise 15.3: How To Customize The Contact List View	15-6
Rearrange The Order Of Columns	15-6
Resize A Column	15-6
Add A Column	15-7
Delete A Column	15-7
Exercise 15.4: How To Customize Columns On A Tab	15-8
Creating Fields	15-8
Field Data Type Options	15-9
Field Behavior Options	15-10
Customize Field Behavior	15-10
Triggers	15-11
Exercise 15.5: Create A Trigger	15-12
Exercise 15.6: How To Create A Drop-Down List Field	15-13
Exercise 15.7: How To Add Items To A Drop-Down List	15-14
Exercise 15.8: How To Edit The Values In A Drop-Down List (From A View)	15-15
How To Add An Item To A Drop-Down List	15-15
How To Modify Or Delete An Item In The Drop-Down List	15-16
Exercise 15.9: How To Modify A User Field	15-16
Exercise 15.10: How To Create A Field	15-17
Deleting Fields	15-18
Managing Priority Types	15-19
Exercise 15.11: Creating Activity Types	15-19
Annual Events	15-20
Exercise 15.12: Create An Annual Event Activity	15-20
Add The Event To Your Calendar	15-21

CUSTOMIZING REPORT TEMPLATES 16-1

Report Design Overview	16-2
Report Creation Options	16-2
Create A Report Based Off Of An Existing Report	16-2
Create A Report From Scratch	16-2
Report Designer	16-3
Report Designer Toolbars	16-3
Sections Of A Report	16-4
Section 1: Report Header	16-5
Section 2: Page Header	16-5
Section 3: Detail	16-5
Section 4: Page Footer	16-5
Section 5: Report Footer	16-5
Customizing Report Templates	16-5

Exercise 16.1: Customizing The Report Templates 16-5
    Field vs Label 16-6
    How To Manually Resize A Field 16-7
Report Designer Toolbox 16-7
How To Add A Field To A Report 16-8
How To Align Fields On A Report 16-9
How To Add Text To A Report 16-9
Properties Window 16-10
How To Add A Summary Field 16-10
Custom Fields 16-12
Exercise 16.2: How To Create A Custom Field 16-13
Hiding Fields On A Report 16-13
Exercise 16.3: Hiding A Report Section 16-14
Exercise 16.4: Adding A Section To A Report 16-15
How To Remove A Section Of The Report 16-16
Exercise 16.5: How To Create A Section Break 16-17
    Create The Cover Page 16-17
    Add A System Field 16-17
    Add A Page Break 16-17
Exercise 16.6: Using The Picture Field 16-18
Exercise 16.7: Create A New Report 16-18
    Create A Custom Report Template 16-18
    Look Up The Records 16-19
Create A Report From Scratch 16-19
Exercise 16.8: Create A Subreport 16-20
    Add The Subreport To The Main Report 16-21
Modifying Labels And Envelopes 16-22
Exercise 16.9: Modify An Envelope (Or Label) Template 16-22
Creating Label And Envelope Templates 16-23

CUSTOMIZING THE MENU AND TOOLBARS 17-1
Modifying Menus 17-2
Exercise 17.1: Using The Customize Dialog Box To Modify Menus 17-2
    How To Add A Command To A Menu 17-2
    How To Create A Custom Menu 17-3
    How To Create A Custom Submenu 17-4
    Rearrange Commands On A Menu 17-5
    How To Delete Commands From A Menu 17-5
Exercise 17.2: Creating Custom Commands 17-5
    Create A Custom Command For A Document 17-6
    Create A Custom Command For An Application 17-6
    Add The Commands To The Menu 17-7
Modifying Toolbars 17-8
Exercise 17.3: Customizing Toolbars 17-8
    How To Add A Command To A Toolbar 17-8
    How To Add A Custom Command To A Toolbar 17-9
    How To Rearrange Commands On A Toolbar 17-9
    How To Customize Toolbar Buttons 17-9
How To Distribute Custom Menus And Toolbars To Other Users 17-10
How To Delete A Command From A Toolbar 17-11
How To Reset Menus And Toolbars 17-12
Exercise 17.4: Creating Keyboard Shortcuts 17-12

    Navigation Pane Customization Options 17-13

USING THE LAYOUT DESIGNER 18-1
    What Is A Layout? 18-2
    ACT! Layouts 18-2
    Layout Designer 18-2
        Layout Designer Formatting Toolbar 18-5
        Layout Designer ToolBox 18-6
    Tabs Overview 18-6
    Exercise 18.1: Create A Tab On A Layout 18-6
        Hiding A Tab 18-7
        Edit Tab Options 18-7
    Exercise 18.2: Adding Fields To A Tab 18-8
    Text Boxes 18-8
    Resizing Fields On A Layout 18-9
    Exercise 18.3: Adding Graphics To A Layout 18-9
    Exercise 18.4: Changing The Background Color Of A Tab 18-10
    Using The Properties Window To Change The Appearance Of A Field Or Label 18-11
    Edit Properties Dialog Box 18-11
    Exercise 18.5: How To Change The Label For A Field On A Layout 18-11
    Exercise 18.6: Create An Annual Event Field 18-12
    Exercise 18.7: Aligning Fields 18-13
    Exercise 18.8: How To Change The Tab Stop Order 18-14

DATABASE MAINTENANCE AND SECURITY 19-1
    Database Maintenance 19-2
    Locking A Database 19-2
    Using The Delete Database Tool 19-3
    The Backup Tool 19-3
    Exercise 19.1: How To Back Up A Database Using The Back Up Command 19-4
        Password Protecting The Backup File 19-5
    Exercise 19.2: How To Back Up Personal Files 19-5
    Check And Repair Tools 19-6
        Reindexing Databases 19-6
        Check And Repair A Database 19-6
    Restoring Databases 19-7
    Exercise 19.3: How To Remove Old Data 19-8
    Finding And Deleting Duplicate Records 19-9
        Using The Copy/Move Contact Data Wizard 19-10
        Deleting Duplicate Records From The Contact List View 19-12
    ACT! Scheduler 19-13
    Exercise 19.4: Schedule A Maintenance Task 19-13
    Security 19-15
    Exercise 19.5: Creating User Accounts 19-15
    Reset Passwords 19-18
    Security Roles 19-18
    Permissions 19-19
    How To Edit User Account Information 19-19
    How To Delete A User Account 19-20
    Data Security 19-21
        Record Access 19-21
        Parent Or Extended Access 19-21
        Public Or Private Access 19-21

Record Manager	19-22
Field Security	19-22
Assigning Field Security	19-22
Password Security	19-23
How Users Change A Password	19-23
Password Policy	19-23
How To Create A Password Policy	19-24
ACT! Diagnostics	19-24

USING CRYSTAL REPORTS WITH ACT! DATABASES 20-1

About Crystal Reports	20-2
Crystal Reports Toolbars	20-3
Standard Toolbar	20-3
Formatting Toolbar	20-4
Insert Tools Toolbar	20-5
Navigation Tools Toolbar	20-6
Expert Tools Toolbar	20-6
Sections Of A Report	20-7
Section 1: Report Header	20-8
Section 2: Page Header	20-8
Section 3: Group Header	20-8
Section 4: Details	20-8
Section 5: Group Footer	20-8
Section 6: Report Footer	20-8
Section 7: Page Footer	20-8
Exercise 20.1: Create Your First Report	20-9
Step 1: Create A Connection To The Data Source	20-10
Step 2: Select The Tables	20-11
Step 3: Select The Fields	20-13
Step 4: Select The Grouping Options	20-14
Step 5: Select The Summary Options	20-15
Step 6: Select The Chart Type	20-16
Step 7: Select The Fields To Filter On	20-16
Step 8: Select A Template	20-17
Step 9: Save The Report	20-18
Exercise 20.2: Create A Contact List Report	20-19
Linking Tables	20-19
Exercise 20.3: Create The State = OH Or FL List Report	20-22

TOC-11

GETTING STARTED WITH SAGE ACT! PRO 2013

The fastest and easiest way to overcome an obstacle is to have someone that has been there, to be by your side every step of the way. That is the goal of this book, to be by your side, while you learn ACT! Pro 2013.

This book is a visual guide that shows you how to create and modify contact, company, group and opportunity records. There are over 675 illustrations in this book that practically eliminate the guess work and let you know that you are doing the steps correctly. Real world examples are provided to help give you an idea of when to use certain features. There is more to ACT! than knowing how to enter contact information. ACT! is robust and has a lot of features.

Learning new tips and shortcuts will allow you to work faster and smarter. The more that you know about ACT!, the easier your day to day contact and customer relationship management experiences will be.

By the time that you complete all of the exercises in this book, you will know more than the basics of ACT!. While you can jump from one section of the book to another, mainly because you paid for the book and can do as you please, I hope that you complete all of the exercises in the order that they are presented, because that will help you gain a better understanding of the features and functionality that ACT! offers. You will also gain more insight into how the features work together.

Sit back and lets get started!

Getting Started With Sage ACT! Pro 2013

What Is ACT! And What Can It Do For Me?

ACT! is a very popular Contact and Customer Relationship Management (CRM) database software package that is used by individuals and companies. In the beginning, ACT! was primarily used by sales people, but over the years the user base and types of companies that use ACT! has expanded. There are millions of ACT! users. CRM software provides a way to keep your contacts, which can be business associates, customers, friends, family, vendors, potential customers and any type of contacts that you have, organized. More importantly to many users, ACT! has the ability to create an audit trail or history for each contact. This makes it easier to remember your relationship with each contact.

ACT! is used to store information like addresses, contact type, to-do lists, meeting and sales information, as well as, other information that will help you maintain existing contacts and develop new contacts. ACT! also has built in applications that allow you to do word processing, send faxes, create and send email. One feature that you may find very useful is the variety of ways that you can look up contact information. Additionally, you can put contacts into groups like friends, sales reps and territory. You can also design and run reports. One of the best features of ACT! is that you can customize it to better meet your needs.

There are two editions of ACT!: ACT! Pro and ACT! Premium. The biggest difference between these two editions is that the latter can be used to access the databases online.

The list of features that ACT! has for managing contacts is extensive. There are over 40 fields that can be used to store general contact information like name, company, email and address. Not only can you keep your contact information organized, you can attach documents that you create in other software packages to the contacts and activities in the database. That is just the beginning of what ACT! offers. The list below provides some of the functionality that ACT! has.

- ☑ Over 50 pre-built reports that present the data in an easy to understand format.
- ☑ The ability to customize existing reports and create your own reports.
- ☑ Automate the creation of a series of tasks that you have to complete for contacts on a regular basis.
- ☑ Put a copy of the database on your laptop to work remotely. When you return to the office, you can sync the copy on your laptop with the live copy of the database that is on a server.
- ☑ Use dashboards, graphs and pipelines to help make business decisions.

ACT! is relatively easy to learn. One reason that ACT! is easy to learn is because it has many of the same options that are in other software packages that you may have already used. This includes options on menus and keyboard shortcuts. When you first start using ACT!, you may think that there are not a lot of features, but there are more features then meets the eye. The majority of people that use ACT!, use it to manage contacts, but there is nothing stopping you from using it to keep track of your book, movie or music collection. If you already know that you need a custom contact management database, you may find it helpful to take notes on the features that you will need to create a database that meets your needs.

If you have read any reviews of ACT!, you have probably read that using the software will make you more efficient and will save you time when it comes to managing your contacts. That is true. What the reviews do not point out or make obvious is that to get the most out of ACT! or any software package for that matter, one has to know more than the basics of the software.

Chapter 1

Overall Objectives

This book is written to accommodate a variety of learning styles. While there are no prerequisites to successfully complete the exercises in this book, having a general knowledge of any of the following would be helpful.

- ☑ Prior version of ACT!
- ☑ Windows environment
- ☑ Database structures
- ☑ Report design

Step-by-step instructions are included throughout this book. This book takes a hands-on, performance based approach to teaching you how to use ACT! and provides the skills required to use the software efficiently. After completing this book you will be able to perform the following tasks and more:

- ☑ Customize ACT!
- ☑ Create, edit and duplicate contact, company, group and opportunity records
- ☑ Use the Lookup command
- ☑ Sort contact records
- ☑ Link company and contact records
- ☑ Run and customize reports
- ☑ Schedule activities and create opportunities
- ☑ Modify report templates and menus
- ☑ Perform database maintenance tasks

Chapter 1 Objectives

In this chapter you will learn about the following:

- ☑ What ACT! can do for you
- ☑ Software support options
- ☑ Creating and copying databases

Conventions Used In This Book

I designed the following conventions to make it easier for you to follow the instructions in this book.

- ☑ The `Courier font` is used to indicate what you should type.
- ☑ **Drag** means to press and hold down the left mouse button while moving the mouse.
- ☑ **Click** means to press the left mouse button once, then release it immediately.
- ☑ **Double-click** means to quickly press the left mouse button twice, then release the mouse button.
- ☑ **Right-click** means to press the right mouse button once, which will open a shortcut menu.
- ☑ Press **CTRL+SHIFT** means to press and hold down the Ctrl (Control) key, then press the Shift key.
- ☑ Click **OK** means to click the OK button on the dialog box.
- ☑ Press **Enter** means to press the Enter key on your keyboard.

Getting Started With Sage ACT! Pro 2013

- ☑ Press **Tab** means to press the Tab key on your keyboard.
- ☑ Click **Save** means to click the Save button in the software.
- ☑ Click **Finish** means to click the Finish button on the dialog box.
- ☑ SMALL CAPS are used to indicate an option to click on or to bring something to your attention.
- ☑ This icon indicates a shortcut or another way to complete the task that is being explained. It can also indicate a tip or additional information about the topic being explained.
- ☑ This icon indicates a warning, like a feature that has been removed or information that you need to be aware of.
- ☑ When you see "YOUR SCREEN SHOULD HAVE THE OPTIONS SHOWN IN FIGURE X-X", or something similar in the exercises, check to make sure that your screen does look like the figure. If it does, continue with the next set of instructions. If your screen does not look like the figure, redo the steps that you just completed so that your screen does match the figure. Not doing so may cause you problems when trying to complete exercises later in the book.
- ☑ "Clear the (name of option)" means to remove the check mark from the option specified in the instruction.
- ☑ The section heading **EXERCISE X.Y:** (where X equals the chapter number and Y equals the exercise number) represents exercises that have step-by-step instructions that you should complete. You will also see sections that have step-by-step instructions that are not an exercise. Completing them as you go through the book is optional, but recommended.
- ☑ [See Chapter 2, Contact Fields] refers to a section in a chapter that you can use as a reference for the topic that is being explained.
- ☑ [See Chapter 2, Figure 2-8] refers to an illustration (screen shot) that you can use as a reference for the topic that is being explained.
- ☑ Many of the dialog boxes in ACT! have OK, Cancel and Help buttons at the bottom of the dialog box. Viewing these buttons on all of the figures adds no value, so they are not shown.
- ☑ VIEW ⇒ CALENDAR ⇒ DAILY, means to open the **VIEW** menu, select **CALENDAR**, then select **DAILY**, as shown in Figure 1-1.

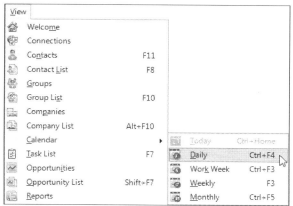

Figure 1-1 Menu navigation technique

Assumptions

Yes, I know one should never assume anything, but the following assumptions have been made. It is assumed that . . . .

- ☑ You are familiar with the Windows environment, including Windows Explorer and are comfortable using a mouse.

Chapter 1

- ☑ You know that the operating system used to write this book is Windows 7 Home Premium. If you are using a different version of Windows, some of the screen shots may have a slightly different look and some of the instructions for Windows tasks may be different.
- ☑ You understand that references to files or folders are files or folders on your computers hard drive and not a server. If your ACT! database is on a server, that is where the default ACT! folders should be located.
- ☑ You will have the My_ACT_Demo database open at the beginning of each chapter, starting with Chapter 2, unless instructed otherwise. You will create this database later in this chapter.
- ☑ You understand that many of the dates in the figures will be different then what you see on your computer screen.
- ☑ You have access to the Internet to download any updates that may be available for ACT! and to download the practice files needed to complete some of the exercises in this book.
- ☑ When you see <smile>, that signifies my attempt of adding humor to the learning process.
- ☑ You understand that from time to time, I will point out functionality that may not work as expected. When I do this, I am not complaining, merely pointing out things that you should be aware of.
- ☑ Optional: That you have access to a printer, if you want to print any of the reports that you run or create.
- ☑ Optional: You have Microsoft Word and Excel, version 2003 or higher installed, if you want to complete the exercises that use these software packages.

Using Microsoft Office 2010 With ACT! Pro 2013
ACT! 2013 is compatible with the 32-bit version of Office 2010, but not the 64-bit version of Office 2010. Hopefully, at some point in the future it will be.

What's Not Covered

Rarely does any one book cover all of the features that a software package has. I cannot speak for every author, but I did not omit features or topics to cheat or mislead you. The size of this book should be proof of that <smile>. It is often a question of time and importance of the topic in relation to what the most used features are of the software. The reason that the following features are not covered in this book is two-fold: They will not prevent you from using over 95% of the features in ACT! and some of the features listed require additional software, hardware or both. Another reason they are not covered is because there are as many different set-ups for the additional software and hardware, as there are people using it.

For example, I may use Brand X PDA and you use Brand Y PDA. What works for me may not work for you. If I wrote instructions that you could not follow, you would think that there is something really wrong with me and even worse, you may think that I did not know what I was doing.

- ☑ Features only found in the Premium edition of ACT!, which aren't many.
- ☑ Sending broadcast faxes.
- ☑ Using ACT! with your PDA.
- ☑ Using ACT! with Microsoft Outlook.
- ☑ Synchronizing databases.
- ☑ Using Connection options.
- ☑ Google integration.

Getting Started With Sage ACT! Pro 2013

What Is A Database?

A **DATABASE** is a repository used to store a collection of related information. An ACT! database is used to store contacts and all of the information for each contact that you have. It seems to be human nature to want to enter as little data as possible, often to save time. ACT!, is more useful in the long run if it has more data. A database has records and fields.

A **FIELD** holds one piece of information, like the contact name or title.

A **RECORD** is a collection of fields about one entity like a contact, company or group.

Exercise 1.1: First Time Opening ACT!

The first time that you open ACT! you will see the window and dialog box shown in Figure 1-2. The dialog box on the right is used to select a database. The Welcome window has two options for selecting a database, as explained below.

① **CREATE A SAGE ACT! DATABASE** This option is used to create a new ACT! database.
② **OPEN AN EXISTING SAGE ACT! DATABASE** Select this option when you want to open an existing database.

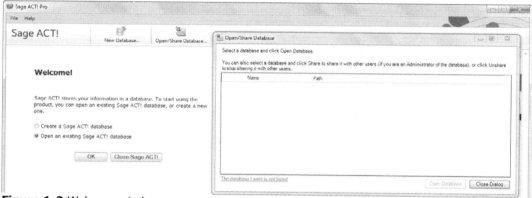

Figure 1-2 Welcome window

1. If you do not see the database that you want to use, click on the link **THE DATABASE I WANT IS NOT LISTED** at the bottom of the dialog box.

2. Navigate to where the demo database file is, then click on the ACT2013Demo file, then click the Open Database button. If this is the first time that you are opening the demo database, it will take a few seconds to open.

Welcome View

When you open an ACT! database you will see the view shown in Figure 1-3. The options in the middle of the window provide quick access to features that may be helpful to new users. The links in the Related Tasks section on the left of the window are explained below. Scroll down where the arrow is in the figure.

Chapter 1

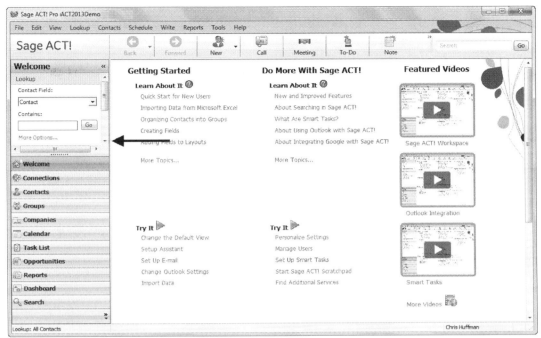

Figure 1-3 Welcome view with database open

Welcome View Related Tasks

WHAT'S NEW IN ACT! Opens the New and Improved Features topic page in the online help file.

ACCESS FEATURES TOURS Opens the Video Feature Tours topic page in the online help file.

VIEW HELP TOPICS Opens the What do you need help with? page in the online help file.

MODIFY PREFERENCES AND SETTINGS Opens the Preferences dialog box. [See Chapter 2, Preferences Overview]

CHANGE COLOR SCHEME OF ACT! Opens the Colors & Fonts tab on the Preferences dialog box. [See Chapter 2, Colors & Fonts Tab Preferences]

CHANGE DEFAULT VIEW Opens the Startup tab on the Preferences dialog box. [See Chapter 2, Startup Tab Preferences]

ACT! Demo Database

ACT! comes with a fully functional demo database that you can use to learn how to use the software. This is the database that you will use to complete the exercises in this book. If you have made changes to the data in the demo database prior to using this book, you should copy the original database to your hard drive (or server, if the demo database is on a network). That way your data and results will match the exercises in this book.

Getting Started With Sage ACT! Pro 2013

Getting Help

As explained below, there are four primary ways to get help if you have a question on how to use a feature or option in ACT!.

① Read this book from cover to cover and complete the exercises. Many of the basic questions that you may have are probably covered in this book.
② The Online Help file. This is an electronic version of the Users Guide. It is helpful for basic definitions.
③ If you have a question about ACT!, you can post a message in the community forum. Help ⇒ Online Support ⇒ Sage ACT! Online Community, will display the forum in your web browser. You can view messages, but not post without an account. If you do not already have an account for the forum, you have to create one to post questions. The account is free. Sage does provide staff to answer questions in the forum. The questions are also answered by other ACT! users.
④ Hire an ACT! consultant. Need I say that this is the most expensive option and you probably will not get an answer to your question as fast as you would like.

Feature Tours

This option is on the Help menu shown in Figure 1-4. It contains tutorials for some of the popular features in ACT!.

Your computer has to be connected to the Internet to view the tours.

Follow the steps below to run the Activities tour.

1. Help ⇒ Feature Tours ⇒ Activities.

2. The tour will start. When you are finished viewing the tour, close the browser window.

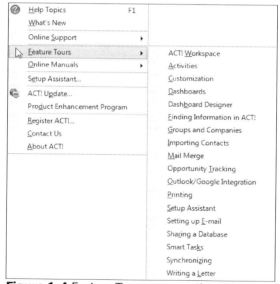

Figure 1-4 Feature Tours menu options

Online Manuals

The manuals that come with the software are installed when ACT! is installed. You can open them from the Help menu shown above in Figure 1-4. To view them, you need to have the free Adobe Acrobat Reader installed. It is probably already installed on your computer. If it is not, the Adobe Reader software can be downloaded from http://get.adobe.com/reader/. You do not have to download and install any of the other software that is on the web page for the Acrobat Reader software to work. You can also use the full version of Adobe Acrobat or another software package that can open and view PDF files.

Request A Feature

As you go through this book and think of a feature that you wish ACT! had, or a feature that you think needs to be improved, it is probably a good idea to post a message explaining the addition or change that you would like to see in future versions of the software.

They do read the messages, but sadly, it may take a few version releases before a suggestion is implemented, depending on when they receive the request. On the link below, click on the Share Ideas tab to post your request.

http://community.act.com/sage/

Setup Assistant Wizard

 In ACT! 2008 and earlier, the Setup Assistant Wizard was called the **GETTING STARTED WIZARD**.

The Setup Assistant option on the Help menu shown above in Figure 1-4 can be used to help you with the following:

① Creating a database to store your contact information in.
② Converting an existing database to work with the current version of ACT!.
③ Checking to make sure that your e-mail and word processor preferences are set up correctly.
④ The setup process to integrate your Outlook calendar with the calendar in ACT!.

While the wizard will complete all of the tasks listed above, you can pick and choose the options that you want to set up.

How To Check For Updates

From time to time, it is a good idea to check to see if there are updates for ACT!. Updates provide changes to the software. Sometimes they are improvements to existing functionality and sometimes they are fixes to features that are not working correctly. This type of update is sometimes called a **HOT FIX**. This menu option does not install hot fixes.

Your computer needs to be connected to the Internet to check for updates. In a multi-user environment, you probably will not have to check for or install updates because this is usually handled by tech support or a Database Administrator. Before installing any update, you should back up any existing databases that you use. The steps below show you how to check for updates.

1. Help ⇒ ACT! Update, is used to check for updates.

If there are no updates available, you will see the message shown in Figure 1-5 in the lower right corner of your computer screen.

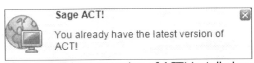

Figure 1-5 Latest version of ACT! installed message

In the lower right corner of your computer screen you may see a message that says to "Click here" for a description and download. If so, click on the option.

Getting Started With Sage ACT! Pro 2013

If you want to read about the update, click on the link on the dialog box otherwise, click the **DOWNLOAD** button.

2. When prompted to continue without backing up your data, click Yes if you have not created any databases yet. If you have created databases and want to back them up, click No.

3. When prompted, close ACT!. The update will be installed and the database will be updated if necessary.

Exercise 1.2: Create A Folder For Your Files

You will create and modify databases in this book. You will also download files. It would be a good idea to store all of the files for this book in the same folder on your computers hard drive so that you can find them easily. You will create a folder at the root of the C drive. If you want to create the folder in another location or under an existing folder, navigate to that location prior to starting step 2 below. The steps below explain how to obtain and download the practice files that are used in this book.

1. All of the files that are used in this book are in a zip file named act2013.zip. To have the link for the zip file sent to you, send an email to act2013@tolanapublishing.com. If you do not receive an email in a few minutes with the subject line ACT! 2013 Files, check the spam folder in your email software.

2. Once you receive the email with the link to the files, open Windows Explorer, then click on the Local Disk (C) drive.

3. File ⇒ New ⇒ Folder, or right-click on the C drive, then select New ⇒ Folder.

4. Type `ACT Book` as the folder name, then press Enter. Leave Windows Explorer open.

 Unless stated otherwise, all of the databases and files that you create in this book should be saved in the folder that you just created. I will refer to this folder as "your folder" through out the book.

5. Go to the web page listed in the email that you received and download the zip file into the folder that you just created.

6. In Windows Explorer, click on the folder that you created. You should see the zip file on the right side of the window.

    Right-click on the zip file and select **EXTRACT TO HERE**, as illustrated in Figure 1-6. The files will be copied to your folder.

Figure 1-6 How to extract the files

What Is The "My Record"?

The My Record is the contact record that is displayed when you first open a database in ACT!. This record contains information about you and is used when you create documents like letters that require information about you, like your name and address. This saves you a lot of time because you do not have to enter this information for every document that you create that needs this information. Each person that uses the database has a My Record in the database.

If the database that you use is also used by other people, your My Record may have already been created for you by the administrator of the database. The first time that you use a database you should make sure that the information on your contact record is accurate and as complete as possible. Having the information filled in on your My Record is really important if you plan to use the templates that come with ACT!. If the information is not filled in on the My Record, a lot of your information that would automatically be filled in, in a mail merge document or template will be missing or inaccurate.

The My Record information is also used to track who created a record, who last modified a record and who deleted a record. This is how different users are designated as the owner (which ACT! calls the Record Manager) of a (contact, company, group or opportunity) record in the database. If the database will be used by more than one person, each person should create a My Record, otherwise they will have to log on as someone else. Logging on as someone else is not the best solution, in my opinion because the other persons name will automatically be filled in when information is added, changed or deleted. This will make it difficult to know which user added or changed information in the database.

If by chance when the database opens and you do not see your contact record, something may be wrong. The things that come to mind are the following:

① The database could be corrupt.
② You did not log on as yourself.
③ Your contact information has been changed by someone else.

Look at the data on the contact record closely to see if your name has been changed and all of the other information is correct. If you are sure that the record is not yours, you should review the maintenance options covered in Chapter 19, to see if any of them will resolve the issue. If not, call the help desk at your company or post a message in the forum.

Database Naming Conventions

At some point, you may have the need to create a database. Like many other things in life, there are rules that you have to follow. Below are the rules for database names.

① The name cannot be more than 32 characters.
② The name cannot contain spaces or any of the following characters:
~ ! @ # $ % ^ & * ( ) + { } | : " < > ? ` - = [ ] \ ; ' , . /
③ The name can have a combination of letters, numbers and the under score.
The underscore is often used in place of a space in the database name.

Exercise 1.3: Create A Database

During the process of creating a database you will create a My Record. The person that creates a database is automatically given administrator security rights to the database. In this exercise you will learn how to create a database from scratch, opposed to using the Setup Assistant Wizard to create the database.

1. Open ACT!, if it is not already open, then click the **NEW DATABASE** button or File ⇒ New Database.

Getting Started With Sage ACT! Pro 2013

2. Type `My_ACT_Database` in the **DATABASE NAME** field on the New Database dialog box.

3. Click the **BROWSE** button, then navigate to your folder.

   Click on the folder illustrated in Figure 1-7.

   (**Hint**: If necessary, click on the plus sign in front of the Computer option shown at the top of the figure to see the C drive.)

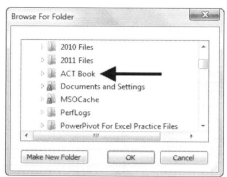

Figure 1-7 Browse For Folder dialog box

4. Click OK. This is the folder that the database will be saved in.

5. If the Currency field is not set to USD - US Dollar, select it from the drop-down list.

6. Check the **SHARE THIS DATABASE WITH OTHER USERS** option.

Sharing A Database Tips
① If this option is not enabled, it usually means that you did not open ACT! as an administrator. To run ACT! as an administrator, right-click on the link (on the Start menu) for ACT! and select **RUN AS ADMINISTRATOR**, as illustrated in Figure 1-8. If the icon for ACT! is on your desktop, follow the instructions in the Database Copy Failed Message tip box on page 1-16.
② When designing a database, one thing that you need to consider is whether or not the database will be used by more than one person. If so, when the database is created, you should put it on a server or shared drive. Creating a database on your computers hard drive and then trying to move it, is more work then it is worth. You would have to back up and restore the database and all associated files to put them on the server.

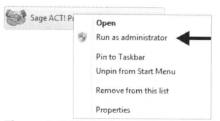
Figure 1-8 Shortcut menu for link on the Start menu

Anyone that you plan to share the database with must be using the same version of ACT! that the database was created with. If you (the creator of the database) are using ACT! Pro 2013, other people that want to use your database have to use the Pro version also. For example, they cannot use an older version of ACT! with a database that was created in ACT! Pro 2013, nor can ACT! Premium 2013 be used.

7. Type your first and last name in the **USER NAME** field.

   Other then your name, you should have the same options filled in that are shown in Figure 1-9.

   If you wanted the database to be password protected, you would enter the password in the last two fields on the dialog box.

   It is not a requirement for ACT! databases to have a password.

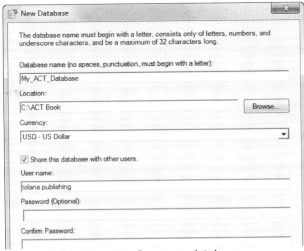

Figure 1-9 Information for a new database

 User names are not case sensitive, but passwords are.

8. Click OK. The database will now be created. When it is finished, there will be one contact record in the database, which is the My Record that is automatically created for the user name on the New Database dialog box, shown above in Figure 1-9. You would add your information to the contact record when you see it on the screen.

9. If you see the message shown in Figure 1-10, click No.

Figure 1-10 Startup view message

10. If you see the message that says that you have successfully shared this database, click OK.

Password Protected Databases

If the database is used by more than one person, you will see the dialog box shown in Figure 1-11 when you open the database.

You would have to enter your user name and password exactly as it was entered on the dialog box shown earlier in Figure 1-9 or how it was set up by the Database Administrator (by default, that is the person that created the database).

Figure 1-11 Log on dialog box

Viewing A Database Structure

Earlier you created a database. You may find it helpful to view the structure and folders of databases in ACT!, so that you will know where files are located.

1. Open Windows Explorer, then navigate to and click on your folder. You should see the files and folders shown in Figure 1-12. You will also see the files that you downloaded, even though they are not shown in the figure.

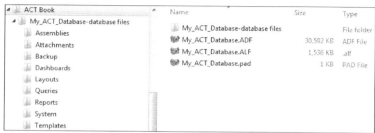

Figure 1-12 Contents of the ACT Book folder

2. Close Windows Explorer.

> **Database Tips**
> Below are some tips that you should know about ACT! databases.
>
> ① The folders shown on the left side of Figure 1-12 above, are automatically created when a new database is created. They are used to store files that are created or used by ACT!.
> ② When a database is created, approximately 20 MB of hard drive space is allocated for it.
> ③ The **.ADF** file is the database file.
> ④ The **.ALF** file is the log file for the database. This file should be backed up. If this file becomes corrupt and you do not have a copy of it, you will need to contact Sage in order to be able to use the database again.
> ⑤ The **.PAD** file is used to open the database. It is a shortcut that points to the database. If you want to share a database that is on a shared server with other people, give them a copy of this file. .PAD stands for Pointer to ACT! database.
> ⑥ ACT! databases store three types of files, as explained in Table 1-1.

File Type	Description
Database	This is the database file that contains the contact records, notes, activities and all of the data that you see when you use ACT!.
Database Supplemental	These files are automatically created when ACT! is installed. Reports and templates are supplemental files. (1)
Personal Supplemental	These are files that you create and save, like letters or spreadsheets. (1)

Table 1-1 ACT! file types explained

(1) Supplemental files are covered in Chapter 9.

Open/Share Database Dialog Box

The dialog box shown in Figure 1-13 displays the databases that you have access to. If you are the Administrator of the database, you will see a Share or Unshare button next to the database.

Clicking a **SHARE** button opens the dialog box shown in Figure 1-14. This dialog box is used to log onto the database that you want to share with other users.

Clicking an **UNSHARE** button also displays the dialog box shown in Figure 1-14. Once your log on information is verified, you will see the message shown in Figure 1-15. It lets you know that the database will no longer be shared.

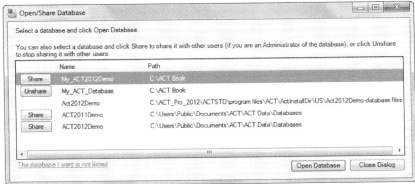

Figure 1-13 Open/Share Database dialog box

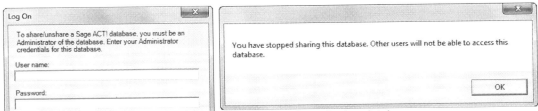

Figure 1-14 Log On dialog box   **Figure 1-15** Stop sharing database message

Exercise 1.4: How To Make A Copy Of A Database

The exercises that you will complete in this book will modify the demo database that comes with ACT!. Therefore, it is a good idea to make a copy of the demo database and use the copy to complete the exercises.

1. File ⇒ Open/Share Database. You will see the dialog box shown earlier in Figure 1-13. You should see the ACT Demo database. If there are other databases that you have access to, you will see them on the dialog box.

2. Click on the ACT Demo database, then click the Open Database button. If you see a message stating that the database needs to be updated, click Yes to create a back up. Click OK on the Back Up Database dialog box. The update process could take a few minutes.

3. When the database opens, File ⇒ Save Copy As, then type `My_ACT_Demo` in the **DATABASE NAME** field.

4. If your folder is not in the Database Location field, click the Browse button. Double-click on your folder, then click OK.

5. Check the option **SHARE THIS DATABASE WITH OTHER USERS**.

   You should have the options shown in Figure 1-16.

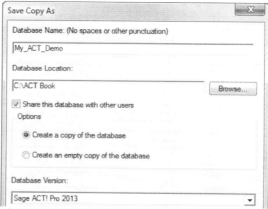

Figure 1-16 Save Copy As dialog box

6. Click OK. It will take what seems like a long time (a few minutes) to save a copy of the database.

 Database Copy Failed Message
If after completing the steps above, you get the Database copy failed error message, follow the steps below.

1. Close ACT!.
2. Right-click on the ACT! icon on your desktop and select **RUN AS ADMINISTRATOR**.
If you want ACT! to always run in administrator mode, select the Properties option on the shortcut menu, then click the **ADVANCED** button on the Shortcut tab on the Properties dialog box. You will see the dialog box shown in Figure 1-17. Select the Run as administrator option, then click OK. Click Apply, then click OK.
3. Repeat all of the steps in this exercise.

Figure 1-17 Advanced Properties dialog box

7. Click OK when you see the "Save As was successful" message. You now have your own copy of the demo database, which you will use in the next chapter.

8. If you see the Alarms dialog box, click the **CLEAR ALARM** button.

A copy of the database does not make your My Record the default My Record. This means that when you open the My_ACT_Demo database that you just created, the default My Record will be the creator of the original database, which is Chris Huffman. Do not change the owner to yourself. The exercises in this book are based on Chris Huffman being the default My Record owner. This is especially important in ACT! 2013 because about 140 of the 200 contacts in the demo database are marked as private for Chris Huffman. I have not seen this in previous versions of the demo database.

ACT! WORKSPACE

 In this chapter you will learn about the ACT! workspace. You will also learn the following:

- ☑ Setting default preferences
- ☑ Changing layouts
- ☑ The views in ACT!
- ☑ Detail view tabs

  Name Changes
From version to version, the name of some options and features can get renamed. Throughout the book I point out these name changes and include the version of ACT! that the name change first appeared in. I do this because I know that everyone does not buy the upgrade version of the software every year. Hopefully, this will keep many people from spending a lot of time looking for a feature or option by a name, not realizing that the name has changed.

CHAPTER 2

ACT! Workspace

Workspace Overview

When you open a database you will see the modified Welcome screen view unless the **STARTUP VIEW** preference option has been changed. The goal of this chapter is to help you learn the various sections of the workspace.

Clicking the Contacts button on the left side of the workspace will display the Contacts detail view shown in Figure 2-1. Table 2-1 explains the sections of the workspace. Parts of the workspace will change, based on the view that is selected.

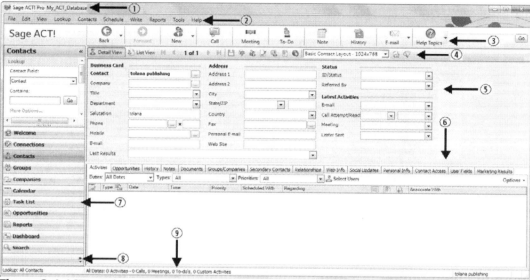

Figure 2-1 ACT! workspace

	Name	Description
①	Title bar	Displays the name of the database that is open. The icon in the left corner of this section opens the Control menu shown in Figure 2-2. The options on this menu are used to close, restore, move, size, minimize or maximize the ACT! window.
②	Menu bar	Contains the default menus and commands for the current view. The menu options are explained in Table 2-2. (1)
③	Global toolbar	Contains buttons for the options that you will probably use the most. The buttons are shortcuts to items on the menu bar. The Global toolbar buttons are explained in Table 2-3.
④	Detail or List view toolbar	The options on this toolbar change, depending on the type of records that are displayed.
⑤	Detail	Contains basic information for the contact, company, group or opportunity. Many of these fields are used in templates and reports, which means that the information should be as accurate as possible. (1)

Table 2-1 Sections of the ACT! workspace explained

Chapter 2

	Name	Description
⑥	Tabs	The fields on each tab contain information for the contact, company, group or opportunity record that is displayed in the top half of the window. The information that you see on the tabs depends on the access rights and security that you have. This means that different people that use the database will see different information. (1)
⑦	Navigation Pane	The buttons in this section are used to display a different view, lookup records and access tasks related to the view. (1)
⑧	Layout button	The options on this button are used to customize the Navigation Pane.
⑨	Status bar	This section is primarily used to provide additional information about the record that is currently displayed. On the Opportunity list view, total dollar amounts are displayed in this section.

Table 2-1 Sections of the ACT! workspace explained (Continued)

(1) This option can be customized.

Figure 2-2 Control menu

Menu Bar

The options on the menu are the same for each view. The options are explained in Table 2-2.

Menu	Description
File	The options are used to open, close, save, import, export, backup and print data.
Edit	The options are used to modify data in the view. The options on this menu change, based on the view that is selected.
View	Is used to select a different view, display the mini calendar, select a tab or refresh data.
Lookup	Is used to select the field to use to search for records in the database and create queries.
Contacts	The name of this menu option changes based on the view that is selected. It has options for the type of data that is displayed. For example, if the Opportunity view is displayed, this menu name changes to Opportunities.
Schedule	The options are used to create an activity, activity series, manage smart tasks, as well as, granting calendar access.
Write	The options are used to create emails, letters and other types of documents.
Reports	The options are used to select a report to run.
Tools	This menu contains options for creating new fields, creating and modifying layouts, database maintenance, converting old databases, synchronizing databases, customizing menus and toolbars and selecting preferences.

Table 2-2 Menu bar options explained

ACT! Workspace

Menu	Description
Help	The options on this menu are primarily used to learn about ACT!. There are also options for updating the software and getting support.

Table 2-2 Menu bar options explained (Continued)

Global Toolbar

Figure 2-3 shows the Global toolbar. The buttons are explained in Table 2-3.

> In ACT! 2009 and earlier, these buttons were on the detail or list view toolbar.

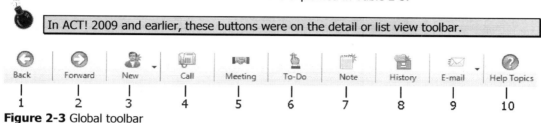

1   2   3   4   5   6   7   8   9   10

Figure 2-3 Global toolbar

Button	This Button Is Used To . . .
1	Display a previous record or view. Clicking on the arrow on this button displays the last nine items that were displayed, as shown in Figure 2-4.
2	Display the previous record or view in the list shown in Figure 2-4. For example, in the figure, the weekly calendar is the current view (it's in bold). When you click this button, the Welcome list view would be displayed.
3	Select the type of new record that you want to create, as shown in Figure 2-5.
4	Schedule a telephone call activity. (2)
5	Schedule a meeting activity. (2)
6	Schedule a To-Do activity. (2)
7	Create a note.
8	Create a history record.
9	Compose and view emails, as well as, select email preferences, as shown in Figure 2-6.
10	Open the Help system.

Table 2-3 Global toolbar buttons explained

(2) This option is for the current record on the detail view. It can be used with multiple records on the list view, if the records are selected or tagged.

Navigation Pane

Table 2-4 explains the buttons on the Navigation Pane. Figures 2-7 to 2-15 show the views.

Button	Displays The . . .
Welcome	View shown in Chapter 1, Figure 1-3.
Connections	View shown in Figure 2-7.
Contacts	Contacts detail view shown earlier in Figure 2-1.
Groups	Groups detail view shown in Figure 2-8.
Companies	Companies detail view shown in Figure 2-9.
Calendar	Calendar view shown in Figure 2-10.

Table 2-4 Navigation Pane buttons explained

Chapter 2

Button	Displays The . . .
Task List	Task List view shown in Figure 2-11.
Opportunities	Opportunity list view shown in Figure 2-12.
Reports	Reports view shown in Figure 2-13.
Dashboard	Dashboard view shown in Figure 2-14.
Search	Search view shown in Figure 2-15.

Table 2-4 Navigation Pane buttons explained (Continued)

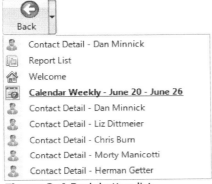

Figure 2-4 Back button list

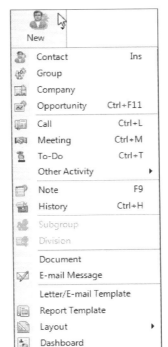

Figure 2-5 New button options

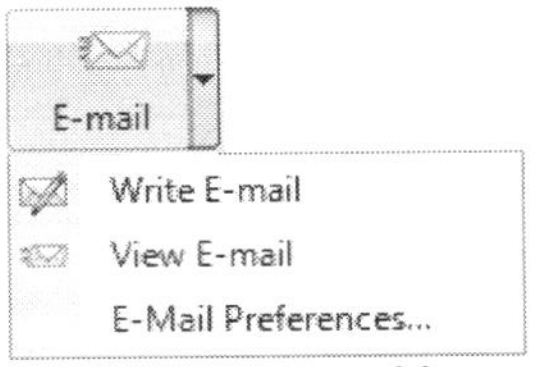

Figure 2-6 E-mail button options

Figure 2-7 Connections view (Only some options are displayed in the figure)

2-5

ACT! Workspace

Figure 2-8 Groups detail view

Figure 2-9 Companies detail view

Figure 2-10 Calendar (weekly) view

Figure 2-11 Task List view

2-6

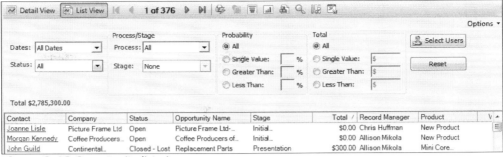

Figure 2-12 Opportunity list view

Figure 2-13 Reports view

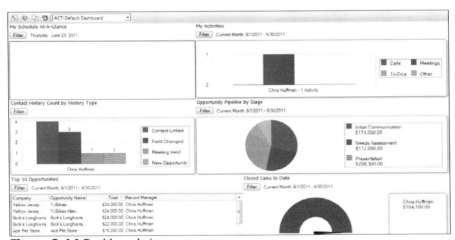

Figure 2-14 Dashboard view

ACT! Workspace

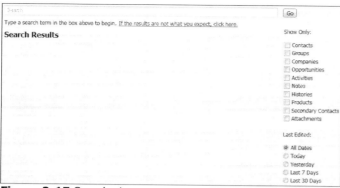

Figure 2-15 Search view

Sage Connection Services

The options in the Connections view, shown earlier in Figure 2-7 are business tools that you can use to contact your customers. Some of the options require a paid subscription to continue using.

Minimize And Restore The Navigation Pane

If you need more space in the workspace, you can minimize the Navigation Pane by clicking on the arrow shown in the upper right corner of Figure 2-16.

Figure 2-16 Minimize Navigation Pane button

When you click this button, the Navigation Pane is reduced, as shown in Figure 2-17. If you click on any of the buttons shown in Figure 2-17, that view will be displayed. If you click in the Contacts section of the Navigation Pane toolbar shown in Figure 2-17, the **LOOKUP** and **RELATED TASKS** section of the Navigation Pane are displayed, as shown in Figure 2-18. Click on the arrow button at the top of the Navigation Pane toolbar to restore it.

 Lookup Section
This section on the Navigation Pane (shown at the top of Figure 2-18) was displayed by default in ACT! 2011, is still available. [See Startup Tab Preferences, later in this chapter]

Related Tasks

The links in this section of the Navigation Pane are shortcuts to tasks that are on menus. The options change depending on the view that is currently displayed. The Related Tasks options are explained at the end of the chapter that the view is covered in.

Chapter 2

Figure 2-18 Lookup and Related Tasks sections of the Navigation Pane restored

Figure 2-17 Navigation Pane minimized to a toolbar

Resizing The Top And Bottom Sections Of Detail Views

The **DETAIL** views have two sections which are sometimes referred to as primary and secondary sections. These sections can be resized as needed. The primary section is at the top of the view and contains basic information like the name and address for the contact, company or group. The top section of a detail view contains fields that you will probably enter a lot of information in. The secondary section is at the bottom of the window and displays the tabs.

As you scroll through the records, the data in both sections will change. This is known as **RELATIONAL DATA** because the data on the tabs is related to the record displayed at the top of the window. You may need to make the bottom half (the Tabs section) longer or shorter. If this is the case, follow the steps below.

1. Place the mouse pointer on the bar illustrated in Figure 2-19.

Figure 2-19 Mouse pointer in position to resize a section of the detail view

2. Press and hold down the left mouse button, then drag the bar up or down as needed.

Detail View Tabs

There are 15 tabs on the Contact detail view: Activities, Opportunities, History, Notes, Documents, Groups/Companies, Secondary Contacts, Relationships, Web Info, Social Updates, Personal Info, Contact Access, Latest Activities, User Fields and Marketing Results. The fields on each of these tabs is used to enter more information for each contact. Click on each of these tabs now to become familiar with the types of data that can be entered for a contact.

The company and group detail views have some of the same tabs as the contact view, plus tabs that the contact detail view does not have. Table 2-5 lists which detail view has which tabs in the Basic layout 1024x768. Table 2-6 explains the type of information on each tab.

Tab	Contacts	Company	Group	Opportunity
Activities	X	X	X	X
Opportunities	X	X	X	
History	X	X	X	X
Notes	X	X	X	X
Documents	X	X	X	X
Groups/Companies	X			X
Secondary Contacts	X			
Relationships	X			
Web Info	X	X		
Social Updates (3)	X			
Personal Info	X			
Contact Access	X			
Latest Activities (4)	X			
User Fields	X			X
Marketing Results	X			
Billing and Shipping		X		
Company Profile (5)		X		
Company Access		X		
Divisions		X		
Contacts		X	X	X
Group Address (6)			X	
Group Access (7)			X	
Subgroups			X	
Products/Services				X
Opportunity Info				X
Opportunity Access				X

Table 2-5 Detail view tabs

(3) This tab is new in ACT! 2013.
(4) This tab is only on the Contact 800x600 layout.
(5) This tab is named **COMPANY INFO** on the ACT Demo layout, which is customized.
(6) This tab is named **ADDRESS** on the ACT Demo layout, which is customized.
(7) This tab is named **GROUP INFO** on the ACT Demo layout, which is customized.

Tab	Contains This Type Of Information . . .
Activities	Scheduled activities. [Chapter 7] (8)
Billing and Shipping	Billing and shipping addresses for the company. [Chapter 5]
Company Access	The person that created and last edited the company record. [Chapter 5] (9)
Company Profile	Tracks the region, revenue, SIC Code and more for each company. [Chapter 5]
Contact Access	The person that created and last edited the contact record. [Chapter 3] (9)
Contacts	List of contacts in the company or group. [Chapter 3]
Divisions	Lists the divisions that are associated to the company. [Chapter 5]
Documents	Lists files that have been attached to the record currently displayed. [Chapter 9] (8)
Group Access	The person that created and edited the group record. [Chapter 6] (9)
Group Address	Address for the group. [Chapter 6]
Groups/Companies	Groups that the contact belongs to. This tab is only available in the Contact detail view. [Chapter 5]
History	Completed and deleted activities, as well as, changes to other types of records. [Chapter 9] (8)
Latest Activities	The date that the last email, call, meeting and letter sent, took place for each contact. [Chapter 3]
Marketing Results	Email, survey and drip marketing E-Marketing tools. [Chapter 9]
Notes	Notes that have been created for a contact, company or group. [Chapter 9] (9)
Opportunities	Open, inactive and closed sales. [Chapter 8] (8)
Opportunity Access	The person that created and edited the opportunity record. [Chapter 10] (9)
Opportunity Info	Competitor and Referred by fields. [Chapter 10]
Personal Info	Home address information, birthday and alternate phone numbers for the contact. [Chapter 3]
Products/Services	Create, edit and delete the items for the opportunity. [Chapter 10]
Relationships	Relationships that the contact has with other contacts in the database. [Chapter 3]
Secondary Contacts	Names of people associated with the contact. [Chapter 9]
Social Updates	The most recent updates by the associated friend or follower.
Subgroups	List of the subgroups for the group. [Chapter 6]
User Fields	Fields that can be customized, so that you can enter any information that does not fit in any other field in the database. [Chapter 3]
Web Info	Social networking web sites for the record currently displayed at the top of the workspace. [Chapter 9]

Table 2-6 Information stored on tabs explained

(8) Depending on the view, the data displayed on this tab is for a contact, company, group or activity. In some instances, the data on this tab displays data from multiple detail views.
(9) Stores the Public/Private status of the contact, company or group. **PUBLIC** status (the default status) means that anyone that opens the database can view the record. **PRIVATE** status means that only the person that created the record can view it.

ACT! Workspace

Preferences Overview

Preferences are used to modify ACT! to work the way that you want or need it to. Some of the preferences require administrator rights. As you go through the preferences, try to think about how you will use ACT! in terms of how the preferences can be modified to work best for you. It may be a good idea to write down the options that you want to change and what you want to change them to. That way, after you have completed this book, you can make the changes in your database.

For example, if you plan to keep most of the databases that you use in one folder, you could set that folder as the one that ACT! looks in first. The default folder for databases is the My Documents folder in Windows. I have watched many people lose work that was stored in the My Documents folder because they were not aware of the pitfalls of storing work in a folder that Windows creates. ACT! allows you to change the default location for databases, documents, reports, queries and any other type of file that you can create or use in ACT!.

Exercise 2.1: View And Modify The Preferences

In this exercise you will learn about the preferences in ACT!. You will also modify some of the preferences for the My_ACT_Demo database.

1. Open the My_ACT_Demo database. If prompted that the database will be verified, click OK. The update process takes a minute or so. When it is complete, click OK.

2. Tools ⇒ Preferences.

General Tab Preferences

The options shown in Figure 2-20 are used to select preferences for the database. The options in the **FILE TYPE** drop-down list shown in Figure 2-21 contain the types of **PERSONAL FILES** that you can set a folder location for. This means that you can store the databases in one folder and the documents that you create in a different folder. If you want to save different file types in the same folder, you have to select the same folder for each file type.

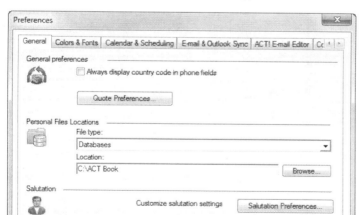

Figure 2-20 General tab preferences

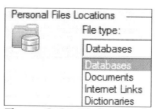

Figure 2-21 File type options

 The **FILE TYPE** and **LOCATION** options are something that you will want to change after you complete the exercises in this book because these options should reflect the location of the database that you use the most.

Chapter 2

The **BACKUP LOCATION** file type option was introduced in ACT! 2010, then removed in ACT! 2011. It was added back in ACT! 2012 and removed again in ACT! 2013.

1. Click the **BROWSE** button shown earlier in Figure 2-20, then navigate to and click on your folder.

2. Click OK to close the Browse For Folder dialog box. The **LOCATION** field should have changed to the folder that you selected in step 1.

3. Select your folder as the location for the Documents file type. You should have the options shown in Figure 2-22.

Figure 2-22 Modified Personal Files Locations options

4. Click the **SALUTATION PREFERENCES** button. Select the option, **USE CONTACT'S FIRST NAME**, if it is not already selected. Click OK, then click the Apply button.

Colors & Fonts Tab Preferences

The options on this tab are used to change the default font, style, text and background colors that are displayed in the workspace.

The options on the right side of the tab shown in Figure 2-23 are used to customize all of the views (lists), tabs, calendar and compositions (the dialog box that you enter notes on) in the **VIEWS** list.

Click on the object that you want to modify in the Views list, then change the options on the right side of the dialog box as needed.

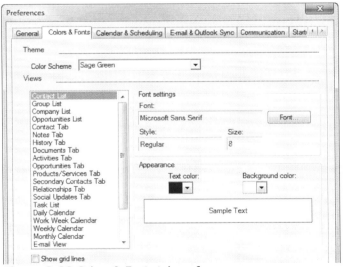
Figure 2-23 Colors & Fonts tab preferences

Changing Multiple Views At The Same Time
If you want to make the same change to more than one view, click on the first view that you want to change. Press and hold the Ctrl key down, then click on the other views, as shown in Figure 2-24. Once you have selected all of the views that you want to customize, select the options that you want. There is no global change option available, so this is the work around that I came up with. This will provide a consistent look when you go from one part of ACT! to another. This means that you will not have the top half of the Contact detail view with a green background and the background color of the tabs on the Contact detail view purple, unless that is what you want.

ACT! Workspace

Figure 2-24 Multiple views selected to be customized at the same time

If available and checked, the **SHOW GRID LINES** option on the Colors & Fonts tab shown earlier in Figure 2-23 will change the layout of data on a tab to look like a spreadsheet, as shown in Figure 2-25.

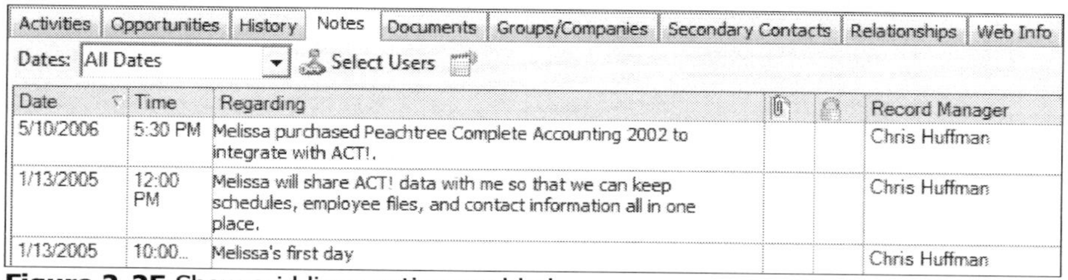

Figure 2-25 Show grid lines option enabled

You may want to change the colors and fonts or add grid lines to the Notes and History tabs because they will contain more data than the other tabs and having color or gridlines may make the entries easier to read.

Themes

As shown in Figure 2-26, there are two color scheme themes that you can select from.

The default is Sage Green. Themes are used to make global color changes to the workspace.

Figure 2-26 Theme Color Scheme options

Calendar & Scheduling Tab Preferences

Each of the buttons shown in Figure 2-27 are used to open a dialog box that has options for a specific preference.

The **CALENDAR PREFERENCES** options are used to set the work days and time period increments for the calendars.

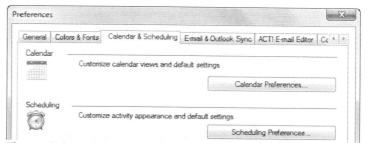

Figure 2-27 Calendar & Scheduling tab preferences

The **SCHEDULING PREFERENCES** options are used to set the default values for each of the activity types.

2-14

Copy Calendar Information Option
In ACT! 2009, this option was on many of the toolbars. It has been removed.

E-mail & Outlook Sync Tab Preferences

This tab has options that provide more functionality between ACT! and Outlook. The options shown in Figure 2-28 are the settings for the e-mail software that you will use with ACT!.

It is not a requirement to configure email software because you can use the Email Editor that comes with ACT!. These settings do not change the options that you currently have set in your e-mail software.

If you do not see any settings on this tab, it means that you have not set up an email package to use with ACT!.

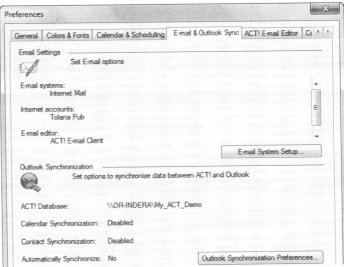

Figure 2-28 E-mail & Outlook Sync tab preferences

The **E-MAIL SYSTEM SETUP** button shown above in Figure 2-28 opens the **E-MAIL SETUP WIZARD**, which is used to configure Internet Mail or Outlook as the email software that you want ACT! to recognize. The email choices that you see may be different, because the choices depend on the email software that ACT! finds and recognizes on your computers hard drive.

ACT! Workspace

The **OUTLOOK SYNCHRONIZATION PREFERENCES** options are used to configure how data will be copied between ACT! and Outlook calendars and contacts.

Clicking this button displays the options shown in Figure 2-29.

The options are used to configure ACT! to work with your contacts in Outlook.

Figure 2-29 Outlook synchronization Preferences dialog box

ACT! E-mail Editor Tab Preferences

The options shown in Figure 2-30 are used to configure the ACT! Email Editor. You will only see this tab when there is at least one email software package configured.

The options on this tab are used to select the incoming and outgoing e-mail settings.

You can even set an option to notify you when you receive e-mail.

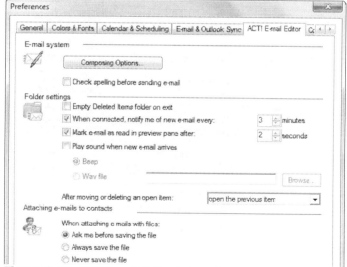

Figure 2-30 ACT! E-mail Editor tab preferences

If the **CHECK SPELLING BEFORE SENDING E-MAIL** option is selected, emails that you compose will be spell checked automatically before they are sent.

Chapter 2

The **COMPOSING OPTIONS** button on the ACT! Email Editor tab opens the dialog box shown in Figure 2-31.

This dialog box contains additional e-mail options that can be selected.

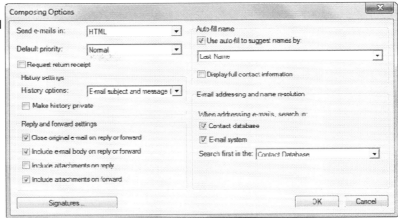

Figure 2-31 Composing Options dialog box

Communication Tab Preferences

The options shown in Figure 2-32 are used to select the default word processor, spell check, fax software and print options that you will use.

The **DIALER PREFERENCES** option requires your computer to be connected to a phone line, similar to using dial-up Internet service. These options allow ACT! to dial phone numbers for you.

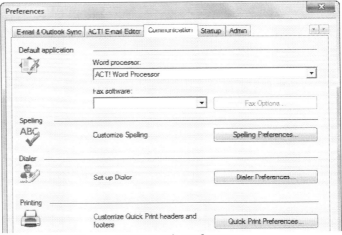

Figure 2-32 Communication tab preferences

The **QUICK PRINT PREFERENCES** button on the Communication tab opens the dialog box shown in Figure 2-33. These options are used to select the header and footer options for printing the lists that you saw earlier in Figure 2-23.

The **FOOTER OPTIONS** button (on the Quick Print Preferences dialog box) opens the dialog box shown in Figure 2-34.

ACT! Workspace

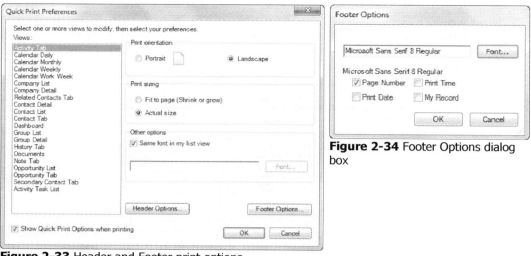

Figure 2-33 Header and Footer print options

Figure 2-34 Footer Options dialog box

1. If the ACT! Word Processor option is not selected, as shown earlier in Figure 2-32, select it now, then click the **SPELLING PREFERENCES** button.

The options in the **UPON SAVING, CHECK SPELLING FOR THE FOLLOWING** section shown in Figure 2-35, are used to select which tabs on the detail views will have spell checking enabled automatically.

If you have a custom dictionary from another application that you want to use in ACT!, you can select it by clicking the Browse button in the **SELECT USER DICTIONARY** section.

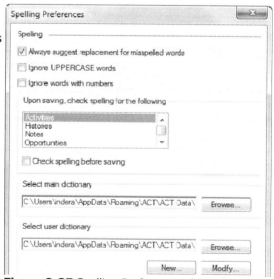

Figure 2-35 Spelling Preferences dialog box

User Dictionaries

User dictionaries are used to save words that are not in the main dictionary. This is helpful because once you save a word in this dictionary, it will not be considered a misspelled word in ACT!. If you use Microsoft Office and have created a custom dictionary, you can use it in ACT!.

You can create several user dictionaries. For example, if you are in the legal field you could create a legal dictionary and store the legal words that you need in it. If you need to add or delete words that are in the **USER** dictionary, click the **MODIFY** button shown above in Figure 2-35.

The options on the dialog box shown in Figure 2-36 are used to add and delete the words in the user dictionary.

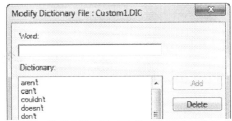

Figure 2-36 Modify Dictionary File dialog box

2. On the Spelling Preferences dialog box, click on the **ACTIVITIES** option in the list, then press and hold down the Shift key.

   Scroll to the end of the list and click on the last option. All of the options should be highlighted, as shown in Figure 2-37.

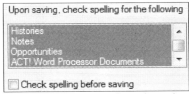

Figure 2-37 ACT! tabs selected

3. Clear the **CHECK SPELLING BEFORE SAVING** option if you do not want to have the spell checker run automatically each time you create an entry on one of the tabs that you just highlighted. You can run the spell checker manually, as needed.

4. Click OK, then click the Apply button on the Communication tab.

Startup Tab Preferences

The options shown in Figure 2-38 determine what will happen each time ACT! is opened and what happens when records are added to the database.

If you primarily use the same ACT! database, you can click the **STARTUP DATABASE** button and select the database that you want to have open automatically when ACT! is opened.

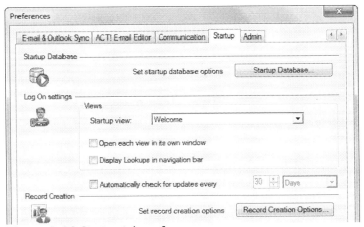

Figure 2-38 Startup tab preferences

If you do not want the database to open with the Welcome view, select the view that you want from the **STARTUP VIEW** drop-down list. You can also select the Dashboard option.

If checked, the **DISPLAY LOOKUPS IN NAVIGATION BAR** option shown above in Figure 2-38 will display the lookup search options in the Navigation bar, as shown earlier in Figure 2-18. Check the option, then click the Apply button.

ACT! Workspace

If checked, the **AUTOMATICALLY CHECK FOR UPDATES EVERY** option is used to let ACT! know how frequently you want to check for software updates. If your database is on a server, you should not select this option because the administrator needs to update the copy of ACT! and the database that is on the server before the desktop copies of ACT! (the copy that is installed on your computer) are updated.

I disable automatic update options in all software because I prefer to create an image of my computers hard drive before installing updates, just in case the update doesn't want to play nice with the other software that I have installed, if you know what I mean. The other reason that I disable this option is because ACT! will open faster because it will not have to check for updates before the software opens.

The **CHECK FOR UPDATES** option should be disabled on remote databases because remote databases should only be updated after the main database has been updated.

The **RECORD CREATION** options are covered in Chapter 9.

Exercise 2.2: Select A Database And View To Automatically Open With ACT!

Earlier you learned that a database could be selected to open automatically when ACT! is opened. You will select the copy of the database that you just created to open automatically when you open ACT!. This will be the database that you use to complete the majority of exercises in this book.

1. Tools ⇒ Preferences ⇒ Startup tab.

2. Click the **STARTUP DATABASE** button.

3. Select the **NAMED DATABASE** option, then click the button at the end of the drop-down list field.

4. Double-click on the My_ACT_Demo.pad file in your folder.

   You should have the options selected that are shown in Figure 2-39.

   Click OK.

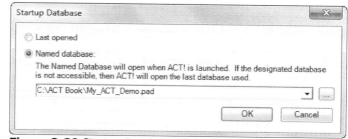

Figure 2-39 Startup Database dialog box options

5. On the Startup tab, open the Startup view drop-down list and select **CONTACTS**.

6. Click Apply. The next time that you open ACT!, the database and view that you selected in this exercise will automatically open.

Admin Tab Preferences

The options shown in Figure 2-40 are used to set default options for features that you will probably use on a regular basis.

The **NAME PREFERENCES** options are covered in Chapter 15.

The **COMPANY PREFERENCES** options are covered in Chapter 5.

The **DUPLICATE CHECKING** options are used to select how ACT! handles duplicate contact, company and group records in the database.

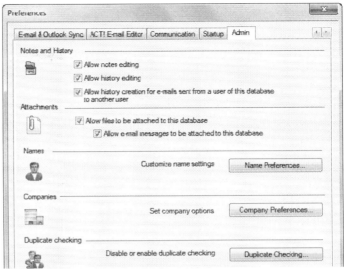

Figure 2-40 Admin tab preferences

 Administrator or manager rights are needed to change the **ALLOW HISTORY EDITING** and **DUPLICATE CHECKING** options.

Using The Duplicate Checking Options

1. Click the **DUPLICATE CHECKING** button on the Admin tab, then open the **RECORD TYPE** drop-down list and select Company.

2. Change the first **THEN ON** field to <None>, as shown in Figure 2-41.

   The options shown will prompt anyone using the database when they enter a company record that has the exact company name as a record already in the database.

Figure 2-41 Duplicate checking options for company records

3. Click OK, then click the Apply button. Click OK to close the Preferences dialog box.

4. File ⇒ Exit, to close ACT!, then reopen it.

The database may need to be verified. This is only done the first time that a database is opened. Look in the upper left corner of the workspace. You should see the name of the database in the Title bar.

ACT! Workspace

If you know that you will use more than one database and have set one database as the default (the one that opens automatically), make sure that you have the one that you need open, before you start adding records. Otherwise, you may find that you have entered data in the wrong database. If you find that this is the case, you can use the Import tool to copy the records to the correct database, then delete the records from the database that they were added to by mistake.

Exercise 2.3: Viewing Layouts

ACT! comes with the two basic layout styles that are shown in Figure 2-42 for the Contact, Group, Company and Opportunity detail views. These two layouts come with new databases that you create. The demo database has an additional layout (ACT Demo) as shown.

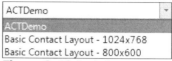

Figure 2-42 Basic layouts

Layouts are the background, fields and tabs in the workspace. These options can be modified to better meet your needs or you can create your own layout. Fields and tabs can be added, re-arranged or hidden as needed.

The options in this drop-down list contain layouts for the type of view (contact, company, group or opportunity) that is currently displayed. Each layout for each view can contain different fields. For example, the Basic Contact Layout 1024x768 displays more fields than the Basic Contact Layout 800x600.

1. Open the **LAYOUT** drop-down list on the Detail View toolbar and select **BASIC CONTACT LAYOUT - 800X600**, if it is not already selected.

2. File ⇒ Save, to save the changes.

It is possible that a database will require more than one layout. Different people or groups of people that are using the database may need to see different fields or may need to have the fields appear in a different order. Images and text can also be added to a layout. You can switch layouts at any time. Modifying layouts is covered in Chapter 18.

The Views In ACT!

There are several views in ACT! (Contacts, Groups, Companies, Calendar, Task List, Opportunities, Reports, and Dashboard) that you can view records and reports in.

The icons on the left side of the workspace on the Navigation Pane are used to switch to a different view.

The view can also be changed from the **VIEW** menu, as shown in Figure 2-43.

 The items on a menu like the one shown in Figure 2-43 that have an icon in the left column means that the option is on at least one toolbar in the software.

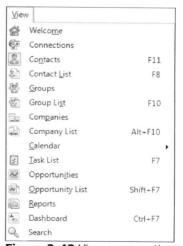

Figure 2-43 View menu options

CREATING AND EDITING CONTACT RECORDS

In this chapter you will learn about contact records, including the following:

- ☑ Adding and deleting contact records
- ☑ Enter information on the Notes, Documents and Personal Info tabs
- ☑ Editing contact information
- ☑ Using the Date field calendar
- ☑ Attaching files on the Documents tab
- ☑ Creating relationships
- ☑ Duplicating contact information

Creating And Editing Contact Records

What Is A Contact?

A contact in ACT! is any person or group of people that you need to have up to date information on. When many people hear the word **CONTACT**, they immediately think of a business contact. It is true that many people use ACT! strictly for managing business contacts, but you can have friends, family members, prospects and vendors, as well as, business contacts in the same ACT! database. As you will see, ACT! handles much more than names and addresses.

If you are brand new to ACT!, this chapter and the next one are probably the most important ones for you to fully understand because creating, editing and looking up contacts are the tasks that you will spend most of your time doing. The key thing to remember when entering data is to be consistent. This will make finding contacts in the database easier and reports more accurate.

Contact Detail View Toolbar

Figure 3-1 show the Contact detail view toolbar. Table 3-1 explains the buttons on the toolbar. The buttons provide quick access to some of the most used options for contacts. Each view (contact, company, group etc) has its own toolbar. For example, the Contact list and Contact detail views have a similar toolbar. You will see that not all buttons are enabled for both views.

Figure 3-1 Contact detail view toolbar

Button	Description
1	Displays the Contact detail view.
2	Displays the Contact list view.
3	Displays the first record. (1)
4	Displays the previous record. (1)
5	The **RECORD COUNTER** displays the record number (By default, contacts are displayed in alphabetical order) of the contact that is currently displayed and how many contact records are in the database. **42 OF 201** means that you are currently viewing record 42 and that there are 201 records in the database. (1)
6	Displays the next record. (1)
7	Displays the last record. (1)
8	Saves the record. (2)
9	Opens the Quick Print Options dialog box, which has options for printing the current screen.
10	Duplicates the current contact record.
11	Opens the word processor.
12	Call the contact on the phone through the Dialer application. (2)
13	Is used to attach a file to the contact record.
14	Opens Internet Explorer to the Google Maps web site and displays a map based on the address of the contact record that is currently displayed.
15	Is used to select a layout for the view. (2)
16	Displays the ACT! E-marketing options. (3)
17	Displays the Sage Business Info for Services for ACT! options. (3)

Table 3-1 Contact detail view toolbar buttons explained

(1) This option is either for the entire database or current lookup, which is a subset of records in the database. Lookups are covered in Chapter 4.
(2) This option is only available from the Contact detail view.
(3) This option requires a paid subscription to use.

Contact List View Toolbar

In addition to the buttons shown above in Figure 3-1, the buttons shown in Figure 3-2 are only available on the Contact list view. Table 3-2 explains the buttons on the toolbar.

Figure 3-2 Contact list view toolbar buttons

Button	Description
1	Is used to customize the columns in the view.
2	Exports the data to an Excel spreadsheet.

Table 3-2 Contact list view toolbar buttons explained

 List View Buttons
The buttons shown above in Figure 3-2 are also available on the Company, Group, Task List and Opportunity list views.

 If you cannot remember the name of a button on the toolbar, hold the mouse pointer over the button. You will see the name of the button, as illustrated in Figure 3-3. This is known as a **TOOL TIP**.

Figure 3-3 Tool tip illustrated

Difference Between The Enter And Tab Keys

You can use both of these keys to move from field to field when adding or editing data. The **TAB** key is used to move from field to field on the layout. The Tab key stops at every field by default.

The **ENTER** key is used to move from field to field also. The difference is that the Enter key does not stop at every field. It stops at the most used fields. The order that these keys move in can be changed.

Exercise 3.1: Creating A New Contact Record

You do not have to enter information in all of the fields, but you should enter enough information to make the contact record meaningful. You will learn how to enter data on several of the tabs on the Contact detail view in this exercise.

1. Click the **NEW** button on the Global toolbar. You will see a blank record. Notice that the record counter has been incremented by one. There should now be 202 records in the database.

 You can also press the **INSERT** key to add a new contact or select Contacts ⇒ New Contact.

CREATING AND EDITING CONTACT RECORDS

2. Type `Sarah Baker` in the Contact field, then press the Tab key.

Notice that the contacts first name has automatically been filled in the Salutation field. That is because you selected the option on the Preferences dialog box, to automatically fill in the salutation field with the contacts first name.

The button at the end of the Contact field on the Contact detail view opens the dialog box shown in Figure 3-4.

This button is called an **ELLIPSIS** button in ACT!. In other software, this is called the Browse button, which provides the same functionality.

By default, ACT! automatically splits a contact name into three fields. Initially, the options on this dialog box display what ACT! thinks the first, middle and last name are, based on the preferences selected on the Contact Name dialog box.

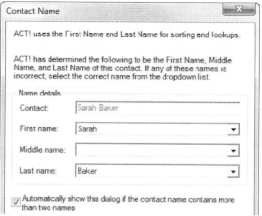

Figure 3-4 Contact Name dialog box

If a name has not been separated correctly, open the drop-down list for the name that is not correct and select the correct one. This may happen when someone's first or last name is two names like Johnnie Mae Westbrook. In this example, the contacts first name is Johnnie Mae. By default, ACT! will interpret it as shown in Figure 3-5. These separation options are what enables contacts to be sorted or used in a lookup by first or last name, even though the first and last name are in the same field.

By default, ACT! has been set up to not use Mr., Mrs., Ms., Esq., MD, PhD and Dr. as part of the first, middle or last name. I entered my name with "Dr" in front of it, then opened the Contact Name dialog box and saw that ACT! separated my name correctly, as shown in Figure 3-6. You can change these options as needed.

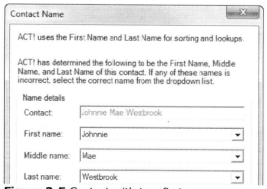

Figure 3-5 Contact with two first names

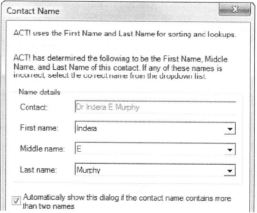

Figure 3-6 Contact name separated correctly

3. Type Capri Book Company in the Company field.

4. Open the Title field drop-down list.

   Scroll down the list and select the Sales Manager title, as illustrated in Figure 3-7.

   The **EDIT LIST VALUES** option is used to add, edit or delete the values in the drop-down list.

Figure 3-7 Title field drop-down list values

5. Switch to the Basic Contact Layout - 1024x768.

6. Type pur in the Department field, then press the Tab key. Notice that the Purchasing department has been filled in automatically.

7. Type 765 555 5330 in the Phone field. (Do not put spaces between the numbers. I typed it that way to make it easier for you to read.) Notice that the phone number was automatically formatted.

Phone Number Formatting

Like the salutation field, the phone number fields also have default formatting. The ellipsis button at the end of the Phone and Mobile fields will open the dialog box shown in Figure 3-8. The options shown are used to change how the phone number will be formatted. The default phone number format is for the US. If you enter a phone number for a different country and do not know the correct format for the country, open the Country field drop-down list shown in Figure 3-8 and select the country. After you click OK on the Enter Phone Number dialog box, the phone number will be formatted for the country that you selected.

The **EDIT FORMATS** button on the Enter Phone Number dialog box opens the dialog box shown in Figure 3-9. You can create your own phone number format or select one of the other formats shown in Figure 3-9 to be the new default format.

Figure 3-8 Enter Phone Number dialog box

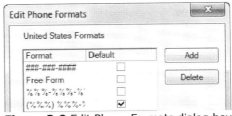

Figure 3-9 Edit Phone Formats dialog box

 Using Country Codes
The **COUNTRY CODE** is the prefix that you have to enter before you dial the area code. The Country Code for the United States is 1, as shown above in Figure 3-8 in brackets. Being able to look up the country code in the Country field drop-down list is helpful if you have contacts in other countries and do not know the country code.

Creating And Editing Contact Records

8. Enter the information in Table 3-3 in the appropriate fields on the Contact detail view.

   The top portion of the contact record should look like the one shown in Figure 3-10.

   This is the contact record that you will use to enter data on various tabs in the remainder of this exercise.

Field	Type This
Address 1	123 Main St
City	Los Angeles
State	CA
Zip	90277
Country	USA
ID/Status	Supplier

Table 3-3 Contact information

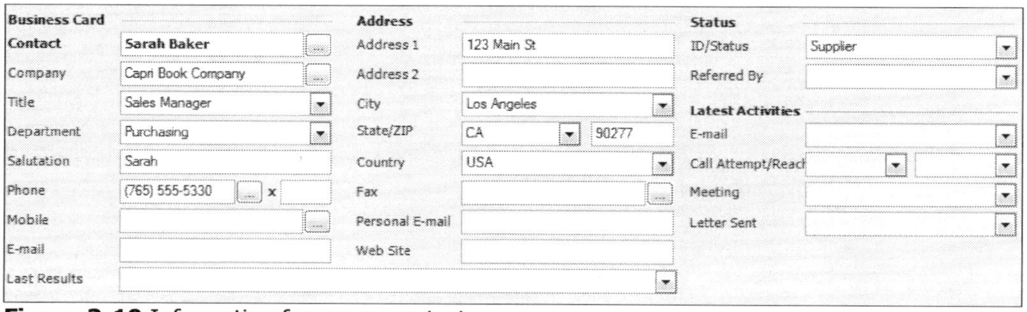

Figure 3-10 Information for a new contact

As shown above in Figure 3-10, there are two address fields. ACT! actually has three address fields. This view only displays two of them. All three fields are for one address, not three different addresses. Often, the physical street address goes in the Address 1 field and the other two address fields are used to enter the floor, suite or room number, for example.

Some company addresses also include a building name. These are examples of the type of address information that could be entered in the second and third address fields. If a contact has more than one company address, like a street address and a PO Box, you could use fields on the User Fields tab as long as the layout for that tab is modified to reflect what the fields are being used for.

The Notes Tab
The data on this tab is a log of each note that you or another user of the database created about the contact, company, group or opportunity. The entries on this tab are created automatically each time a note is created. An unlimited number of notes can be created.

Insert Note Dialog Box Toolbar
Table 3-4 explains the buttons on the Insert Note dialog box toolbar shown in Figure 3-11.

Figure 3-11 Insert Note dialog box toolbar

Chapter 3

Button	Description
1	Prints the note.
2	Displays the note to show how it will look when it is printed.
3	Spell checks the note.
4	Change the font for in the note.
5	Change the font size for the note.
6	Change the font color of the note.
7	Makes the selected text in the note bold.
8	Makes the selected text in the note italic.
9	Underlines the selected in the note text.
10	Draws a line through the selected text. This is usually done to indicate text that you want to delete.
11	Left aligns the text in the body of the note. This is the default alignment for text.
12	Centers the text in the body of the note.
13	Right aligns the text in the body of the note.
14	Creates a bulleted list in the body of the note.

Table 3-4 Insert Note dialog box toolbar buttons explained

1. On the **NOTES** tab, click the **INSERT NEW NOTE** button illustrated in Figure 3-12. Notice that the Date and Time fields are filled in automatically on the Insert Note dialog box. If you had created a My Record in this database, your name would be in the **RECORD MANAGER** field.

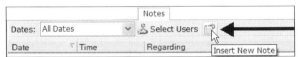

Figure 3-12 Insert New Note button illustrated

2. In the field at the bottom of the dialog box type This is my first note. It has an attachment and is associated to 3 contacts at Liberty.

The **CONTACT** button on the Insert Note dialog box opens the dialog box shown in Figure 3-13.

If you need to attach the same note to other contacts, select the other contacts on this dialog box.

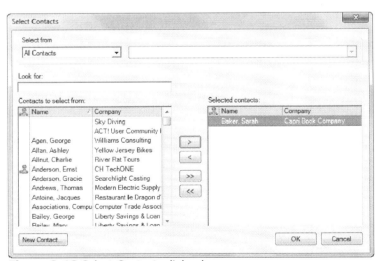

Figure 3-13 Select Contacts dialog box

Creating And Editing Contact Records

Sorting Contact Records On The Select Contacts Dialog Box
If you click on the Name or Company column headings in the **CONTACTS TO SELECT FROM** list or the **SELECTED CONTACTS** list, you can sort the contacts in ascending or descending order.

New Contact Dialog Box

Clicking the **NEW CONTACT** button shown above in Figure 3-13 opens the dialog box shown in Figure 3-14. This dialog box is used to create a new contact record.

Figure 3-14 New Contact dialog box

Add/Remove Dialog Box

The ellipsis button at the end of the **SHARE WITH** field on the Insert Note dialog box opens the dialog box shown in Figure 3-15.

Figure 3-15 Add/Remove dialog box

The options on this dialog box are used to share the note with everyone in a group, company or opportunity. By default when you click the button at the end of the Share with field, you will see a message about sharing public notes. Click OK to close the message window.

The Add/Remove dialog box replaces the Select Group/Company dialog box in ACT! 2009 and earlier.

3. Click the Contact button on the Insert Note dialog box.

4. Select the three contacts at Liberty Savings & Loan, as shown in Figure 3-16, by clicking on the first contact at the company, then press and hold down the Shift key and click on the last contact at Liberty.

Figure 3-16 Contacts selected to add the note to

5. Click the **ADD** button shown above in Figure 3-16.

   There should be four names in the **SELECTED CONTACTS** list on the Select Contacts dialog box, as shown in Figure 3-17.

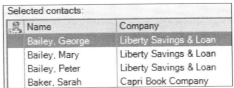

Figure 3-17 Contacts that will have the note attached

6. Click OK to close the dialog box.

How To Attach A File To A Contact Record

The **ATTACH** button on the Insert Note dialog box provides two options to attach a file to a note, as shown in Figure 3-18. The options are explained below.

Figure 3-18 Attach button options

① Selecting the **FILE** option stores a copy of the file with the note. Select this option if you know for sure that you will not need to see any changes that may be made to the original document, when the document is opened from inside of ACT!. This option also increases the size of the database.

② The **SHORTCUT** option creates a link to a file. The link is not dynamic, which means that if the file is moved to another folder, renamed or deleted, the shortcut will no longer work.

If the attached file needs to be opened by other users of the database and the shortcut attachment option is selected, the file needs to be in a location (a folder) that other users have access to, like a server. I don't know how the computers in your office are networked, but I doubt that the person down the hall from you has access to the hard drive on your computer. If you find out that they do, you need to call your IT department immediately and have them change the status of your hard drive to not be shared <smile>.

1. Click the **ATTACH** button on the Insert Note dialog box, then select the File option.

Creating And Editing Contact Records

2. Double-click on the **C3 ATTACH** file in your folder.

   The Insert Note dialog box should look like the one shown in Figure 3-19. You will have a different date and time.

   Checking the **PRIVATE** option will prevent other people that use the database from viewing the note. You would be the only person that could see this note.

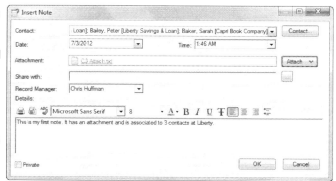

Figure 3-19 Insert Note dialog box

3. Click OK to close the Insert Note dialog box.

4. Click OK on the **SPELL CHECK STATUS** dialog box if you enabled the automatic spell checker option on the Preferences dialog box. If you wanted to spell check the note manually, click the **SPELL CHECK** button on the Insert Note dialog box toolbar. The entry on the Notes tab should look like the one shown in Figure 3-20.

Figure 3-20 Information added to the Notes tab

Attached Documents
When you attach a file in ACT!, a copy of the file is placed in the Attachments folder of the database. The original copy of the file is still where is was before you attached it. If you make changes to the original file (the one outside of ACT!), you will not see the changes when you open the attachment in ACT!. The opposite is also true. Changes made to the attached copy of the file will not be seen in the original file. You can edit the attached documents, as well as, view, email and print them. Chapter 9 covers how to edit attached documents. You have the three options explained below to manage attachments:

① You can reattach the original file to the note if the original file was changed and you need the changes attached to the note.
② You can copy the original file that you changed, to the Attachments folder in ACT!, as long as the original file still has the same file name. This will overwrite the file in the Attachments folder.
③ You can make the changes to the copy in the Attachments folder.

Tips For Viewing And Deleting Attachments On The Notes Tab
① By default, notes are displayed with the most recent one at the top of the list.
② To view an attachment, double-click on the note that has the attachment, then click on the **ATTACHMENT** link on the Edit Note a dialog box.
③ To delete an attachment from a note, double-click on the note. Click the Attach button, then select **FILE**. You will see the message shown in Figure 3-21. Click Yes and the attachment will be deleted.

Figure 3-21 Remove Attachment message

Attaching Files On The Documents Tab

Earlier you attached a document to a note. The Documents tab displays the documents that are associated with the current contact. The documents on this tab cannot be linked to another contact from this tab. There is an option on the Documents tab that is also used to attach a document to the current contact.

A file that is attached to a note does not appear on the Documents tab.

1. On the **DOCUMENTS** tab, click the **ADD DOCUMENT** button, then select the File option. You can also right-click in the white space on the Documents tab and select Add Document.

2. Double-click on the **C3 DOCUMENTS TAB** file in your folder.

   You will see a reference to the document, as shown in Figure 3-22.

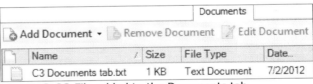
Figure 3-22 File added to the Documents tab

Tips For Viewing And Deleting Attachments On The Documents Tab
① To view an attachment on the Documents tab, double-click on the attachment.
② To delete an attachment from the Documents tab, right-click on it and select **REMOVE DOCUMENT**.

Relationships

This tab is used to create and display contact relationships. The Relate Contact dialog box looks similar to the Insert Note dialog box.

1. On the **RELATIONSHIPS** tab, click the **RELATE CONTACT** button. At the top of the dialog box, you should see the name Sarah Baker.

CREATING AND EDITING CONTACT RECORDS

If you want to relate the contact to one other contact, open the first drop-down list and select the contact. If you want to relate the contact to more than one contact at the same time, like all contacts in a company or group and all of them have the same relationship, follow the steps below.

2. On the Relate Contact dialog box, Contacts button ⇒ Select Contacts. You will see the Select Contacts dialog box.

3. Open the Select from drop-down list and select Companies. Open the drop-down list to the right and select Verge Records.

4. Add all of the contacts from the company to the Selected Contacts list, then click OK.

5. Open the drop-down list for Sarah Baker and select Business Partner.

6. Open the last drop-down list and select Vendor.

7. In the Notes field at the bottom, type `This relationship is for the record company to write a jingle for a commercial.`

8. Your dialog box should look like the one shown in Figure 3-23.

   Click OK.

   You will see a separate entry for each contact at the record company on the Relationships tab, as shown in Figure 3-24.

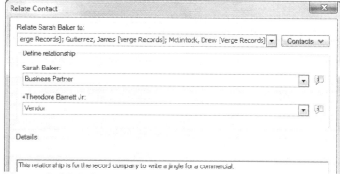

Figure 3-23 Relate Contact dialog box

Figure 3-24 Contacts added to the Relationships tab

 In ACT! 2010, the Relate Contact dialog box had a formatting toolbar. The toolbar was removed in ACT! 2011.

Chapter 3

Entering Information On The Personal Info Tab

 In ACT! 2008 and earlier, this was called the **HOME ADDRESS** tab.

In addition to the fields for the contacts home address, the following fields are also available on this tab:

① The **PERSONAL E-MAIL** field should not be used for the business e-mail address, especially if you plan to use the Mail Merge wizard to create an email mail merge. The wizard does not use this field. (4)

② The **MESSENGER ID** field is used to store the contacts Instant Messenger ID or screen name.

③ The **WEB SITE** field is used to store the contacts personal web site. (4)

(4) The location of this field varies, depending on the layout. On the 800x600 layout, this field is on the Personal Info tab. On the 1024x768 layout, this field is on the top portion of the window.

 Editing The Web Site And Personal E-mail Fields
These fields among others, can be edited differently then most of the contact fields.
You can delete the contents of the field and re-type it or you can right-click in the field and select **EDIT WEB SITE**, as shown in Figure 3-25 or **EDIT PERSONAL E-MAIL**. If selected, these options select (highlight) the information in the field so that you do not have to delete it before you start typing in the field.

Figure 3-25 Edit Web Site field shortcut menu

1. Select the 800x600 layout.

2. On the **PERSONAL INFO** tab, type `1899 Payton Place Village Drive` in the Address 1 field.

3. Add the information in Table 3-5 to the record.

Field	Type This
City	Sacramento
State	CA
Zip	99990
Home Phone	7815551308

Table 3-5 Home Address information

3-13

Creating And Editing Contact Records

Using The Date Field Calendar

Date fields, like the Birthday field, will have a calendar like the one shown in Figure 3-26. You can use the calendar to select the date or you can type the date in the field. Find the month and year in the calendar, then click on the day that you need, by using the options that are explained below.

Figure 3-26 Date field calendar

The **TODAY** button will add the current date to the field.

Clicking the **LEFT ARROW** button at the top of the calendar will display previous months.

Clicking the **RIGHT ARROW** button will display future months.

What I like about date fields is that you do not have to type a four digit year or type a zero as the first digit of a month or day. You can type 6/2/09 and ACT! will convert it to the date shown in Figure 3-27.

Figure 3-27 Date field converted

The **BIRTHDAY** field does not require you to enter the year the contact was born. Entering the day and month is sufficient. The current year will be filled in automatically if you do not enter it. Chapter 4 covers this and other **ANNUAL EVENT** fields and how to use them as a lookup field.

4. Click on the arrow at the end of the Birthday field, then select your next birthday on the calendar. The information on the Personal Info tab should look similar to the information shown in Figure 3-28.

   Notice that the phone number was not automatically formatted. That is because the Home Phone field is a Free Form format field. [See Phone Number Formatting, earlier in this chapter]

Figure 3-28 Personal Info tab fields

Contact Access Tab

 In ACT! 2008 and earlier, this was called the **CONTACT INFO** tab.

3-14

Chapter 3

The majority of fields shown in Figure 3-29 are filled in and updated automatically. The values cannot be changed.

The **RECORD MANAGER** field lists the current owner of the contact record.

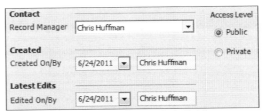
Figure 3-29 Contact Access tab fields

The **CREATED ON/BY** fields store the date that the record was created and the name of the user that created the contact record. I do not know why the Created On field has a drop-down list because this field is filled in automatically when the record is created and it can't be changed.

The **EDITED ON/BY** fields store the date that the record was last edited and the user that edited the record. These fields cannot be changed.

The **ACCESS LEVEL** options are used to make the contact record **PUBLIC** (anyone with rights to the database can view it) or **PRIVATE** (only the Record Manager can view it). This is the only option on the tab that can be changed.

Latest Activities Tab

The fields shown in Figure 3-30 store the last time that a user of the database was in touch with the contact. Except for the Last Results fields, the other fields are filled in automatically.

Figure 3-30 Latest Activities tab fields

User Fields Tab

The fields shown in Figure 3-31 are free form. They are used to enter data that does not fit into any of the fields that currently exist in the database.

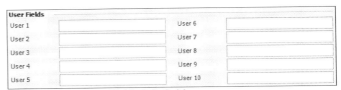
Figure 3-31 User Fields tab fields

Later in the book you will learn how to change the labels of these fields to something meaningful for the data that you enter on this tab.

While the fields on the User Fields tab seem like a good idea to use, they can be dangerous if more than one person is using the database. That is because by default, any user that has rights to modify the layout, add, edit or delete information, can do just that.

For example, one user may decide to use the User 2 field to store an alternate email address for the contact. Another user may use the User 2 field to store the date that they mailed the contact a sample product. If this happens, one of these types of data will have to be moved to a different field. This may have to be done manually, record by record, which is probably not something that you want to do.

Creating And Editing Contact Records

Saving Data
If any of the fields on the view that you are using have the **GENERATE HISTORY** option enabled, a history record will be created and will appear on the History tab when the record is saved. There are two ways to save the data that you enter, as explained below.

① Move to another record.
② Click the Save Changes button on the toolbar.

Exercise 3.2: Duplicating Contact Information
In Exercise 3.1 you created a contact record with a company that was not already in the database. In this exercise you will create a contact record based on information from an existing contact record. This is known as duplicating a contact. This will save you time because you do not have to retype the company information. Duplicating a contact record that has the company information that you need, duplicates data in some of the fields in the top half of the Contact detail view. There are two ways that you can duplicate records, as explained below:

① You can duplicate the primary fields, which are the company, phone, fax, address, city, state, zip code, country and web site fields. These are the primary fields that ACT! sets up as the default. You can make other fields primary fields as needed.
② All of the fields can be duplicated. If this option is selected, the only fields not duplicated are the contact name and e-mail address fields.

Opportunity fields cannot be used as primary contact fields.

Creating A New Contact Based On The Primary Fields

1. Switch to the 1024x768 layout, then display the contact Jonathan Jenkins. (**Hint**: If you have the Lookup Search options displayed in the Navigation bar you can type the name in the **CONTAINS** field, then click the Go button.)

2. Click the **DUPLICATE CONTACT** button on the Contacts toolbar.

   You should see the dialog box shown in Figure 3-32.

   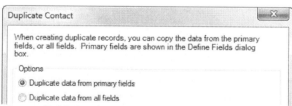

   Figure 3-32 Duplicate Contact dialog box

3. Select the option **DUPLICATE DATA FROM PRIMARY FIELDS**, if it is not already selected, then click OK. You should see a new record with the primary fields filled in.

4. Click Yes, when prompted that the changes affect the lookup/sort criteria.

5. Add the information in Table 3-6 to the new contact record. The top half of the contact record should look like the one shown in Figure 3-33. Keep the record displayed to complete the next exercise.

Field	Type This
Contact	Dan Day
Title	Analyst
Department	Engineering

Table 3-6 Duplicate contact information

Chapter 3

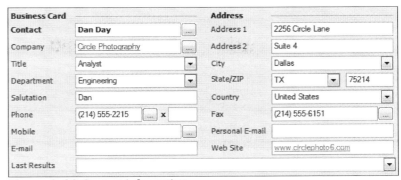

Figure 3-33 Contact information

 Other Ways To Open The Duplicate Contact Dialog Box
① Right-click on a blank space in the top half of the Contact detail view and select **DUPLICATE CONTACT**.
② Contacts ⇒ Duplicate Contact.

Contact Detail View Related Tasks

The options shown in Figure 3-34 are primarily found on the detail view. Some of the options are also on list view. The options are explained below.

Figure 3-34 Contact detail view related tasks

VIEW ALL CONTACTS Is the same as selecting Lookup ⇒ All Contacts. This option is helpful when you have already created a lookup and now want to display all of the records. It is quicker to use this link, then opening the Lookup menu and selecting the option. It may just be my laptop, but the View All Contacts link takes longer to display all of the records then the option on the Lookup menu does.

CREATING AND EDITING CONTACT RECORDS

WRITE LETTER Opens the ACT! Word Processor and displays a letter template, as shown in Figure 3-35.

This template is in the ACT Demo layout.

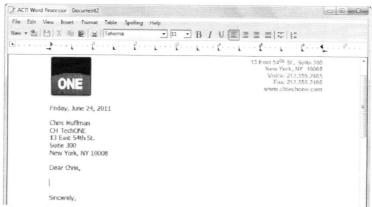

Figure 3-35 Letter template

PRINT CURRENT SCREEN Opens the Quick Print Options dialog box so that you can select options for how the screen will be printed.

PRINT MAILING LABELS & ENVELOPES Opens the Print dialog box that has options for printing labels and envelopes.

MODIFY LAYOUT Opens the current contact detail view layout in the Layout Designer, so that the layout can be changed.

SCHEDULE ACTIVITY SERIES [See Chapter 7, Activity Series]

ADD CONTACT TO GROUP Opens the Add/Remove dialog box to select groups and companies to add the contact to.

RELATE TO ANOTHER CONTACT Opens the Relate Contact dialog box. [See Relationships, earlier in this chapter]

VIEW GROUPS/COMPANIES Opens the dialog box shown in Figure 3-36.

 In ACT! 2010, this dialog box was removed, but in ACT! 2012 it was back.

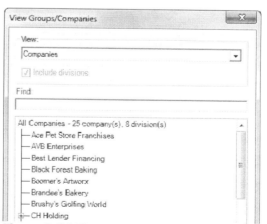

Figure 3-36 View Groups/Companies dialog box

MANAGE SMART TASKS [See Chapter 14, Using Smart Tasks]

Contact List View Related Tasks

The options shown in Figure 3-37 are for the Contact list view. The options that are only on the list view are explained below. The others were explained in the previous section.

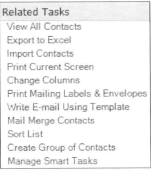

Figure 3-37 Contact list view related tasks

EXPORT TO EXCEL Exports the contacts that are displayed on the list view to Excel.

IMPORT CONTACTS Opens the Import Wizard, which lets you import data from a variety of sources, as shown in Figure 3-38.

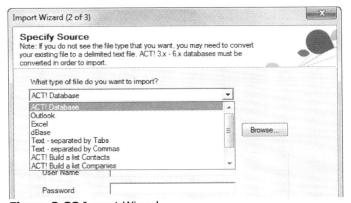

Figure 3-38 Import Wizard

CHANGE COLUMNS Opens the Customize Columns dialog box. [See Chapter 15, Exercise 15.3]

WRITE E-MAIL USING TEMPLATE Opens the Template folder (for the database) so that you can select a template to use for the email that you want to create. Once you select the template, a new email window will open with the template that you selected.

MAIL MERGE CONTACTS Opens the Mail Merge Wizard.

SORT LIST Opens the Sort dialog box to sort the contacts displayed in the view.

CREATE GROUP OF CONTACTS Displays the Group detail view. All of the contacts displayed in the view will be added to the group that you create.

FINDING CONTACTS IN A DATABASE

In this chapter you will learn how to use the following search techniques:

- ☑ Lookup options on the Navigation Pane
- ☑ Lookup command
- ☑ Keyword Search lookups
- ☑ Multiple field lookups
- ☑ Narrow lookup option
- ☑ Add to lookup option
- ☑ Universal search feature
- ☑ Annual Events lookup

You will also learn the following:

- ☑ How to modify more than one record at the same time
- ☑ How to sort records
- ☑ How to delete records

Finding Records

Having a database with hundreds or thousands of contacts is great. Being able to find the contacts that you need to access quickly, is a core reason of putting information into a database. ACT! comes with several lookup options to find contacts. Depending on the contacts that you need to find, one lookup option is probably a better solution then the other lookup options. Many of the lookup options are covered in this chapter. Some are specifically for contacts and others can be used to look up other types of records.

Lookup Options On The Navigation Pane

At the top of the Navigation Pane is a lookup section, as shown in Figure 4-1, if the lookup option is enabled on the Preferences dialog box.

This section of the Navigation Pane is used to find records. This drop-down list field (the Contact Field in Figure 4-1) contains all of the fields that can be searched.

Figure 4-1 Contacts Navigation Pane lookup options

Each of the other views on the Navigation Pane also has a lookup section. The options in the drop-down list change, depending on the view that is currently displayed. The options in this section provide quick access to some of the lookup options in ACT!.

The drop-down list is used to select the field that you want to search on. The fields on the tabs of the detail views are also included in this list.

The **MORE OPTIONS** link opens the Lookup dialog box.

The steps below demonstrate how to use the lookup options.

1. Open the drop-down list and select the field that you want to search on.

2. Type the value in the Contains field that the field that you selected must have, then click the Go button.

Exercise 4.1: Using The Lookup Options On The Navigation Pane

1. In the Related Tasks section of the Navigation Pane, click the View All Contacts link.

2. Open the Contact Field drop-down list, then select Company.

3. Type `Circle` in the **CONTAINS** field, then click the Go button. You will see all of the contact records in the Contact list view that have Circle in the Company field.

The Lookup Command

The Lookup command is used to find records based on the criteria that you select. Other software packages use the term **QUERY** when discussing finding specific records. You can find all contacts in one state or all contacts that have the same title. You can use the Lookup command to find contacts by Company, First Name, Last Name, Phone Number, City, State, Zip Code or ID/Status. Later you will learn how to find contacts using other fields. The biggest limitation to lookups is that the criteria

Chapter 4

cannot be saved. After you complete the lookup exercises, you will better understand why it is so important to enter data correctly and to enter as much data as possible for each record that you create.

Lookup Contacts Dialog Box Options

This dialog box provides several options to help you find the records that you need. The options are explained below. The options shown in Figure 4-2 are used to select how to find the records. These options are used to include or exclude records.

The options shown in Figure 4-3 are used to select the type of records to search, to find the contacts that you are looking for.

The **CURRENT LOOKUP** options shown in Figure 4-4 are used to determine the type of lookup that you want to create. The options are explained in Table 4-1.

Figure 4-2 Search criteria options

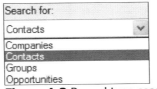

Figure 4-3 Record type search options

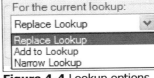

Figure 4-4 Lookup options

Option	Description
Replace Lookup	This is the default option. It creates a new lookup.
Add to Lookup	Adds the contacts from the lookup that you are creating now, to the previous lookup that you created.
Narrow Lookup	Searches the records from the previous lookup to exclude (remove) records from it, based on the criteria that you select in the current lookup.

Table 4-1 Current lookup drop-down list field options explained

Exercise 4.2: Using The Lookup Command

1. Lookup ⇒ State.

2. Open the drop-down list to the far right and select NY or type NY in the field.

3. Click on the button before the words **SHOW MORE OPTIONS** on the dialog box. You should have the options shown in Figure 4-5.

   Click OK.

   You should see that record 1 of 26 is displayed.

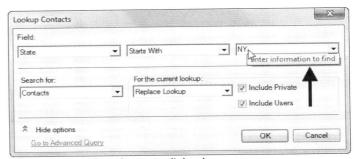

Figure 4-5 Lookup Contacts dialog box

4-3

Finding Contacts In A Database

Notice the field in the upper right corner Figure 4-5 with the tool tip. I will refer to that field as the Search field. The **INCLUDE PRIVATE** option is used to search your private records. The **INCLUDE USERS** option is used to retrieve other database users "My Records", if they meet the search criteria.

The result of a lookup will only display records that match the criteria that you select. Notice that the view changed to the Contact list view. If you click the Detail View button on the toolbar, you will be able to see more information for each of the contacts that were retrieved by the lookup.

Notice that the information on the Status bar in the lower left corner of the workspace displays **LOOKUP: STATE**. This lets you know what field was selected for the current lookup.

4. Lookup ⇒ All Contacts, or click the View All Contacts link in the Related Tasks section of the Navigation Pane. All of the contacts will be displayed.

5. Click the Detail View button on the Contacts toolbar.

> **Contact Detail View Lookup Shortcut**
> Using the lookup options on the menu or clicking the **MORE OPTIONS** link in the Lookup section of the Navigation Pane is probably how most people create a lookup, but there is another way. Right-click in the field on the Contact detail view that you want to use as the lookup field and select **LOOKUP [FIELD NAME]**, as illustrated in Figure 4-6. The Lookup Contacts dialog box will open. This also works on fields on tabs that you can enter data, like the fields on the Personal Info tab.

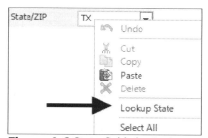
Figure 4-6 State field shortcut menu

Exercise 4.3: Using Keyword Search Lookups

Keyword search lookups are used to find records based on information in any field. You can perform a keyword search for a word or phrase in any field, including fields on the tabs. This is different from the lookup that you created in the previous exercise. The lookup that you created in the previous exercise searched for records that **START WITH** the value that you typed in or selected. Keyword searches are different. They retrieve records that have the value any place in a field.

This is very helpful when you remember a word or phrase, but do not remember what field it is in. Depending on how many tables you select to search in, the keyword search could take a while because all of the fields are searched, including fields on the System tabs, which each have their own table in the database. [See Chapter 18, Tabs Overview]

1. Lookup ⇒ Advanced ⇒ Search on Keywords. You should see the Search on Keywords dialog box.

2. Type `Sales` in the **SEARCH FOR** field.

Chapter 4

3. Select the **CONTACTS** type option, then clear the **OPPORTUNITIES** option in the Look in section.

   You should have the options selected that are shown in Figure 4-7.

Figure 4-7 Search on Keywords dialog box

These options will search for the word "Sales" in all contact, activity, history, notes and relationships fields.

The **FIELDS** option in the Look in section includes all fields for the record type that is selected. For example in Figure 4-7 above, selecting the Fields option will cause all of the contact fields to be searched.

4. Click the **FIND NOW** button. The records shown at the bottom of the dialog box match the criteria that you selected.

You should see that the keyword search criteria "Sales" was found 374 times. Currently, there are not 374 records in the database. This is not the number of records that have the search criteria. It is the number of fields that have the word "Sales" in it. This means several records have the word "Sales" in more than one field.

Viewing The Keyword Search Results

When you view records retrieved from the search, the Search on Keywords dialog box stays open. This allows you to go back to it to select other records to view in detail. You can also change the search options and perform another search. There are several options that you can select from to view the results in the Contact detail view, as explained below.

① You can scroll through the list of records at the bottom of the Search on Keywords dialog box. You may recognize the records that you are looking for.
② If you right-click on a single record at the bottom of the dialog box and select **GO TO RECORD**, as illustrated in Figure 4-8, the detail record will be displayed.
③ You can select more than one record to view by clicking on one record, then pressing and holding down the **CTRL** key and clicking on the other records that you want to view, as shown in Figure 4-9. Once the records are selected, right-click and select **LOOKUP SELECTED RECORDS**.
④ Click the **CREATE LOOKUP** button at the top of the Search on Keywords dialog box. This option will create a lookup to display every record (on the Contact List view) with the record type that you selected on the dialog box.

Figure 4-8 Keyword Search shortcut menu options

4-5

Finding Contacts In A Database

Figure 4-9 Multiple records selected to view

5. Select the first 10 records on the Search on Keywords dialog box, then right-click on any of the highlighted records and select **LOOKUP SELECTED RECORDS**.

Notice that the dialog box is minimized in the lower left corner of the screen. The reason that there are only five contact records is because some of these contact records have more than one field that has the word "Sales" in it.

6. Close the Search on Keywords dialog box. Lookup ⇒ All Contacts, when you are finished viewing the contact records.

> **Keyword Search Viewing Tips**
> ① Selecting the **LOOKUP ALL** option on the shortcut menu shown earlier in Figure 4-8 is the same as clicking the Create Lookup button.
> ② Double-clicking on a record in the bottom half of the Search on Keywords dialog box is the same as right-clicking on a record and selecting Go To Record.
> ③ To select several adjacent records, click on the first one, then press and hold down the **SHIFT** key and click on the last record that you want to view.

Exercise 4.4: How To Create A Lookup Using Multiple Fields

Exercise 4.2 covered how to perform a lookup using one field. In this exercise you will learn how to look up records using more than one field. If you wanted to email managers that are in Boise, you would have to search two fields. You would have to search the City field for "Boise" and you would have to search the Title field for "Manager".

If you open the Lookup menu you will see the City field. You will not see the Title field. It appears that you cannot search the Title field. The **OTHER FIELDS** option on the Lookup menu contains the fields that are not listed on the Lookup menu. You can also right-click in the Title field on the view and select the lookup option from the shortcut menu.

1. Lookup ⇒ City.

2. Type `Boise` in the Search field, then press Enter. There are three contacts in Boise. Notice that two contacts have the Manager title.

Using The Narrow Lookup Option

Until now, when you performed a lookup, the Replace Lookup option was used. The Replace Lookup option tells ACT! to remove the records from the previous lookup and start over.

The **NARROW LOOKUP** option is used to reduce the number of contacts that are from the result of the previous lookup. In this exercise, the previous lookup selected all contacts in Boise. Now you want to find the managers in Boise. If you selected the Replace lookup option you would get all managers, no matter what city they are in. This is not what you want in this exercise. The Narrow Lookup option will only search the records that were retrieved from the previous lookup.

1. Lookup ⇒ Other Fields. Open the Field drop-down list and select Title.

 The **OTHER FIELDS** option does not provide any additional fields to search on, that are not already in the Field drop-down list. If the field that you want to search on, is not on the Lookup menu, you can select any field to open the Lookup Contacts dialog box and select the field that you need from the **FIELD** drop-down list.

2. Open the Search drop-down list and select Manager.

3. Select the **NARROW LOOKUP** option.

   The Lookup Contacts dialog box should have the options shown in Figure 4-10.

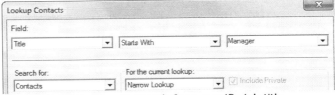

Figure 4-10 Options to search for a specific job title

4. Click OK. You should now have two records in the lookup. This means that one of the three original contact records retrieved does not have "Manager" in the Title field.

This may seem like a lot of work to remove one record. If the database retrieved thousands of records that met your initial lookup criteria, being able to perform another lookup to remove 1,000 records from the search automatically, makes this a good feature to use.

Exercise 4.5: Using The Add To Lookup Option

If you wanted to find contacts with a Texas address or were sales reps, using the Replace lookup and Narrow lookup options together would not give you the results that you are looking for. The **ADD TO LOOKUP** option is used to combine the results from different lookups. The records from the various lookups do not have to be related. This is the type of lookup that you will learn how to create in this exercise.

1. Lookup ⇒ State. Type TX in the Search field.

2. Make sure that the **REPLACE LOOKUP** option is selected. Click OK. 14 records should have been retrieved.

3. Lookup ⇒ Other Fields. Select Title from the Field drop-down list, then select Sales Representative from the Search drop-down list.

When performing lookups, you should select an item from the Search drop-down list as much as possible, even though the Search field will allow you to type in an entry. If you type in an entry and what you type in is not used on any record, you will not retrieve the records that you expect.

4. Select the **ADD TO LOOKUP** option. Click OK. There should be 20 records displayed. All of the records in the lookup either have "TX" in the State field or "Sales Representative" in the Title field. If someone typed "Texas" in the State field on contact records, those records would not be retrieved in this search.

Finding Contacts In A Database

Universal Search

At the right side of the Global toolbar is the Search tool. It can be used to search for any information regardless of the view that is currently displayed. For example, you could search for opportunities from a Group view.

Operators like "AND" and "OR" can also be used to combine terms that you want to search for. The question mark (used to replace one character) and asterisk (used to replace two or more characters) wildcard characters can also be used in the Universal search field. The steps bellow show you how to use this search feature.

1. From any view that has the Search field at the end of the Global toolbar, type in the phrase, words or terms that you want to search for.

2. Click the Go button. You will see the screen shown in Figure 4-11.

Figure 4-11 Screen results window

The **SHOW ONLY** options are used to select (filter) the search results by record type.
The **LAST EDITED** options are used to select a date range.
These options are optional. To view a record, click on a link in the Name column.

Finding Contact Records That Are Missing Information

The goal of Exercise 4.4 was to find contacts that meet specific criteria to send an email to. In order to send the contacts an email, they need to have an email address. You can use the Lookup command to find contacts that do or do not have an email address. Searching for records that do not have data in certain fields is a good way to keep contacts from having data missing.

Exercise 4.6: Find Contacts Without An Email Address

In this exercise you will find all contacts that do not have an email address.

1. Lookup ⇒ E-mail Address.

   Select the **DOES NOT CONTAIN DATA** option, illustrated in Figure 4-12.

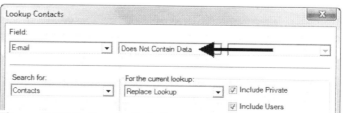

Figure 4-12 Options to find all contacts without an email address

Chapter 4

2. Click OK. To verify that the records do not have an email address, click the Detail View button. View a few records and look at the E-mail field. You will see that the field is empty.

The reason that I had you view the records on the Contact detail view is because the E-mail field is not displayed by default on the Contact list view. You will learn how to modify a layout to display the fields that you need.

Exercise 4.7: Finding Contacts That You Added To The Database

One way to help keep data accurate and consistent is to review it. Everyone that uses the database should do this periodically. The frequency that data is checked and verified depends on how many records are added and how often data is modified.

In this exercise you will create a lookup that finds all contacts that you added to the database in the last month. The fields that you need for this search are the Record Creator and Create Date fields on the Contact Access tab. In Chapter 16 you will create a report to print this data.

1. Lookup ⇒ Other Fields.

   Select the options shown in Figure 4-13. You have to type in the Record Creators name.

   Click OK.

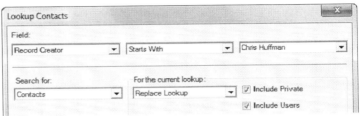
Figure 4-13 Record Creator field lookup criteria

2. Lookup ⇒ Other Fields.

   Select the options shown in Figure 4-14.

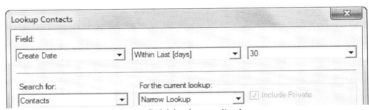
Figure 4-14 Create Date field lookup criteria

3. Click OK. You should see the two records shown in Figure 4-15. These records should look familiar because you created them earlier.

Figure 4-15 Contacts that you added to the database in the last 30 days

Annual Events Lookup

Annual events is another type of lookup. Examples of annual events are anniversaries, birthdays and yearly salary reviews. By default, annual events do not appear on calendars, but they can be added to a calendar. Creating a lookup is one way to be able to view annual events.

 Annual event fields only search the month and day portion of the date field, because they are tracked from year to year.

Finding Contacts In A Database

Exercise 4.8: Lookup Annual Events

In this exercise you will create a lookup to find all contacts with a birthday between January 1, 2010 and March 31, 2010.

1. Lookup ⇒ Annual Events.

   The options in the **SEARCH FOR** drop-down list shown in Figure 4-16 display all of the types of annual events that are currently being used in the database.

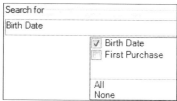

Figure 4-16 Annual event types

2. Accept the Birth Date search option, then select the **DATE RANGE** option.

3. Open the first date drop-down list field and select January 1, 2010, as shown in Figure 4-17. Open the second date drop-down list field and select March 31, 2010. You should have the options selected that are shown in Figure 4-18.

Figure 4-17 Date field calendar

Figure 4-18 Birth Date annual event search options

4. Click the **FIND NOW** button. You will see the contacts that have a birthday in the date range that you selected.

5. Close the Annual Events Search dialog box, then display all of the contacts.

If you click the **SCHEDULE TO-DO** button, you can create an activity for the contact that is selected at the bottom of the Annual Events Search dialog box. The contacts name will appear on the Schedule Activities dialog box. This option will not recognize more than one selected contact.

 Annual Events Search Viewing Tips
The records shown at the bottom of the Annual Events Search dialog box match the criteria. The options explained below are how you can view the results.

① You can search for more than one annual event at the same time. As shown earlier in Figure 4-16, you can check more than one annual event type or you can select the **ALL** option to lookup all of the annual event types that are in the database.
② If you right-click on a single record at the bottom of the Annual Events Search dialog box and select **GO TO CONTACT**, the record will be displayed.

Chapter 4

> **Annual Events Search Viewing Tips** (Continued)
> ③ Click the **CREATE LOOKUP** button. This button will create a lookup to display every record that is displayed at the bottom of the Annual Events Search dialog box in the Contact detail view.
> ④ Double-clicking on a record is the same as right-clicking and selecting **GO TO CONTACT**.

ACT! Annual Events Report

The **PRINT LIST** button on the Annual Events Search dialog box prints the report shown in Figure 4-19.

Figure 4-19 ACT! Annual Events report

Contact Activity Lookup

This type of lookup is used to find contacts whose records were or were not updated since a certain date. The lookup searches on any or all of the following tabs: Notes, History, Activities, Opportunities and Contact Access. This lookup is useful if you have a lot of contacts that you need to keep up with on a regular basis. It is also a good way to make sure that the data is accurate and that none of your contacts are being neglected or have fallen off of your radar, as they say.

Exercise 4.9: Find Contacts That Have Not Been Updated

In this exercise you will search for contacts that have not had the notes, opportunities or activities updated since February 1, 2010.

1. Lookup ⇒ Contact Activity.

2. Change the **SINCE DATE** to 2/1/2010.

   > I am not sure why, but the value in the **SINCE DATE** field is saved in ACT!. This means that the next time that you open this dialog box, the date that you selected the last time that you used the dialog box will automatically be in this field.

3. Clear the following options: Contact fields and Histories. Select the Activities option. You should have the options selected that are shown in Figure 4-20.

   > The Histories and Activities options allow specific categories to be searched for, as shown in Figure 4-21.

4-11

Finding Contacts In A Database

Figure 4-21 Activity options

Figure 4-20 Contact Activity dialog box options

4. Click OK. There should be 34 records on the Contact list view. This would be the list that you would work from, because the contact records have not been updated in a long time.

> **Contact Activity Lookup Tips**
> ① Lookups are not case sensitive. Typing "Marketing" or "marketing" will return the same results.
> ② LOOKUP ⇒ PREVIOUS displays the last nine searches that you ran, as shown in Figure 4-22. You can select the search that you want to run again. When you reopen ACT!, these searches will not be available because they are not saved.
> ③ Right-click in a field in the top half of the Contact detail view and select Lookup (Field Name) to open the Lookup dialog box.
> ④ When only one record meets the lookup criteria, it is displayed in the Contact detail view. You do not have to display all contacts before creating a lookup.

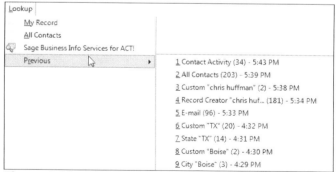

Figure 4-22 Previous searches

Modifying Several Records At The Same Time

You may have the need to change the data in the same field on several records. You could make the changes one record at a time or you could create a lookup to retrieve all of the records that you need to change and change all of them at the same time.

Chapter 4

 If you do not create a lookup first, the changes will be made to every record in the database.

If you have several company contacts at the same address and the company moves, you could look up the company address that you need to change and change all of the records at the same time, if the address fields are not linked. You can also change data on the User Fields, Personal Info and Secondary Contacts tabs this way.

The **REPLACE FIELD** command is used to change the data in a field for multiple records at the same time.

Exercise 4.10: How To Modify Several Records At The Same Time

In this exercise you will change the value in the Last Results field and add a note to a user defined field for all contacts in NY. The tasks that you will learn in this exercise are helpful for updating several records at the same time, as well as, keeping the data consistent and accurate.

 It is a good idea to make a back up copy of the database before modifying several records at the same time. This is known as a **GLOBAL** change. This type of change cannot be undone with a mouse click. You do not have to create a back up copy now because this is a practice database.

Change The Last Results Field

1. Create a lookup to find all contacts in NY. The lookup should retrieve 26 records.

2. Edit ⇒ Replace Field. You will see the Replace Data dialog box.

3. Open the Replace contents of field drop-down list and select the **LAST RESULTS** field.

4. Open the Value drop-down list and select **DISCUSSED OPPORTUNITIES**, as shown in Figure 4-23.

Figure 4-23 Replace data options for the Last Results field

5. Click OK. When you see the Replace/Swap/Copy message that lets you know that all records in the current lookup will be modified, click Yes to modify the records.

Change The Value In A User Defined Field

In this part of the exercise you will use the Replace Field command to change the value in a user defined field. User defined fields are free form fields that are used to enter data that there is no existing field for.

1. Switch to the 800x600 layout, then Edit ⇒ Replace Field.

Finding Contacts In A Database

2. Select the User 10 field from the first drop-down list, then type Should this record be private? in the **VALUE** field, as shown in Figure 4-24.

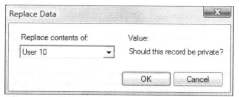

Figure 4-24 Replace data options for the User 10 field

3. Click OK, then click Yes to modify the records.

Observe the following information about the 26 records in the lookup, by clicking the Detail View button.

① The **LAST RESULTS** field on the Latest Activities tab has been set to Discussed opportunities. On the 1024x768 layout, this field is on the top portion of the view, instead of on a tab.
② The **EDITED ON** field on the Contact Access tab has today's date.
③ The **USER 10** field on the User Fields tab has the text that you typed in the Value field shown above in Figure 4-24.

Exercise 4.11: How To Delete Data From Several Records At The Same Time

Just like you can add or change data in a field for multiple records, you can also delete data from a field for multiple records at the same time. You will learn how in this exercise.

1. With the 26 NY records still in the lookup, Edit ⇒ Replace Field.

2. Select the User 10 field from the first drop-down list and leave the Value field empty. Leaving the Value field empty will overwrite the data in the field with blanks, which produces the same effect as deleting data in the field.

3. Click OK, then click Yes. You can view the information on the User Fields tab. You will see that the User 10 field for the 26 records is now blank.

Using The Contact List View

Until now, you have been using the Contact detail view to look at records. This view only displays one record at a time. The Contact list view resembles a spreadsheet and displays all of the contacts that you have the right to see. Options not covered on the Contact list view in this chapter are covered in Chapter 9. [See Chapter 9, Tagging Contacts]

The first two columns on the Contact list view shown in Figure 4-25, are used to visually bring records to your attention.

The first column will have an icon in it if the contact record is a user of the database.

The second column will display a lock icon if the record was marked private by the current user (you).

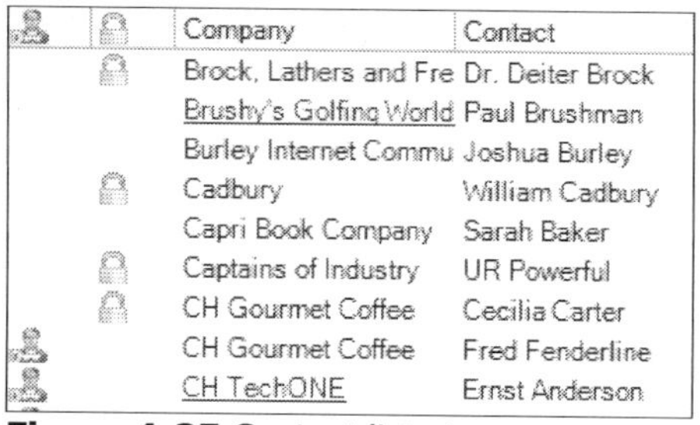

Figure 4-25 Contact list view

Chapter 4

Sorting By Columns In The Contact List View

You can sort the records in the Contact list view by clicking on the column heading that you want to sort on. The default sort order is based on the Company field.

1. Lookup ⇒ All Contacts. On the Contact list view, click on the Contact column heading.

Notice that the records are now sorted by the contacts last name, even though the first and last names are in the same column. The Last name field is the field that the Contact column actually sorts on.

You should see a triangle in the Contact column heading. If the triangle points up like this ▲, the records are sorted in ascending (A to Z or 1 to 10) order. If the triangle points down like this ▼, the records are sorted in descending (Z to A or 10 to 1) order.

 If your database has hundreds or thousands of records, you may not want to scroll down the list even though the records are currently sorted to find the contact that you need. If that is the case, the steps below show you how to find to a specific record in the list without scrolling.

2. Open the Options drop-down list shown in Figure 4-26 at the far right and select Show Look For.

Figure 4-26 Options drop-down list

3. Click on the column heading, not the arrow on the column heading, of the field that has the value that you want to look for to sort the list. In this exercise, click on the Contact column.

4. Type the first few letters of what you are looking for. In this example, type `York`, because that is a contacts last name.

You will see the first contact in the list that matches what you typed in, is highlighted. Also notice that the letters that you typed in are in the **LOOK FOR** field even though you did not click in this field before you typed in the information.

The more letters that you type, the closer ACT! will be able to find the record that you are looking for. This works for all columns, as long as the list is sorted on that column before you start typing in the search criteria.

View Detail Information From The Contact List View

If you want to view all of the data for a contact from the Contact list view, double-click on the contact that you want to view. If you click on a field that is hyperlinked (blue), like the company or web site fields, you will open the Company detail record or the web site.

How To Select And View Specific Records

If you have a database with thousands of records, you will probably not want to see all of the records in the Contact list view. You can select (highlight) any of the records and only view the records that you select.

Finding Contacts In A Database

1. Click the List View button. Click on the Company column heading. The records should be in alphabetical order by company. If not, click on the Company column heading again.

2. Click on the first record with the company name A1 Services. Press and hold down the Shift key, then click on the last record with the same company name.

3. Press and hold down the Ctrl key, then select all of the Beautiful Friendship company records.

   The Contact list view should look like the one shown in Figure 4-27.

Figure 4-27 Contact list view with records selected

4. Right-click in the Contact list view on a highlighted record and select the option, **LOOKUP SELECTED CONTACTS** on the shortcut menu, as illustrated in Figure 4-28.

   In the Contact list view you should now only see the eight records that you selected.

Figure 4-28 Contact list view shortcut menu

Exercise 4.12: Sorting Records

Earlier, you learned how to sort records in the Contact list view by clicking on a column heading. That is how to sort on a single column. If you want to sort on more than one column or sort on a column that is not displayed on the Contact list view, you have to use the Sort dialog box. Follow the steps below to sort records in the Contact list view.

1. Lookup ⇒ All Contacts.

2. Edit ⇒ Sort. You should see the Sort dialog box.

3. Open the **SORT BY** drop-down list. You will see all of the fields on the current layout. Select the State field, then select the **ASCENDING** sort order option.

4. Open the **AND THEN BY** drop-down list and select the Referred By field (which is not displayed on the Contact list view), then select the Descending sort order option.

5. You should have the options selected that are shown in Figure 4-29.

   Click OK.

   The records are now sorted by the State and Referred By fields.

Figure 4-29 Sort dialog box options

Exercise 4.13: How To Delete Contacts From The Database

If you no longer need to keep information on a particular contact or secondary contact, you can delete the record. Once you delete a record, it is gone forever unless you restore it from a back up copy of the database. The contact record is deleted from all companies that it is associated or linked to. The contact record is also deleted from any group that it is a member of. When deleting a contact you have the following options:

① Delete the current contact.
② Delete all of the contacts in the current lookup.
③ Select the contacts on the list view, then right-click and select Delete Contact.

When you delete a contact, the Notes and History records for the contact are also deleted. The programmer in me knows that just deleting records from a database is usually not the best solution. A better solution would be to export the records that you do not need to another database. You can name this database anything that you like. This second database is sometimes referred to as a **HISTORY** or **ARCHIVE DATABASE**, meaning that it does not contain any current or active records. Once you export the records from the live database to the second database, you can delete them from the live database.

How To Delete One Record

1. Right-click on the record for William Cadbury that does not have a company name and select **DELETE CONTACT**.

2. Click the Delete Contact button shown in Figure 4-30, then click Yes to confirm that you want to delete the record.

Figure 4-30 Delete contact confirmation dialog box

How To Delete Multiple Records At The Same Time

If you need to delete several records, create a lookup to find the records that you want to delete.

1. Lookup ⇒ Company. Type A1 in the Search field.

2. Press Enter or click OK. Five records should be displayed.

4-17

Finding Contacts In A Database

3. Contacts ⇒ Delete Contact.

4. Click the **DELETE LOOKUP** button, then click Yes to confirm that you want to delete the five records in the lookup.

5. In a few seconds, you will see a message that tells you that no more records match the lookup criteria. Click OK.

View The My Record

Now that you have edited and deleted records, you can check the History tab to see the entries for the changes that you made to the database.

1. Lookup ⇒ My Record.

2. On the History tab, the first seven entries should be for the records that you deleted or changed, as shown in Figure 4-31.

    The **REGARDING & DETAILS** column is used to let you know what the change to the record is.

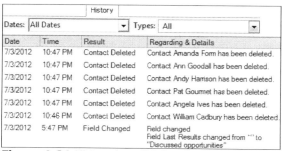

Figure 4-31 History log of deleted and changed records

3. Lookup ⇒ All Contacts. There should be 197 records in the database.

CREATING COMPANY AND DIVISION RECORDS

In this chapter you will learn about the following company and division record options:

- ☑ Using the Companies tree
- ☑ Creating company and division records
- ☑ Associating and linking contacts to companies
- ☑ Duplicating company and division records
- ☑ Using the Company Lookup command

Company And Division Records Overview

Company records allow contacts associated with a company to be managed easier. If a company has a lot of contacts, it may be easier to manage the contacts if divisions were created for the company. Brick and mortar companies have divisions, departments and business units. Companies in ACT! can have them also. You can create companies and divisions that best meet your needs. It is also possible that you may not need any companies or divisions. Figure 5-1 shows the Company detail view.

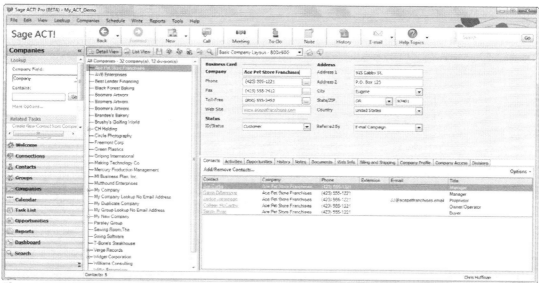

Figure 5-1 Company detail view

The **COMPANY** record type is used to keep track of contacts in the same company. In a way, a company record is similar to a group. This may be why the groups and companies are on the same tab on the Contact detail view. You can see all of the companies and groups except dynamic groups that a contact is a member of. It would be nice if there was a way to know if the entries on this tab are a company or group. Contacts can be associated with more than one company.

An example of when you would associate a contact to more than one company would be if one consultant (a contact) did work for multiple companies that are in your database. You can create activities, notes and opportunities, as well as, attach documents to a company record. In ACT!, any of the following are acceptable ways to categorize contacts in a company. These categories would be divisions that you create. I am sure that you can come up with several others.

① By department.
② By title.
③ By contacts home state.

Keep in mind that company records in ACT! do not have the same limitations as brick and mortar companies. Company records in ACT! function more like folders, meaning that the contact records associated to a company, do not have to have anything related. While the company records displayed in the Companies tree have the name of a company, you can create a company record with any name that you want. You could create a company record that has your first name as the company name.

In addition to being able to create 15 levels of divisions per company record, you can also create
SUBDIVISIONS. Subdivisions are used to further divide the contacts into categories per company, which makes it easier to manage hundreds or thousands of contacts associated with the company.

An example of when it would be appropriate to create subdivisions would be for a company that has 1,000 sales reps. I would create a division called "Sales Reps". I would then create subdivisions for each of the product lines the company has like telephones, digital cameras, camcorders and televisions. I would add the sales reps to the appropriate subdivisions based on the product lines that the sales rep sells. As you can see, divisions and subdivisions can be used to organize contacts in the way that works best for you. A contact that is in a division does not have to also be part of the company. This means that you can add a contact to a division without being required to associate it to the company. Divisions are independent of the company that they are created under.

Company vs Group Records

In this chapter you will learn how to create company records. In the next chapter you will learn how to create group records. On the surface, company and group records may appear to be the same and have the same functionality, but there are some differences.

Company records have more functionality than group records. For example, company records have more fields that can be used to automatically fill in fields on a contact record. The opposite is also true. Fields on a contact record can be used to fill in fields on a company record.

Creating a group is like saving a lookup because the records do not have to have the same data in a specific field. When you view contacts from the Company detail view you can see the notes, activities and opportunities for all of the contacts in the company on the same tab. The same is true if contact records are viewed from the Group detail view.

Company Detail View Toolbar

Many of the buttons on the Company detail view toolbar are the same as the contact and group toolbars. Figure 5-2 shows the Company detail view toolbar. Table 5-1 explains the buttons on the toolbar.

Figure 5-2 Company detail view toolbar

Button	Description
1	Displays the Company detail view.
2	Displays the Company list view.
3	Saves the record. (1) (2)
4	Opens the Quick Print Options dialog box.
5	Adds or removes a contact from a company. (2)
6	Updates the linked contacts for the selected company.
7	Attach a file. (2)
8	Creates a lookup of the selected company.
9	Is used to select a different layout. (1)

Table 5-1 Company detail view toolbar buttons explained

CREATING COMPANY AND DIVISION RECORDS

Button	Description
10	Displays the ACT! E-marketing options. (3)
11	Displays the Sage Business Info for Services for ACT! options. (3)

Table 5-1 Company detail view toolbar buttons explained (Continued)

(1) This option is only available from the Company detail view.
(2) This option applies to companies and divisions.
(3) This option requires a paid subscription.

Companies Tree

The Companies tree is on the left side of the Company detail view. At the top of the Companies tree, the number of companies and divisions are displayed. The tree displays all of the companies, divisions and subdivisions in the database, as illustrated in Figure 5-3.

A plus sign in front of an entry in the tree means that there is at least one division below it.

If you click on an entry in the tree, you will see the detail information for it on the right side of the window. The companies and divisions at this level are recognized as divisions.

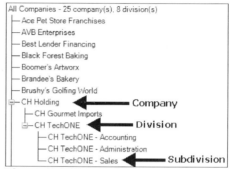

Figure 5-3 Companies tree

Company records in the Companies tree may or may not contain the same companies that you see in the Contacts view. For example, in the Contact list view you will see the following companies, Cadbury, County Tennis Supplies and Liberty. If you look in the Companies tree, you will not see an entry for these companies. It is not a requirement that every company have a company record.

You can use the tree to complete several tasks including moving, creating and deleting a company.

Any task that you can do for a company, you can also do for a division or subdivision. Like other features in ACT!, the Companies tree has a shortcut menu, as shown in Figure 5-4.

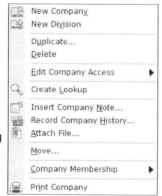

Figure 5-4 Companies tree shortcut menu

Exercise 5.1: Create New Contact Records

To complete some of the company exercises, you need to add more contact records to the database.

1. Create contact records for the following names. You only have to enter the name in each record. John Doe, Jennifer Doe, Charles Smith, Mary Wood and Bill Grant.

2. Create contact records for the following names: Laura Smith and Tom Wood. Type `Lookup` in the Company field for these two records. They will be used later in this chapter to lookup contacts and link them to a company.

Chapter 5

Exercise 5.2: Create A Company Record

1. Click the **COMPANIES** button on the Navigation Pane.

2. Click the **NEW** button on the Global toolbar, then create records for the two companies in Table 5-2.

   The first record should look like the one shown in Figure 5-5 in the 800x600 layout.

Field	Company #1	Company #2
Company	My Company	My Other Company
Address 1	123 Main St	456 South St
City	Hitsville	Hollywood
State	CA	CA

Table 5-2 Company record data

Figure 5-5 New company record

ACT! tries to prevent you from creating duplicate records.

If you enter a company name that already exists as a company record in the database, you will see the warning message shown in Figure 5-6 when you try to go to another company record.

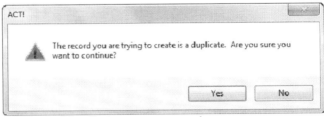

Figure 5-6 Duplicate company warning message

If you recall, in Chapter 2 you changed how ACT! checks for duplicate companies.
If you click Yes, the company record that you just created will be added to the database.
If you click No, you will have to change the company name to save the record.

Exercise 5.3: Create Divisions For A Company

Creating a division uses the same screen as the one for creating a company record.

1. Display the company (or division) record that you want to create a division for. For this exercise click on the company, My Company in the Companies tree.

2. Right-click on the Company Name in the tree and select **NEW DIVISION**, then type the division name in the Company field. For this exercise type `Finance` in the Company field.

3. If you click on the company in the tree you will see the division. You will also see the **HIERARCHY** of the company and its divisions on the Divisions tab, as illustrated at the bottom of Figure 5-7.

Creating Company And Division Records

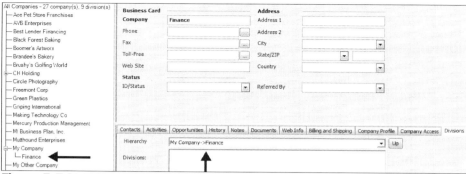

Figure 5-7 Division associated to a company

4. Create the divisions in Table 5-3 under the company listed.

Division	Company
Technology Division	My Company
Marketing	My Other Company
Sales Division	My Other Company

Table 5-3 Divisions to create

Associating Contacts To Companies And Divisions

Contacts can exist in an ACT! database without being linked or associated to a company. Companies can be in the database without having contacts linked to them. There is no requirement that contacts and companies be linked or associated, so do not be alarmed if you have contact records that are not linked to company records or vice versa. Although, I am not sure why someone would create a company and not associate any contacts to it, it is acceptable in ACT!. There are two ways to associate contacts to companies as explained below.

① **Manually** This method entails creating the link between a contact and a company. ACT! refers to this type of link as a **STATIC** link. That is because the link will remain intact until you manually change it.

② **Automatically** This method entails creating a query that selects the contact records that will be linked to a company. ACT! refers to this type of a link as a **DYNAMIC** link because the contacts associated to a company will change automatically, depending on whether or not the data in the contact record meets the criteria in the query. A contact record can meet the criteria in the query this week and not meet the criteria next week, if the data in any of the contact record fields that the query uses, changes. Creating queries is covered in Chapter 13.

Exercise 5.4: Associate A Contact To A Company Record

There are several ways to associate contacts to a company record. In this exercise you will learn different ways to accomplish this task. Contact records can be associated to companies from the contact record. The opposite is also true. Contact records can be associated to companies from the company record.

1. Open the company record for My Other Company in the Company detail view. On the Divisions tab, you should see the two divisions that you created for the company.

2. Click the Add/Remove Contacts to Company button on the Company toolbar.

Chapter 5

3. Click the **CONTACTS** button on the Add/Remove Contacts dialog box, then type Doe in the Look for field.

4. Select the contact record for John Doe, then click the Add button.

5. Click OK.

   The contact should be in the **STATIC MEMBERS** section of the dialog box, as shown in Figure 5-8.

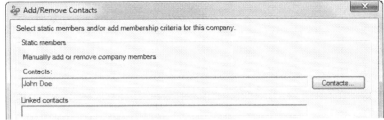

Figure 5-8 Add/Remove Contacts dialog box

6. Click OK. You will see the contact John Doe on the Contacts tab on the Company detail record.

> **More Ways To Open The Add/Remove Contacts Dialog Box From A Company View**
> ① Companies ⇒ Add/Remove Contacts.
> ② Right-click on the company name in the Companies tree or Company column (in the Company list view) and select Company Membership ⇒ Add/Remove Contacts.
> ③ On the Contacts tab, click the Add/Remove Contacts button.
> ④ On the Contacts detail view, on the Contacts tab, on a blank space in the Contact List section, right-click and select Company Membership ⇒ Add/Remove Contacts, on the shortcut menu.

> **How To Open The Add/Remove Dialog Box From A Contact View**
> Below are several ways to open the Add/Remove dialog box shown in Figure 5-9.
>
> ① Contacts ⇒ Add Selected to Company.
> ② On the Contact list view, right-click and select Add Contacts to Company from the shortcut menu.
> ③ On the Contacts detail view, on the Groups/Companies tab, select Companies and Divisions from the **SHOW FOR** drop-down list field, then click the Add/Remove Companies button, illustrated in Figure 5-10.

The entries in the list on the right are companies, divisions, subdivisions and groups that the contact is a member of.

I find this dialog box helpful because you can add and remove companies, divisions and groups for the contact at the same time.

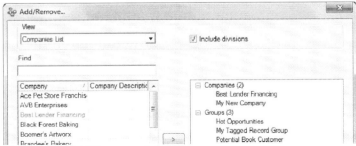

Figure 5-9 Add/Remove dialog box

5-7

Creating Company And Division Records

Figure 5-10 Company options on the Groups/Companies tab on the Contact detail view

Exercise 5.5: Create A Company Record From A Contact Record

Earlier you created a company record from scratch. Creating a company record from a contact record that has the address information for the company will keep you from having to type the same information in again. You can create a company record from a contact record by following the steps below.

 Create Company From Contact Option
Selecting this option on the Contacts menu generated the error message shown in Figure 5-11, prior to ACT! 2013. Thankfully, it has been fixed. The way to fix this error if you get it in the future is to open the Define Fields dialog box, select the Customer ID field in the Contacts table and change the Permission to Full Access, as shown in Figure 5-12.

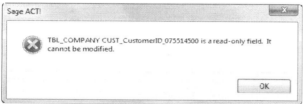

Figure 5-11 Read only error message

Figure 5-12 Field security options

1. Select the contact that has the information for the company record that you want to create. In this exercise select the contact Jane Bellamy of Boomers Artworx.

2. Contacts ⇒ Create Company from Contact.

The Company detail view will open and the company name and address fields will automatically be filled in. If you needed to make any changes to the information for the new company record, you could. Notice in the Companies tree that the company name is similar to another company. The difference is the apostrophe in the other company name.

5-8

Chapter 5

Exercise 5.6: Create A Contact Record From A Company Record

Creating a contact record from a company record that has the address information will keep you from having to type in the same information again. You can create a contact record from a company record by following the steps below.

1. Select the company in the Companies tree that has the information for the contact record that you want to create. In this exercise select the company Circle Photography.

2. Companies ⇒ Create Contact from Company. The Contact detail view will open and the company name and address fields will automatically be filled in.

3. Type `Test Record` in the Contact field, then display another record.

Refreshing Linked Data In Contact Records

It is possible that you may not be viewing the most current data in the database. This happens when there are several people adding and editing records in the database. To make sure that you are viewing the most current data, refresh the data of the contact record that is displayed in the Contact detail view.

Contacts ⇒ Update Linked Contact, will refresh the data. If this option is not enabled on the menu, it means that the contact is not linked to a company record.

Linking Company And Contact Records

If you scroll through the contact records you will see that some company names are blue and underlined and others are not. The company names that are blue and underlined are hyperlinked. You can click on this link to open the company, division or subdivision record.

Fields on the contact record that are linked will automatically be updated when the corresponding field in the company record is updated. This means that if the company name field on the company record changes from DEF Company to HIJ Company, any contact records that are linked to the DEF company on the company name field will automatically be updated if the **AUTOMATICALLY LINK NEW CONTACTS TO THEIR COMPANY RECORD** option is checked, as shown in Figure 5-13.

Tools ⇒ Preferences ⇒ Admin tab ⇒ Company Preferences button, will open the Company Preferences dialog box shown in Figure 5-13.

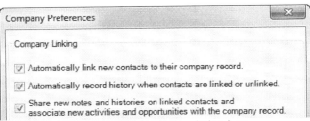

Figure 5-13 Company Preferences dialog box

Creating Company And Division Records

The ellipsis button at the end of the Company field on a contact record that is not already linked, opens the dialog box shown in Figure 5-14.

If the contacts company name already exists in the database, you can link the contact to the company by selecting the company name on the dialog box.

If the contact record is linked to a company, the dialog box shown later in Figure 5-30 opens.

Figure 5-14 Link To Company dialog box

Associate vs Linking

On the surface, these terms sound like they have the same functionality. Understanding the difference is important if you have the need to make some contacts private. In ACT!, associating and linking have different functionality as explained below. I find it somewhat deceiving how the "Private" option works.

In "My world", when you mark a contact as private, whether or not the contact is "linked" to a company, any information that you enter on any of the tabs for the contact is also marked as private by default. The exception would be if you manually override the private option for a specific piece of information. If a history record is created, the history record would also be automatically marked as private. Well, I started this paragraph off by saying in "My world".

The scenario that I just described is **NOT** how the private option works in ACT! if the contact record is marked as private and "linked" to a company record. When a note or history record is created for a contact that is linked to a company record, the note or history record is visible (available for other users to see) from the company record by default. If this is not what you want to happen, mark the note as private on the Insert Note dialog box.

Depending on a users rights, they may not be able to see all of the contact information that is displayed under the company record. Users that have rights to the contact record will be able to view the activity and opportunity records that are displayed under the company record.

> **Linking Issues**
> Overall, linking contacts to companies is a good feature to have and use. Depending on how sensitive some of the contact data is, you may not want it to be shared. Some contact data is automatically shared. I think that it is important that you understand how linking works.
>
> By default, contact notes, history, activity and opportunity records are displayed under the company record that they are linked to. I thought that if the link between a contact and company was removed, that the contacts history, activity and opportunity records would also be removed from the company record, but that is not the case.
>
> I can understand why they are not automatically removed because the primary purpose of company records is to build a profile of the company, which includes the interactions with all of the contacts associated or linked with the company. I just wanted to let you know that the contacts linked data is not automatically removed from the company record when the contact record is unlinked.

Chapter 5

> **Linking Issues** (Continued)
> **Solutions**
> Fortunately, there are ways to prevent notes and history records that you want to remain private, from being displayed under the company record.
>
> ① As you already learned, when you create a note you can mark it as **PRIVATE**.
> ② If you know that you do not want any contact note and history records to be displayed under company records, clear the **SHARE NEW NOTES AND HISTORIES ON LINKED CONTACTS...** option shown earlier in Figure 5-13. With this option cleared (not checked), you can share a specific note if you have the need to do so.

 Contacts can be associated to multiple companies and divisions, but can only be linked to one company.

Associating Companies And Groups

You can associate companies and groups to the following types of records: Activity, history, notes and opportunity with relative ease, as you will learn throughout this book. Each of the dialog boxes listed below have an **ASSOCIATE WITH** or **SHARE WITH** field. Click the ellipsis button at the end of these fields, then select the companies and groups that you want to associate to the record.

① Schedule Activities [See Chapter 7, Figure 7-1]
② New History [See Chapter 9, Figure 9-16]
③ Edit History [See Chapter 9, Figure 9-20]
④ Insert Note [See Chapter 3, Figure 3-19]

Exercise 5.7: Creating Manual Links Between Contacts And Companies

In this exercise you will learn several ways to link contact and company records.

Manually Link A New Contact With A Company

In this part of the exercise you will create the contact record and then link it to a company.

1. Open a new contact record and enter the name `Jane Doe`.

2. Click the ellipsis button next to the Company field, then select the company, My Company and click OK. You will see that the company name is a link on the Contact detail view.

3. Click the Save Changes button. If you click on the company link, you will see the company record on the Company detail view.

Manually Link An Existing Contact With A Company

In this part of the exercise you will learn how to link an existing contact to a company.

1. Right-click in the Contact field in the Contact detail view and select **LOOKUP CONTACT**.

2. Type `Charles Smith` in the Search field, then press Enter.

5-11

Creating Company And Division Records

3. Click the ellipsis button next to the Company field. Select the company, My Company, then click OK.

> **Link Or Associate Contacts To Divisions Or Subdivisions**
> You can link or associate a contact to a division or subdivision the same way that you link a contact to a company. In both parts of Exercise 5.7 above, instead of selecting the company, select the division or subdivision.

Exercise 5.8: Link Multiple Contact Records To A Company Record

This type of linking is another example of the static link option that you read about earlier. This is one way that you can change the company that several contacts are linked to, at one time.

1. Create a lookup that retrieves records that have **LOOKUP** in the Company field.

2. Select (highlight) both records in the Contact list view, then Contacts ⇒ Link to Company.

3. Select the company, My Other Company, then click OK.

4. Click OK when prompted that no more records match the search criteria.

If you look at the My Other Company record on the Company detail view, you will see that both contacts (Laura Smith and Tom Wood) have the new company name. Their old company name was "Lookup".

Exercise 5.9: Understanding The Power Of Linking

In the previous exercise you linked two contact records to a company record. Figure 5-15 shows the company and contacts associated with it. Notice that the Company field for John Doe is blank. This is how you can visually tell which contacts are linked to a company and which ones are associated to a company. In this exercise you will rename the company.

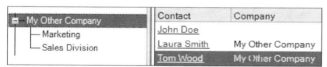

Figure 5-15 Contacts linked and associated to the same company

1. Open the My Other Company record in the Company detail view.

2. Change the Company name to My New Company.

3. View ⇒ Refresh. This will update the company name throughout the database.

Linking And Unlinking Contact And Company Fields

You have learned that you can link the company name field on the contact record to the company name field in the company record. This is also true for other fields on the contact record.

An important concept to remember about linking fields is that the fields that you want to link should be the same data type or a compatible data type. Otherwise, you will have trouble linking the fields. For example, you should not try to link a date field to an email field.

Chapter 5

 If you created a linked company record field it is applied to all company records, not just a particular record. The same is true if you unlink a company record field.

Viewing Linked Fields

Companies ⇒ View Linked Fields, will display how company fields are linked to contact fields, as shown in Figure 5-16.

The **DEFINE FIELDS** button opens a dialog box that is used to create, edit or delete fields. You will learn more about this option in the next exercise.

Figure 5-16 View Linked Fields dialog box

Exercise 5.10: Create A Linked Billing Address Field

In this exercise you will modify the Billing Address 1 field in the company record so that it is linked to the contact User 5 field. This is not a link that you would create in a live database because it really does not make a lot of sense. The fields that are normally linked between contact and company records are already linked in this database, as shown above in Figure 5-16. Therefore, I had to select fields that were not already linked, to demonstrate how to use the linking feature.

1. Tools ⇒ Define Fields.

   Notice that the database is locked, as illustrated in Figure 5-17.

   Figure 5-17 Locked database notification illustrated

2. Open the **VIEW FIELDS FOR** drop-down list on the Define Fields dialog box and select Companies, if it is not already selected.

3. Click on the Billing Address 1 field.

   Click the **EDIT FIELD** link, illustrated in Figure 5-18, then click Next.

   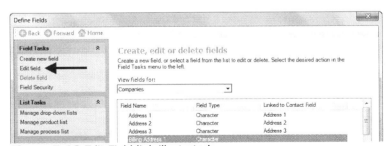

   Figure 5-18 Edit Field link illustrated

4. On the Customize field behavior screen, check the **LINK TO CONTACT FIELD** option, then open the drop-down list. Notice that some fields are not enabled in the drop-down list. You cannot select these fields to link to, because they have already been linked to a field.

5-13

Creating Company And Division Records

5. Scroll down the list and select the User 5 field, then click Finish.

   In Figure 5-19, you will see that the Billing Address 1 field is linked to the User 5 contact field.

   Click Close.

Figure 5-19 Billing Address 1 field linked to the User 5 contact field

Billing And Shipping Tab

 In ACT! 2008 and earlier, this was called the **ADDRESSES** tab.

The fields shown in Figure 5-20 are used to store the billing and shipping address of the company, division or subdivision.

Figure 5-20 Billing and Shipping tab fields

Updating Contact Address Fields From The Linked Company Record

If a company moves, you would update the address fields on the company record. The next step is to update the contact records that are linked to the company record so that they display the updated address information. Before changing the company record, it is a good idea to view the linked contacts to make sure that they have the address that you are about to change.

Companies can have several locations which means that there would be different addresses for the same company. You could create divisions under the company or create a different company record for each location. The steps below show you how to change the address on the company record and update the linked contact records. For now you can read the steps. In the next exercise you will be able to practice this technique.

1. Open the company record and change the information in the linked field, then save the changes.

2. Click the **UPDATES LINKED CONTACTS FOR THE CURRENT COMPANY** button on the Companies toolbar.

3. Click **YES** when you see the message shown in Figure 5-21.

Figure 5-21 Update linked contacts message

Chapter 5

Exercise 5.11: Test The Linked Field That You Created

To test the linked field, you will enter data in the Company Billing Address 1 field and observe how the linked contact records are updated.

1. Select the company My New Company, then click on the Billing and Shipping tab.

2. Type `Test field link` in the Billing Address 1 field.

3. Click the **UPDATES LINKED CONTACTS FOR THE CURRENT COMPANY** button on the Companies toolbar. Click Yes when you see the message shown above in Figure 5-21. The contact records will now be updated.

 If you click the Save Changes button after making the change in step 2 above, instead of clicking the Updates button, you will also see the message shown above in Figure 5-21.

4. On the Contacts tab on the Company detail view, double-click on one of the records that has the company name, My New Company.

5. On the User Fields tab of the contact record, you should see the text that you entered in the Billing Address 1 field in the User 5 field, as shown in Figure 5-22.

Figure 5-22 User 5 field updated

 User Fields Tab
In the exercise that you just completed you added data to a user field. If this were a live database you would rename the user field and update the layout. If you do not do this, other people that use the database may not know what type of data should be entered in the field.

Company Profile Tab

The fields shown in Figure 5-23 track the region, industry, revenue, SIC Code and more for each company, division and subdivision.

Figure 5-23 Company Profile tab fields

Creating Company And Division Records

Company Access Tab

 In ACT! 2008 and earlier, this was called the COMPANY INFO tab.

The fields shown in Figure 5-24, except for the Access Level options are updated by ACT! automatically. These fields store when the company record was created, by who and when it was last changed.

The **RECORD MANAGER** field can be manually changed to another user by the current record owner.

Figure 5-24 Company Access tab fields

The **EDITED ON/BY** fields contain when and who last updated the record.

Unlink A Company Record Field

If you have a company record field that is linked, but no longer need it to be linked, follow the steps below. You do not have to complete these steps now.

1. Tools ⇒ Define Fields.

2. Select the field that you want to unlink, then click the **EDIT FIELD** link.

3. Click Next, then clear the **LINK TO CONTACT FIELD** option shown in Figure 5-25.

   Click Finish, then click Close.

   Previously linked contact record fields that have data will keep the data even though the field is no longer linked to a company record field.

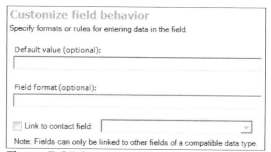

Figure 5-25 Customize field behavior options

Adding Contacts To Divisions

There are several ways to add contacts to divisions, as explained below. It would be easier if we could use drop and drag to add or move a contact record from one company or division to another one.

① Right-click on the division in the Companies tree and select **COMPANY MEMBERSHIP** ⇒ **ADD/REMOVE CONTACTS**. (4)
② Right-click on the contact on the Company detail view and select **COMPANY MEMBERSHIP** ⇒ **ADD/REMOVE CONTACTS**. (4)
③ Right-click on the contact on the Company detail view and select **COMPANY MEMBERSHIP** ⇒ **ADD SELECTED TO COMPANY**. You will see the Add/Remove dialog box.

(4) You will see the Add/Remove Contacts dialog box, shown earlier in Figure 5-8.

Exercise 5.12: Using The Companies Tree To Move A Division

You can drag divisions from one company to another. You can also drag a company to another company and make it a division.

1. In the Companies tree, expand the two companies that you created earlier in this chapter by clicking on the plus sign in front of them.

2. Drag the Finance division from the first company to the second company.

    Click Yes when prompted if you are sure that you want to move the company, in this case a division, to a new location.

    The Companies tree should look like the one shown in Figure 5-26.

Figure 5-26 Division moved from one company to another

Exercise 5.13: Duplicating Company And Division Records

You can duplicate a company that has divisions, but the divisions are not duplicated. This is known as **DUPLICATING** a company. The process is similar to duplicating contacts.

1. In the Company detail view, right-click on the company, My New Company and select Duplicate.

2. On the dialog box shown in Figure 5-27, select the option **DUPLICATE DATA FROM ALL FIELDS**, then click OK.

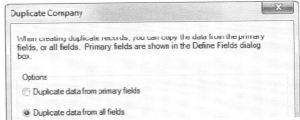

Figure 5-27 Duplicate Company dialog box

3. Click the Save Changes button. Click Yes when prompted to continue.

4. You will see a company record that looks like the one that you duplicated. Type My Duplicate Company in the Company field.

5. View ⇒ Refresh. Click on the new company in the tree.

Notice that there are no divisions and that the contact John Doe is a member. That is because this contact is not linked to the company, My New Company. You will not see the two other contacts shown earlier in Figure 5-15 because they are linked to the company, My New Company (formerly My Other Company).

Creating Company And Division Records

Looking Up Companies

Looking up companies is similar to looking up contacts. Lookup ⇒ Name, will display the Lookup Companies dialog box, which is similar to the dialog box that you use to look up contacts. The differences are explained below.

① The Title bar on the dialog box has "Lookup Companies" instead of "Lookup Contacts".
② The fields in the first drop-down list are company related fields.

Exercise 5.14: Finding Companies

It is really important to make sure that the company data is as accurate as possible. Often, when adding a new company, you may not know or have all of the information that you want to enter for the company. From time to time it is a good idea to either look up records that do not have data in certain fields or create reports that show records that are missing data. If your company does a variety of promotional campaigns, it may be important to track how each contact was obtained. You could use the Referred By field to store this information. In this exercise you will find companies where the Referred By field is empty.

1. Lookup ⇒ Other Fields.

2. Open the Field drop-down list and select Referred By.

3. Open the second drop-down list and select the option **DOES NOT CONTAIN DATA**, then click OK.

The companies and divisions that you see in the Company list view do not have the Referred By field filled in. Someone should try to fill in this information.

Create A Company Note And Attachment

Creating a note for a company is the same process as creating a note for a contact. Creating a note for a company uses the same Insert Note dialog box that is used for creating notes for contacts. Creating a note with an attachment is also the same process as attaching a file to a contact record. Right-click on the company in the Companies tree that you want to create a note for and select **INSERT COMPANY NOTE**. The company name will automatically be filled in the Share with field on the Insert Note dialog box.

Viewing Company Notes

Over time, the number of notes for companies can grow. If contacts are associated with a company, the Notes tab on the Company detail view will have even more notes for you to sift through.

As shown in Figure 5-28, the Notes tab on the Company detail view has the **SHOW FOR** drop-down list filter.

Figure 5-28 Notes tab on the Company detail view

ALL displays both company and company contact notes.
COMPANY only displays notes that are created from a company record.
COMPANY CONTACTS only displays notes that were created for a contact associated with the company. The difference between the Company and Company Contacts options are the level that the notes are created at.

Moving Companies And Divisions

Earlier in this chapter you read that in the Companies tree you can drag companies and divisions to new locations. If you do not like to drag them, you can use the **MOVE** option on the shortcut menu. You can complete this task from either company view. The steps below explain the process.

1. Right-click on the company or division that you want to move and select **MOVE**.

2. Select one of the options explained below.

    ① On the dialog box shown in Figure 5-29, select the **PROMOTE DIVISION TO COMPANY** option to make the division that you selected a company.

    ② Select the **CHANGE TO BE DIVISION OF** option if you want the company or division that you selected to be a division of another company.

If you select a company before opening this dialog box and select the Promote option, nothing will change. Some of the text on the dialog box is different then what is shown in Figure 5-29.

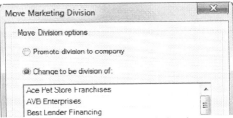

Figure 5-29 Move Division dialog box

3. Select the company that you want to move it to on the Move Division dialog box, then click OK.

> **Deleting A Company Record**
> If you need to delete a company record, any division records under it will be promoted to a company record, unless you delete the division records first. You will not receive a warning that the company record that you are deleting has division records.

Removing Links Between Contact And Company Records

If a contact record is linked on the Company (name) field, it cannot be changed until you remove the link. You already learned that contact notes and history records that appear under the company record are not automatically removed. Removing the link between the contact and company is how the contact notes and history records remain under the company record. When you have the need to remove links, you can follow the steps below.

1. Open the contact record (in the Contact detail view) that you want to remove the company link from.

2. Click the ellipsis button at the end of the Company field. You will see the dialog box shown in Figure 5-30.

    The **UNLINK FROM COMPANY** option will remove the link between the contact and company records.

Figure 5-30 Unlink from Company dialog box

Creating Company And Division Records

The **LINK TO A DIFFERENT COMPANY** option shown above in Figure 5-30, is used to link the contact to a different company. This would be helpful if the contact needs to be moved to a different company.

Selecting this option, then clicking OK, opens the dialog box shown in Figure 5-31. It is used to select the company that you want to move the contact to.

Figure 5-31 Link To Company dialog box

The company or division that you want to move the contact to, must already have a record in the database.

3. Click OK on the Unlink from Company dialog box. The link will be removed from the Company field.

Company Detail View Related Tasks

The related tasks options shown in Figure 5-32 are primarily on the detail view. Some options are also on the list view. The options are explained below.

Figure 5-32 Company detail view related tasks

CREATE NEW CONTACT FROM COMPANY Opens a new contact record with the company fields filled in, that are filled in on the company record that was selected before clicking on the link.

LOOKUP COMPANY CONTACTS Displays the contacts that are on the Company Contacts tab on the Contact list view.

VIEW FIELDS LINKED TO CONTACTS Opens the View Linked Fields dialog box.

UPDATE FIELDS LINKED TO CONTACTS Displays the message shown earlier in Figure 5-21, which is used to update the linked field data for contacts linked to the company that is selected.

WRITE E-MAIL USING TEMPLATE Opens the Template folder (in the database) so that you can select a template to use for the email that you want to create. Once you select the template, a new email window will open with the template that you selected. If you selected multiple contacts on the Contacts tab, a mail merge document will be created for each contact.

SCHEDULE ACTIVITY SERIES [See Chapter 7, Activity Series]

MODIFY LAYOUT Opens the current company detail view layout in the Layout Designer, so that the layout can be changed.

VIEW GROUPS/COMPANIES Opens the View Groups/Companies dialog box, which displays a list of the companies, divisions and groups in the database.

Using The Company List View

While the Company detail view is probably the company view that you will use most often, the Company list view provides the same functionality. The Company list view shown in Figure 5-33 has the same shortcut menu options as the Companies tree. Actually, the shortcut menu in the Company list view has more options. Like the Contact list view, you can sort on the column headings in the Company list view. If there are a lot of companies in the list you may have a need to filter them.

Figure 5-33 Company list view

The **EDIT MODE** option is used to modify records in the Contact list view.

The **INCLUDE DIVISIONS** option displays all of the divisions and subdivisions in the database. The problem is that the default options on the Company list view do not provide a visual way to know which record is a company, division or subdivision or which company a division or subdivision record belongs to.

If you customize the view and add the **HAS DIVISIONS, DIVISION** and **HIERARCHY LEVEL** fields to the view, you will be able to tell a division from a company, but not which company a division belongs to, as shown in Figure 5-34.

Hierarchy Level 0 is a company record.

Hierarchy Level 1 is a company or division record.

Hierarchy Level 2 is a division record.

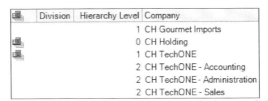
Figure 5-34 Company list view with division fields

Create A New Division

To create a new division from the Company list view, right-click on the company that you want to create the division for and select **NEW DIVISION**.

Company List View Related Tasks

The options shown in Figure 5-35 are for the Company list view. The options that are only on the list view are explained below.

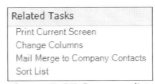
Figure 5-35 Company list view related tasks

5-21

Creating Company And Division Records

PRINT CURRENT SCREEN Opens the Quick Print Options dialog box so that you can select options for how the screen will be printed.

CHANGE COLUMNS Opens the Customize Columns dialog box, which allows you to add, remove and change the order that the columns are displayed on the company list view.

MAIL MERGE TO COMPANY CONTACTS Opens the Mail Merge Wizard, shown in Figure 5-36.

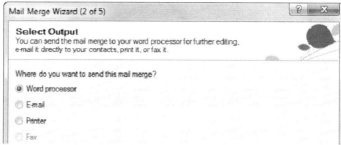

Figure 5-36 Mail Merge Wizard

SORT LIST Opens the Sort dialog box to sort the companies displayed in the view.

GROUPING CONTACTS

In this chapter you will learn about the following group and subgroup record options:

- ☑ Using the Groups tree
- ☑ Creating groups
- ☑ Adding contacts to a group or subgroup
- ☑ Managing group notes and attachments
- ☑ Saving the result of a lookup as a group or company
- ☑ Creating subgroups
- ☑ Converting a group to a company
- ☑ Using the Convert Groups to Companies Wizard

Grouping Contacts

Groups Overview

Grouping records is another way for you to be able to categorize and find contacts. You have learned how to use the lookup command to find contacts. The limitation to using the lookup command is that all of the contact records that you want to find have to have the same information in the same field. You could think of the group option as a free form way to classify or categorize contacts, because the contacts that you add to a group do not have to have any data in common. Like company records, group records can have 15 levels. You can create as many groups as you need.

If you wanted to group certain contacts together because they are all involved in the same project, you could create a group. You can add a contact to as many groups as needed. Grouping helps you find and organize contacts quickly. The main benefit to creating groups over creating lookups, is that the group information is saved. Figure 6-1 shows the Group detail view.

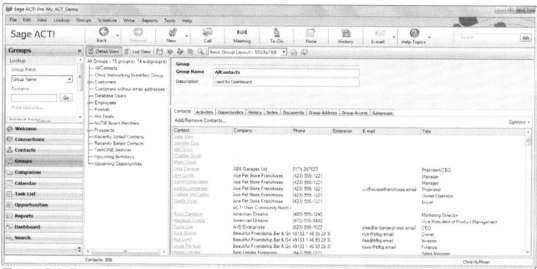

Figure 6-1 Group detail view

The top right section of the Group detail view displays the group name and description of the group that is selected in the tree. The bottom right section displays different information depending on which tab is selected. For example, the Group Access tab shows information about when the group was created, whether or not the group is private and who created it. The names on the Contacts tab are the contacts or companies that are in the group.

Group Detail View Toolbar

Figure 6-2 shows the Group detail view toolbar. Table 6-1 explains the buttons on the toolbar.

Figure 6-2 Group detail view toolbar

Chapter 6

Button	Description
1	Displays the Group detail view.
2	Displays the Group list view.
3	Saves the record. (1)
4	Opens the Quick Print Options dialog box.
5	Adds or removes a contact from a group. (2)
6	Attach a file. (2)
7	Creates a lookup of the group that is selected.
8	Is used to select a layout. (1)
9	Displays the ACT! E-marketing options. (3)
10	Displays the Sage Business Info for Services for ACT! options. (3)

Table 6-1 Group detail view toolbar buttons explained

(1) This option is only available on the Group detail view.
(2) This option applies to groups and subgroups.
(3) This option requires a paid subscription.

Good Groups And Not So Good Groups

These are the types of groups that you can create. An example of a not so good group would be a group that contains contacts in the same state. This is not a good use of a group because you can create a lookup by state to accomplish this.

An example of a good group would be a group that contains contacts that attended an insurance seminar that you were a guest speaker at. This is a good group because there is no existing field that you could create a lookup on to find these contacts. You could create an activity for the contacts in the group. It would appear on the Activities tab for the group.

Groups Tree

The Groups tree is on the left side of the Group detail view. At the top of the Groups tree, the number of groups and subgroups are displayed, as shown earlier in Figure 6-1. If you click on a group in the tree, you will see the subgroups on the Subgroups tab.

A plus sign in front of a group means that there is at least one subgroup below it. The Employees group shown in Figure 6-3 has two subgroups; International Employees and USA Employees. The International Employees group has two subgroups; AsiaPac Employees and European Employees.

Figure 6-3 Groups and Subgroups on the Subgroups tab

 The **UP** button illustrated above in Figure 6-3 is enabled if the group or subgroup that is selected is part of a larger group. Clicking this button will move up the hierarchy, one level at a time. This button is also on the Company detail view. If you double-click on any subgroup shown, the detail record for the subgroup will be displayed.

Grouping Contacts

Exercise 6.1: How To Create A Group

1. Click the **GROUPS** button in the Navigation Pane.

2. Click the **NEW** button on the Global toolbar. You should see a new group record at the top, on the right of the window.

 You can also right-click on a blank space in the Groups tree and select **NEW GROUP**.

3. Type `Potential Customer` in the Group Name field.

4. Press the Tab key, then type `This group contains contacts that are interested in the next version of the book` in the Description field.

 The Description field can have up to 128 characters.

5. Click the Save Changes button.

   Click on the Subgroups tab.

   The group record should look like the one shown in Figure 6-4.

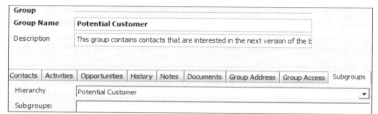
Figure 6-4 New group record created

Notice that the **HIERARCHY** field was filled in automatically and that the group appears on the left side of the window.

Adding Contacts To A Group

The ways that you can add contacts to a group (or subgroup) are explained below.

① You can scroll through the entire list of contacts in the Contact list view and select the contacts that you want, one by one and add them to a group. This is known as a **STATIC** group. The contacts stay in the group until you remove them.

② If possible, you can use the lookup command to find at least some of the contact records that you want to add to a group.

③ Select an existing group and add contacts from the existing group to the new group.

④ Contacts can automatically be added to a group if they meet the criteria of the query. This is known as a **DYNAMIC** group because contacts are added and removed based on whether or not they meet the criteria. There is no intervention on your part after creating the query. This type of group is updated each time the Groups/Companies tab on the Contact detail or Group detail view is displayed.

An example is a group for contacts that have the Sales Rep title. Contacts added to the database that have this title would automatically be added to the group. Any contact in the group whose title changes from Sales Rep would automatically be removed from the group. Chapter 13 covers creating this type of group.

Chapter 6

The benefit of using the last three options explained above to add contacts to a group is that you do not have to scroll through all of the records in the database to select contacts to add to a group.

 When you add a contact that has a note to a group, the contacts notes are displayed on the Groups Notes tab, unless the note is marked private. The owner of the private note will see the note on the Groups Notes tab, but other database users will not.

Exercise 6.2: How To Add Contacts One By One To A Group

The contacts that you will add to the group in this exercise are static.

1. Select the group that you want to add contacts to. In this exercise select the Potential Customer group.

2. Click the **ADD/REMOVE CONTACTS TO GROUP** button on the toolbar or click the **ADD/REMOVE CONTACTS** button on the Contacts tab. You will see the Add/Remove Contacts dialog box.

3. Click the Contacts button.

4. Click on the contact Ashley Allan, then press and hold down the **CTRL** key and click on the following names: Bruce Baker, Sarah Baker and Kirby York.

5. Click the **ADD** button.

    The four contacts that you selected should be displayed in the **SELECTED CONTACTS** list, as shown in Figure 6-5.

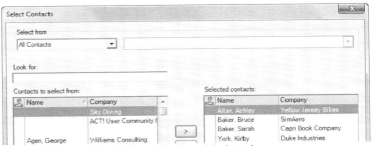

Figure 6-5 Contacts selected to be added to the group

The options in the **SELECT FROM** drop-down list and the (Group names) drop-down list to the right of it, are used to narrow or widen the number of names that appear in the **CONTACTS TO SELECT FROM** list. If you select the **GROUPS** option from the first drop-down list and the Customers group from the second drop-down list you will see the contacts shown on the left of Figure 6-6.

If the database has a lot of names and you do not want to scroll through the list, you can type the name that you want to add to the group in the **LOOK FOR** field.

Figure 6-6 Contacts from an existing group

6-5

Grouping Contacts

 If you scroll through the list of names on the left, you will see that the names that you have already selected for the group are grayed out. This lets you know that the contact is already a member of the current group or has been selected to be a member of the current group.

6. Click OK. You should see the contacts in the **STATIC MEMBERS** section of the Add/Remove Contacts dialog box.

7. Click OK. The contacts will now be added to the Potential Customer group. You will see the contacts at the bottom of the Contacts tab, as shown in Figure 6-7.

Contact	Company	Phone	Extensio	E-mail	Title
Sarah Baker	Capri Book Company	(765) 417-5330			Sales Manager
Kirby York	Duke Industries	310-622-1506		kirby.york@dukeindustry.ema	
Bruce Baker	SimAero	(480) 555-2144		Bruce@simaero360.email	Chief Designer
Ashley Allan	Yellow Jersey Bikes	(619) 555-8890		ashley@yjbikes.email	VP of Sales

Figure 6-7 Contacts added to the group

 To add a contact to a group, you can right-click on a contact record on either contact view and select **ADD CONTACT TO GROUP**.

Looking Up Groups

Looking up groups is similar to looking up companies. Lookup ⇒ field name from a group view or Lookup ⇒ Groups ⇒ Select an option from a different view, will display the same dialog box that is used to look up contacts. The differences on the Lookup dialog box for groups are the same as the differences between contacts and companies. [See Chapter 5, Looking Up Companies]

Exercise 6.3: Finding Group Records

You have already learned how to find (look up) all of the contacts that were associated with a company. Looking up contacts that are in the same group is basically the same process. In this exercise you will create a lookup for groups that do not have data in the Address 1 field.

1. Lookup ⇒ Other Fields.

2. Open the Field drop-down list and select the Address 1 field.

3. Open the next drop-down list and select the **DOES NOT CONTAIN DATA** option, then click OK.

You will see the groups that do not have any information in the Address 1 field. If you double-click on any group in the Group list view and then click on the Group Address tab, you will see that the Address 1 field is empty.

Exercise 6.4: How To Rename A Group

The steps below show you how to rename a group. If you need to rename a subgroup, select the subgroup in step 1 instead of a group.

1. Click on the group that you want to rename in the Groups tree. In this exercise click on the Potential Customer group.

Chapter 6

2. Type in the new group name. Type the word `Book` after the word **POTENTIAL** in the Group Name field on the right.

3. Click the Save Changes button. The group will be renamed and the new name is displayed on the Groups tree.

 The reason that I click the Save Changes button is because it refreshes the view. If you clicked on another group or subgroup in the tree and then come back to the group that you changed, you would see that the group was renamed.

Exercise 6.5: Add Contacts To An Existing Group

In this exercise you will find contacts in Arizona and add them to the Potential Book Customer group. To add contacts to a subgroup, select the subgroup in step 3 below instead of a group.

Create The Lookup And Add The Contacts To The Group

1. Create a lookup to find all contacts in AZ. There should be 19 records in the Contact list view.

2. Select (highlight) all of the records, then right-click on the highlighted records and select **ADD CONTACTS TO GROUP**, as illustrated in Figure 6-8.

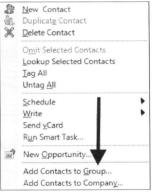

Figure 6-8 Option to add the contacts to a group illustrated

 If you do not want to right-click on the records, you can use Contacts ⇒ Add Selected to Group.

3. Click on the Potential Book Customer group shown in Figure 6-9, then click OK.

Figure 6-9 Group selected to add the contacts to

Grouping Contacts

View The Contacts In The Group

1. Click the Groups button on the Navigation Pane, then click on the Potential Book Customer group in the Groups tree.

2. On the Contacts tab, you should see the contacts that you just added, plus the contacts that you added in a prior exercise. Click the Save Changes button.

Exercise 6.6: Use The Lookup Command To Add Contacts To A Group

You can use this option when you have several records that have something in common that you want to add to the same group or subgroup. In this exercise you will create a lookup to find all contacts that have the Sales Representative title. After that, you will create a group and add the contacts to a group.

1. Create a lookup that finds all contacts that have Sales Representative as the title. Five records should have been retrieved. (**Hint**: Lookup ⇒ Contacts ⇒ Other Fields)

2. Click the arrow on the New button on the Global toolbar and select Group, as shown in Figure 6-10.

Figure 6-10 New button options

3. Type `Sales Reps` in the Group Name field, then type `This group contains all of the sales reps` in the Description field.

4. Click the Add/Remove Contacts button on the Contacts tab, then click the Contacts button.

5. Select the **CURRENT LOOKUP** option from the first drop-down list.

   You should only see the contacts from the lookup that you created, in the list of names on the left side of the dialog box, as shown in Figure 6-11.

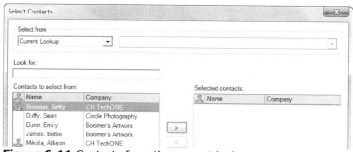

Figure 6-11 Contacts from the current look up

6. Click the **ADD ALL>>** button. All of the contacts should be in the **SELECTED CONTACTS** list on the right side of the dialog box. Click OK twice to close both dialog boxes.

7. In the Group detail view click on the Sales Reps group in the Groups tree, if it is not already selected. On the Contacts tab you will see the five contacts that are in the group.

How To View The Groups That A Contact Is A Member Of

1. Click on the link for Emily Dunn.

2. On the Groups/Companies tab in the Contact detail view, open the **SHOW FOR** drop-down list and select Groups and Subgroups, if it is not already selected. You will see that this contact is a member of the Sales Rep group that you just created and the Potential Book Customer group that you created earlier in this chapter.

Exercise 6.7: How To Manage Group Notes And Attachments

The Notes tab on the Group detail view is used to view notes for the group, just like you can view notes for a contact. If you create a note for the group, you only have to type it in once and it will be associated with all contacts in the group. You can also assign a contacts note to a group. There are several ways to create a note for a group.

 All of the group management of notes and attachments discussed in this exercise also apply to creating, editing and maintaining company notes and attachments.

How To Create A Group Note And Attach A File To The Group Note

In addition to adding a note to a group, you can attach files like charts, spreadsheets or sales literature to a group. Doing this allows you to keep all of the attachments for the group in one place.

1. Click the Groups button, then click on the Potential Book Customer group.

2. On the Notes tab, click the **INSERT NEW NOTE** button. You should see the Potential Book Customer group name in the Share with field on the Insert Note dialog box.

3. Type `These contacts have requested a book catalog` in the field at the bottom of the dialog box.

4. Select the text that you just typed and change the font to Comic Sans MS, then change the font size to 12.

5. Change the color to red. The color option is to the right of the Font size drop-down list. Leave the dialog box open to complete the next part of the exercise.

How To Attach A File To A Group

Attaching a file to a group record is the same process as attaching a file to a contact record.

1. Click the **ATTACH** button, then select File.

Grouping Contacts

2. Double-click on the C3 Attach file in your folder.

   The note should look like the one shown in Figure 6-12. Click OK.

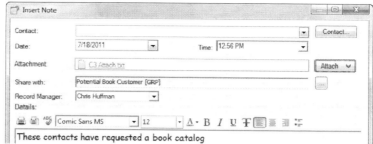

Figure 6-12 Group note

View The Group Notes And Attachments

1. On the Notes tab, open the **SHOW FOR** drop-down list and select Group. The entry should be the one for the note shown above in Figure 6-12.

2. Click on the Attachment icon for the note. The attached file will open. Close the attached file.

Exercise 6.8: Assign A Contact Note To A Group And Individual Contacts
In this exercise you will complete the following tasks:

① Create two notes for a contact that is in a group.
② Associate one of the notes to contacts in the group that the contact in the task above is a member of.
③ Associate one of the notes to one contact that is not in the group.
④ Associate the second note to a group that the contact in the first task above is not a member of.

Add The Contact To Another Group

1. Click on the Potential Book Customer group on the Group detail view.

2. On the Contacts tab, right-click on the contact Sarah Baker and select Group Membership ⇒ Add Selected to Group.

3. Scroll down the list of groups on the left of the dialog box and select the Prospects - Hot Opportunities group, then click the Add button. The contact should be a member of the two groups shown on the right of Figure 6-13. Click OK.

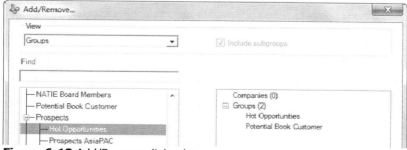

Figure 6-13 Add/Remove dialog box

Create The Notes

In this part of the exercise you will create the notes for Sarah Baker.

1. Open the Contact detail view for the contact Sarah Baker. (**Hint**: If you are in the Group detail view, click on the contacts name on the Contacts tab).

2. Click on the Notes tab, then create the notes in Table 6-2.

Note	Regarding Field	Formatting
1	This is the first contact note for S. Baker. It will be applied to individual contacts in 2 groups and 1 contact that is not in a group.	Change the font size to 10. Change the text color to green and bold.
2	This is the second contact note for S. Baker. It will be applied to the group via the Insert Note dialog box.	Change the color of the text to purple, bold and italic. Complete steps 3 and 4 below, before closing this note.

Table 6-2 Notes to create for Sarah Baker

3. Click the button at the end of the Share with field on the Insert Note dialog box, then click OK to share the note, as indicated in Figure 6-14.

Figure 6-14 Sharing a public note message

4. Select the Potential Book Customer group and add it to the note, then click OK. You should have the options shown in Figure 6-15.

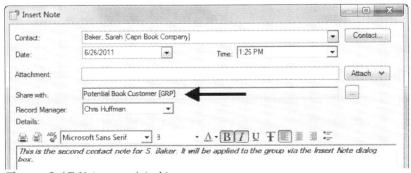

Figure 6-15 Note associated to a group

5. Click OK to close the Insert Note dialog box.

Grouping Contacts

Associate The Notes

In this part of the exercise you will associate the two notes that you just created to other contacts.

1. Locate the first note that you created in Table 6-2 above for Sarah Baker in either the Contact detail or Group detail view, then double-click on the note.

2. Click the **CONTACT** button on the Edit Note dialog box, then add the contact George Bailey to the Selected contacts list.

3. Open the **SELECT FROM** drop-down list on the Select Contacts dialog box and select Groups, then select the Sales Reps group from the next drop-down list. You will see the contacts for the group on the left side of the dialog box.

4. Add Bettie James to the contact list.

5. Select the Prospects group from the second drop-down list at the top of the dialog box, then add the contacts Mary Bailey and Kirby York.

   You should have the contacts selected that are shown in Figure 6-16.

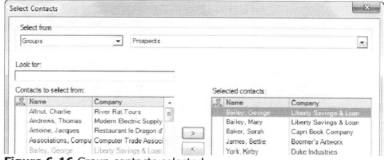

Figure 6-16 Group contacts selected

6. Click OK twice to close both dialog boxes.

   When you see the dialog box shown in Figure 6-17 select the first option, then click OK.

Figure 6-17 Edit shared note options

Editing A Shared Note
After creating a note, you may need to update the information in the note. When you modify a note that is shared with groups or contacts, you will see the dialog box shown above in Figure 6-17. Select the option for how you want the changes that you make to the note to be applied.

View The Notes

1. Create a contact lookup by last name. Search for Bailey. You will see three contacts.

Chapter 6

2. Switch to the Contact detail view. George and Mary Bailey will have the first note in Table 6-2 above (in green). Peter Bailey does not. This is correct.

3. Switch to the Group detail view. The note with green text should also be available in the Prospects group. If you do not see the note, select **GROUP CONTACTS** in the Show for drop-down list.

4. View the Potential Book Customer group notes. You will see the second note that you created in Table 6-2 above. You will also see the first note because it was created by Chris Huffman (aka you) who is a member of the Potential Book Customer group.

Show For Drop-Down List Options

The options in the **SHOW FOR** drop-down list shown in Figure 6-18 are available on the Notes, History, Activities and Opportunities tabs in the Group detail view.

The options are used to filter the records that are displayed on the tab. [See Chapter 5, Viewing Company Notes]

Figure 6-18 Show For drop-down list options

 By default, group level notes cannot be viewed on the Notes tab in the Contact detail view. To know if there is a group note for the contact, click on the Groups/Companies tab on the Contact detail view. Double-click on the group, then click on the Notes tab in the Group detail view.

Preview Area

If the note is long, you will not see all of it on the Notes tab. If you look to the far right of the workspace, you should see a shaded area. This is the Preview area.

If you click on a note, you will see the entire note on the right side in the Preview area. You can resize the Preview area by placing the mouse pointer in the position illustrated in Figure 6-19, then drag the mouse pointer in the direction that you want to resize the window to.

If you do not want to have the Preview area visible, you can hide it by clicking on the Options button shown in Figure 6-19 and clearing the **SHOW PREVIEW** option, shown on the right of the figure. You can do this on any Notes tab.

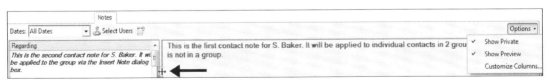

Figure 6-19 Preview area illustrated

Exercise 6.9: How To Save The Result Of A Lookup As A Group Or Company

If you create a lookup that you will need to use over and over, you can save it as a Group or Company by following the steps below. The number of records in this type of group or company can change. If the value in the field that the lookup is using changes and now meets the criteria, the contact record will automatically be added to the group or company. If the value in a contact record field changes and no longer meets the lookup criteria, the record will automatically be removed from the group or company.

6-13

Grouping Contacts

In this exercise you will save the results of the lookup as a group and a company. On your own, you do not have to save the same lookup results both ways. Select the option that works best for you.

1. Create an Email Address lookup for contacts that do not have an email address. 99 records should be retrieved.

2. Lookup ⇒ Groups ⇒ Save Lookup as Group.

3. Type `My Group Lookup No Email Address` as the group name, then View ⇒ Refresh, or press the F5 key.

4. Lookup ⇒ Companies ⇒ Save Lookup as Company.

5. Type `My Company Lookup No Email Address` as the company name, then View ⇒ Refresh or press the F5 key.

If you view the records under the company and group that you just created, you will see that both have the same records. Normally, you would not save the same records to a group and company. It is done here for illustration purposes so that you can learn both methods of saving the result of a lookup.

Subgroups

A subgroup is usually a subset of the contacts in the group. In the previous exercise you created a group that contains contacts that do not have an email address. If you wanted to further categorize the contacts in the group by company, title, state, status or just about anything that you can think of, you can create a subgroup. Subgroups can be 15 levels deep, meaning subgroups can have subgroups. Subgroups are similar to the divisions that companies have.

Exercise 6.10: Creating Subgroups

In this exercise you will create two subgroups for the My Group Lookup No Email Address group: One for sales reps and one for title.

1. In the Group detail view, right-click on the My Group Lookup No Email Address group in the Groups tree and select **NEW SUBGROUP**.

2. Type `Sales Reps with no email` in the Group Name field.

3. In the Description field, type `This subgroup contains sales reps that do not have an email address.`

4. Click on the My Group Lookup No Email Address group in the Groups tree. You should see the subgroup in the Groups tree.

5. Create another subgroup under the My Group Lookup No Email Address group. Use `No Title` as the subgroup name.

Chapter 6

6. In the Description field, type

   These contacts do not have a title.

   You should have the subgroups shown in Figure 6-20.

Figure 6-20 Subgroups

Exercise 6.11: Moving Contact Records Between Groups And Subgroups

After the subgroups are created, it is a good idea to move the appropriate records from the group to a subgroup, if applicable. In this exercise you will move contacts that have the Sales Rep title to the corresponding subgroup and contacts that do not have a title to a different subgroup. There are two ways to move contact records between groups and subgroups, as explained below:

① Move the contacts manually using the Add/Remove dialog box.
② Use a query.

Moving Records Manually

Currently, moving contacts from one group to another and removing them from the original group is a two step process, as explained below.

① Add the contacts from the first group to the second group.
② Remove the contacts (that are linked to a company) from the original group unless you need the contact in the group and related subgroup. There is no way currently to complete this step from the Group detail view.

> **Moving Contact Records**
> Keep in mind that when the term "move" is used, you are actually copying records in one group to another group. This means that the records are in two groups. Currently, the only automated work around for this is to create dynamic groups. I think that it would be very useful to be able to move records by dropping and dragging them between groups.

Step 1: Add The Contacts To The New Group

In this part of the exercise you will add records to each of the subgroups that you created.

1. Click on the My Group Lookup No Email Address group, then click on the Contacts tab.

2. Sort the contacts by the Title field. The contacts that do not have a title should be at the top of the list.

3. Select all of the contacts without a title, then right-click on the selected contacts. Select Group Membership ⇒ Add Selected to Group.

Grouping Contacts

4. Scroll down the list and select the **NO TITLE** subgroup, illustrated in Figure 6-21, then click OK.

Figure 6-21 Subgroup illustrated

5. In the My Group Lookup No Email Address group, select the three contacts with Sales Representatives in the Title field.

6. Right-click on the selected records. Group Membership ⇒ Add Selected to Group.

7. Scroll down the list and select the **SALES REPS WITH NO EMAIL** subgroup.

8. If you click on the Sales Reps with no email subgroup you will see the contacts that you added, as shown in Figure 6-22.

Figure 6-22 Contacts in a subgroup

Step 2: Remove The Contacts From The Original Group

As stated earlier, there is no way to remove linked contacts from a group from the Group detail view. They have to be removed from the Contacts Groups/Companies tab. In this part of the exercise you will remove the three contacts that you added to the Sales Reps with no email subgroup from the My Group Lookup No Email Address group.

1. Click on the Sales Reps with no email group, then click on the Contacts tab.

2. Click on the first contacts name. The Contact detail view will open.

3. Click on the Groups/Companies tab, then click the Add/Remove Groups button.

Chapter 6

4. On the right side of the Add/Remove dialog box, you will see the groups that the contact is a member of, as shown in Figure 6-23.

   Click on the second group shown, then click the Remove button.

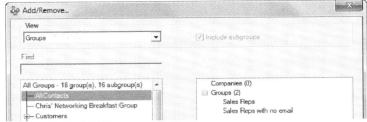

Figure 6-23 Add/Remove dialog box

5. Click OK. The group should be removed from the contact. Repeat these steps for each contact that you want to remove from the group.

Deleting Groups Or Subgroups

You may have a need to delete a group or a subgroup. When you delete a group or subgroup, the contacts in the group or subgroup, their notes and attachments are not deleted. The groups notes, history records and attachments are deleted.

Subgroups of the group that will be deleted are not deleted. The subgroup is automatically promoted to a group. If you need to delete a group or subgroup, you can follow the steps below. For now, you can read the steps because you do not need to delete a group or subgroup.

1. Right-click on the group or subgroup in the Group detail or Group list view and select Delete.

2. Click Yes when prompted to delete the current group or subgroup.

Removing Contacts That Are Not Linked From Companies Or Groups

Exercise 6.1 covered how to remove contacts that were linked to a company from a group. There may be times when you need to remove contacts that are not linked from a company, division, group or subgroup. Examples would be if the contact leaves the company or you copied a contact in a group to a subgroup. If this is the case, you can follow the steps below to remove contacts that are not linked to a company, division or group record. For now, you can read this section because you do not need to remove a contact from a company or group.

1. Right-click on the company, division, group or subgroup that has contacts that you want to remove in the tree, then select the appropriate option below.

    ① Company Membership ⇒ Add/Remove Contacts.
    ② Group Membership ⇒ Add/Remove Contacts.

2. Click the Contacts button on the Add/Remove Contacts dialog box.

3. Select the names that you want to remove in the **SELECTED CONTACTS** list, then click the Remove button.

4. Once you have removed the contact records, click OK twice to close both dialog boxes.

Converting A Group To A Company

Groups and subgroups can be converted to a company. If the group or subgroup that you convert has subgroups, the subgroups are not converted by default. They move up the hierarchy and quite possibly become a group. Contacts that are in the group or subgroup that is being converted, automatically become members of the company.

One reason that you may convert a group to a company is because you need to use a feature (for the contact records that are currently in a group) that only a company record has. In the next exercise you will convert the My Group Lookup No Email group to a company.

 Once you convert a group to a company, it cannot be converted back.

Exercise 6.12: Using The Convert Groups To Companies Wizard

1. In the Group detail view, right-click on the My Group Lookup No Email Address group and select **CONVERT TO COMPANY**.

2. Click Next on the first screen of the wizard. You will see the screen shown in Figure 6-24.

    The **SELECT GROUPS** screen is used to select the groups that will be converted to a company.

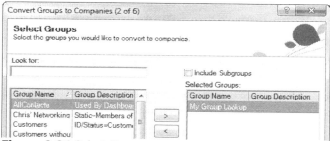

Figure 6-24 Select Groups screen

Because you selected the group before opening the wizard, the group is already selected and is in the **SELECTED GROUPS** list on the right. This means that the group is ready to be converted to a company.

If the group has subgroups that you also want to convert, check the **INCLUDE SUBGROUPS** option. If the group has more than one subgroup, the wizard does not allow you to select a specific subgroup to convert. You can convert the subgroups separately if you do not select the group first.

 Groups ⇒ Convert To Company, will also open the Convert Groups wizard.

3. Click Next.

   The **MAP FIELDS** screen shown in Figure 6-25 is used to select the field in the company record that data from a field in the group record will be moved to.

   If you need to select a different company field, click in the company field that needs to be changed and select the field that you need from the drop-down list, as shown on the right in Figure 6-25.

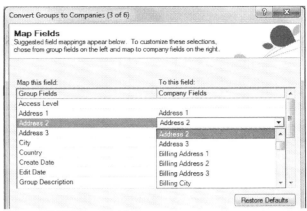

Figure 6-25 Map Fields screen

If you modified the group view by adding fields to it, you will not see a corresponding field in the list of company fields. You will have to add a field to the company table first.

4. The fields are mapped correctly.

   Click Next on the Map Fields screen.

   The screen shown in Figure 6-26 displays the groups that will be converted.

   Click Next on the screen shown in the figure.

   The Convert Groups to Companies screen informs you when the group has been converted.

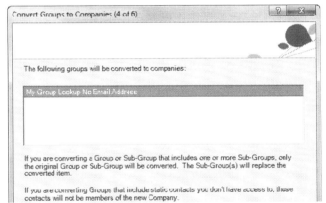

Figure 6-26 Groups to be converted screen

5. Click Next after the group has been converted. Click Finish on the last screen of the wizard.

The group record has been removed. If you look in the Company detail view you will see the My Group Lookup No Email Address company. If you need to change the company name you can.

Move Group Option

This option is used to promote a subgroup to a group or make a group a subgroup of another group. The steps below demonstrate how to move a group or subgroup.

1. In either group view, click on the group or subgroup that you want to move (promote).

Grouping Contacts

2. Groups ⇒ Move Group. On the dialog box shown in Figure 6-27, select one of the options explained below.

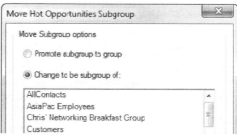

Figure 6-27 Move Group dialog box

 ① **PROMOTE SUBGROUP TO GROUP** This option is only available for subgroups. When selected, the subgroup is promoted to a group and the contacts are retained in the group.
② **CHANGE TO BE SUBGROUP OF** Select this option to make the group (or subgroup) a subgroup of a different group.

> The **MOVE** option is also available for companies.

Group Address Tab

The fields shown in Figure 6-28 are used to enter an address for the group if applicable.

Figure 6-28 Group Address tab fields

Group Access Tab

> In ACT! 2008 and earlier, this was called the **GROUP INFO** tab.

The fields shown in Figure 6-29 are filled in and updated by ACT! automatically.

The fields were explained in Chapter 3. [See Chapter 3, Contact Access Tab]

Figure 6-29 Group Access tab fields

6-20

Group Detail View Related Tasks

The related tasks options shown in Figure 6-30 are primarily on the detail view. Some options are also on list view. The options are explained below.

Figure 6-30 Group detail view related tasks

MODIFY GROUP MEMBERSHIP Opens the Add/Remove Contacts dialog box.

WRITE LETTER TO GROUP CONTACTS Opens the Template folder (in the database) so that you can select a letter template. Once the template is selected, a mail merge of contacts in the group is created and displayed in the word processor.

VIEW CONTACTS WITHIN GROUP Displays the contacts in the selected group in the Contact list view. If there is only one contact in the group, it will be displayed in the Contact detail view.

WRITE E-MAIL USING TEMPLATE Opens the Template folder (in the database) so that you can select a template to use for the email that you want to create. Once you select the template, a new email window will open with the template that you selected.

MODIFY LAYOUT Opens the current group detail view layout in the Layout Designer, so that the layout can be changed.

DUPLICATE GROUP Opens the dialog box shown in Figure 6-31, which is used to select which group fields will be duplicated on the new group record.

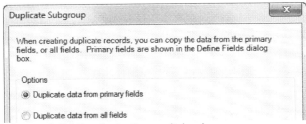

Figure 6-31 Duplicate Group dialog box

VIEW GROUPS/COMPANIES Opens the View Groups/Companies dialog box, which displays a list of the companies, divisions and groups, currently in the database.

Group List View

This view provides an easy way to see groups and subgroups, as shown in Figure 6-32.

Figure 6-32 Group list view

Grouping Contacts

The icon in the first column indicates that the group has subgroups, which is a benefit over the Company list view. If you do not want to see the subgroups, clear the **INCLUDE SUBGROUPS** option.

Group List View Related Tasks

The options shown in Figure 6-33 are for the Group list view. The options that are only on the list view are explained below.

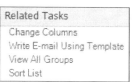

Figure 6-33 Group list view related tasks

CHANGE COLUMNS Opens the Customize Columns dialog box, which allows you to add, remove and change the order that the columns are displayed on the group list view.

VIEW ALL GROUPS Displays all of the groups in the database. It is the same as selecting Lookup ⇒ All groups.

SORT LIST Opens the Sort dialog box to sort the groups displayed in the view.

SCHEDULING ACTIVITIES

In this chapter you will learn the following scheduling activity features:

- ☑ Timeless activities
- ☑ Scheduling a To-Do
- ☑ Scheduling the same activity for multiple contacts
- ☑ Sending email to activity contacts
- ☑ Scheduling activities for other users
- ☑ Using the alarm
- ☑ Rescheduling an activity
- ☑ Handling activity conflicts
- ☑ Group activities
- ☑ Creating and deleting recurring activities
- ☑ Scheduling random activities
- ☑ Filter and sort activities
- ☑ Creating and editing an Activity Series

Scheduling Activities

Activities Overview

Activities are more formal than notes. I think of activities as a really large, well thought out and detailed to-do list for your contacts. Activities let you keep up with your contacts. While it is tempting to only enter a little information for each activity, you may not remember everything that you know now, when the time comes to complete the task that an activity is for.

There are different types of activities that you can schedule. Some activities that you will schedule with contacts are business related and others are personal. The default activity types that you can schedule with contacts are meetings, telephone calls and to-do's. Each of these activities are basically created the same way. Activities are reminders of tasks that you need to complete. You can also create your own activity types.

It is a good idea to display the contact that you want to schedule the activity with before you open the Schedule Activity dialog box. This is not a requirement because there is an option on the dialog box to select the contact. If you want to schedule the same activity for more than one contact, select the group or create a lookup that will display the contacts that you want to schedule the activity for. You can also create the same activity for people that are not part of the same group or lookup at the same time. In addition to being able to view activities on the Activities tab on detail views, you can also view activities on the calendar and Task List.

Figure 7-1 shows the Schedule Activity dialog box.

Table 7-1 explains the options on the Schedule Activity dialog box.

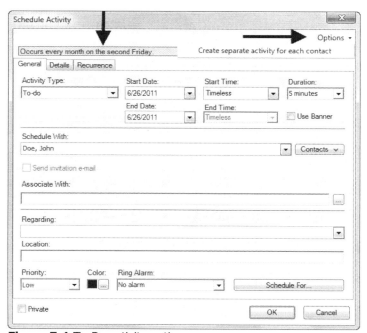

Figure 7-1 To-Do activity options

Option	Description
Create separate activity for each contact	This option is shown in the upper right corner of Figure 7-1 above. It will create an activity for each contact listed in the Schedule With field.
Activity Type	Select or change the type of activity that you are creating or editing. This field will initially be filled in based on the option that you select to open this dialog box. For example, if you click the Schedule Meeting button, "Meeting" will be the value displayed in this field when the dialog box is first opened, but you can change it.
Start Date	The date that the activity should start. The default value is today's date.
Start Time	The time that the activity should start. The default value is **TIMELESS**.
End Date/Time	This field will change automatically when the duration is selected.
Duration	Select the length of time needed to complete the activity.
Use Banner	Displays a banner on the daily calendar if the duration of the activity meets the requirement of the **SHOW FULL DAY** banner calendar preferences option. The banner is also displayed at the top of the Schedule Activity dialog box, as illustrated at the top of Figure 7-1. You can view partial activity entries in the banner section.
Schedule With	By default, this field contains the contact that was displayed before the dialog box was opened. Other contacts can be added.
Contacts Button	The options on this button are used to select contacts for the activity. (1)
Send invitation e-mail	If checked, this option will display a message in the banner at the top of the Schedule Activity dialog box stating that contacts will receive an email notification of the activity and users will receive a calendar email invitation. Once the activity is set up, the appropriate emails and invitations will be sent automatically.
Associate With	Select the groups, subgroups, companies and divisions that need to be included on the activity.
Regarding	Is used to provide a description of the activity. The options that will be displayed in the drop-down list depend on the activity type that is selected. (2)
Location	A free form field that is used to enter where the activity will take place.
Priority	Select how important the activity is. Setting a priority is optional.
Color	Select the color for the priority. (3)
Ring Alarm	If a time is selected from this drop-down list, your computer will beep the number of minutes selected, before the activity is scheduled to start.
Schedule For Button	Select a user in the database to assign the activity to. Activities can be scheduled for more than one user. (4)
Private	If this option is selected on any tab on the Schedule Activity dialog box, other users of the database will not be able to view the activity.

Table 7-1 Schedule Activity dialog box options explained

(1) This button opens the menu shown in Figure 7-2. The options are explained below.
The **SELECT CONTACTS** option is used to select the contacts that the activity is for.
The **NEW CONTACT** option is used to create a new contact, which you can add to the activity.
The **MY RECORD** option is used to add yourself to the activity. If you need to use this option, select it first, then add the other contacts. This option will remove contacts that are already in the Schedule With field, including the original contact that was there.

Scheduling Activities

(2) Figure 7-3 shows the Regarding field drop-down list options for the Meeting activity type. Figure 7-4 shows the Regarding field drop-down list options for the To-Do activity type.
If none of the options in the drop-down list meet your needs, you can type in a new description, which can be up to 256 characters. If you know that you will do a lot of searches or use this field as criteria for a query or report, you should customize it so that only options from the drop-down list can be selected.

(3) By default, each priority level is a different color. If you want to change the color, click the button next to the option. You will see the dialog box shown in Figure 7-5. Keep in mind that the color is associated to a priority level and not the specific activity. If you change the color, the color that you select will automatically be applied to all activities with the same priority, going forward.

(4) Click the **SCHEDULE FOR** button when you need to schedule the activity for another user of the database. In order to schedule an activity for another user, you must have rights to do so.
If you have rights to schedule activities for other users and click this button, you will see the dialog box shown in Figure 7-6. Select the person that you want to schedule the activity for. The activity will display on the users calendar and task list. Don't be surprised when the user (probably a co-worker) does not thank you for giving them more work <smile>.

Figure 7-2 Contacts button options

Figure 7-3 Meeting options

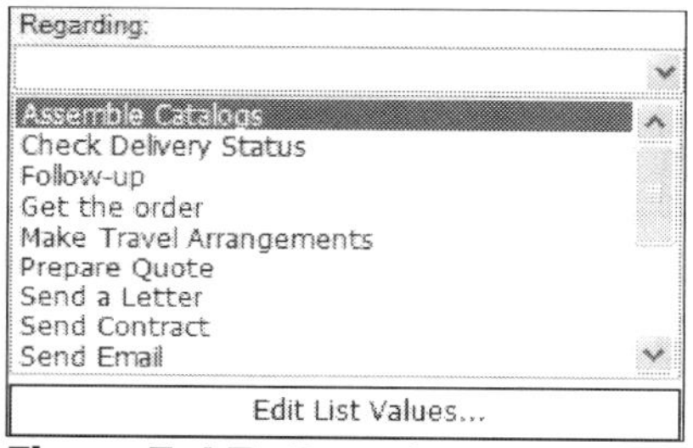

Figure 7-4 To-Do options

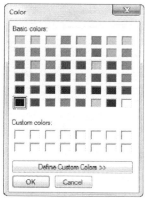

Figure 7-5 Color dialog box

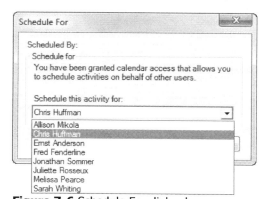

Figure 7-6 Schedule For dialog box

 You will only see users that you have the rights to schedule activities for in the drop-down list on the Schedule For dialog box, shown above in Figure 7-6. Chapter 11 covers how to grant calendar access, which in addition to being able to view entries on another users calendar, also allows you to create activities and assign them to other users.

Chapter 7

Activity Types

There are seven types of activities that you can create, as explained in Table 7-2.

Activity	Is Used To Schedule . . .
Appointment	An Outlook appointment. This is the only place in ACT! that you can select this option to create this type of activity. (5)
Call	A telephone call.
Meeting	A meeting.
To-Do	A task that needs to be completed.
Marketing Call	A telephone call. You could use this option for cold call telephone sales. (5) (6)
Personal Activity	A non business related task. (5) (6)
Vacation	Vacation time. (5) (6)

Table 7-2 Activity types explained

(5) There is no button on the toolbar for this activity type.
(6) Schedule ⇒ Other, as shown in Figure 7-7 displays the entry point for these activity types.

If you do not want to use the menu options to access these activity types, you can click on any of the schedule activity icons on the toolbar to open the Schedule Activity dialog box and then select the activity type from the drop-down list.

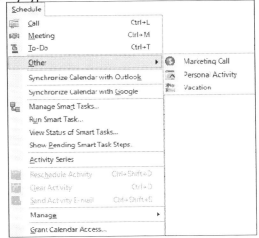

Figure 7-7 Schedule menu options

Timeless Activities

This type of activity is one that does not have a time associated with it. Many types of To-Do activities, like sending an email or fax can be timeless. When you create a To-Do activity, you will see that the default start time displayed is **TIMELESS**. You can change the start time to a specific time if you need to. You can select the timeless option as the default for any type of activity on the Preferences dialog box.

Public Or Private Activities

This option is only useful if more than one person uses the database. If the contact record is marked as private, the activities for the contact are marked as private by default. You can make activities private, even if the contact is not. The symbol illustrated in Figure 7-8 on the Activities tab, denotes that the activity is private.

Scheduling Activities

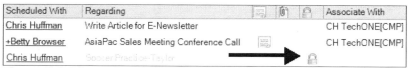

Figure 7-8 Private activity illustrated

Keep the following in mind when deciding whether or not to make an activity private.

① Private activities will partially appear on other users calendars when your name is part of the filter that they use. The actual contents of the activity does not appear, but the word **PRIVATE** appears next to your name.
② When you clear a private activity, it is still marked as private when it is moved to the History tab.
③ Private activities are not displayed in other users Task List.

Exercise 7.1: How To Schedule A To-Do Activity

In this exercise you will create a To-Do activity. Write down the date that you work on this exercise because you will use the same date in Chapter 11 for another exercise.

1. Look up the contacts that have "Customer" in the **ID/STATUS** field.

2. Double-click on the record for Jim Curtis.

3. On the Activities tab of the Contact detail view, click the **TO-DO** button on the Global toolbar. You will see the Schedule Activity dialog box.

4. Open the **REGARDING** drop-down list and select Send Quote.

5. Change the **PRIORITY** to High. Leave the dialog box open to complete the next part of this exercise.

Selecting Who To Schedule The Activity With

You cannot schedule an activity without associating it to a contact in the database.

1. The **SCHEDULE WITH** drop-down list should look like the one shown in Figure 7-9. For now, leave the current contact selected.

   If you click on the Name or Company column heading in the drop-down list, you can change the sort order.

   Clicking the **MY RECORD** button at the bottom of the drop-down list will add the My Record as the person that you want to schedule the activity with.

Figure 7-9 Schedule With drop-down list

How To Schedule An Activity For A New Contact

As mentioned earlier, you can schedule the activity for more than one contact. If the contact that you want to schedule the activity with is not in the database you have to add the contact to the database and then associate it to the activity. This is done by clicking on the Contacts button on the Schedule Activity dialog box and selecting New Contact as shown earlier in Figure 7-2. Selecting this option will open the New Contact dialog box.

How To Add A New Contact To An Activity From The Schedule Activity Dialog Box

In this part of the exercise you will create a new contact for the activity.

1. Click the Contacts button on the Schedule Activity dialog box, then select New Contact. You should see the New Contact dialog box.

2. Enter the information in Table 7-3 for the new contact, then click OK.

   The address fields are on the Business Address tab.

Field	Type This
Company	Spice Plus
Contact	Jennifer Milton
Address	456 Treasury St
City	Astoria
State	PA
Zip	10210

Table 7-3 Information for the new contact

How To Select Multiple Contacts

1. Click the **CONTACTS** button on the Schedule Activity dialog box, then select the Select Contacts option. You will see the Select Contacts dialog box.

    Notice that you can add a new contact from the Select Contacts dialog box also.

You can assign the activity to all contacts, contacts in the current lookup, a group or company. You can also assign the activity on a contact by contact basis, by selecting names from the list.

2. Open the **SELECT FROM** drop-down list and select Current Lookup. You will see the names that are from the ID/Status = Customer lookup that you created earlier in this exercise.

3. Click the **ADD ALL>>** button. You will see all of the contacts from the current lookup in the Selected contacts list.

    If you wanted to assign this activity to other contacts, you could add them now. ACT! will not add names to the Selected contacts list if they have already been selected to be added to the activity.

4. Select the **GROUPS** option from the Select from drop-down list, then open the drop-down list to the right and select the Sales Reps group.

5. Select the first three names from the Sales Reps group by holding down the **CTRL** key and clicking on each name, then click the **ADD>** button. Click OK.

Scheduling Activities

6. Click the Options button in the upper right corner of the Schedule Activity dialog box and select the option, **CREATE SEPARATE ACTIVITY FOR EACH CONTACT**. This will create an entry on the Activities tab of each contact record.

7. Check the **USE BANNER** option. (**Hint**: It is below the Duration field.)

   You should have the options selected that are shown in Figure 7-10.

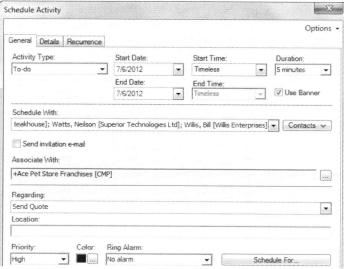

Figure 7-10 General tab activity options

 Activity Linking Issue
When an activity is cleared from a contact that is linked to a company record, by default, the history record that is created for the activity can be viewed from the contact record. To prevent this from happening, clear the **ASSOCIATE WITH** field, shown above in Figure 7-10.

Details Tab Options

The options on this tab are used to add comments, as well as, add an attachment to the activity. The Details tab is used to enter more text than the Regarding field on the General tab can store.

8. On the Details tab, type `This is a To-Do activity`, as shown in Figure 7-11.

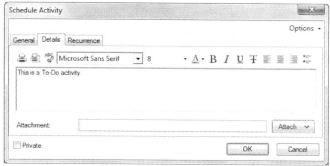

Figure 7-11 Details tab options

Recurrence Tab Options

The options on this tab are used to select the frequency of the activity, as well as, the start and end date for a recurring activity.

Chapter 7

9. No options need to be selected on this tab. Click OK.

View The Activity

10. On the Activities tab, scroll through the records. You will see the To-Do activity that you created, as illustrated in Figure 7-12.

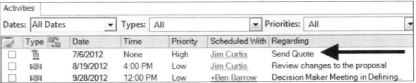

Figure 7-12 To-Do activity illustrated in the Contact detail view

You may be asking yourself, what if I schedule an activity for a future date? How will I remember it? On the Task List view, you can view all of the activities that are scheduled in the future.

Send Invitation E-Mail Option

If you select this option on the Schedule Activity dialog box and have email software configured to work with ACT!, once you click OK on the Schedule Activity dialog box, the email will be generated.

Your email software will open and you will see an email similar to the one shown in Figure 7-13.

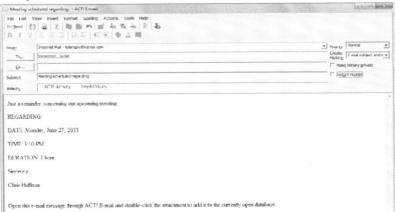

Figure 7-13 Activity e-mail that will be sent to the contacts

Viewing An Activity With Multiple Contacts

If the same activity is assigned to more than one contact, you will not see all of the contact names in the **SCHEDULED WITH** column on the Activities tab. You will see a plus sign at the beginning of the list of names, as illustrated in Figure 7-14. If you click on this link, all of the contacts associated with the activity will be displayed in the Contact list view.

Figure 7-14 Multiple contacts for an activity illustrated

Scheduling Activities

> **Why I Think It's Best To Schedule Phone Calls Individually**
> Looking at the activity illustrated above in Figure 7-14, you will not know how many people need to be called, if this was a telephone call activity. You would have to view them on the Contact list view or open the Schedule Activity dialog box to see the contact names, which adds an extra step to the process. If you call some of the contacts but cannot reach other contacts, it will be difficult to know which contacts you still have to call because there is no way to mark some contacts on the activity as completed and leave others open.
>
> If you do not call all of the contacts, but mark the task as being complete, you may not remember that you still need to call other contacts that are listed on the activity because the activity will no longer appear on the Activities tab or Task List. This is the other reason why I think it is best to schedule phone calls individually. If you want to automatically have activities assigned to multiple contacts scheduled individually, select the option on the Scheduling Preferences dialog box. [See the Modifying Scheduling Preferences section later in this chapter]

Exercise 7.2: Scheduling Activities For Other Users

The **SCHEDULE FOR** button at the bottom of the General tab on the Schedule Activity dialog box is used to create an activity for another user of the database. For example, if you wanted a sales manager in your company to send a thank you note to all of your suppliers, you could schedule the activity for the sales manager. Won't the sales manager be thrilled!

How To Schedule A Call

This activity type is used to create a reminder to call a contact. In this exercise you will schedule a phone call activity for another user of the database.

1. Look up the contact George Agen.

2. Click the **CALL** button on the Global toolbar.

3. Change the Priority to Medium, then select the Regarding option, Confirm Appointment.

4. Click the **SCHEDULE FOR** button. Open the drop-down list and select Allison Mikola, then click OK.

5. You will see the banner shown in Figure 7-15 at the top of the Schedule Activity dialog box.

   Click OK.

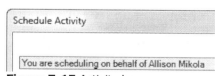
Figure 7-15 Activity banner

Exercise 7.3: Using The Alarm

This feature is designed to remind you of a scheduled activity. ACT! has to be open in order for the alarm to notify you of an activity. If ACT! is open, the Alarms dialog box will pop up. If ACT! is open, but minimized, the ACT! button on the Windows Taskbar will flash. Your computer will beep if you have the Ring Alarm option enabled. If you only select the Set Alarm option, you will only be notified at the time that activity starts, not before.

The alarm also has a snooze option, which you can use to be reminded of an activity. It works like the snooze button on an alarm clock, by notifying you in advance of the activity. You can reset the alarm to go off again at a later time. You can also clear the alarm option to turn it off completely. Turning off the alarm does not clear the activity.

The snooze option is useful if you need time before the activity to prepare for it. If you want a snooze time that is not in the Ring Alarm field drop-down list, you can type it in. For example, you can enter any of the following times in the field: 46 minutes, 46 hours or 46 days.

1. Lookup the contact Jim Curtis.

2. Click the **CALL** button on the Global toolbar.

3. Open the Start Time drop-down list. Scroll down the list and click in the time slot that is to the nearest, next half hour. (If it is currently 8:20 PM, select 8:30 PM. If it is 4:35 PM, select 5 PM.)

4. Select the Regarding option Confirm Appointment, then change the Priority to Medium.

5. Open the **RING ALARM** drop-down list and select 5 minutes. This means that you will be notified five minutes before this activity starts.

6. You should have the options selected that are shown in Figure 7-16.

    You will see a different date and time.

    Click OK.

    If there is a conflict alert, select the closest available time in the future.

    You should now see an entry for this activity on the contact record for Jim Curtis.

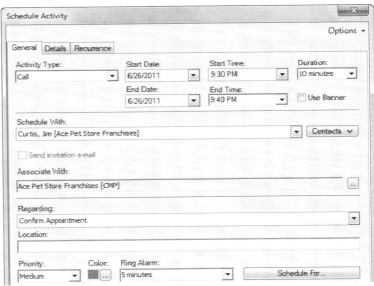

Figure 7-16 Telephone call activity options

When the Alarms dialog box shown in Figure 7-17 appears, come back to the section below: Alarm Notification Options.

For now, continue going through the book by going to Exercise 7.5: Handling Activity Conflicts or you can go get a snack <smile>.

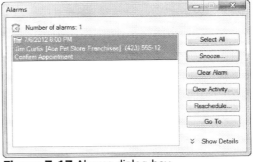

Figure 7-17 Alarms dialog box

Scheduling Activities

Alarm Notification Options

You should now see the dialog box shown above in Figure 7-17. The alarm options explained below are available.

Select All Is used to set the same option for all of the activities that are displayed on the Alarms dialog box.

Snooze Is used to reset the snooze time on the dialog box shown in Figure 7-19.

Clear Alarm Turns the alarm off for the rest of the day. The activity will still stay on your calendar.

Clear Activity Opens the Clear Activity dialog box so that you can mark the activity as being complete.

Reschedule Opens the Schedule Activity dialog box, which is used to select a different date or time for the activity.

Go To Displays the contact record that the alarm is for.

Show Details Displays the Activity Details section, shown in Figure 7-18. It is at the bottom of the Alarms dialog box.

When the details are displayed, the Show Details button will change to **HIDE DETAILS**.

Figure 7-18 Activity details on the Alarms dialog box

Setting The Snooze Alarm

1. Click the Snooze button.

   You should see the dialog box shown in Figure 7-19.

Figure 7-19 Snooze Alarm dialog box

2. Select the **10 MINUTES** option, then click OK. 10 minutes from now you will be notified again of the meeting that you have scheduled.

Exercise 7.4: Rescheduling An Activity

Rescheduling allows you to change when an activity will take place.

1. On the Alarms dialog box, click on the activity for Jim Curtis.

2. Click the **RESCHEDULE** button. You will see the Schedule Activity dialog box for the activity. If you were doing this for real, you would select a new date or time on the Schedule Activity dialog box.

3. For now, click the Cancel button.

4. Click the **CLEAR ALARM** button on the Alarms dialog box, then close the dialog box. Look up the contact Jim Curtis.

5. Double-click on the Confirm Appointment activity. Change the **RING ALARM** option to **NO ALARM**, then click OK.

Exercise 7.5: Handling Activity Conflicts

ACT! will warn you of activity conflicts and try to keep you from scheduling two activities at the same time. If this occurs, you will be notified when you are creating an activity that conflicts with an existing activity. You will have the option to reschedule the time and/or date of the new activity. In this exercise you will schedule a meeting activity for a time when an activity already exists.

1. Look up the contact Jim Curtis.

2. Click the **MEETING** button on the Global toolbar.

3. Change the Start date to 8/19/2012. (Yes, I know that this is a date in the past, but bear with me.) You can do this by typing the date in the field or by using the calendar attached to the field. Change the Start time to 4:30 PM.

4. Set the Duration to 2 hours.

5. Select the **PRESENTATION** Regarding option.

   You should have the options shown in Figure 7-20.

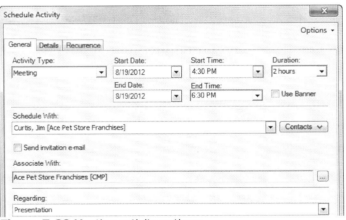

Figure 7-20 Meeting activity options

6. Click OK. You should see the message shown in Figure 7-21.

Normally, you would not see this dialog box because you would not be trying to schedule an activity for a date in the past, unless you typed in a date in the past by mistake. It is being done here on purpose to demonstrate how to handle activity conflicts.

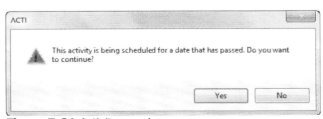

Figure 7-21 Activity warning message

Scheduling Activities

7. Click Yes to continue. You will see the dialog box shown in Figure 7-22.

   This dialog box is telling you that the activity that you are trying to schedule is conflicting with an existing activity.

   The figure shows that an activity has already been scheduled with the contact on 8/19/2012 starting at 3:30 PM.

   Therefore, it is probably a good idea to reschedule this activity for another date or time.

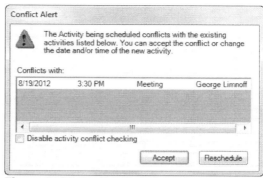

Figure 7-22 Conflict Alert dialog box

If you still want to schedule this activity, click the **ACCEPT** button. If you want to change the date or time of the activity, click the **RESCHEDULE** button.

How To Reschedule A Conflicting Activity

1. Click the **RESCHEDULE** button on the Conflict Alert dialog box shown above in Figure 7-22.

2. Change the Start date to 9/19/12. Change the Start time to 11:30 AM, then click OK. This date and time does not conflict with other activities for the contact.

3. Click Yes when prompted that the activity has been scheduled for a date in the past.

Exercise 7.6: Group Activities

You can schedule an activity for a group. Doing this means that each contact in the group will be associated to the group activity. The group activity will appear on the Activities tab of each contact in the group.

In this exercise you will create a group activity for the Sales Reps group. The majority of the steps to create a group activity are the same as creating an activity for one contact.

1. Open the Group detail view, then click on the Sales Reps group.

2. Click the Meeting button on the Global toolbar, then change the Start Date to tomorrow.

Notice that the group name is in the Associate With field on the Schedule Activity dialog box. You can also add individual contacts and other groups to the activity.

3. Click the Contacts button, then select the Select Contacts option.

4. Open the Select From drop-down list, then select Groups.

5. Open the next drop-down list and select the group, Sales Reps with no email. Add all of the contacts in the group to the list, then click OK.

6. Select the **FOLLOW-UP ON PRESENTATION** Regarding option, then click OK. If you click on the Activities tab for the Sales Reps group, you will see the activity that you just created.

Chapter 7

Recurring Activities

Recurring activities are activities that are repeated on a consistent frequency. The four types of recurring activities that can be created are explained below. The recurring options look somewhat similar, but the fields perform differently. To make sure that you have selected the correct options, read the information in the banner at the top of the dialog box. It briefly explains what the options that you selected represent.

The **EVERY** field determines how many days, weeks, months or years are between each occurrence of the activity.

The **STARTS** field is the date that you want the first occurrence of the recurring activity to begin.

The **ENDS** field is the date that you want the last occurrence of the activity to happen.

There are two ways that recurring activities can be scheduled, as explained below:

① Activities that occur on a regular basis, like monthly staff meetings.
② Activities that occur randomly, like processing payroll every other Friday.

Recurring Activity Types Explained

① **Daily** Select this option if the interval for the recurring activity is in days.

For example, the options shown in Figure 7-23 are for an activity that will happen every five days.

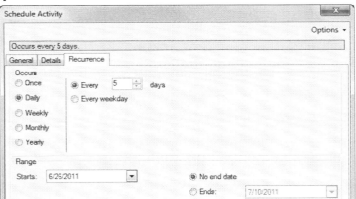

Figure 7-23 Daily recurring activity type options

② **Weekly** Select this option for activities that you want to occur weekly.

The options shown in Figure 7-24 are for a weekly meeting that will take place every Thursday and Friday, indefinitely.

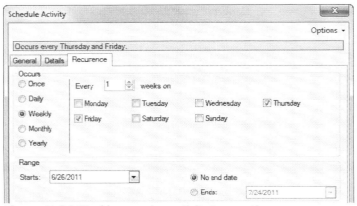

Figure 7-24 Weekly recurring activity type options

Scheduling Activities

③ **Monthly** Select this option for activities that you want to occur monthly.

The options shown in Figure 7-25 will create a monthly activity that takes place on the second Tuesday of every month.

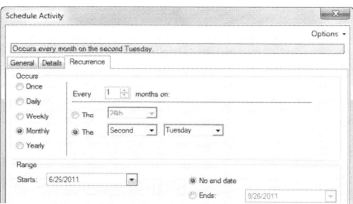

Figure 7-25 Monthly recurring activity type options

④ **Yearly** Select this option for activities that you want to occur yearly.

The options shown in Figure 7-26 will create a yearly activity that takes place on the last Tuesday in March.

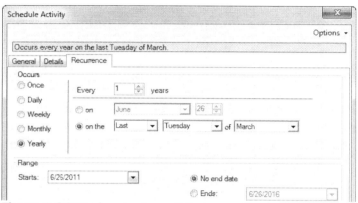

Figure 7-26 Yearly recurring activity type options

Exercise 7.7: How To Schedule Recurring Activities

If you know that you will need to have monthly meetings, you can schedule the meeting once and have ACT! automatically schedule the rest of the monthly meetings for the time frame that you specify.

1. Look up the contact Rick Blaine, then click the Meeting button.

2. Select the options in Table 7-4 for the meeting activity.

Option	Change To
Start Date	The 24th of next month
Start Time	3 PM
Duration	2 hours
Regarding	Contract Negotiations

Table 7-4 Meeting activity options

3. On the **RECURRENCE** tab, select the Monthly option, then change the first **THE** option to the 24th, if it is not already.

7-16

Chapter 7

4. Select the ENDS option and type in the date a year from today.

   You should have options selected that are similar to the ones shown in Figure 7-27.

   These options will schedule a meeting the 24th of each month for the next year.

Figure 7-27 Recurrence tab options

5. Click OK. If there is a conflict, reschedule the activity and change the Start date on the Schedule Activity dialog box to the 25th.

   On the Activities tab for Rick Blaine, you will see a recurring meeting that starts on the 24th of next month, as shown in Figure 7-28.

Figure 7-28 Recurring meeting illustrated

The recurring activity symbol is illustrated.

Only the next occurrence of recurring activities will appear on the Activities tab and Task List. All of the occurrences of a recurring activity will appear on your calendar. This means that you will see each occurrence of a weekly meeting on a calendar, but you will only see the next occurrence of the weekly meeting on the Activities tab.

Exercise 7.8: How To Schedule Random Activities

Scheduling random activities allows you to schedule a conference call on the last day of the month. If you select the 31st, ACT! will schedule the recurring activity on the last day of the month, no matter what the actual last date of the month is.

1. Look up the My Record.

2. Click the CALL button, then select the options in Table 7-5.

Option	Change To
Start Time	5 PM
Duration	15 minutes
Regarding	Discuss legal points
Priority	High

Table 7-5 Schedule call activity options

Scheduling Activities

3. On the Recurrence tab, select the Monthly option.

   Open the first drop-down list and select the 31st.

   If you wanted the activity to end, you would enter a date in the ENDS field.

   You should have similar options to those shown in Figure 7-29. Click OK.

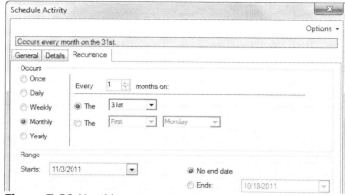

Figure 7-29 Monthly recurrence settings

On the Activities tab of the My Record (for Chris Huffman), you should see a phone call scheduled for the last day of the current month. If the current month does not have 31 days, the activity will appear on the last day of the month. This may or may not be a workday.

Scheduling An Activity For The Last Workday Of The Month

In the previous exercise you created a random recurring activity that would automatically be scheduled for the last calendar day of the month.

If you need to schedule a monthly activity for the last workday of the month, select the monthly options illustrated in Figure 7-30.

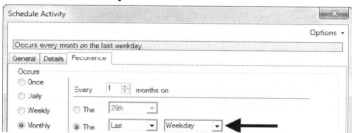

Figure 7-30 Options for a last workday of the month activity

> **Other Ways To Open The Schedule Activity Dialog Box**
> The majority of the activities that you created in this chapter used a button on the toolbar to open the Schedule Activity dialog box. There are other ways to open the Schedule Activity dialog box, as explained below.
>
> ① Double-click on a time slot on the calendar. This is helpful because it can help prevent you from trying to schedule conflicting activities.
> ② Open the Schedule menu.
> ③ On the Activities tab of a detail view, right-click in the list of activities and select Schedule ⇒ Meeting, as shown in Figure 7-31.

Figure 7-31 Activities tab shortcut menu

7-18

Deleting Recurring Activities

If you have scheduled a recurring activity and either no longer need the remaining activities or need to clear (delete) a recurring activity for a specific date, you can.

Exercise 7.9: How To Clear All Future Recurring Activities

In this exercise you will learn how to delete all of the remaining occurrences of an activity.

1. If the My Record is not displayed, display it now.

2. On the Activities tab, right-click on the monthly Discuss Legal Points activity that you just created for the current month. Select the **ERASE ACTIVITY** option.

3. You will see the dialog box shown in Figure 7-32 letting you know that this is a recurring activity.

    Select the **DELETE ALL OCCURRENCES** option, then click OK.

    If your email software opens, close it.

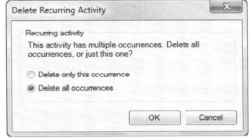

Figure 7-32 Delete Recurring Activity dialog box

Exercise 7.10: How To Clear A Single Recurring Activity

In this exercise you will learn how to clear one occurrence of the remaining occurrences of an activity.

1. Look up the contact Jim Curtis.

2. Right-click on the presentation activity on 9/19/2012 that you created earlier in this chapter and select **CLEAR ACTIVITY**.

3. Select the **ERASE** option on the Clear Activity dialog box, as illustrated in Figure 7-33, then click OK. The activity will be deleted.

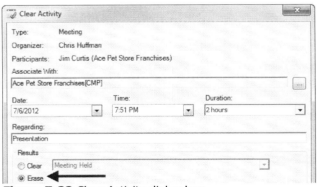

Figure 7-33 Clear Activity dialog box

Scheduling Activities

Clearing Activities

It is good practice to clear activities once you complete them. When you clear an activity, a record is automatically created on the History tab of the contact that the activity belongs to. This way, if you need to know whether or not an activity was completed or ever existed, you will be able to easily tell.

> **Recurring Activities**
> When you use the **CLEAR ACTIVITY** option on recurring activities that were created prior to installing ACT! 2013, the recurring activities automatically duplicate themselves.

Other Reasons To Clear Activities

① Some reports are based on history records that are created when an activity is cleared. Without history records, the reports will not produce the correct output.
② Allows you to schedule follow up activities.
③ You will not be reminded of the activity.
④ Fields on the Latest Activities tab are updated.

How To Clear Activities

You have already learned how to clear recurring activities from the Activities tab. Clearing other types of activities is basically the same process. You can right-click on an activity any place except the History tab, then select Clear Activity. The other ways to clear an activity are explained below:

① On the Task List, click in the check box illustrated in Figure 7-34.
② On any Calendar view, click in the check box illustrated in Figure 7-35.
③ Select the activity on the Activities tab that you want to clear, then Schedule ⇒ Clear Activity.

Figure 7-34 Task List option to clear an activity

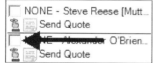

Figure 7-35 Calendar view option to clear an activity

Exercise 7.11: Clear An Activity For A Contact

When you clear an activity you can leave the options the way that they are or you can add or change information about the activity as needed. You should make changes that will help you remember more about the activity in the future.

1. Right-click on the Contract Negotiations activity for Rick Blaine, then select **CLEAR ACTIVITY**.

2. Click the **FOLLOW-UP** button. The follow-up option is used to schedule another activity for the contact. (Amazingly, this is called a follow up activity <smile>.) This is the equivalent of creating a paper trail.

3. Open the **REGARDING** drop-down list and select the Follow-up on Presentation option, then click OK.

4. Select the **MEETING NOT HELD** results option on the Clear Activity dialog box.

Chapter 7

5. Check the **ADD ACTIVITY DETAILS TO HISTORY** option, if it is not already checked.

   You should have the options shown in Figure 7-36.

   Click OK.

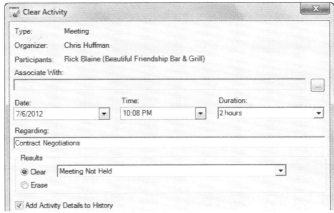

Figure 7-36 Clear activity options

The activity for Contract Negotiations with today's date is no longer on the Activities tab. You should see a new activity with today's date that has "Follow-up on Presentation" in the Regarding field. On the History tab, you will see an entry for the meeting not held activity.

 How To Clear More Than One Activity At The Same Time
You can clear more than one activity on the Activities tab or the Task List at the same time by selecting the activities that you want to clear, then right-click on them and select **CLEAR MULTIPLE ACTIVITIES**, as illustrated in Figure 7-37.

Figure 7-37 Task List multi select shortcut menu

Exercise 7.12: Clear An Activity For A Group

The steps below show you how to clear a group activity. In this exercise you will clear the group activity that you created earlier in this chapter. Clearing a group activity is the same process as clearing an activity for a contact.

1. Click the Groups button, then click on the Activities tab for the Sales Rep group.

2. You should see a Follow-up on Presentation activity with tomorrows date. It may be a date in the past if you completed Exercise 7.6 before today. Right-click on the activity and select **CLEAR ACTIVITY**.

3. Click OK on the Clear Activity dialog box because none of the information for the activity needs to be changed.

Scheduling Activities

Exercise 7.13: How To Filter Activities

You may only want to see certain types of activities or activities in a certain date range. Filtering is used to accomplish both of these tasks. In this exercise you will learn how to filter activities.

1. Look up the My Record. On the Activities tab, open the **TYPES** drop-down list and clear the Vacation option. If there are vacation activities, they will not be displayed now.

2. Right-click in the Activities tab and select Filter Activities on the shortcut menu.

3. You should see the Filter Activities dialog box. Open the Dates drop-down list and select **TODAY AND FUTURE**.

4. Open the Types drop-down list and clear the Personal Activity option.

   You should have the options selected that are shown in Figure 7-38.

   Click OK.

   There should be less activities displayed now then when you first started this exercise.

Figure 7-38 Filter Activities dialog box

Sorting Activities
You can sort the activities on the Activities tab in ascending or descending order by clicking on the column heading of the field that you want to sort on.

Exercise 7.14: How To Delete An Activity

If you have an activity that you do not need anymore or will not complete, you can delete it. If you delete an activity, it is not automatically recorded on the History tab, but it is removed from your schedule.

1. Look up the contact Rick Blaine. Display all of the activities by changing the **DATES** option to All Dates. Change the **TYPES** option to All.

2. Click on the activity that has today's date or the most recent date if you completed the prior exercises in this chapter before today, then press the Delete key.

3. Select the Erase option on the Clear Activity dialog box, then click OK. Select the option to delete all occurrences if prompted, then click OK.

Activity Series

ACT! comes with two activity series that you can use. You can also create your own activity series. Activity series remind me of a project plan or mini to-do list that has all of the tasks that you need to do, to complete a project. An activity series is used to schedule pre-defined activities with contacts. An activity series saves you time because you do not have to remember all of the tasks or create a series of activities manually for each contact. Like other features in ACT!, the activity series can be public or private.

The key to understanding how an activity series works is understanding the concept of the **ANCHOR DATE**. The anchor date is the date the activities in the series use as a starting point. It is the date that all activities in the series are based from. You can schedule activities, days, weeks or months before or after the anchor date. If you are trying to figure out when you would have the need to schedule an activity before the anchor date, hopefully, the following scenario will help.

If you are planning to have a product launch, a lot of activities need to be completed weeks and months before the product is actually launched. Some of the tasks that need to be completed prior to the product launch include the following: Inviting the media, finding and booking a location for the launch, creating and inviting potential customers, creating and executing an advertising campaign and hiring a caterer. These activities would have a date prior to the anchor date. In this scenario, the anchor date would be the date of the product launch.

The **ACTIVITY SERIES TEMPLATE CREATION WIZARD** can be accessed from any view. It is used to create a list of activities to complete. You can create as many activity series as you need. Having a list makes it easier to remember what the next task is that needs to be completed.

Another example of an activity series would be the tasks that have to be completed when you obtain a new customer. The following items could be the activities that need to be completed for new customers.

① Verify the contact information. (Send email)
② Send the customer a welcome kit. (Send literature)
③ Call the customer five days after the welcome kit is sent out. (Confirm shipment)
④ Set up another opportunity for the customer. (Send quote)

Exercise 7.15: Create An Activity Series

In this exercise you will create an activity series that will be used as the guidelines for changing a prospect to a customer. The series will include the four activities listed above.

1. Schedule ⇒ Manage ⇒ Activity Series Templates.

    You will see the dialog box shown in Figure 7-39.

    Select the first option, then click Next.

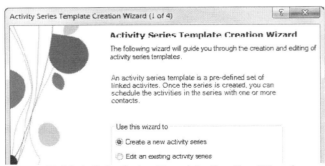

Figure 7-39 Activity Series Template Creation Wizard

 Select the **EDIT AN EXISTING ACTIVITY SERIES** option on the first wizard screen, shown above in Figure 7-39, when you want to view the existing activities. You will see the screen shown in Figure 7-40. You would also select this option if you need to edit an activity series.

Scheduling Activities

Figure 7-40 Existing activity series screen

2. Type `My Activity Series` in the Name field.

   Type `New Customers Welcome Kit` in the Description field, as shown in Figure 7-41, then click Next.

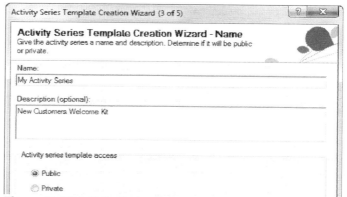

Figure 7-41 Activity Series Name screen

3. Click the Add button on the third wizard screen.

   Open the Activity Type drop-down list and select To-do.

   Select the **SEND EMAIL** Regarding option.

   Change the Ring Alarm option to No Alarm.

   You should have the options shown in Figure 7-42.

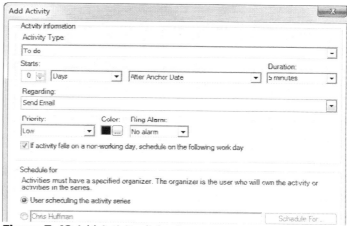

Figure 7-42 Add Activity dialog box

The **STARTS** field is how many days, weeks or month's from the Series Anchor date that you want the activity to begin.

The options in the next drop-down list are used to select the interval (days, weeks or months) that the activity needs to be completed in.

7-24

Chapter 7

The third drop-down list is used to select whether the activity should start **BEFORE** or **AFTER** the Anchor date.

4. Click OK. You should see the activity that you just created.

5. Create the activities in Table 7-6.

Field	Activity #1	Activity #2	Activity #3
Activity Type	To-do	Call	Marketing Call
Starts	1	6	8
Regarding	Send Literature	Confirm Shipment	Follow up per email
Ring Alarm	No Alarm	No Alarm	No Alarm

Table 7-6 Activities for the series

6. When you are finished, the Activity Series screen should look like the one shown in Figure 7-43.

   If necessary, you can resize the columns on this screen just like you can on the tabs on a detail view.

   Click Next.

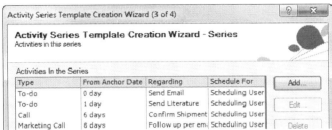

Figure 7-43 Activities in the series

7. The option **YES, SCHEDULE NOW** should be selected, as shown in Figure 7-44.

   Click Finish.

   You will see the Schedule Activity Series dialog box.

Figure 7-44 Activity Series Finish screen

Assign The Activity Series To Contacts

You can assign the activities in the series to one or more contacts as soon as you create the activity series, by following the steps below.

1. Click the Contacts button on the Schedule Activity Series dialog box and select the first option.

2. Assign the activities to all of the contacts in the Sales Reps with no email address group, then click OK.

3. Change the **SERIES ANCHOR DATE** to next Monday.

7-25

Scheduling Activities

4. You should have the options shown in Figure 7-45.

   The only difference should be the anchor date.

   Click the Schedule button.

Figure 7-45 Schedule Activities Series dialog box

5. Look up the contact Emily Dunn, then click on the Activities tab.

   You should see the four activities from the series, as illustrated in Figure 7-46.

   Notice that they are in date order.

Figure 7-46 Activities from the series

Exercise 7.16: How To Edit An Activity Series

In this exercise you will modify the activity series that you just created. You will also assign users to tasks in the activity series.

1. Schedule ⇒ Manage ⇒ Activity Series Templates. Select the **EDIT AN EXISTING ACTIVITY SERIES** option, then click Next.

2. Select the activity series that you created, then click Next.

3. Add the following to the Description field. – (Select the anchor date to equal the date that you will send the literature), as shown in Figure 7-47, then click Next.

7-26

Chapter 7

The reason that I include information about the anchor date in the Activity Series description is so that I will know which activity is the one driving the series. Doing this is optional.

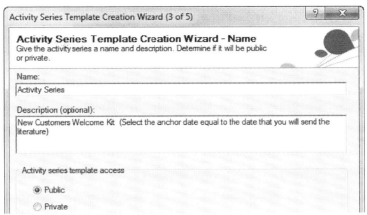

Figure 7-47 Modified activity series description

4. Select the Send Literature activity, then click the Edit button.

5. Click the last option in the **SCHEDULE FOR** section, then click the **SCHEDULE FOR** button.

6. Open the drop-down list on the Schedule For dialog box and select Allison, then click OK twice to return to the Activity Series wizard.

7. Repeat the steps above to assign a user to the activities in Table 7-7.

Activity	Assign To
Confirm Shipment	Ernst
Follow up per email	Jonathan

Table 7-7 Activities to assign to users

8. Change the Starts field of the Send Email activity to 2, then select **BEFORE ANCHOR DATE** from the drop-down list, as illustrated in Figure 7-48.

   Click OK.

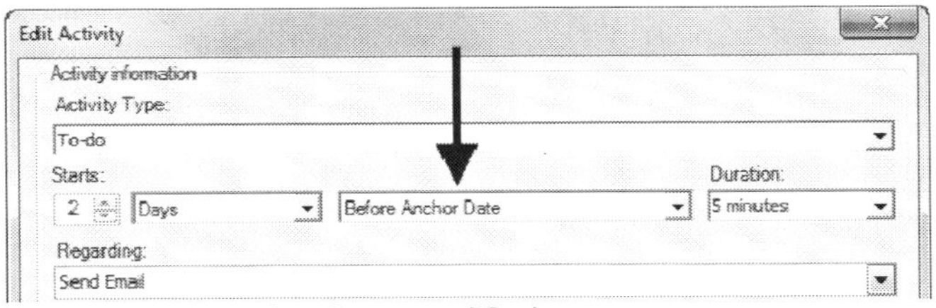

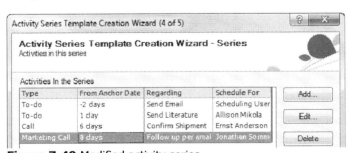

Figure 7-48 Anchor Date modified

When you are finished, the **SCHEDULE FOR** column on the wizard screen should look like the one shown in Figure 7-49.

Notice that the first To-do activity has **-2 DAYS** in the From Anchor Date column. That is because you selected the Before Anchor Date option, which means that this activity should be started two days before the anchor date.

Figure 7-49 Modified activity series

9. Click Next. Select No, schedule later, then click Finish.

7-27

RUNNING REPORTS

In this chapter you will learn the following about running reports:

- ☑ Selecting report criteria
- ☑ Custom date ranges
- ☑ Printing calendars, address books, labels and envelopes
- ☑ Using the Quick Print options

Running Reports

Reports Overview

ACT! comes with several reports already created that you can use. They are on the Reports menu. In this chapter you will learn how to run some of the reports. The reports that you run can be printed and saved. Reports are probably a key feature in ACT! because we are a report driven society. For many, reports are the only reason they enter contact information in ACT!. Once you have been using ACT! for a while you will probably see that you are running the same reports on a regular basis. Take some time once you have run reports for about a month and carefully look at the data. Are there columns on the report that do not have any data or very little data? Is the report providing the level of detail that you need? If not, you may need to modify the report and/or enter more data.

The label and envelope options are on the Print dialog box, which is accessed from the File menu. The calendar and address book print options are with the labels and envelopes. Some people think that it is strange that these options are not on the Reports menu, but if you think about it, they are not reports in the true sense of the word.

The Reports menu shown in Figure 8-1 is how you access the reports. Notice the **OTHER REPORTS** options. (For example, Other Contact Reports and Other Group Reports). The wording gives the impression that these options would display more reports.

As a programmer, I was not misled by this wording because these options do not have a triangle like the Group, Company and Opportunity Reports menu options have. A programming standard when a menu option will open a submenu is to put a triangle next to the option.

If you look closely, you will see that the "Other Reports" menu options have three periods (called an **ELLIPSIS**) after them. This is another programming standard. This is used to signify that selecting the option will open a dialog box.

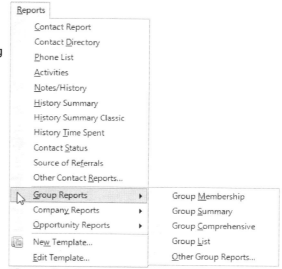

Figure 8-1 Reports menu

When you select any of the "Other Reports" options, you will see the **SELECT REPORT** dialog box which has all of the reports that came with ACT!. If you modify reports or create new ones and other people will use the reports, you could save them in this folder or add them to a menu so that other people can access them. OK, the programming chapter for today is over!

Define Filters Dialog Box

The Define Filters dialog box should reduce any anxiety that you may have about selecting options to run reports because it is used to select the criteria for each report. Options that are not available for a report are not enabled. You have to create the lookup or run a saved query before selecting a report to run if you do not want to be limited by the options on the Define Filters dialog box. If you know that a certain report needs a lookup or query, you should create it and save it. It would be a nice feature to be able to select a saved lookup or query from the Define Filters dialog box when selecting other report criteria.

Chapter 8

Activity, Notes, History And Opportunity Reports
The default date range option for these reports is **CURRENT MONTH**. If left unchanged, this may produce unexpected results by not displaying all of the data that you would expect to see. For example, you create a lookup or run a query that retrieves contact records that have a create date from last year.

If you leave the default date range of the current month selected, the report will not display any activity, note, history or opportunity data from any other time period. Only data for the current month will be displayed on the report. More than likely, you would also be expecting to see data for these types of records from previous years.

Tips For Running Reports In This Chapter
① Unless stated otherwise, make sure that the **SEND THE REPORT OUTPUT TO** option on the General tab on the Define Filters dialog box is set to Preview for the report exercises, unless you want to print the report. The remaining report output options are explained in Table 8-1.
② Make sure that the **EXCLUDE 'MY RECORD'** option is checked on the General tab on the Define Filters dialog box. Selecting this option will keep the My Record from printing.
③ Save any report that you want to keep in your folder.
④ Close the report when you are finished viewing it.

File Type	Select This File Type If The Report . . .
Rich-Text	Needs to be edited in a word processor.
HTML	Will be posted on the Internet.
PDF	Will be distributed to someone that does not have ACT!. Either the full version of Adobe Acrobat or the free Adobe Reader is needed to view a PDF file.
Text	Needs to be in plain text format. Non text objects like image files are not saved in this format.
Printer	Will be printed on paper.
Email	Will be sent via email.

Table 8-1 Report output file types explained

Exercise 8.1: The Contact Report

This report will print a profile for each contact that is selected. You can filter the report to include or not include the notes, history, opportunities and activity information.

1. Reports ⇒ Contact Report.

Running Reports

2. On the General tab, select the **ALL CONTACTS** option.

   You should have the options selected that are shown in Figure 8-2.

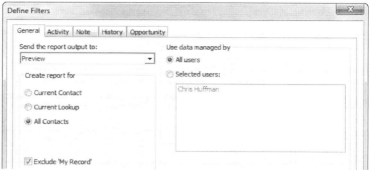

Figure 8-2 General tab options for the Contact report

 If you created a lookup for the records that you want to appear on the report prior to opening the report, select the **CURRENT LOOKUP** option. If you only want the report to use the contact record that you have open, select the **CURRENT CONTACT** option.

3. On the Activity tab, clear the **MEETINGS** option. Clearing this option will keep the meeting activities from printing on the report.

4. Open the **DATE RANGE** drop-down list and select Past.

 The **PAST** date range option will only print activities that have a date in the past. The **CUSTOM** button is used to select a specific date range for the activities that you want to include on the report.

5. Clear the **INCLUDE CLEARED ACTIVITIES** option.

   You should have the options selected that are shown in Figure 8-3.

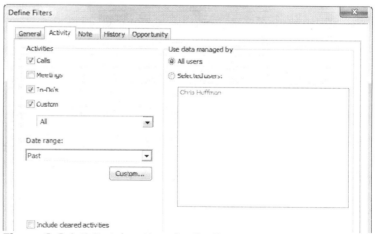

Figure 8-3 Activity tab options for the Contact report

6. On the Note tab, clear the Notes option.

7. On the History tab, clear the Email and Attachments options, then select the **ALL** date range option.

8. On the Opportunity tab, clear the Closed-Won, Closed-Lost and Inactive options.

Chapter 8

9. Change the Date Range to All, then click OK. The report will open in its own window. In the lower left corner of the Print Preview window you will see the report pages being created.

Report Print Preview Toolbar

Like many other windows in ACT!, the Print Preview window has a toolbar, as shown in Figure 8-4. Table 8-2 explains the buttons on the toolbar.

Figure 8-4 Report print preview toolbar

Button	Description
1	Saves the report.
2	Prints the report.
3	Is used to change the paper size, margins and orientation of the report.
4	The Show Navigation Bar button displays the report pages in the thumbnail view, as shown in Figure 8-5.
5	The Hand Tool button is used to move the report page around in the window.
6	The Zoom In Tool button is used to change the magnification of the report displayed on the screen.
7	The Select Text button is used to select text in the report that you want to copy to another document.
8	Displays the first page of the report.
9	Displays the previous page of the report.
10	Displays the next page of the report.
11	Displays the last page of the report.
12	The Actual Size button is used to enlarge the report on the screen.
13	The Full Page button is used to display an entire page of the report, whether or not it is readable.
14	The Page Width button is used to resize the report so that it is the size of the Print Preview window.
15	The Two Pages button is used to display two pages of the report in the window at the same time, as shown in Figure 8-6.
16	The Four Pages button is used to display four pages of the report in the window at the same time. (1)
17	Cancels the print preview process from generating the entire report.

Table 8-2 Report print preview toolbar buttons explained

Running Reports

Viewing Other Pages In A Report

Most reports have more than one page. If you want to move around the report quickly, the easiest way to do that is to click the **SHOW NAVIGATION BAR** button on the toolbar.

This will let you view a thumbnail of each page of the report, as shown in Figure 8-5. This option is useful if the report is large. You can scroll down the thumbnails and click on the page that you want to view.

Scrolling down the thumbnails and clicking on page 32 is faster then clicking the Next Page ▶ button 31 times if the current page is the first page of the report.

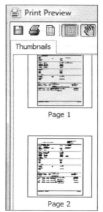

Figure 8-5 Report preview thumbnail option

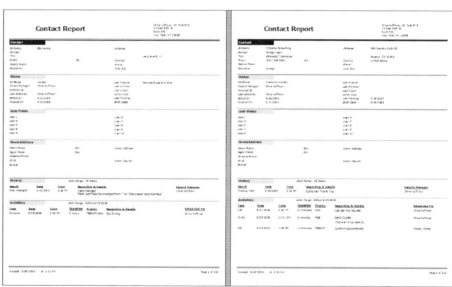

Figure 8-6 Two pages of the report visible at the same time

(1) Clicking on the arrow at the end of the **FOUR PAGES** button displays the grid shown in Figure 8-7. This is used to select how many pages of the report to display in the window.

When you want to display a specific number of pages in the report, click in the first square in the upper left corner of the grid, then drag the mouse to the right and then down until you see the number of rows and columns that you need. In the example shown, 12 pages of the report will be displayed on the screen.

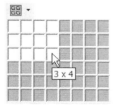

Figure 8-7 Four Pages button options

Preview And Save The Report

1. Click the **ZOOM IN TOOL** button, then click on the report three times. The report will be displayed much larger. Compare this report to the report shown earlier in Figure 8-6.

2. Click the **FILE SAVE** button on the Print Preview window toolbar. You should see the folder that you created. For now, you can accept the default file name, then click the Save button.

The Contact Directory Report

This report is similar to the contact report in the previous exercise.

The difference is that the information on the Activities, Notes, History and Opportunities tabs will not print on the Contact Directory report.

This report prints the contact address information, as shown in Figure 8-8.

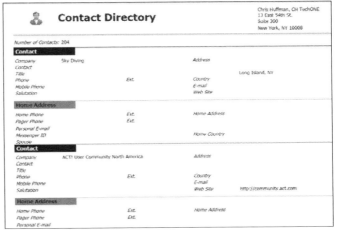

Figure 8-8 Contact Directory report

Exercise 8.2: The Phone List Report

This report will print the company, contact, phone, mobile phone and extension fields. Earlier in this chapter you learned that if you wanted to only print records based on the result of a lookup or contacts in a specific group, you have to create the lookup or select the group before you run the report. In this exercise you will create a lookup before running the report.

1. Create a lookup to find all contacts in the state of Washington. You should have six records displayed.

2. Reports $\Rightarrow$ Phone List.

3. Select the Current lookup option if it is not already selected, then click OK. The report should look like the one shown in Figure 8-9.

Phone List

Chris Huffman, CH TechONE
13 East 54th St.
Suite 300
New York, NY 10008

Number of contacts: 6

Company	Contact	Phone	Phone Ext
Marxsys Financial	Alexander O'Brian	(206) 555-4247	
Verge Records	Theodore Barrett Jr	(206) 555-4414	
Verge Records	Theodore Barrett Sr	(206) 555-4410	
Verge Records	James Gutierrez		
Verge Records	Paul Henderson		
Verge Records	Drew McLintock		

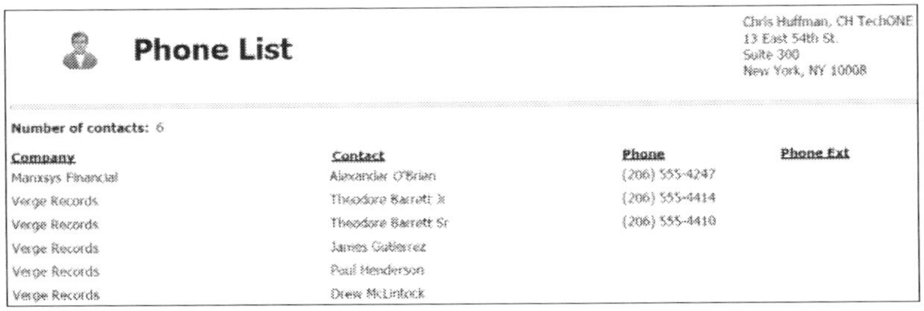

Figure 8-9 Phone List report

Running Reports

Exercise 8.3: The Activities Report

This report will print the activities that are scheduled and completed with contacts. The default option is to print the report for all users in the database.

1. Reports ⇒ Activities.

2. On the General tab, select the All Contacts option.

3. On the Activity tab, clear the To-Do's and Include cleared activities options.

How To Create A Custom Date Range

Often, you may have the need to print a report to include information for a few weeks or a few months. To do this you need to create a custom date range.

1. On the Activity tab, click the **CUSTOM** button. You will see the Select Date Range dialog box.

2. Click the < arrow on the **FROM** calendar until you see June 2012, then click on the 1st.

3. Type 11/20/2012 in the **TO** field, then press the Tab key.

   You should have the options shown in Figure 8-10.

   Click OK.

Figure 8-10 Date range options selected

4. You should have the options selected on the Activity tab that are shown in Figure 8-11.

   Click OK.

   The report should look similar to the one shown in Figure 8-12.

Figure 8-11 Activity tab options

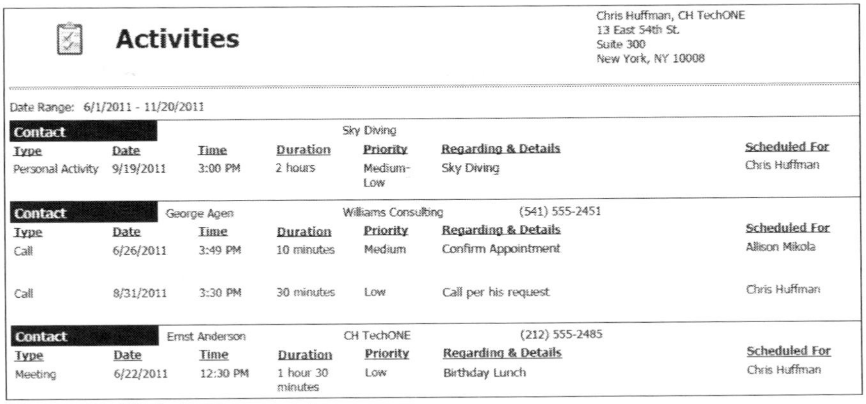

Activities

Chris Huffman, CH TechONE
13 East 54th St.
Suite 300
New York, NY 10008

Date Range: 6/1/2011 - 11/20/2011

Contact			Sky Diving			
Type	Date	Time	Duration	Priority	Regarding & Details	Scheduled For
Personal Activity	9/19/2011	3:00 PM	2 hours	Medium-Low	Sky Diving	Chris Huffman

Contact	George Agen		Williams Consulting		(541) 555-2451	
Type	Date	Time	Duration	Priority	Regarding & Details	Scheduled For
Call	6/26/2011	3:49 PM	10 minutes	Medium	Confirm Appointment	Allison Mikola
Call	8/31/2011	3:30 PM	30 minutes	Low	Call per his request	Chris Huffman

Contact	Ernst Anderson		CH TechONE		(212) 555-2485	
Type	Date	Time	Duration	Priority	Regarding & Details	Scheduled For
Meeting	6/22/2011	12:30 PM	1 hour 30 minutes	Low	Birthday Lunch	Chris Huffman

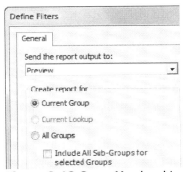

Figure 8-12 Activities report

Exercise 8.4: The Group Membership Report

This report will print the contacts in each group. This enables you to see which contacts are in what group. This would be a report that you may want to create a lookup or saved query for. The contacts name, company, title, phone and email fields are printed on the report.

1. Select the Sales Reps group in the Groups tree.

2. Reports ⇒ Group Reports ⇒ Group Membership.

3. Select the **CURRENT GROUP** option shown in Figure 8-13.

   Click OK. The report should look like the one shown in Figure 8-14.

Figure 8-13 Group Membership report filter options

Group Membership

Chris Huffman, CH TechONE
13 East 54th St.
Suite 300
New York, NY 10008

Group Name	Sales Reps				
Contact	Company	Title	Phone	Ext.	E-mail
Betty Browser	CH TechONE	Sales Representative	(212) 555-2485		bbrowser@CHTechONE.email
Sean Duffy	Circle Photography	Sales Representative	0164 262546		
Emily Dunn	Boomer's Artworx	Sales Representative	(602) 555-4874		
Bettie James	Boomer's Artworx	Sales Representative			
Allison Mikola	CH TechONE	Sales Representative	(212) 555-2485		Allison@CHTechONE.email

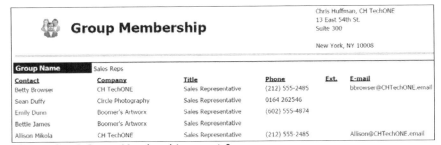

Figure 8-14 Group Membership report for one group

Running Reports

Exercise 8.5: The Company Comprehensive Report

This report will display the following data for a company: Contacts, notes, history, activities and opportunities. This report can be used to produce a company profile. You can select options including a date range for each type of data. For example, you can select the All date range for history records and the last year date range, for notes. The good thing is that the date range that you select for each type of data, prints at the beginning of that section of the report. The Company Summary report, which is similar, does not print contacts or notes.

1. Create a company lookup for Ace Pet Store Franchises.

2. Reports ⇒ Company Reports ⇒ Company Comprehensive.

3. On the General tab, select the Current lookup option.

4. On the Activity tab, create a date range for all of 2012.

5. On the Note tab, select the date range All.

6. On the History tab, select the date range 1/1/2008 to 12/31/2011.

7. On the Opportunity tab, create a date range for 1/1/2011 to 12/31/2012, then click OK. Figure 8-15 shows the first page of the report.

Figure 8-15 First page of the Company Comprehensive report

Other Reports

The reports that you have run so far in this chapter are just the beginning. Below are two more reports that you many find useful.

Source Of Referrals Report

This report is based on the value in the Referred By field.

The report includes the total number of referrals, as illustrated in Figure 8-16.

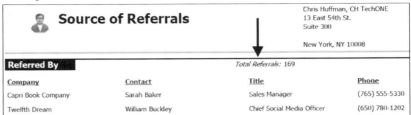

Figure 8-16 Source of Referrals report

The first section of the report will list all contacts that the Referred By field is blank, which does not make sense to me. To get around this, create a lookup to exclude contact records if the Referred By field is blank.

Notes/History Report

This report prints the notes and history records for the contacts that you select, as shown in Figure 8-17.

Figure 8-17 Notes/History report

Reports View

This view displays all of the reports that you have access to. Reports that you run frequently can be added to the Favorites section of the view by checking the box in the **FAVORITE REPORTS** column shown at the bottom of Figure 8-18.

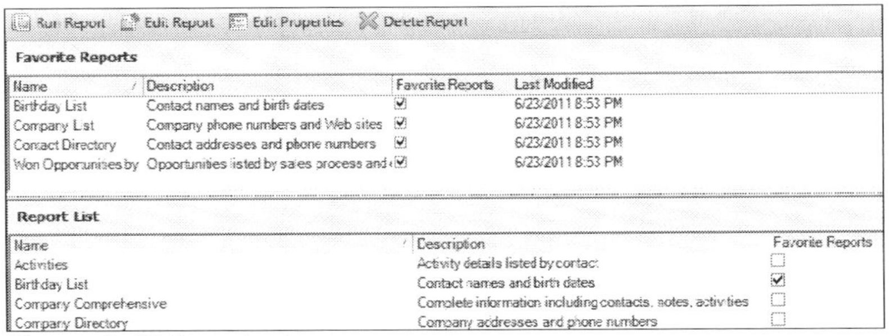

Figure 8-18 Reports view

Running Reports

Reports View Toolbar

Figure 8-19 shows the Reports view toolbar. Table 8-3 explains the buttons on the toolbar.

Figure 8-19 Reports view toolbar

Button	Description
1	Displays the Define Filters dialog box to run the selected report.
2	Displays the report in the Report Designer, so that it can be modified.
3	Opens the dialog box shown in Figure 8-20. The report name displayed in the Reports view can be changed and a description can be added or changed.
4	Is used to delete the report for all users. This option will delete the report from the hard drive. Use this option with caution.

Table 8-3 Reports view toolbar buttons explained

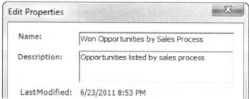

Figure 8-20 Edit Properties dialog box

The **OPTIONS** button is used to customize the columns in the Reports view. Each section of the Reports view can be customized individually. Columns can be added, renamed and reordered. At the top of Figure 8-18 shown earlier, the Last Modified column was added to the Favorite Reports section.

Printing In ACT!

So far in this chapter you have learned how to print reports that come with ACT!. Reports are not the only thing that can be printed from ACT!. The remaining exercises in this chapter show you how to print labels, envelopes, an address book and how to use the Quick Print options on the File menu.

Exercise 8.6: How To Print Labels

There are several label templates that you can select from. There is also a template that you can use to create a custom label.

 If you do not use Avery brand labels, you may be able to find the Avery label size equivalent that you use on your box of labels.

1. File ⇒ Print.

2. Select the **LABELS** Printout type, then select the Avery 5160 (label size) Paper type.

3. Click the Print button.

Chapter 8

4. Select the appropriate **CREATE REPORT FOR** option on the Define Filters dialog box, then click OK.

   The labels should look similar to the ones shown in Figure 8-21.

Figure 8-21 Labels

> **Selecting Where To Start Printing Labels**
>
> Unless you print the same number of names and addresses that the sheet of labels has, you will always have sheets of partially used labels. You can select where the labels should start to print on the sheet.
>
> The options on the **POSITION** tab (File ⇒ Print ⇒ Select the label size, then click the Print button) on the Define Filters dialog box shown in Figure 8-22 are used to select the Row and Column that the labels should start printing on. If you need to start printing labels on the first row, third column, you would select the options shown in Figure 8-22.
>
> It would be nice if the layout of the sheet of labels was displayed on the dialog box so that you could make sure that you selected the correct row and column before you previewed the labels. If you selected the options shown in Figure 8-22 and previewed the labels, they would look like the ones shown in Figure 8-23.

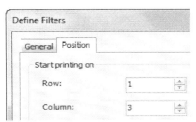

Figure 8-22 Position tab options

8-13

Running Reports

Figure 8-23 Labels with Position tab options changed

Exercise 8.7: How To Print Envelopes

In this exercise you will learn how to print envelopes using an envelope template.

1. File ⇒ Print.

2. Select the **ENVELOPES** Printout type, then select the envelope size in the Paper type list shown in Figure 8-24.

    The options in the **PAPER TYPE** section are the envelope sizes.

Figure 8-24 Envelope options

> The **ENABLE PREVIEW** option on the Print dialog box shown above in Figure 8-24 may not always work for labels, envelopes and reports. Some people claim that updating the printer drivers may cause this option to work. I found that when this option works, it can take a while to display the address book.

3. Click the Print button.

4. Select the appropriate **CREATE REPORT FOR** option, then click OK.

Chapter 8

The envelope should look like the one shown in Figure 8-25. Notice that the return address information has been filled in.

You may have a different addressee on the envelope, depending on which record was displayed before you started this exercise.

Figure 8-25 Envelope in print preview

5. Close the Print Preview window.

Exercise 8.8: How To Create And Print An Address Book

Printing an address book is useful if you need to have contact information from the database when you do not have access to a computer. You can select up to three additional fields to print in the address book. If you use a Day Timer or Day Runner, you can print the contacts in these address book formats. There are several print options that you can select from.

1. File ⇒ Print. Select the **ADDRESS BOOK** Printout type, then check the **ENABLE PREVIEW** option.

2. Select the Day-Timer Folio (2 Col) Paper type option.

   The preview may take a few seconds to display, but should look like the one on the right side of Figure 8-26.

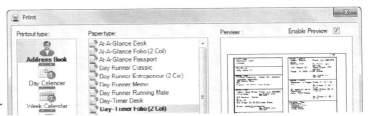

Figure 8-26 Print dialog box

3. Click the **OPTIONS** button, then clear the Alternate Address and Secondary Contacts options, if they are checked.

4. Select the Primary Address, Phone Numbers and E-mail Address options if they are not already selected.

5. Check the **LETTER AT THE TOP OF EACH PAGE** option in the Print Settings section.

6. Open the first **ADDITIONAL FIELDS** drop-down list and select Fax Phone.

7. Change the Sort Order to **CONTACT LAST NAME**, then select the All Contacts **CREATE PRINTOUT FOR** option.

Running Reports

8. Change the font size to 10. You should have the options shown in Figure 8-27.

   If you create a field it will not be listed in the **PRINT** section of the Options dialog box.

   You have to select a field that you create from one of the three **ADDITIONAL FIELDS** drop-down lists.

   Click OK.

   If you want to print the address book, click the Print button on the Print dialog box.

Figure 8-27 Address Book options

How To View The Address Book Without Printing It

If you want to see what the address book will look like without printing it and you have the full version of Adobe Acrobat installed, select the Adobe PDF option in the Name drop-down list on the Print dialog box, as illustrated in Figure 8-28.

Figure 8-28 Print dialog box options

If you have another software package installed that creates PDF files, select it from the drop-down list.

Doing this will create a PDF version of the address book, as shown in Figure 8-29. You can view the PDF file on the screen or print it.

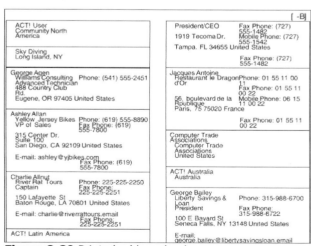

Figure 8-29 Printed address book

8-16

Chapter 8

 If you click the Cancel button on the Print dialog box shown earlier in Figure 8-28, not only will that dialog box close, but so will the Print dialog box shown earlier in Figure 8-24. This means that all of the options that you selected to configure what you wanted to print will be lost, so you will have to select them again when you open the dialog box. This appears to be a bug because the Print dialog box shown earlier in Figure 8-24 should not close.

Exercise 8.9: Using The Quick Print Options

The **QUICK PRINT CURRENT WINDOW** and **QUICK PRINT SELECTED** options are useful if you just want to print what is on the screen. Both of these options, as well as, the Print Current Screen option in the Related Tasks section of many views, displays the dialog box shown in Figure 8-30.

The **SAME FONT IN MY LIST VIEW** option is only available when a list view is displayed. When cleared, you can select the font that you want to use to print the report by clicking the Font button. If you are going to print the data on a tab, it is probably a good idea to resize the columns on the tab so that the data is not cut off.

The Quick Print options print data exactly as it appears. It is not perfect, but it may handle your basic printing needs.

Figure 8-30 Quick Print Options dialog box

The steps below show you how to print the data in the current window.

1. Look up the My Record.

2. Make sure the Contact detail view is open, then click on the Activities tab.

3. File ⇒ Quick Print Current Window. You will see the Quick Print Options dialog box. If you click the Set Options button you can change the printing options as needed.

If you printed the data on the Activities tab that is visible, it would look similar to the data shown in Figure 8-31.

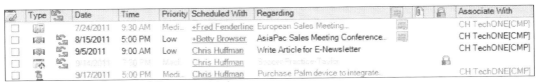
Figure 8-31 Quick print of the current tab

Reports View Related Tasks

The **NEW REPORT TEMPLATE** option shown in Figure 8-32 opens the Report Designer, which you can use to create a new report.

Figure 8-32 Reports view related tasks

8-17

WRAP UP OF THE BASICS

In this chapter you will learn the about following features in ACT!:

- ☑ Tagging records
- ☑ Copying data
- ☑ Swapping data
- ☑ Supplemental files
- ☑ Promoting secondary contacts
- ☑ Editing notes
- ☑ Filtering notes
- ☑ Record creation options
- ☑ Web Info tab
- ☑ Marketing Results tab
- ☑ Export contact data to Excel
- ☑ Adding graphics to ACT! notes
- ☑ Editing attached documents
- ☑ Using the scratchpad

Shameless Book Plug #1
If you have the need to export ACT! data to Excel to create PivotTables and PivotCharts, you may find my book, Getting Started With PowerPivot For Excel 2010 (ISBN 978-1-935208-13-6) helpful because PowerPivot can connect to ACT! databases, which means that you will have more control over the ACT! data that is imported into Excel.

Because you purchased this book on ACT!, you can order the PowerPivot book for 50% off of the list price. For more information go to www.tolana.com/books/act.html.

CHAPTER 9

Wrap Up Of The Basics

Wrap Up Overview

This chapter concludes the basics of ACT!. The majority of tasks that you will use the most in ACT! are covered in the first 8 chapters of this book. The remaining chapters contain tasks that you may use a lot when first creating a database, but may use much less frequently over time. The exceptions to this are the opportunities, dashboard and backing up a database, which, depending on how frequently data is modified, you may need to do daily. The topics covered in this chapter are important to know, but in my mind were better left out of the previous chapters because they were not essential to learning and mastering the core concepts of ACT!.

Understanding The ID/Status And Referred By Fields

The majority of fields on the Contact detail view are pretty straight forward. The fields discussed below may not be as straight forward.

The **ID/STATUS** field is most often used to categorize contacts. This means that you can enter customers, prospects, friends, vendors and lawyers in the same database. Many people would keep each of these types of contacts in different databases or spreadsheets. Using this field allows you to maintain an unlimited number of types of contacts in the same database. This field provides an informal way to group or categorize contacts. You can add to and edit the options that are in this drop-down list.

When you first enter names of potential customers in the database, you would select the "Prospects" ID/Status if the goal was to get the contact to purchase a product or service from you. If they purchase a product, you would change the value in the ID/Status field to Customer. When the value in this field is changed, an entry is automatically created on the History tab unless you change the option to not record a history record. Having this field generate a history record can be helpful if you need to know when the status of contacts change. During a marketing campaign, you could look up all of the contacts that are still "Prospects" and contact them by phone or email to see whether or not they received your mailing.

What may not be obvious is that the ID/Status field is what ACT! refers to as a **MULTI-SELECT** field. This means that the field can store more than one value. Multi-select fields look like the one shown in Figure 9-1. Open the drop-down list and check the options that you want to categorize the contact by.

The **REFERRED BY** field shown in Figure 9-2 is used as a way to know how the contact was acquired. You could have purchased a mailing list of leads from two companies and need to track which company the lead (contact) came from. You could also have contacts from a newsletter subscription service. How will you know how each contact was acquired if this field was left blank?

Figure 9-1 Multi-select drop-down list field

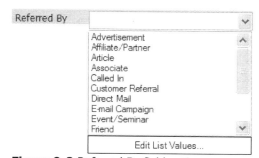

Figure 9-2 Referred By field options

Why Are Drop-Down Lists Important?

Drop-down lists contain the most used values that would be entered in a field. Drop-down lists are important because they help ensure that the data in a field is entered the same way for every record. Consistent data is especially helpful if the field will be used in queries, reports or sorting.

For example, one user types "USA" in the Country field and another user types "United States" in the Country field. When you run a query that looks for all records with "USA" in the Country field, the query will skip records that have "United States" in the field. This means that the result of the query will not contain all of the records that it should. In Chapter 3, I had you type USA in the Country field instead of selecting United States from the Country drop-down list. [See Chapter 3, Figure 3-10]
If the entries in the drop-down lists do not have the types of information that you need, you can create new entries. Later in the book you will learn how to add and delete entries in drop-down lists.

ACT! has two types of drop-down lists as shown above in Figures 9-1 and 9-2. The drop-down list shown in Figure 9-1 allows more than one option to be selected. The drop-down list in Figure 9-2 only allows one option to be selected. This is the more popular type of drop-down list and the one that you are probably the most familiar with. Both types of drop-down lists can be used to select or type in the value that you want. If the value that you enter is already in the list, after typing in enough characters to make the value unique, it will automatically be filled in the field.

> Drop-down lists are used to add information to a field without typing. You can also type the first letter of the value that you are looking for. Doing this will bring you to the first entry that matches the letter that you typed in. You do not have to open the drop-down list to select an entry if you already know what you are looking for. You can type in the first few letters.

> If you enter text in a field that has a drop-down list like the City, Country or Department fields, the text that you type in may or may not be accepted. It depends on whether the **LIMIT TO LIST** option on the Define Fields dialog box is enabled for the field. This option will force the user to select an option from the list or leave the field blank. This is done to ensure the accuracy of data in the field.

Tagging Contacts

There may be times when you need to select contacts that do not have any data in common. Tagging records is used to create a manual lookup. If you have tried to create a lookup for contacts but can't find a common denominator, you can tag the records. To tag a record, enable the tag mode, then manually click on the records. After you tag the records that you need, you can create a lookup of the tagged records. With a small database like the demo database that you are using to complete the exercises in this book, manually viewing all of the records to find the ones to tag is bearable. If the database has 5,000 records, it could take a while to find the records that you need if the records do not have common data.

Exercise 9.1: Tagging Contacts

In this exercise you will tag random contact records, add a note to the records and save them as a group. It is not a requirement to group tagged records.

1. Create a group called `My Tagged Record Group`.

Wrap Up Of The Basics

2. Open the Contact list view. Sort the contacts by state, then check the **TAG MODE** option illustrated in Figure 9-3.

Figure 9-3 Tag options

The **LOOK FOR** field is used to search for a contact based on the field that the list is sorted on. If the Contact List is sorted on the Company field, you would enter the company name that you were looking for in this field.
The **EDIT MODE** option is used to modify records in the list view.
The **TAG MODE** option turns the tag functionality on and off.
The **TAG ALL** button will mark all of the contacts displayed in the list as tagged.
The **UNTAG ALL** button will remove the tag from all of the selected contacts.
The **LOOKUP SELECTED** button creates a lookup of the records that have been tagged.
The **OMIT SELECTED** button is used to remove the tagged contacts from the view. This option does not delete the records from the database.

 If you click on a record that you do not need to tag, click on the record again to remove the tag. When in tag mode, records that are tagged are highlighted, as shown in Figure 9-4.

Company	Contact	Phone	Extension	Title	Address 1	Address 2	City	State	ZIP Code
Circle Photography	Test Record				2256 Circle Lane	Suite 4	Dallas	TX	75214
Circle Photography	Dan Day	(214) 555-2215		Analyst	2256 Circle Lane	Suite 4	Dallas	TX	10053
Circle Photography	Jonathan Jenkins	(214) 555-2215		Owner	2256 Circle Lane	Suite 4	Dallas	TX	75214
Continental Detective A	John Guild	406-202-4400		Chief Investigator	26 W Granite St		Butte	MT	59701
Continental Detective A	Nick Charles	406-202-4400		Owner	26 W Granite St		Butte	MT	59701
Continental Energy	Herman Getter	(918) 555-2451		Vice President Of	54 S. Utica	Suite 220	Tulsa	OK	74137
Corleone's Pasta Comp	Morty Manicotti	(480) 555-4512		Director of Manuf	8800 Pasta Way	Suite 200	Scottsdale	AZ	85258

Figure 9-4 Tagged records

3. Tag the first record in each of the following states: AZ, CA and LA.

4. Click the **LOOKUP SELECTED** button.

At this point you could add the same note to the contact records that are tagged, create an activity that included these records, save them as a group, subgroup, company or division.

5. Click the Note button on the Global toolbar, then type This contact is a tagged record that is in the Tagged Record Group.

6. Click the button at the end of the **SHARE WITH** field on the Insert Note dialog box, then click OK on the Public Note message box.

7. Select the My Tagged Record Group and add it to the list on the right, then click OK.

8. The dialog box should have the options that are shown in Figure 9-5. Click OK to close the Insert Note dialog box.

9. Right-click on the tagged records and select Add Contacts to group. Select the My Tagged Record Group option.

10. Click OK, then clear the Tag Mode option. Now when you need to access these records you can select the group that they are in. If you view the tagged group, you will see the three contacts.

Chapter 9

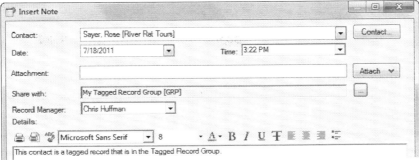

Figure 9-5 Insert Note dialog box

Using The Omit Selected Option

If there are records that you do not want to view, you can remove them from the list view. Removing records from a view does not delete them from the database. Using the Omit Selected option has the same effect as creating a lookup. The difference is that the Omit Selected option does it record by record, manually. To restore the records, lookup all of the contacts.

1. On the Contact list view, display all of the contacts.

2. Click on the first record in the Contact list view. The record should now be highlighted.

3. Click the **OMIT SELECTED** button on the toolbar. The record should not be visible in the window. You will see that the record count decreases by one.

Copying Data From One Field To Another

You may have a need to copy data from one field to another. Instead of doing this manually, record by record, you can create a lookup for the records that you want to copy the data to, then use the **COPY FIELD** command. Not creating a lookup first means that data will be copied to every record in the database. It is not a requirement to create a lookup first.

Exercise 9.2: How To Copy Data

In this exercise you will look up the Liberty Savings company and copy the data in the Title field to the User 6 field.

1. Create a lookup for the Liberty Savings company.

2. On the Contact detail view, Edit ⇒ Copy Field.

3. Open the **COPY CONTENTS OF** drop-down list and select the Title field, then open the **TO** drop-down list and select the User 6 field. You should have the options shown in Figure 9-6.

    Click OK.

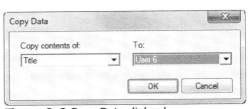

Figure 9-6 Copy Data dialog box

Wrap Up Of The Basics

4. Click Yes when you see the Replace/Swap/Copy message, which lets you know that all of the records in the current lookup will be modified.

You will see the message shown in Figure 9-7. This message lets you know that the **TARGET** field (User 6) size is smaller than the **SOURCE** field (Title). If the target field is smaller, some of the data in the source field will not be copied to the target field.

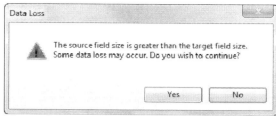

Figure 9-7 Data Loss message

5. Click Yes on the Data Loss message window. Normally you would not want to have data loss and would click No if you see the message shown above in Figure 9-7.

View The Copied Data

6. Click the Contact detail view button.

   On the User Fields tab, you will see the title in the User 6 field, as shown in Figure 9-8.

Figure 9-8 User Fields tab

Swapping Data

This command is used to swap the data in one field with data from another field. Like the Copy Field command, if the target field is smaller, all of the data will not be copied to the target field. You may find that from time to time, using this feature will cause ACT! to hang (stop working).

Exercise 9.3: How To Swap Data

In this exercise you will swap the data in the Alternate Phone field with the data in the Home Phone field.

1. Create a lookup for the city of Scottsdale. You should see six records in the Contact list view.

2. Edit ⇒ Swap Field.

3. Open the **SWAP CONTENTS OF** drop-down list and select the Alternate Phone field, then open the **WITH CONTENTS OF** drop-down list and select the Home Phone field, as shown in Figure 9-9.

Figure 9-9 Swap Data dialog box

4. Click OK. Click Yes to modify records in the current lookup.

9-6

Chapter 9

View The Swapped Data

1. Click the Contact detail view button, then click on the Personal Info tab.

2. Scroll through the records.

You will not see a phone number in the Home Phone field because none of the records had data in the Alternate Phone field. If any of the records had data in the Alternate Phone field, it would have been swapped (moved) to the Home Phone field.

 It is recommended that you back up the database before using the **COPY FIELD** or **SWAP FIELD** command.

What Are Supplemental Files?

Supplemental files are files that ACT! uses that are not saved in the database (**.ADF**) file.
The database file only stores the data that you see in the views. Examples of supplemental files include attachments, templates, reports and layouts. Many of these supplemental files are installed when ACT! is installed. ACT! has two supplemental file types, as explained below.

① **Database** This file type includes the templates, reports and layout files that you see when you first open ACT!. These files are only available when ACT! is open. They are stored in folders. The default main folder name is **Name of database-database files**. Under this folder are folders for each type of file. [See Chapter 1, Figure 1-12] If you copy a database, these files are also copied. If the ACT! database is stored on a server, more than likely, the database supplemental files are stored on the same server.

② **Personal** This file type includes files that are not associated to records in the database. Personal files are not backed up when a database is backed up. If you create a file that you do not want to share with other users of the database, save it in your personal supplemental folder. The other option is to create a folder outside of the default ACT! folders and save files that you do not want to share in that folder. An example of this would be the folder that you created for this book.

What Are Secondary Contacts And Why Should I Use Them?

Secondary contacts are contacts that are associated to a primary contact in the database. Examples of secondary contacts include an alternate contact if the primary contact is unavailable or a primary contacts assistant. You can also create secondary contact records to store the primary contacts spouse and children.

It would be helpful if the Secondary Contacts tab would automatically change colors as soon as one secondary contact was added to a primary contact record. That would make it easier to know if there were any secondary contacts associated to the primary contact.

Exercise 9.4: Entering Information On The Secondary Contacts Tab

You can create a separate secondary contact record for the contacts children, assistant and spouse. Keep the following two things in mind when creating secondary contact records.

① Secondary contact records cannot be used in a mail merge using the wizard.

② Activity, note, opportunity and history records cannot be created or associated with secondary contact records.

Wrap Up Of The Basics

1. Lookup the contact Sarah Baker.

2. On the **SECONDARY CONTACTS** tab shown in Figure 9-10, click the **NEW SECONDARY CONTACT** button.

Figure 9-10 Secondary Contacts tab

3. Enter the information in Table 9-1 in the appropriate fields on the Secondary Contacts dialog box.

Field	Type This
Contact	Terry London
Title	Purchasing Agent
E-mail	tlondon@xcapri.com
Web site	www.xcapri.com

Table 9-1 Secondary contact information

4. The dialog box should look like the one shown in Figure 9-11.

   Click OK.

   You should see the contact on the Secondary Contacts tab of the contact record.

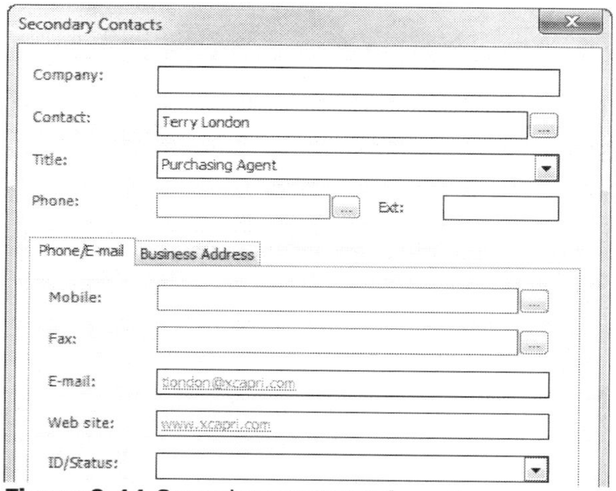

Figure 9-11 Secondary contact information

Exercise 9.5: Promoting A Secondary Contact

There may be a time when a secondary contact needs to become a primary contact. Instead of creating a new primary contact record for the secondary contact (which would also leave the secondary contact record in place if you did not delete it) you can promote the secondary contact to a primary contact by following the steps below. When a secondary contact is promoted, it is automatically deleted from the primary contact record.

1. Add a secondary contact record to the contact John Doe, by clicking the **NEW SECONDARY CONTACT** button on the Secondary Contacts tab.

   Add the secondary contact information shown in Table 9-2.

Field	Type This
Company	Secondary Contact
Contact	Chris Graham
Title	Assistant
ID/Status	Employee

Table 9-2 Secondary contact information

2. Click on the secondary contact that you want to promote. In this exercise select the secondary contact record that you just created, then click the **PROMOTE** button shown earlier in Figure 9-10. You will see the dialog box shown in Figure 9-12.

The **DUPLICATE DATA** option will copy data from the primary contacts record (like the company name and address fields) to the record that you are promoting.

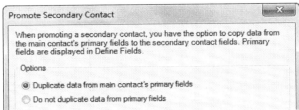

Figure 9-12 Promote Secondary Contact dialog box

3. For this exercise select the Duplicate data option, then click OK. You will see that the record is no longer on the Secondary Contacts tab and has become a contact.

Deleting A Secondary Contact

If a secondary contact should no longer be associated to the primary contact and you currently do not have a replacement contact, you should delete the secondary contact by following the steps below. For now you can just read the steps to become familiar with the process.

1. On the Secondary Contacts tab, right-click on the secondary contact that you want to delete, then select **DELETE SECONDARY CONTACT**.

2. Click Yes to permanently delete the secondary contact.

Notes And History Tabs

You have learned a little about these tabs and what types of data they have. You will see that they have a lot in common.

Notes Tab

The Notes tab contains details including business and personal information about contacts, companies and groups. The goal of entering notes is to build a profile of your relationship with the contact, company or group. Notes can be edited unless the **ALLOW NOTES EDITING** option is not enabled. [See Chapter 2, Admin Tab Preferences]

The Notes tab may be under utilized because many people are use to writing messages on a note pad or on a loose piece of paper or worse, think that they will remember details of a phone call or meeting. Days later when they need this information they cannot find the piece of paper that it was written on or they mentally draw a blank. I fall into the category of not being able to find the envelope that I wrote the information on. If you start off using the Notes tab when you first start using ACT!, the easier it will be to continue the good habit.

Whether you think that you are going to use ACT! daily or not, it may help if you open ACT! when you first turn your computer on. What I do is open the Contact list view and sort it by last name, then when I need to add a note, I do not have to wait to open ACT! and find the contact record. By the time I waited for ACT! to open, I would forget what I wanted to put in the note <smile>.

Wrap Up Of The Basics

Attaching A Document To An Existing Note

Chapter 3 covered how to add an attachment to contact records and how to attach a document on the Documents tab. Chapter 6 covered how to attach a document to a group record. Attaching a document to an existing note is similar. On the Notes tab, open the note that you want to attach a document to, then click the Attach button.

How To Copy A Note From One Contact Record To Another

If you attach a note to a contact record and want to attach the note to a different contact record, you can, by following the steps below. Both records need to be displayed before you start step 1.

1. On the Notes tab, click on the note that you want to copy, then press **CTRL+C**.

2. Click on the Notes tab of the contact record that you want to copy the note to, then press **CTRL+V**.

Editing A Shared Note

If you edit a note that is shared, you will see the Edit Shared Note dialog box, when you click OK after editing the note. The options on this dialog box are to save the changes for all contacts that are associated with the note or to create a new note for the contact record that you opened the note from, to edit. You can try this by editing the note with green text that you created in Chapter 6 for George and Mary Bailey.

Filtering Notes

Over time, contact, company or group records can accumulate a lot of notes. While they can be sorted, it may be more effective to filter the notes.

If you right-click in the detail section of the Notes tab on the Contact or Company detail view and select **FILTER NOTES**, you will see the dialog box shown in Figure 9-13 on the Contact detail view and Figure 9-14 on the Company detail view.

Figure 9-13 Contact Filter Notes dialog box

While filters narrow and reduce the number of records displayed (in this case notes), filters can be tricky and give the appearance that records are lost.

If you cannot find records, check the filter options on the tabs and change them to display all of the records.

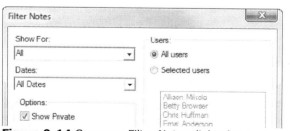

Figure 9-14 Company Filter Notes dialog box

History Tab

You have already viewed records on the History tab for the My Record. History records display changes that you have made to records in the database. The History tab picks up where the Notes tab leaves off. The entries on the History tab are a chronological recap of the communication and events for contacts, companies, groups and opportunities. The majority of entries on this tab come from other tabs, but you can manually create a History record.

Some entries on the History tab are created automatically when you delete a contact, when the Last Results field is updated, create a mail merge, change the value in the ID/Status field or complete an activity. The date and time are automatically added to each entry that is added to the History tab.

You can add an entry to the History tab from any detail view by right-clicking in the detail section of the History tab and selecting **RECORD HISTORY** on the shortcut menu shown in Figure 9-15.

You will see the dialog box shown in Figure 9-16. It looks similar to the Schedule Activity dialog box. You can also create a history record from the list views. The **FOLLOW-UP** button opens the Schedule Activity dialog box.

Figure 9-15 History tab shortcut menu

 New History Dialog Box
In ACT! 2010 and earlier, this dialog box was called the **RECORD HISTORY DIALOG BOX**.

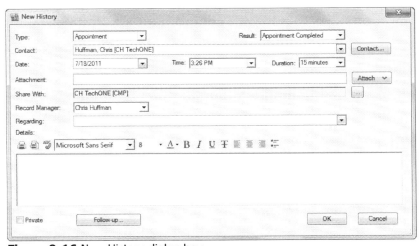

Figure 9-16 New History dialog box

Automatic Additions To The History Tab

As you just learned, you can manually add records to the History tab. By default, ACT! has designated the ID/Status and Last Results fields as history fields when you create a new database. When the data in a history field is changed, a record is automatically created and added to the History tab. You will learn how to designate a field as a history field. [See Chapter 15, Field Behavior Options]

Wrap Up Of The Basics

Finding Records On The History Tab

At the top of the Companies History tab shown in Figure 9-17, there are options that you can use to find specific records as explained below.

Figure 9-17 Companies History tab

The Dates Field

The options in this drop-down list are used to select the date range for the records that you want to view on the History tab. As time goes on, you will have more and more entries on the History tab, but you may not want to see all of them all the time.

You can reduce the number of records displayed by selecting a date range. You can also create a **CUSTOM** date range to select history records like you can to create reports. The same Select Date Range dialog box is used. [See Chapter 8, Figure 8-10]

History Record Types

The History record type options are shown in Figure 9-18. The options include the opportunity histories and system changes options.

Within each type you can select specific items to display or hide on the History tab, as illustrated.

There are several types of history records that you can view, as explained in Table 9-3.

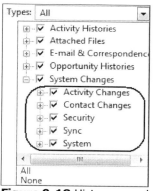

Figure 9-18 History record options

Type	This Type Of History Record Is Created When . . .
Activity Histories	You change the value in a field that has been designated to automatically have a history record created.
Attached Files	A document is attached to a contact, company or group record.
E-mails & Correspondence	You send an email message.
Opportunity Histories	When an opportunity or quote is created.
System Changes	One of the options illustrated above in Figure 9-18 changes.

Table 9-3 History record options explained

Select Users Button

This option is useful if more than one person is using the database.

The dialog box shown in Figure 9-19 is used to select which users entries you want to view on the History tab.

To select multiple users calendars to view, select the first user then press and hold down the Shift key, then click on the other users names. The maximum number of users that you can select is 10.

Figure 9-19 Select Users dialog box

Using The New History Tool

This tool is used to create a history record for tasks that you complete that do not have a scheduled activity. This is helpful when you need to remember something like an email or phone conversation that you had with a contact that was not scheduled. History records can also be created from the company and group views.

> **Merge Documents And History Records**
> Prior to ACT! 2010, a history record was generated when merged documents were printed in Microsoft Word. That does not happen now. The work around is posted on Sage's web site. Search for Answer ID 26851.

How To Open The New History Tool

Earlier in Figure 9-16 you saw the New History dialog box. You can open this dialog box by doing any of the following:

① Pressing the Ctrl+H keys.
② On the History tab of a detail view, right-click and select Record History.
③ On the History tab of a detail view, click the **NEW HISTORY** button.
④ Click the History button on the Global toolbar.

How To Create A History Record For Multiple Contacts

Just like you can schedule one activity with multiple contacts, you can create a history record for multiple contacts at the same time. There are two ways to accomplish this, as explained below.

① Open the New History dialog box, click the Contact button, then select the contacts that you want to create the history record for.
② Tag the records that you want to create the history record for, then open the New History dialog box. Earlier in this chapter you learned how to tag records.

How To Edit History Records

After viewing the history records that ACT! creates, you may decide that they need more information or that the information needs to be changed. If this is the case, double-click on the history record that you want to change. You will see the dialog box shown in Figure 9-20. Make the changes that are needed, then click OK.

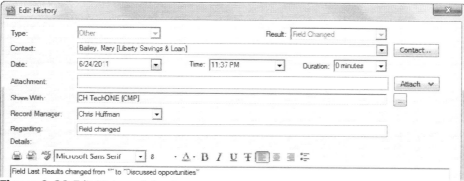

Figure 9-20 Edit History dialog box

How To Edit A History Record Associated With Multiple Contacts

After you create a history record that is associated with multiple contacts you may have the need to change it. After you make the change, you will see the dialog box shown in Figure 9-21. These options are used to select whether to save the change for the current contact or for all contacts associated with the history record.

Select the option that fits your need, then click OK.

These options are similar to the options on the Edit Shared Note dialog box. [See Chapter 6, Figure 6-17]

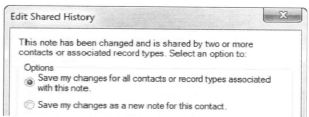

Figure 9-21 Edit Shared History dialog box

Preventing History Records From Being Deleted

You can delete history records. If you are the only person that is using the database, it may not be necessary to prevent history records from being deleted. If other people will be using the database, you may want to consider preventing history records from being deleted by clearing the **ALLOW HISTORY EDITING** option on the Admin tab on the Preferences dialog box.

Documents Tab

If you will attach a lot of documents to contact, company and group records, this section will give you a better understanding of the features that the Documents tab offers. The Documents tab is the repository for attachments in the database. Unless an attachment is marked as private, all users of the database will have access it. The attachments are usually stored in the Attachments folder for the database.

Figure 9-22 shows the Documents tab with several types of attached documents. The first column displays the icon for the file type. Sometimes the icons are not correct. An example is the E2.1 document listed in Figure 9-22. It has the icon for ACT!. The file was created in a software package called Crystal Reports, which it seems ACT! partially recognizes.

The **FILE TYPE** column will automatically be filled in as long as the file type is one that ACT! recognizes. Now that ACT! has functionality to have its databases attached to, in Crystal Reports, I was expecting to see "Crystal Reports" in the File Type column. Table 9-4 explains the buttons on the Documents tab.

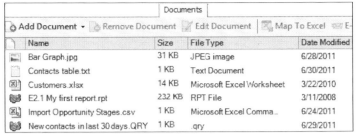

Figure 9-22 Documents tab

Button	Description
Add Document	Attach a document. If the **FILE** option is selected, remote database users can access the document.
Remove Document	Delete the selected attachment. This action deletes the document from the Documents folder. (1)
Edit Document	Opens the attached document so that it can be viewed or edited. To view or edit the document, you have to have the software that the document was created in installed on your computer. For example, in Figure 9-22 above the last document was created in Crystal Reports. If you do not have this software installed, you will not be able to open this document.
Map To Excel	Map fields in the database to fields in an Excel spreadsheet.
E-mail Document	Used to send the selected file via email.

Table 9-4 Documents tab buttons explained

(1) If you do not have another copy of the document on your hard drive, the file cannot be retrieved after it is deleted. Unlike many Windows applications, deleting files from ACT! does not send the deleted files to the Recycle Bin in Windows.

You can also right-click on the document (on the Documents tab) that you want to delete and select **REMOVE DOCUMENT**, as shown in Figure 9-23.

When you select this option you will see the message shown in Figure 9-24. Click Yes to delete the document. You can also delete an attachment from the History tab by right-clicking on the file and selecting **DELETE SELECTED**, as shown earlier in Figure 9-15.

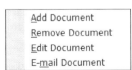

Figure 9-23 Documents tab shortcut menu options

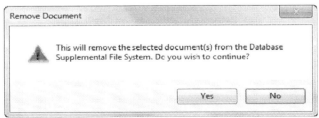

Figure 9-24 Remove Document message

Wrap Up Of The Basics

Record Creation Options

The options shown in Figure 9-25 are used to make contact, company, group and opportunity records public or private by default. If you know that one of these types of records needs to be private, most or all of the time, select the **PRIVATE** option on this dialog box.

Tools ⇒ Preferences ⇒ Startup Tab ⇒ Record Creation Options button, opens this dialog box.

Figure 9-25 Record Creation Options dialog box

 Internet Services And MapQuest
In ACT! 2010, these options were removed.

Web Info Tab

The options on this tab include Sage Business Info Services for ACT!. This is a paid subscription that lets you download contacts from Hoovers™ database.

The options shown in Figure 9-26 are used to create and view web content information for a contact or company. This tab is an internal browser (to ACT!) that is used to display web pages. The options are used to display information from web sites like Yahoo™, Google™, Facebook™ and more, that the contact or customer is listed on or is a member of.

Clicking the **EDIT LINKS** button shown in the figure opens the dialog box shown in Figure 9-27. You can add and edit the links that will display on the Web Info tab.

Figure 9-26 Web Info tab

Chapter 9

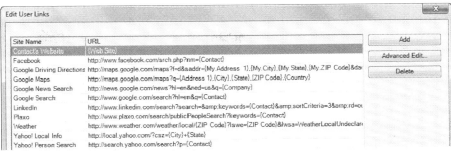

Figure 9-27 Edit User Links dialog box

Marketing Results Tab

The options shown in Figure 9-28 are used to create and view the marketing efforts that have been made to the contact. The marketing options include email, surveys, forms and drip marketing. To utilize these features, you need a paid subscription account with Swiftpage. There is a link for this company on the tab.

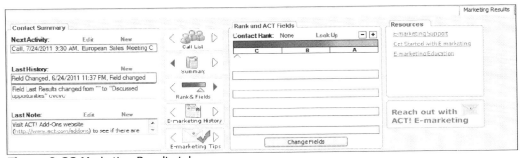

Figure 9-28 Marketing Results tab

Exporting Data To Excel

If you need to work with contact, company or group data in a spreadsheet, you can export the data to Excel.

> The **EXPORT TO EXCEL** option is only available on the Contact, Company, Group, Task List or Opportunity list views. To view the exported records, you need to have Excel installed. The only columns that are exported are the ones that are visible. If you want to export data that is not currently visible, add the columns of data that you want to export to the view before exporting data, then remove the columns that you added if you no longer need them in the view, once the export is completed.

Exercise 9.6: Export Contact Data To Excel

In this exercise you will export all of the contacts for a specific company to Excel.

1. Create a lookup for the `CH TechONE` company. Nine records should be displayed.

2. Click the **EXPORT CURRENT LIST TO EXCEL** button on the toolbar. The records from the lookup will be exported to Excel, which will automatically open and display the records, as shown in Figure 9-29. When you are finished viewing the spreadsheet close Excel.

9-17

Wrap Up Of The Basics

	A	B	C	D	E	F	G	H	I	J	K	L
1	Contact Type	Private	Company	Contact	Phone	Extension	Title	Address 1	Address 2	City	State	ZIP Code
2	Contact	Public	CH TechONE	Jane Chan	(212) 555-4447		Controller	13 East 54th St.	Suite 300	New York	NY	10008
3	User	Public	CH TechONE	Allison Mikola	(212) 555-2485		Sales Representative	13 East 54th St.	Suite 300	New York	NY	10008
4	User	Public	CH TechONE	Melissa Pearce	(212) 555-2485		Assistant	13 East 54th St.	Suite 300	New York	NY	10008
5	User	Public	CH TechONE	Juliette Rosseux	(212) 555-2485		CFO	13 East 54th St.	Suite 300	New York	NY	10008
6	User	Public	CH TechONE	Betty Browser	(212) 555-2485		Sales Representative	13 East 54th St.	Suite 300	New York	NY	10008
7	User	Public	CH TechONE	Sarah Whiting	(212) 555-2485		Vice President European Operations	13 East 54th St.	Suite 300	New York	NY	10008
8	User	Public	CH TechONE	Jonathan Sommer	(212) 555-2485		Vice President AsiaPac Operations	13 East 54th St.	Suite 300	New York	NY	10008
9	User	Public	CH TechONE	Ernst Anderson	(212) 555-2485		Vice President of US Operations	13 East 54th St.	Suite 300	New York	NY	10008
10	User	Public	CH TechONE	Chris Huffman	212-555-2485		CEO	13 East 54th St.	Suite 300	New York	NY	10008

Figure 9-29 Exported contact records in Excel

Adding Graphics To ACT! Notes

You can add graphics or images to notes by following the steps below.

1. Open an existing note or create a new one. Leave the note open.

2. Open the graphic file that you want to add to the note in a graphics viewer or other software package that will let you see the graphic.

3. Right-click on the graphic and select Copy (or Edit ⇒ Copy), then right-click in the note in ACT! and select Paste.

    Your note field should look similar to the one shown at the bottom of Figure 9-30.

Figure 9-30 Graphic file added to a note

How To Edit Attachments

The steps are the same to edit word processing documents and other types of attachments. Attachments can be on the Notes, History, Activities or Documents tab. The only difference is that you need the software that other file types were created in. There are two ways to open attachments, as explained below.

① Clicking on the attachment icon for the document that you want to edit.

② Double-clicking on the row that has the attachment that you want to edit will open the Edit dialog box. Click on the attachment.

Using The Scratchpad

This tool (introduced in ACT! 2012) can be used whether or not ACT! is open. Once you open the Scratchpad, you can leave it open while you are using ACT! or any other software package.

Chapter 9

Open The Scratchpad

Select one of the following ways to open the Scratchpad shown in Figure 9-31.

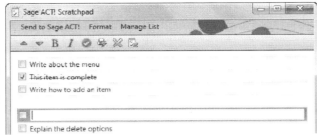

If you have ACT! open before opening the Scratchpad and the scratchpad application does not open, close ACT!, then open the scratchpad.

Figure 9-31 Sage ACT! Scratchpad

① In ACT!, Tools ⇒ Sage ACT! Scratchpad.
② Double-click on the Sage ACT! Scratchpad icon on your desktop.
③ Windows Start button ⇒ Programs ⇒ Sage ACT! Pro ⇒ Sage ACT! Scratchpad.

SEND TO SAGE ACT! The options shown in Figure 9-32 are used to create an activity, note or history record in ACT!.

The **FORMAT** options are used to make the item bold or italic.

The **MANAGE LIST** options shown in Figure 9-33 are for the selected item.

Figure 9-32 Send to Sage ACT! options

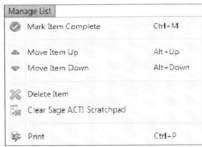

Figure 9-33 Manage List options

The options on the toolbar shown in Figure 9-34 are explained in Table 9-5.

Figure 9-34 Scratchpad toolbar

Option	Description
1	Moves the selected item up in the list each time the button is clicked.
2	Moves the selected item down in the list each time the button is clicked.
3	Makes the item bold.
4	Makes the item italic.
5	Marks the item as complete.
6	Prints the items on the scratchpad.

Table 9-5 Scratchpad toolbar buttons explained

Wrap Up Of The Basics

Option	Description
7	Deletes the selected item.
8	Deletes all of the items on the scratchpad.

Table 9-5 Scratchpad toolbar buttons explained (Continued)

Adding An Item

To add an item, click in an empty row and start typing. To add another item, click in the next empty row or any empty row, as shown earlier in Figure 9-31. Items are automatically saved when the cursor is placed in another row or when you press Enter.

Editing An Item

Click in the row of the item that you want to change or select the text in the row that you want to change, then make the changes. To make an item bold or italic, click in the row, then click the Bold or Italic button. To remove the bold or italic, click on the line that you want to remove the formatting from, then click the Bold or Italic button.

Delete An Item

To delete an item, click in the row that you want to delete, then click the Delete button.

Mark An Item As Complete

Click on the check box at the beginning of the row of the item that you want to mark as complete. Once checked, the strike through feature will be applied to the item, as shown on the second row earlier in Figure 9-31.

Create A Record From An Item In The List

Activity, note and history records can be created in ACT! from an item in the Scratchpad by following the steps below.

1. Leave the Scratchpad application open, then open ACT! if it is not already open.

2. Click in the row in the Scratchpad of the item that you want to use to create a record in ACT!.

3. Click the Send to Sage ACT! button on the toolbar, as shown earlier in Figure 9-32, then select the type of record that you want to create in ACT!.

   The corresponding dialog box in ACT! will open. The content of the item in the Scratchpad is added to the Regarding field on the dialog box, as illustrated in Figure 9-35.

Figure 9-35 Scratchpad item used to create a record in ACT!

4. Fill in the fields to create the record, then save the record.

OPPORTUNITIES

In this chapter you will learn the following tasks that will show you how to create and manage opportunities.

- ☑ Schedule a follow up activity for an opportunity
- ☑ How to edit the Product List
- ☑ How to view an opportunity
- ☑ How to associate an opportunity to a company
- ☑ Lookup opportunity options
- ☑ Export opportunities to Excel
- ☑ Creating quotes
- ☑ Change the status of an opportunity
- ☑ Opportunity reports
- ☑ Create opportunity graphs and pipelines
- ☑ Customize products and processes
- ☑ Creating process lists and stages
- ☑ Importing and exporting stages
- ☑ Importing and exporting products

Opportunities

What Is An Opportunity?

An opportunity is a sale in progress, meaning there is some likelihood that the contact may make a purchase. Opportunities automate the sales process. You can run reports that display what stage opportunities are in and which opportunities you have the best chance of turning into a sale. Like activities, opportunities create history records when they are created or when certain fields like the Status or Close Date is changed.

Tracking Potential Sales

ACT! provides a way to manage and track potential sales through opportunities. The tracking process is quite extensive. You can track opportunities through each stage of the process. There are six stages that you can monitor in the CHT1 Sales process that comes with ACT!. You can track opportunities by dollar amount, sales rep, status and more. You can also customize the opportunity process and products that come with ACT!. You can create your own opportunity processes and import processes that are created in another software package. Opportunities can be exported, which will allow you to analyze the data in different ways.

Opportunity Detail View

The Opportunity detail view shown in Figure 10-1 is used to create and edit sales. The options are explained in detail in Exercise 10.1, as you create an opportunity. Four of the tabs are specific to opportunities. The data types on these tabs are explained below.

Figure 10-1 Opportunity detail view

Opportunity Detail View Tabs

① **Products/Services** This tab stores the basic information about the opportunity, as shown in Figure 10-2.
② **Opportunity Info** Figure 10-3 shows the fields on this tab. The fields that you may want to fill in when creating an opportunity are the Referred By and Competitor fields. Entering data on this tab is optional.
③ **Opportunity Access** The options shown in Figure 10-4 are the same as the ones on the Contact Access tab. [See Chapter 3, Contact Access Tab]
④ **User Fields** Some of the fields on this tab, shown in Figure 10-5, are similar to fields on the User Fields tab on the Contact detail view because most of them have the character field type, which is free form. You can use the fields to store data that does not fit in any of the other fields on the Opportunity view. The Opportunity Field 2 has the Date data type by default. You can rename these fields in the layout.

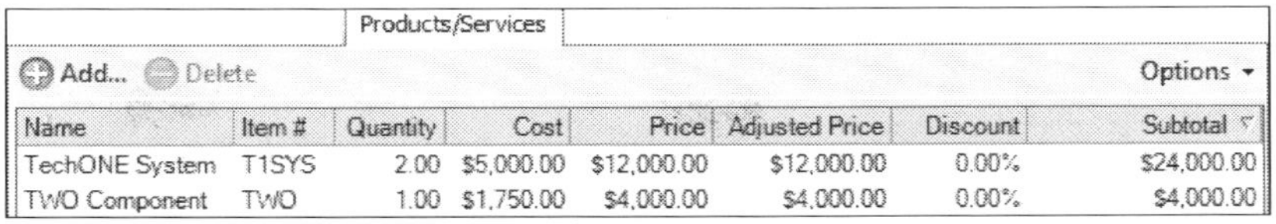

Chapter 10

Figure 10-2 Products/Services tab

 Products/Services Tab Subtotal Field
I am not sure why the subtotal field is so far to the right and can't be resized like the other columns on this tab can. I had to make the workspace smaller to be able to include the subtotal field in the screen shot. The other option is to move the Subtotal field to the left, before the Discount field.

Figure 10-3 Opportunity Info tab

Figure 10-4 Opportunity Access tab

Figure 10-5 User Fields tab

The options in the Opportunity Field 1 drop-down list, shown in Figure 10-6, are different types of payments that can be accepted to pay for the order.

The option in the Opportunity Field 2, shown in Figure 10-7 is a calendar. This field can be used as a date field for a date that is not already captured in any of the other opportunity fields.

Figure 10-6 Opportunity Field 1 drop-down list options

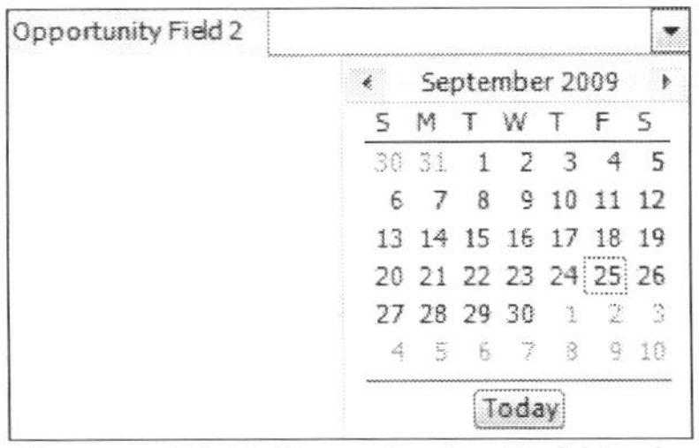

Figure 10-7 Opportunity Field 2 drop-down list

10-3

Opportunities

Opportunity Detail View Toolbar

Figure 10-8 shows the Opportunity detail view toolbar. Table 10-1 explains the buttons on the toolbar.

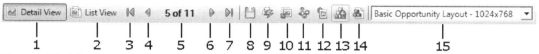

Figure 10-8 Opportunity detail view toolbar

Button	Description
1	Displays the opportunities in detail view.
2	Displays the opportunities in list view.
3	Displays the first opportunity in the view.
4	Displays the previous opportunity in the view.
5	Displays the record number currently displayed and the total number of records displayed in the view.
6	Displays the next opportunity in the view.
7	Displays the last opportunity in the view.
8	Save the changes.
9	Opens the Quick Print Options dialog box.
10	Duplicates the current opportunity.
11	Is used to add or remove contacts for the opportunity.
12	Creates a quote for the opportunity.
13	Is used to create or edit a product that you will use in the opportunity.
14	Opens the Manage Product List dialog box.
15	Is used to select a layout.

Table 10-1 Opportunity detail view toolbar buttons explained

Opportunity List View

You have the option of viewing all or some of the opportunities for contacts that you have access to. You can filter opportunities. You can also print opportunities, as well as, customize the Opportunity list view.

1. Click the Opportunities button on the Navigation Pane. Clicking on a contact name will open the Contact detail view for the contact.

Opportunity List View Toolbar

Figure 10-9 shows the Opportunity list view toolbar. Table 10-2 explains the buttons on the toolbar, that are not on the Opportunity detail view toolbar.

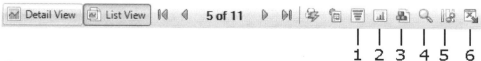

Figure 10-9 Opportunity list view toolbar

Chapter 10

Button	Is Used To . . .
1	Create an opportunity pipeline.
2	Create an opportunity graph.
3	Open the Manage Product List dialog box.
4	Create an automatic lookup of contacts associated to the opportunities that are displayed.
5	Customize the columns at the bottom of the Opportunity list view.
6	Export the opportunities that are displayed in the view to Excel.

Table 10-2 Opportunity list view toolbar buttons explained

 The buttons for E-Marketing and Business Info Services that were available of the Opportunity list view toolbar in ACT! 2012 were removed in ACT! 2013.

Using The Opportunity List Filters

The filter options for the Opportunity list view are shown in Figure 10-10. They are helpful if there are a lot of opportunities displayed and you only need to see certain ones. Like other views, you can sort the data on the bottom half of the view by clicking on the column headings. The filter options are explained below.

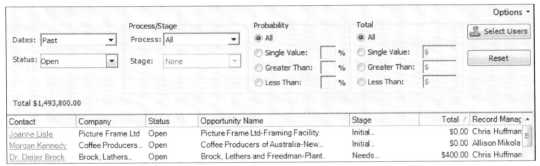

Figure 10-10 Opportunity list view

① The **DATES** drop-down list options shown in Figure 10-11 are used to select the date range that you want to see opportunities for.
② The **STATUS** drop-down list options shown in Figure 10-12 are used to select the statuses that you want to see opportunities for.
③ The **PROCESS** drop-down list options shown in Figure 10-13 are used to select the process that the opportunities must have in order to be displayed. The options shown are the processes in the demo database.
④ The **STAGE** options are only available once a process has been selected. The options in the drop-down list shown in Figure 10-14 are specific to the process that is selected. The default stage is **ALL**. The stage options shown are for the CHT1 Service process.
⑤ The **PROBABILITY** options are used to select a single value and percent for opportunities that you want to see. If you only wanted to see opportunities that have a 91% or greater probability of closing (making the sale), you would select the options shown in Figure 10-15. The 90% shown in the **GREATER THAN** field will NOT return probabilities that are 90%, only probabilities that are greater. If you wanted to include 90%, you would have to enter 89% in the Greater Than field.

10-5

Opportunities

⑥ The **TOTAL** options are used to select the total dollar amount that the opportunity must have to be displayed. If you only wanted to see opportunities that have a total amount less than $1,000, you would select the options shown in Figure 10-16.

⑦ The **SELECT USERS** button opens a dialog box that is used to select the users that you want to see opportunities for.

⑧ The **RESET** button will clear all of the filter options that are currently selected. I tend to click this button as soon as I open the Opportunity list view so that all of the opportunities are displayed before I apply any filters.

⑨ The **OPTIONS** button is used to select whether or not private opportunities should be displayed. You can also customize the columns in the Opportunities list by selecting the **CUSTOMIZE COLUMNS** option on this button.

Figure 10-11 Date options

Figure 10-12 Status options

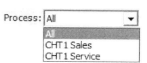

Figure 10-13 Process options

Figure 10-14 Stage options

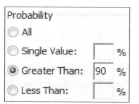

Figure 10-15 91% or greater probability options

Figure 10-16 Total amount less than $1,000 options

> **Additional Ways To Filter Contacts On The Opportunity List View**
> ① Right-click in the list of opportunities and select **CREATE LOOKUP**.
> ② Click the **CREATE LOOKUP FROM OPPORTUNITY** button on the toolbar.

Status Bar

Figure 10-17 shows the information that is displayed in the Status bar. You will see the total number of opportunities, the weighted and grand total dollar amounts of the opportunities that are displayed. The **WEIGHTED TOTAL** field is calculated based on the product total and the probability of closing the opportunity.

```
Lookup: All Opportunities        376 Opportunities, $1,437,875.00 Weighted Total, $2,785,300.00 Grand Total
```
Figure 10-17 Opportunity status bar

Opportunity List View Shortcut Menu

The Opportunity list view shortcut menu is shown in Figure 10-18.

The **FILTER OPPORTUNITIES** option opens the dialog box shown in Figure 10-19. It is another way to filter the opportunities. It contains the same options that are at the top of the Opportunity list view.

The **PRINT OPPORTUNITY LIST** option creates the report shown in Figure 10-20. This report contains all of the opportunities that are displayed on the list view.

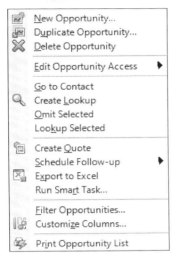

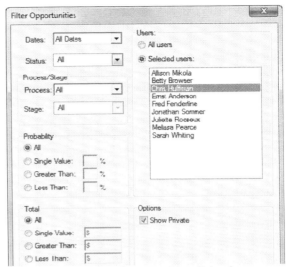

Figure 10-18 Opportunity list view shortcut menu

Figure 10-19 Filter Opportunities dialog box

Figure 10-20 Opportunity List report

Exercise 10.1: Create An Opportunity

If you have viewed the Opportunity Tracking tour in the Help system, you may think that creating an opportunity is complicated. You can view the tour or look at the examples, but the process probably won't "click" until you create a new opportunity, which is the best way to fully understand each component of an opportunity.

> Opportunities inherit the security that the contact has.

1. Open the contact record for Mary Wood in the Contact detail view.

2. On the Opportunities tab, click the **NEW OPPORTUNITY** button, illustrated in Figure 10-21.

Figure 10-21 Opportunities tab options

3. Type `My first opportunity` in the Name field.

> Many people use a purchase order number or the contacts company name and a sequential number for the name of the opportunity.

Opportunities

Select The Probability

The probability is a percent. It signifies to what degree you think that the opportunity will result in a sale. Throughout the opportunity process, the probability can change.

4. Type 80 in the Probability field.

Days Open Section

The options in this section are dates for the opportunity.

OPEN DATE Is the date that the opportunity record was created.

DAYS OPEN This field is updated automatically. It displays the number of days between the Open date and the Act. Close date.

The **EST. (ESTIMATED) CLOSE DATE** field is the date that you would like to have the sale closed by. Like the Probability field, the value in this field can change during the course of the opportunity process.

The **ACT. (ACTUAL) CLOSE DATE** field should be filled in when the contact buys the product or service, or when the Closed-Lost status is selected.

> The **EST. CLOSE DATE** is a field used in date range criteria for filters, lookups and reports for open and inactive opportunities. The **ACT. CLOSE DATE** field is used in date range criteria for closed opportunities.

Status Options

There are four status options as explained below.

① **Open** This is the default status for a new opportunity. This status means that there is activity for the opportunity. Often, the activity is you hearing from the contact or you contacting them.
② **Closed-Won** Select this option when the opportunity results in a sale.
③ **Closed-Lost** Select this option if the opportunity did not result in a sale and there is currently no activity for the opportunity.
④ **Inactive** Select this option if there is currently no activity for the opportunity, but there is still a chance that a sale may happen.

Association Section

This section displays the contacts, groups and companies that are associated with the opportunity.

5. Enter a date that is a month from today in the Est. Close Date field. The top half of the Opportunity detail view should look like the one shown in Figure 10-22. The only difference should be the date in the field.

Chapter 10

Figure 10-22 Options for a new opportunity

What Is A Process List?

A Process List contains the tasks that need to be completed for a sale. If you or your company has a set of tasks for a sale or part of a sale, you should create a process list so that everyone that creates an opportunity will complete the same set of tasks for each opportunity that is created. A process list may remind you of an activity series.

For example, you or your company may have a process for new prospect contacts like call the contact, send the contact a brochure and go see the contact. These three tasks would be a process list that you could create. You can also incorporate an existing process list.

Select The Process

The processes shown earlier in Figure 10-13 come with ACT!. Each process has its own list of stages. Later in this chapter you will learn how to create your own process list.

Select The Stage

The stage options are based on the process that is selected. The stage indicates where the opportunity is in the sales process. This can be used to let you know which opportunities need your immediate attention.

6. Select the Needs Assessment stage.

Products And Services

The fields that you just filled in are the basic fields for an opportunity. The options on the Products/Services tab are the items for the opportunity that the contact will hopefully purchase.

It is not advised, but you can also type a new product in. It will only be available for the current opportunity. The reason that you should add the product to the list is to help keep the products consistent for all opportunities.

The **NAME** drop-down list (on the Add/Edit Product dialog box shown later in Figure 10-24) shown in Figure 10-23 contains all of the products and services that can be sold.

When new products and services are added, they will be displayed in this drop-down list.

Figure 10-23 Name drop-down list items

Opportunities

Select The Products And Services For The Opportunity

1. On the Products/Services tab, click the Add button.

2. Open the Name drop-down list and select the service, ONE Component.

It is not a requirement that products or services have an item number. Item numbers should be set up when the product is added to the list. If the information is incorrect in the Product List you can change it in the opportunity that you are working on. Changing it here would only apply the change to the opportunity that you have open. It is best to make the changes in the product list.

3. Type 2 in the Quantity field.

Price Considerations

The cost and price are automatically filled in because they are stored in the product list. If these values are not correct, you have two options to correct them, as explained below.

① Edit the fields on the Opportunities detail view. This option only changes the values in the current opportunity.
② Edit the data in the product list. This option will change the price throughout the database.

Adjusted Price

Filling in this field is optional. It is used to give the contact a discount or price that is different then the default price for the product or service. If you change the price in this field, the discount percent is automatically recalculated.

4. You should have the options shown in Figure 10-24.

   The Display Fields button is used to add, remove and reorder the fields on the Products/Services tab.

   Click OK.

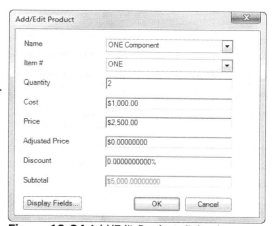

Figure 10-24 Add/Edit Product dialog box

Add A Service

In this part of the exercise you will add a service product to the opportunity and learn how to set up a discount.

1. Click the Add button, then select the Service Contract product.

2. Change the discount to 20%, then click OK. You should have the products shown in Figure 10-25.

Chapter 10

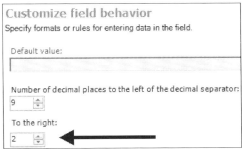

Figure 10-25 Products and Services added to the opportunity

 Changing The Discount Field Decimal Places
If the number of decimal places after the decimal point in the Discount column shown above in Figure 10-25 annoy you, you can edit the Products Discount field on the Define Fields dialog box. On the Customize field Behavior screen, change the **TO THE RIGHT** field to 2, as illustrated in Figure 10-26. The Discount field will then be displayed as illustrated in Figure 10-27. If you change the field to zero, no zeroes will appear after the decimal point.

Figure 10-26 Discount Field Customize Field Behavior screen options

Figure 10-27 Modified discount field

 Giving A Discount For The Entire Order
As you just learned, you can discount each item on the opportunity. It would be nice if we could also give a discount off of the entire order. For example, "Spend $100, get $20 off". I could not find a way to create this type of discount.

 The Opportunity Details Tab
In ACT! 2009 and earlier, the Details tab on the Opportunity detail view was used to enter notes. That functionality has been removed from the opportunity process. Instead, use the Notes tab.

Add A Note

If there is information that does not fit in any of the existing fields, you can use one of the fields on the User Fields tab or you can enter it in a note.

1. On the Notes tab, click the Insert New Note button.

2. Type `This is my first opportunity` in the field, then click OK.

3. Click the Save Changes button. Leave the opportunity open.

Opportunities

Exercise 10.2: Schedule A Follow Up Activity For The Opportunity

The default follow up opportunity activity is a phone call. The default value for the Regarding field is the opportunity name. If there is a stage, it is automatically included in the Regarding field, as illustrated at the bottom of Figure 10-28.

Scheduling an activity for an opportunity is the same as scheduling other activities. In this exercise you will schedule a phone call activity for tomorrow for the opportunity.

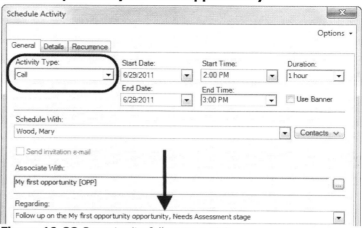

Figure 10-28 Opportunity follow up activity

1. On the Contacts tab, click the **FOLLOW UP** button.

2. Change the Start Date to tomorrow, then change the Start time to 2 PM.

3. Click OK to close the Schedule Activity dialog box.

Exercise 10.3: Edit The Product List

In this exercise you will learn how to add a new product to the Product list.

1. Tools ⇒ Define Fields. Click on the **MANAGE PRODUCT LIST** link.

> **Other Ways To Open The Manage Product List Dialog Box**
> ① Click the Manage Product List button on the Opportunity list view toolbar.
> ② Opportunities ⇒ Manage Product List.
> ③ Click the Modify Fields for Product Tab link in the Related Tasks section of the Opportunity detail view.

2. Click the Add button, then type ACT! Book in the Name field.

3. Press the Tab key and type BK-0001 in the Item Number field, then type 10 in the Cost field.

4. Type 49.95 in the Price field.

   The item should look like the one illustrated in Figure 10-29.

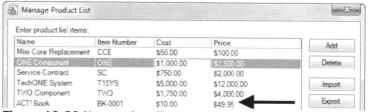

Figure 10-29 New product illustrated

10-12

5. Click OK, then click Close on the Define Fields dialog box.

Exercise 10.4: How To Associate An Opportunity To A Company
In this exercise you will associate the opportunity that you created in Exercise 10.1 to a company.

1. On the Activities tab of the opportunity, double-click on the opportunity that is scheduled with Mary Wood.

2. Click the button at the end of the **ASSOCIATE WITH** field.

3. Open the View drop-down list and select Companies. Scroll down the list and select My New Company, then click the Add button.

4. Click OK. You will see the company in the Associate With field. Click OK to close the Schedule Activity dialog box.

> **Opportunity Linking Issue**
> As you have learned in previous chapters, linked contacts that are marked as private can still have data from various tabs displayed under the company record that it is linked to. Opportunity records of linked contacts will not be visible from the company record, but opportunity history records will be visible from a company record. If you do not want the opportunity history records of private contacts visible, you have to clear the **AUTOMATICALLY RECORD HISTORY WHEN CONTACTS ARE LINKED OR UNLINKED** option on the Company Preferences dialog box. [See Chapter 5, Linking Company And Contact Records]

Exercise 10.5: Lookup Opportunities
The Lookup Opportunity options are similar to the opportunity filter options because they are used to narrow down the opportunities that will be displayed on the screen. By default, the opportunities that are displayed from the lookup are the ones for the current user (you). If you want to view opportunities for all users or specific users, you have to select the users. In this exercise you will perform three opportunity lookups.

Figure 10-30 shows the Opportunity lookup menu options. Most of the options shown were explained earlier in this chapter in the Using The Opportunity List Filters section. The other options are explained below.

The **NAME** option uses the name of the opportunity that you want to search for.

The **PRODUCT** option uses the Name field on the Products/Services tab for the product that you want to search for.

Figure 10-30 Opportunity lookup menu options

Lookup Opportunity #1
In this lookup exercise you will find opportunities for all users that are in the Initial Communication stage of the CHT1 Sales process.

1. From the Opportunity detail view, Lookup ⇒ Other Fields.

10-13

Opportunities

2. Select the **PROCESS** field to search on.

3. Type `CHT1 Sales` in the Search for field. You should have the options shown in Figure 10-31.

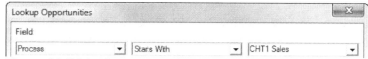

Figure 10-31 Lookup opportunity options to find a process

4. Click OK. You will see fewer opportunities because all of the opportunities are not in the process that you selected in the lookup.

Lookup Opportunity #2

In this lookup exercise you will find opportunities that have been open for more than 30 days. This requires two lookups: one to find opportunities with the number of days greater than 30 and one to narrow down the opportunities to only those that are open. When the lookup requires searching on more than one field, the efficient lookup rule of thumb is to select the field that will eliminate the most records first. In databases with thousands of records, this will greatly speed up the search process. Being able to see a list of these opportunities will allow you to follow up to see what you can do to close the sale.

1. Lookup ⇒ Other Fields, then select the **DAYS OPEN** field to search on.

2. Select the **GREATER THAN** option, then type `30` in the Search field. You should have the options selected that are shown in Figure 10-32.

   Click OK.

Figure 10-32 Lookup Opportunity options to find opportunities greater than 30 days

> **Status Field Lookup**
> When you need to create a lookup for the status field, you cannot type in the status name. If you do, you will see an error message that says "The value you typed is greater than the max field length". This did not happen in ACT! 2009 and earlier versions. You could type in the name. I suspect that the developers hooked the status field up to the ID field, which by default is a numeric field, instead of a text field.
>
> Until this is fixed, you have to enter a number for the status, as shown below. You will see these options at the top of the Lookup dialog box, as shown in Figure 10-33.
> 0 (zero) = Open, 1 = Closed Won, 2 = Closed Lost, 3 = Inactive

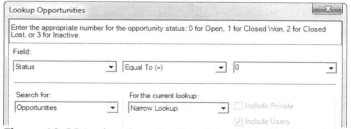

Figure 10-33 Lookup Opportunities dialog box with status field options

10-14

Chapter 10

3. Lookup ⇒ Status.

4. Type 0 (for the Open status) in the Search field.

5. Change the Current lookup option to Narrow Lookup, then click OK. You will see the opportunities that have been open for more than 30 days.

Table Names

As shown in Figure 10-34, the table name (in brackets) is visible for fields that are not in the main table for the lookup.

The two fields shown at the bottom of the drop-down list are from the Opportunity table, which is the main table for this lookup.

Figure 10-34 Table name as part of the field

Lookup Opportunity #3

In this lookup exercise you will find opportunities that have a specific product.

1. Lookup ⇒ Product.

2. Type `Two Component` in the Search field, then click OK.

As shown in Figure 10-35, you cannot see all of the products for the opportunity. To see the products, you have to double-click on an opportunity. The way to tell if an opportunity has more than one product is when you see an ellipsis (three periods) at the end of the field, as illustrated in the figure.

Opportunity Name	Stage	Total	Record Manager	Product	Weighted Total
Bick's Longhorns-East Texas Operations	Initial...	$22,000.00	Chris Huffman	Service Contract...	$2,200.00
Django Consulting-New Opportunity	Negotiation	$4,000.00	Allison Mikola	TWO Component	$4,000.00
Boomer's Artworx-Upgrade to Loft	Commitment to Buy	$4,000.00	Ernst Anderson	TWO Component	$4,000.00

Figure 10-35 Result of the lookup

How To Close An Opportunity

This is the part of the opportunity process that will probably make you happy. When a contact makes a purchase they become a customer and their opportunity needs to be closed. If a contact does not make a purchase for whatever reason, the opportunity should be closed indicating that. The steps below show you how to close an opportunity.

1. Display the opportunity that you want to close.

2. Select the appropriate closed status. [See Status Options earlier in this chapter]

3. Select or type in a **REASON** if applicable, on the Opportunity Info tab.

Opportunities

4. You can also add comments on the **NOTES** tab. Once a closed status is selected and you click the Save Changes button, history records similar to the ones shown in Figure 10-36 will be created for the opportunity.

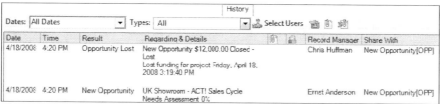

Figure 10-36 History record for a closed opportunity

Exercise 10.6: Export Opportunities To Excel

In this exercise you will export opportunities to Excel. Exporting the opportunity data will allow the data to be analyzed, as well as, create charts.

1. Lookup all of the opportunities.

2. Click the Export Current List To Excel button on the toolbar. The opportunity records will be exported and Excel will open automatically.

If you look at the bottom of the spreadsheet you will see three tabs. The first tab displays the data from the Opportunity list view.

The second tab on the spreadsheet displays a Pivot chart of the data. My Pivot chart looks like the one shown in Figure 10-37. The Pivot Table Field List dialog box shown on the right side of the figure, displays all of the fields that were exported to Excel. You can drag any of those fields to the chart.

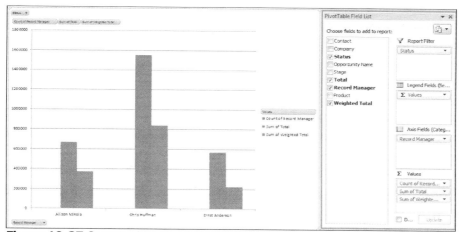

Figure 10-37 Opportunities PivotChart

The third tab displays the summary information in a PivotTable that is displayed on the Pivot chart. The Opportunities Pivot tab should look like the one shown in Figure 10-38. If you change the options on this tab, the chart will automatically be updated to reflect the changes. You can select

Chapter 10

different options in the drop-down lists (Status and Record Manager) to filter the data like you can on the Pivot chart. Doing this will cause the following to happen.

① The data will be recalculated on the Pivot Sheet tab.
② The Pivot chart will change.

Status	(All)		
	Data		
Record Manager	Count of Record Manager	Sum of Total	Sum of Weighted Total
Allison Mikola	97	$667,600.00	$374,575.00
Chris Huffman	181	$1,552,800.00	$840,555.00
Ernst Anderson	99	$571,500.00	$224,395.00
Grand Total	377	$2,791,900.00	$1,439,525.00

Figure 10-38 Opportunities PivotTable

3. Leave the spreadsheet open if you want to follow along in the next section. You can save the spreadsheet in your folder if you want. It is not mandatory to save it because you will not need it to complete any other exercise.

Crash Course In Pivot Table Data

This is truly a crash course in pivot table data. Hopefully it is enough for you to understand the basic functionality if you have not used this tool in Excel before. The Pivot Chart tab displays the summary opportunity data graphically. ACT! displays the data in detail.

In the upper left corner of the chart is the **STATUS** drop-down list. If you select a different status, the data will be recalculated based on the status that you select and the chart will change. At the bottom of the chart is the **RECORD MANAGER** drop-down list. When you select a user from the list, the opportunities that the user created will appear on the chart.

Figure 10-39 shows the Pivot chart with the Status changed to **CLOSED-WON**.

The **VALUES** button is used to filter the following total fields: Count of Record Manager, Sum of Total (the Grand total) and the Sum of Weighted Total.

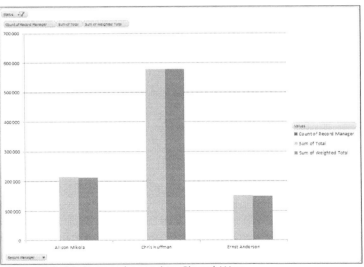

Figure 10-39 Status changed to Closed-Won

10-17

Opportunities

You can move the buttons around on the Opportunity Pivot tab, as shown in Figure 10-40.

B	C	D	E
Record Manager	(All)		
Status	Closed - Won		
	Data		
	Count of Record Manager	Sum of Total	Sum of Weighted Total
Total	120	$944,200.00	$941,200.00

Figure 10-40 Record Manager button moved on the Opportunities Pivot tab

Compare this to Figure 10-38 shown earlier.

If you move the Record Manager button before the Status button on the Opportunities Pivot tab and then view the chart, it will look like the one shown in Figure 10-41.

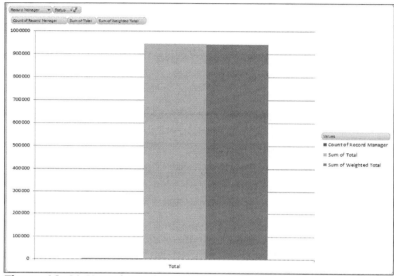

Figure 10-41 Pivot chart after the Record Manager button is moved

Generating Quotes

Often you may need to send the opportunity that you create to a contact when they request a quote. To generate a quote in ACT! you have to have Microsoft Word and Excel installed.

Quote Preferences

There are preferences for quotes that you can set. Tools ⇒ Preferences ⇒ General Tab ⇒ Quote Preferences button, will open the Quote Preferences dialog box.

If the option **PROMPT FOR QUOTE NUMBER WHEN GENERATING** is checked, you can select a prefix for quote numbers, as shown in Figure 10-42.

Adding a quote prefix means that all quotes that you create will start with the same characters and numbers that you enter in the **QUOTE PREFIX** field. You can enter the prefix of your choice or leave it blank if you want to enter a free form quote prefix.

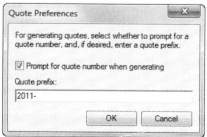

Figure 10-42 Quote Preferences dialog box

10-18

Exercise 10.7: Create A Quote

1. On the Opportunity list view, double-click on the quote that you created for Mary Wood.

2. Click the **CREATE QUOTE** button on the toolbar. The document shown in Figure 10-43 will open in Microsoft Word. If you want to save the quote, save it in your folder.

If you plan to use the quote document, you may want to customize it a little by adding fields or changing the font.

Notice that the shipping and handling charges have not been filled in. You have to fill this in manually.

To modify the shipping and handling field, double-click in the section that has the products. The Excel spreadsheet shown in Figure 10-44 will appear. It has the formulas for the calculations.

The tax rate that you enter should be the tax rate for your state.

This quote template is really two files, as explained below.

Figure 10-43 Quote

① The **QUOTE.ADT** file is the portion of the quote created as a Word template, which you can modify.
② The **QUOTE.XLT** file is the portion of the quote created in Excel, as shown in Figure 10-44. You should not modify the structure of this part of the quote template.

Figure 10-44 Spreadsheet in the Word document

 Some people have reported that they do not see the portion of the quote shown above in Figure 10-44. Make sure that the Quote.xlt spreadsheet is the only spreadsheet in the Templates folder for the database. Any other spreadsheets in that folder need to be moved or deleted.

Opportunities

Exercise 10.8: How To Change The Status Of An Opportunity
Earlier in this chapter you learned that an opportunity can have one of four statuses. When you need to change a status, follow the steps below.

1. On the Opportunity list view, double-click on the opportunity that you want to change the status of. In this exercise select the opportunity for Mary Wood.

2. Select the status that you want. Select Closed-Won for this exercise.

3. On the Opportunity Info tab, type `Purchased service` in the Reason field, then click the Save Changes button.

Viewing Opportunities From The Opportunities Tab
You have created opportunities, viewed them and learned how to filter them from the Opportunities list view. In addition to being able to view opportunities from the Opportunities list view, you can view opportunities from the Opportunities tab on detail views. Like other tabs that you have read about, you can also customize the layout of the Opportunities tab.

As shown in Figure 10-45, some of the filter options that are available on the Opportunities list view are available on the Opportunities tab. If you need more filter options, right-click in the opportunities and select **FILTER OPPORTUNITIES**. You will see the dialog box shown in Figure 10-46. This dialog box is a scaled down version of the one that you saw earlier in Figure 10-19.

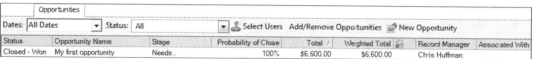

Figure 10-45 Opportunities tab on the Contact detail view

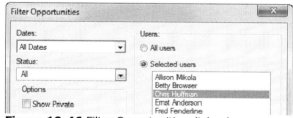

Figure 10-46 Filter Opportunities dialog box

Opportunity Reports
ACT! comes with reports that are specifically for opportunities. In addition to being able to preview and print the reports, there are five other output options that you can select from. You can save the reports and send them as an attachment in an email. You can also save them as a PDF file. The benefit of saving the report in PDF format is that anyone with the free Adobe Reader can view or print the report without having ACT! installed.

Report Options

 After running some of the reports on the Opportunity Reports submenu, I noticed that the Define Filters dialog box for some opportunity reports have the options on the General tab that are usually on the Opportunity tab of this dialog box for other reports like the Company Comprehensive report. The following reports are like this: Sales Analysis by Record Manager, Total By Status, Adjusted for Probability, Pipeline Report and Opportunities By Record Manager.

Exercise 10.9: Sales Analysis By Record Manager Report

This report will display any or all of the available status categories, as well as the number and percent for each category selected. It also has a Closed-Won analysis that provides the average and total amounts for the date range and employees that you select.

1. Reports ⇒ Opportunity Reports ⇒ Sales Analysis By Record Manager.

2. Select **PAST** as the Date Range. The filter options for this report are used to select opportunities based on the status and date range.

3. Click OK. Your report will look similar to the one shown in Figure 10-47.

   Your report will have more records because you are running the report after I did.

Figure 10-47 Sales Analysis By Record Manager report

Exercise 10.10: Opportunities Adjusted For Probability Report

This report will allow the reader to look for trends in the opportunities that they are currently working on. For each status that is selected, the opportunity records will be printed. The total order amount and weighted total amount per status is calculated and printed.

1. Reports ⇒ Opportunity Reports ⇒ Adjusted for Probability.

2. Select all of the opportunity status options, then select the **PAST** Date Range.

3. Click OK. Your report should look like the one shown in Figure 10-48.

Figure 10-48 Opportunities Adjusted for Probability report

Opportunities

Opportunity Graphs And Pipelines
In addition to opportunity reports, ACT! has the ability to create graphs and pipelines for opportunity data. These options are accessed from the Opportunity list view. Graphs and pipelines can be printed and saved in different file formats.

Exercise 10.11: Creating Graphs
The graphs for opportunities that you can create have several options that you can use to customize the graph, like the type of graph and date range of data displayed on the graph.

Create A Bar Graph
In this part of the exercise you will create a bar graph for opportunities created in the second half of 2012.

1. On the Opportunity list view, click the **OPPORTUNITY GRAPH** button.

2. On the General tab, select the options below.
   - Display data for all users
   - Graph by month
   - Starting 6/1/2012
   - Ending 12/31/2012

Your dialog box should have the options shown in Figure 10-49.

Depending on the data that is needed to create the graph, you may need to create a lookup first.

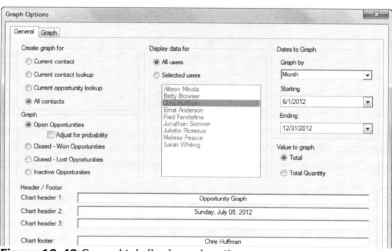

Figure 10-49 General tab (bar) graph options

3. On the Graph tab, select the options below.
   - Allow graph to scroll
   - Show horizontal grid lines
   - 3-D Style

4. Click the button at the end of the **GRAPH** color option and select a different color.

   Your dialog box should have the options shown in Figure 10-50.

Figure 10-50 Graph tab options

5. Click the **GRAPH** button at the bottom of the dialog box.

   The Graph button creates a graph based on the options that are selected.

   Your graph should look like the one shown in Figure 10-51.

   You may have to use the scroll bar below the graph to see the charted data.

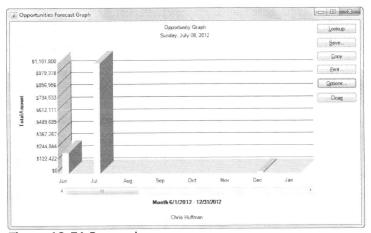

Figure 10-51 Bar graph

The **LOOKUP** button will open the Opportunity list view and display the opportunities that are depicted in the graph.

The **SAVE** button is used to save the graph in .BMP or .JPG graphic file format. Save all of the graphs and pipelines that you create in this chapter in your folder, in .JPG format, as illustrated below in Figure 10-52.

The **COPY** button sends a copy of the graph to the clipboard in Windows. This allows you to paste a copy of the graph into a document like the ACT! Word Processor or a Power Point presentation.

The **PRINT** button will print the graph.

The **OPTIONS** button opens the Graph Options dialog box shown earlier in Figure 10-49, so that you can make changes and recreate the graph.

Opportunities

6. Save the graph as `Bar Graph`, as illustrated in Figure 10-52, then close the Opportunities Forecast Graph dialog box.

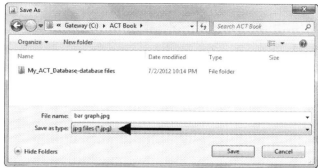

Figure 10-52 Save options for the graph

Create A Line Graph

In this part of the exercise you will create a line graph for opportunities in a specific date range.

1. On the Opportunity list view, click the Opportunity Graph button on the toolbar.

2. On the General tab, select the options below. When finished, your dialog box should have the options shown in Figure 10-53.

    - Display data for all users
    - Graph by week
    - Starting 9/1/2012
    - Ending 12/31/2012
    - Chart header 1 `Opportunity Line Graph`

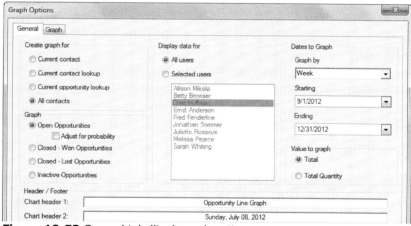

Figure 10-53 General tab (line) graph options

3. On the Graph tab, select the options below. When finished, your dialog box should have the options shown in Figure 10-54.

    - Line graph
    - Allow graph to scroll
    - Show horizontal grid lines
    - Show vertical grid lines
    - 3-D Style
    - Change the background color to light yellow

10-24

Chapter 10

Figure 10-54 Graph tab options

4. Click the Graph button.

   Your graph should look like the one shown in Figure 10-55, if you scroll to the right.

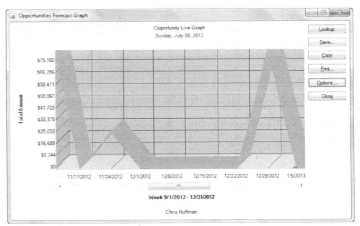

Figure 10-55 Line graph

5. Save the graph as `Line Graph`.

6. Close the Opportunities Forecast Graph dialog box.

Pipelines

Pipelines graphically display opportunities that have an "Open" status for a specific process at each stage. The options to create a pipeline graph are similar to the ones to create a bar or line graph.

Exercise 10.12: Create A Pipeline Graph

1. On the Opportunity list view, click the Opportunity Pipeline button.

Opportunities

2. Select the options below.
   - All contacts
   - All users
   - Graph header 3
     `My First Pipeline`

   Your dialog box should have the options shown in Figure 10-56.

   If the opportunity has more than one process that you want to change the colors of, after you make the color changes for the first process, open the **PROCESS** drop-down list and select the next process that you want to change colors for.

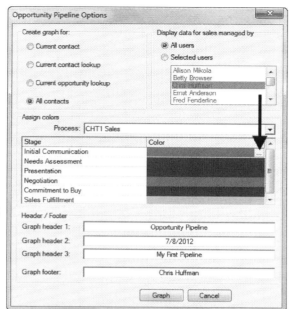

Figure 10-56 Opportunity Pipeline Options dialog box

 To change a color on the pipeline graph for a stage in the process, click the ellipsis button at the end of the stage in the **COLOR** column, as illustrated above in Figure 10-56.

3. Click the Graph button.

   You should see the pipeline graph shown in Figure 10-57.

   Save the pipeline graph as `Pipeline Graph`, then close the Opportunity Pipeline dialog box.

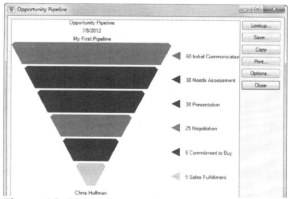

Figure 10-57 Pipeline graph

How To Create And Customize Product And Process Lists

Like the drop-down lists on the Contact detail view, the Opportunity products and processes drop-down lists can be customized. Earlier in Exercise 10.3, you learned how to add a new product. The remaining exercises in this chapter show you how to modify opportunity products and processes, as well as, how to import and export stages and products.

Chapter 10

Exercise 10.13: Creating Process Lists And Stages

In this exercise you will create a process list and the stages for the process.

1. On an Opportunity view, Opportunities ⇒ Manage Process List.

2. Click on the **CREATE NEW OPPORTUNITY PROCESS** link in the Process Tasks section.

3. Type `My first process` in the Opportunity Process field, then type `This process has 3 stages` in the Description field, as shown in Figure 10-58.

Figure 10-58 Manage Process Lists screen

4. Click Next. Click in the Name field, then type `First Stage`.

5. Press the Tab key twice, then type `80` in the Probability field.

6. Click the Add button, then add the two other stages shown in Figure 10-59.

   The **MOVE UP** and **MOVE DOWN** buttons are used to change the order of the stages.

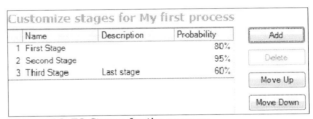

Figure 10-59 Stages for the process

7. Click Finish. You will see the process that you created. In the **PROCESS TASKS** section, notice that there are options to edit and delete processes. Leave the Manage Process Lists window open to complete the next exercise.

Exercise 10.14: Importing Stages

In the previous exercise you created an opportunity process. You also created three stages for the process. If you have a lot of stages for a process or prefer to create them in a spreadsheet, which would allow you to spell check them, you can import the spreadsheet with the stages into ACT!.
In this exercise you will import three stages for the process that you created in the previous exercise. The **MANAGE PROCESS LISTS** window should already be open.

1. Select the **MY FIRST PROCESS** opportunity process, then click on the Edit Opportunity Process link.

2. Change the description to have six stages, then click Next.

Opportunities

3. Click the **IMPORT OPPORTUNITY STAGES** link. In your folder, double-click on the Import Opportunity Stages file.

   You will see the three new stages, as shown at the bottom of Figure 10-60. If you needed to, you could rearrange the order of the stages.

	Name	Description	Probability
1	First Stage		80%
2	Second Stage		95%
3	Third Stage	Last stage	60%
4	Fourth Stage	Add to catalog maili	90%
5	Fifth Stage	Placed Order	95%
6	Sixth Stage	Order Shipped	95%

   Figure 10-60 Imported stages

4. Click the Finish button. Leave the Manage Process Lists window open to complete the next exercise.

Exercise 10.15: Exporting Stages

You can export the opportunity stages to a **.csv** file, which is a file format that you can open in Excel. The **MANAGE PROCESS LISTS** window should already be open.

1. Select the Opportunity Process for the stages that you want to export. In this exercise select the **CHT1 SALES** process, then click on the Edit Opportunity Process link.

2. Click Next. Click the Export Opportunity Stages link.

3. Type `My Export Stages` in the File name field, then press Enter.

4. If you open this file in Excel, it will look like the one shown in Figure 10-61. The reason column B is empty is because the stages that were exported do not have any descriptions.

	A	B	C
1	Initial Communication		10%
2	Needs Assessment		25%
3	Presentation		40%
4	Negotiation		65%
5	Commitment to Buy		80%
6	Sales Fulfillment		90%

   Figure 10-61 Exported stages

   Close the Manage Process Lists dialog box, then close the Manage Process Lists window.

Exercise 10.16: Importing Products

If you need to add a lot of products to the database or have the products in an existing file, you can import them into the database. This means that you can create the product list in Excel and save it in .csv format. In this exercise you will learn how to import data.

1. On the Opportunity list view, click the **MANAGE PRODUCT LIST** button.

2. Click the **IMPORT** button, then click the **BROWSE** button on the Import Products dialog box.

3. Double-click on the Products To Import file in your folder. If you cannot see it, change the Files of type option to **CSV FILES (*.CSV)**.

Chapter 10

4. Check the Source file has column headers option shown in Figure 10-62.

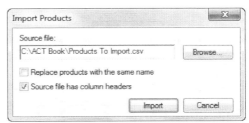

Figure 10-62 Import Products dialog box

The **REPLACE PRODUCTS WITH THE SAME NAME** option overwrites products that are already in the Product list with the changes in the file that you import. This is how you can update existing product information.

The **SOURCE FILE HAS COLUMN HEADERS** option will not import the first row of data in the file. Check this option if the file that you are importing has column headings. If you are not sure, open the file before importing it. You can also view the products on the Manage Product List dialog box and delete the product that has the column headings.

5. Click the Import button on the Import Products dialog box.

    Click OK when prompted that the products have been successfully imported.

    You should see the three products illustrated at the bottom of Figure 10-63.

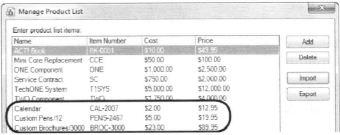

Figure 10-63 Manage Product List dialog box

6. Leave the dialog box open to complete the next exercise.

How To Create A Product List In Excel

If the need arises, the steps below show you how to create a product list in Excel. For now, you can just read through the steps.

1. Create four columns: Name, Item Number, Cost and Price. Typing in the column names is optional. If you type them in, make sure that you do not import the first row of the spreadsheet.
2. Enter the information for each product.
3. Change the Save as type to **CSV (COMMA DELIMITED) (*.CSV)**, as illustrated in Figure 10-64, then save the file.

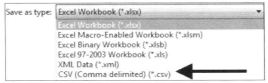

Figure 10-64 CSV file type illustrated

Opportunities

Exercise 10.17: Exporting Products

Exporting products can be useful if you need to change data in several records. You can export the products, make the changes in Excel for example and then import the list back into ACT!. In this exercise you will export products.

1. Open the Manage Product List dialog box if it is not already open, then click the **EXPORT** button.

2. Type My Exported Products as the file name, then press Enter.

3. You can open the exported file in Excel to view it, if you want. Close the Manage Product List dialog box.

Opportunity Detail View Related Tasks

The related tasks options shown in Figure 10-65 are primarily on the detail view. Some options are also on the list view. The options are explained below.

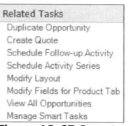

Figure 10-65 Opportunity detail view related tasks

DUPLICATE OPPORTUNITY Opens the dialog box shown in Figure 10-66.

It is used to select which opportunity fields will be duplicated on the new opportunity record.

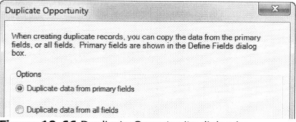

Figure 10-66 Duplicate Opportunity dialog box

CREATE QUOTE [See Exercise 10.7 earlier in this chapter]

SCHEDULE FOLLOW-UP ACTIVITY Opens the Schedule Activity dialog box. Information from the opportunity record is automatically filled in on the activity record.

SCHEDULE ACTIVITY SERIES [See Chapter 7, Activity Series]

MODIFY LAYOUT Opens the current opportunity detail view layout in the Layout Designer, so that the layout can be changed.

MODIFY FIELDS FOR PRODUCT TAB Opens the Define Fields dialog box so that you can modify the fields on the Products/Services tab, as well as, other tabs on the Opportunity detail view.

VIEW ALL OPPORTUNITIES Displays all of the opportunities in the Opportunity list view.

MANAGE SMART TASKS [See Chapter 14, Smart Tasks]

Opportunity List View Related Tasks

The options shown in Figure 10-67 are for the Opportunity list view. The options that are only on the list view are explained below.

Figure 10-67 Opportunity list view related tasks

EXPORT TO EXCEL Exports the opportunities that are displayed in the view to Excel.

PRINT OPPORTUNITIES Opens the Quick Print Options dialog box so that you can select options for how the screen will be printed.

CHANGE COLUMNS Opens the Customize Columns dialog box.

SORT LIST Opens the Sort dialog box to sort the opportunities displayed in the view.

USING THE TASK LIST AND CALENDAR

In this chapter you will learn the following Task List and calendar features:

- ☑ How to use the Task List view to work with activities
- ☑ How to use the calendar views
- ☑ How to filter activities in a calendar view
- ☑ Granting calendar access

Using The Task List And Calendar

Task List View

You have learned how to create activities and view them. You have also learned how to view several contacts at the same time using the Contact list view. If you need to view activities for several contacts at the same time, you can use the Task List view. The entries displayed in the Task List are linked to the current My Record. This means that by default, each person that uses the database has their own Task List and calendar that only displays activities that they scheduled and activities that are assigned to them.

In the Task List view you can add and delete columns, sort by column headings and change the order of the column headings, just like you can with the Contact list view. In addition to being able to view activities for several contacts in the Task List view, you can also modify, sort, filter, clear, schedule and delete activities, the same way that you can on the Activities tab.

Task List Toolbar

Figure 11-1 shows the Task List toolbar.
Table 11-1 explains the buttons on the toolbar.

Figure 11-1 Task List toolbar

Button	Description
1	Prints the current view.
2	Create a lookup.
3	Opens the Customize Columns dialog box, which is used to modify the order of the columns on the Task List.
4	Exports the Task List to Excel.

Table 11-1 Task List toolbar buttons explained

Status Bar

At the bottom of the Task List window is the status bar shown in Figure 11-2. It displays the date range and totals for each type of activity that is displayed on the Task List view.

All Dates: 277 Activities - 35 Calls, 76 Meetings, 98 To-do's, 68 Custom Activities

Figure 11-2 Task List status bar

When you click the Task List button on the Navigation Pane you will see the view shown in Figure 11-3.

Figure 11-3 Task List view

 If you double-click on an activity in the Task List, you can edit it or see more information about the activity.

11-2

Filter Options

The filter options for the Task List are explained in Table 11-2.

Filter	Is Used To . . .
Dates	Select the date or date range that you want to see activities for, as shown in Figure 11-4. If none of the options shown fit your needs, select the **CUSTOM** option at the bottom of the drop-down list.
Types	Select the activity types that you want to see and clear the check mark of the options that you do not want to see, as shown in Figure 11-5.
Priorities	Select the priority of the activity types that you want to see. Clear the check mark of the options that you do not want to see, as shown in Figure 11-6.
Select Users	View the public activities of others users in the database. If you select other users, keep in mind that their activities will continue to be displayed in your Task List until you remove the user from your view.

Table 11-2 Task List filter options explained

Figure 11-4 Date filter options

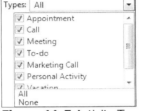
Figure 11-5 Activity Types options

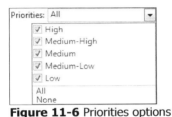
Figure 11-6 Priorities options

Options Button

The options shown in Figure 11-7 are other options that can be selected to filter activities on the Task List view. They are explained below.

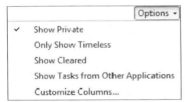

① **Show Private** Displays or hides private activities.
② **Only Show Timeless** Hides tasks that have a time.
③ **Show Cleared** Displays tasks that have been cleared, but not deleted. Cleared tasks have a line through them, as illustrated in Figure 11-8.

Figure 11-7 Task List Options button options

④ **Show Tasks From Other Applications** Displays tasks that were imported or synched from Microsoft Outlook or Google. This option was introduced in ACT! 2012.
⑤ **Customize Columns** Opens the Customize Columns dialog box.

Figure 11-8 Cleared tasks illustrated

Exercise 11.1: Create A Task List Lookup Using Filters

By default, the activities are in ascending order by date. If you have hundreds of activities, you will probably not want to see all of them. You can create a lookup to only display certain activities.

Using The Task List And Calendar

1. Open the Dates drop-down list, then select the **CUSTOM** option at the bottom of the list. You will see the Select Date Range dialog box.

2. Select the range 9/1/2012 to 9/8/2012, then click OK. You should only see activities that have a date in the range that you selected. Select the All Dates option.

3. Display all of the activities, then clear the Activity Type options that you do not want to see. In this exercise clear all of the options except Call and To-Do.

4. Select the priority of the activities that you want to see. For this exercise, select all of the options except Medium-High.

5. If you want to see activities for other users, click the **SELECT USERS** button. Select the first two users, then click OK.

6. View all of the activities and all users.

 If you prefer to see all of the Task List filter options in one place, use the dialog box shown in Figure 11-9. Click the **FILTER LIST** link in the Related Tasks list to display this dialog box.

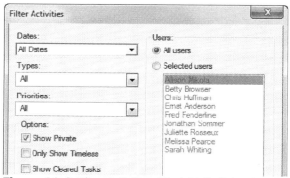

Figure 11-9 Filter Activities (Task List) dialog box

Exercise 11.2: Clearing Tasks From The Task List View

Once you have completed a task or no longer need it, you can clear the activity. You can also create a follow up task. Use the activity dated 2/25/2012 that is scheduled with Lucy Connor to complete this exercise.

1. Click in the **CLEARED** column (the column with the ✓) next to the activity that you want to clear. You will see the Clear Activity dialog box.

Chapter 11

2. In the Details field type `Clearing this task,` as illustrated in Figure 11-10.

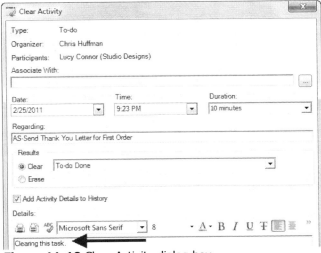

Figure 11-10 Clear Activity dialog box

3. Click OK. You will not see the task in the list unless the **SHOW CLEARED** option is selected on the Options button.

How To Print The Task List

The Task List can be printed by following the steps below.

1. From the Task List view, click on the Print Current Screen link in the Related Tasks list.

2. Select any options that are needed on the Quick Print Options dialog box, then click OK.

Looking Up Records On The Task List

If you like working from the Task List view, you can accomplish the same tasks that you can from other views by using the options on the shortcut menu shown in Figure 11-11.

Like other views, you can look up contacts from the Task List. If you do, the contacts will open in the Contact list view.

There are two ways to create a lookup from the Task List view as explained below.

① Use the options on the Lookup menu.

② Right-click in the Task List view and select Create Lookup, as shown in Figure 11-11.

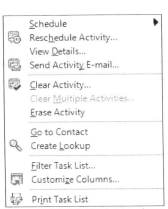

Figure 11-11 Task List shortcut menu

11-5

Using The Task List And Calendar

Customizing The Task List View

The columns on the Task List view can be customized by following the steps below.

1. Open the Task List view.

2. Right-click in the view and select **CUSTOMIZE COLUMNS**. You will see the Customize Columns dialog box.

Adding the **SCHEDULED BY** field to the Task List will display who created the activity. Adding the **SCHEDULED FOR** field will display who the activity has been assigned to.

These two fields are useful to see on the Task List view if you view other users activities on a regular basis. Figure 11-12 shows these two fields.

Regarding	Scheduled By	Scheduled For
Prospect Call	Chris Huffman	Allison Mikola
Demonstration	Chris Huffman	Juliette Rosseux
Network Breakfast	Chris Huffman	Chris Huffman

Figure 11-12 Modified Task List view

Task List View Related Tasks

The options shown in Figure 11-13 are for the Task List view. The options are explained below.

Figure 11-13 Task List view related tasks

SCHEDULE ACTIVITY SERIES [See Chapter 7, Activity Series]

EXPORT TO EXCEL Exports the tasks that are displayed to Excel, as shown in Figure 11-14.

	A	B	C	D	E	F	G	H	I	J	K	L	M
1	Cleared	Type	Recurring	Date	Time	Priority	Scheduled With	Regarding	Location	Details	Duration	Attachment	Private	Associate With
2	False			3/4/2011 1:00 AM	None	Low	Lucy Connor	AS-Follow-up to First			10 minutes			
3	False			5/1/2011 1:01 AM	None	Low	Brian David	Find out about permitting			14 hours 18 minutes			YJBikes-Louisiana
4	False			5/17/2011 12:30 PM	12:30 PM	Low	Sarah Whiting	Birthday Lunch			1 hour 30 minutes			CH TechONE[CMP]
5	False			5/17/2011 12:30 PM	12:30 PM	Low	Sarah Whiting	Birthday Lunch			1 hour 30 minutes			CH TechONE[CMP]

Figure 11-14 Tasks exported to Excel

VIEW ALL RELATED CONTACTS Displays the contacts (in the contacts list view) that are related to at least one task that is displayed.

PRINT CURRENT SCREEN Opens the Quick Print Options dialog box so that you can select options for how the screen will be printed.

CHANGE COLUMNS Opens the Customize Columns dialog box.

EDIT PRIORITY LEVELS [See Chapter 15, Managing Priority Types]

FILTER LIST [See Figure 11-9, earlier in this chapter]

Chapter 11

Calendar Preferences

Chapter 2 covered preferences that you can set for the calendar views. ACT! has calendar options that you can customize as needed.

Calendar Views

The default date when you open any calendar is today's date. Each calendar view has a daily check list and date selector. **TIMELESS** activities are not displayed on calendars. They are displayed under the calendar on the right side of the workspace with the rest of the activities. There is also a mini calendar that you can use. The calendar can also be used to schedule and modify activities.

Calendar Toolbar

Figure 11-15 shows the Calendar toolbar. Table 11-3 explains the buttons on the toolbar.

Figure 11-15 Calendar toolbar

Button	Description
1	Highlights today in any calendar view except the daily calendar.
2	Displays the daily calendar.
3	Displays the work week calendar.
4	Displays the weekly calendar.
5	Displays the monthly calendar.
6	Displays the previous day, week or month, depending on which calendar view is open.
7	Displays the next day, week or month, depending on which calendar view is open.
8	Prints the calendar.
9	Displays the contacts from the current calendar view in the contact list view.

Table 11-3 Calendar toolbar buttons explained

Mini-Calendar

This calendar is used to view calendars for the previous month, current month and next month. This is a quick way to display activities from previous or future months. The single arrows will move to the previous and next month. The double arrows will move to the previous and next year. You can use this calendar to navigate to a day, week or month, by clicking on it.

1. Click the Calendar button on the Navigator Pane.

2. View ⇒ Mini-Calendar, or press F4. You will see the calendar shown in Figure 11-16.

If you click on a date and the weekly calendar view is open, you will see the weekly calendar for the date that you click on.

If necessary, close the mini calendar by clicking on the X in the upper right corner of the calendar.

Figure 11-16 Mini-calendar

11-7

Using The Task List And Calendar

> **Calendar Tips**
>
> **Mini-Calendar** and **Recap List Calendar** If you right-click on the month name in the mini calendar shown above in Figure 11-16, you will see the Recap List calendar shown in Figure 11-17. You can view one of the months in the list. The dates in bold on the mini-calendar have activities. If you right-click on a date that is bold, you will see all of the activities for that day. If you right-click on a date that is bold in either calendar, you will see the dialog box shown in Figure 11-18.
>
> **Shortcut Menu** If you right-click on an activity in the calendar, you will see the shortcut menu shown in Figure 11-19. Many of the options that you will use the most are on this shortcut menu.
>
> The **Filter Calendar** option on the Calendar shortcut menu opens the dialog box shown in Figure 11-20. This dialog box contains all of the filter options that are at the top of a calendar view.
>
> **Drop And Drag An Activity** You can move an activity from one day or time to another day or time by dragging the activity to a new location. If you select an activity to move, that is part of a recurring activity, you will be prompted to change all occurrences of the activity or only the current occurrence. If you click OK to move the activity, it will no longer be part of the recurring activities, as shown by the message in Figure 11-21.

Figure 11-17 Recap List calendar

Figure 11-18 Activities list

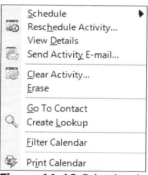

Figure 11-19 Calendar shortcut menu

Figure 11-20 Filter Calendar dialog box

Chapter 11

Figure 11-21 Remove Instance message

Daily Calendar

The daily calendar displays activities and tasks for one day. By default, the day is divided into 30 minute intervals. You can change the time interval on the Preferences dialog box.

1. Display the My Record, then click on the Calendar button on the Navigation Pane.

2. View the daily calendar for the date that you completed Exercise 7.1, by clicking the **DAILY** button and then selecting the day in the mini calendar. The top of the calendar should look similar to the one shown in Figure 11-22.

Figure 11-22 Daily calendar view

Notice that all of the activities in the **RECAP LIST** (which is under the calendar on the right) are for one day, as shown in Figure 11-23.

The items in this section are from the Task List. This list is helpful when there are activities that you can't see without scrolling.

When you click on a different day on the Recap calendar, the activities in the Recap list will change.

When you need to view a different date in the daily calendar, click on the date in the Recap calendar.

Figure 11-23 Recap list

Banner Option

The banner option will display a single line entry at the top of the daily calendar. This lets you see more information about the activity. The banner option can be disabled on the Schedule Activity dialog box. Double-clicking on a banner, like the one shown earlier at the top of Figure 11-22, will open the Schedule Activity dialog box for the activity.

11-9

Using The Task List And Calendar

Calendar Pop-Ups

If you hold the mouse pointer over an activity on a calendar you will see a pop-up like the one shown in Figure 11-24. This allows you to see some of the information about the activity.

Figure 11-24 Calendar pop-up illustrated

Today (Calendar) Button

When clicked, this button will display today's date in the calendar view that you are in, except for the daily calendar view. For example, if today is September 19, 2011 and you are viewing the monthly calendar for June 2010, if you click the **TODAY** button, the September 2011 monthly calendar will be displayed and September 19th will be highlighted.

Work Week Calendar

The work week calendar view shown in Figure 11-25 displays all activities and tasks that have a start time between Monday and Friday or the work days that are selected in the calendar preferences. If you double-click on the day of the week at the top of the calendar, that day will open in the daily calendar. Double-clicking on an activity will open the Schedule Activity dialog box.

Figure 11-25 Work Week calendar view

Weekly Calendar

The weekly calendar view shown in Figure 11-26 displays all activities for the week. The activities under the Recap calendar on the right are for the day that is selected in the calendar.

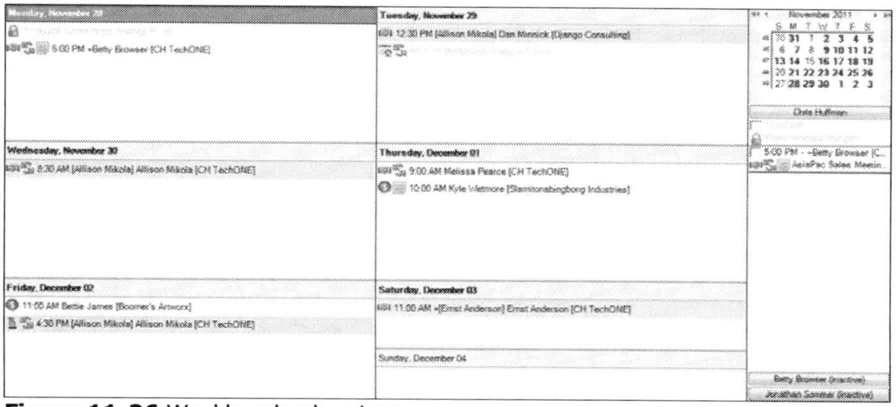

Figure 11-26 Weekly calendar view

11-10

Chapter 11

 If you double-click on a date header on the weekly calendar you will open the daily calendar for the day that you double-click on.

Monthly Calendar

The monthly calendar displays all activities and tasks that have a start time in the month selected, as shown in Figure 11-27. If you click on the button illustrated in the figure, the daily calendar will be displayed.

Figure 11-27 Monthly calendar view

 Cool Calendar Tip
I stumbled across this by accident, with the slip of the mouse. By default, the Recap calendar on the right side of the calendar view only displays one month. The border to the left of this calendar moves. Who knew? Place the mouse pointer in the position illustrated in Figure 11-28, then drag the mouse to the left until you see as many months as you need, as shown in Figure 11-29. You can also display more calendars below, by dragging the bottom of the calendar down.

Figure 11-28 Mouse pointer in position to display more calendars

Figure 11-29 Multiple calendars displayed

 The numbers to the left of the calendar references the week of the year.

11-11

Using The Task List And Calendar

Status Bar

At the bottom of each calendar view is a status bar, as shown in Figure 11-30.

| 14 Activities - 2 Calls, 5 Meetings, 3 To-do's, 4 Custom Activities |

Figure 11-30 Status bar for the weekly calendar

The status bar displays a count of the activities that are scheduled, based on the view that is displayed.

Filtering Activities In A Calendar View

Some calendar views are better able to handle a lot of activities then others. You may only want to view a certain type of activity on a calendar. If either of these options is what you want to do, you can filter the activities that appear on calendars. You can filter activities in a calendar the same way that you filter activities on the Activities tab. The filter that you select will be applied to each calendar view until you remove or change the filter. You can select which activity types and priorities to display.

Calendar Filter Options

Figure 11-31 shows the calendar filter options. They are explained below. They are similar to the Task List view filters that you learned about earlier in this chapter.

Figure 11-31 Calendar filter options

① **TYPES** The options in this drop-down list are used to select the activity types that you want to display. The default is to display all activity types. Clear the check box of the activities that you do not want to display.

② **PRIORITIES** This option is used to select the priority of the activity types that you want to display.

③ **SELECT USERS** This button opens the Select Users dialog box.

④ **OPTIONS** This button is used to display private and cleared activities.

How To Filter Activities On The Calendar

1. Select a month that has a lot of activities, like January 2013.

2. Only display the scheduled meetings that have a low priority. You will see fewer activities.

Using The Calendar To Schedule Activities

In addition to being able to schedule activities from a contact view, activities can also be scheduled from any calendar view. A benefit of scheduling activities from a calendar view is that you are able to see if the start date and time are already booked. I find the daily calendar the easiest to use to schedule activities because you can select the start and end times before opening the Schedule Activity dialog box.

1. Display the start date of the activity that you want to create on a calendar.

Chapter 11

2. If you are using the daily or work week calendar, double-click on the time that you want the activity to start. If you are using the weekly or monthly calendar, right-click on the day that you want to schedule the activity on, then select the schedule option and the type of activity that you want to create.

 If you highlight the start and end time for the activity that you want to create in the daily calendar, as illustrated in Figure 11-32, before you double-click on a time, you will not have to type this information in on the Schedule Activity dialog box.

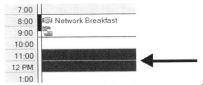
Figure 11-32 Activity time range selected

3. Enter the remaining information for the activity, then click OK.

Exercise 11.3: Granting Calendar Access

This tool is used to give another user access to your calendar. Granting access is helpful when you need to allow someone to schedule or manage your appointments or activities.

 All users of the database can view everyone's calendar. By default, only administrators and managers have the security level to schedule activities for other users.

1. Schedule ⇒ Grant Calendar Access.

   The names that you see in Figure 11-33 are the people that currently have rights to use the database.

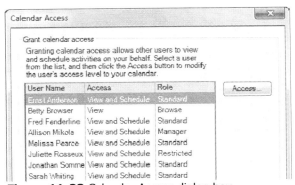
Figure 11-33 Calendar Access dialog box

2. Select the people that you want to have access to your calendar. For this exercise select the five Standard users by holding down the Ctrl key and clicking on the names.

3. Click the **ACCESS** button, then click OK to grant access to **VIEW AND SCHEDULE** activities for the users that you selected, as shown in Figure 11-34.

   Click OK again to close the Calendar Access dialog box.

Figure 11-34 Edit Access dialog box

11-13

Using The Task List And Calendar

Viewing Other Users Calendars

When you have the access to view other users calendars and have selected users on the Select Users dialog box, one day in the weekly calendar will look similar to the one shown in Figure 11-35. Activities for other users will have their name in brackets after the time.

If you look under the calendar on the right side of the window you will see a button for each users activities that you have access to, as shown in Figure 11-36. If you click on one of these buttons, you will see the activities for the user below the button.

Figure 11-35 Calendar with multiple users

Figure 11-36 Buttons to select a user

Exercise 11.4: Printing Calendars

ACT! provides several options to print calendars. If you already use Day Runner or Day-Timer products, you can print calendars in these formats in addition to printing calendars on plain paper. ACT! has three types of calendars that you can print: Daily, Weekly and Monthly.

1. Open the daily calendar.

2. File ⇒ Print. The Day Calendar option should be selected in the **PRINTOUT TYPE** section of the Print dialog box.

3. Select the **PLAIN LETTER FULL PAGE (P) (2 COL)** option in the Paper Type section, as shown at the bottom of Figure 11-37.

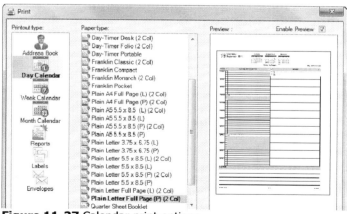

Figure 11-37 Calendar print options

11-14

4. Click the Options button. The options shown in Figure 11-38 are used to customize how the calendar will print.

If you want to print the Activity Details or Column for Priorities for each calendar entry, check the option.

The **START HOUR** field is the hour of the day that you want the calendar to start printing from.

The **FILTER** button opens the Filter Calendar Printout dialog box shown below in Figure 11-39. These options are used to filter the activities that will print on the calendar. You can select which users activities, the date range and activity options, including the type and priority that you want to print on the calendar.

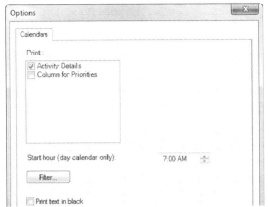

Figure 11-38 Calendar options

By default, the users calendars that you have access to are selected when this dialog box is opened.

PRINT TEXT IN BLACK This option is for color text items on the calendar that you want to print in black.

5. Check the Activity Details **PRINT** option, then clear the Column for Priorities option, if it is checked.

6. Select 7 AM in the **START HOUR** field. You should have the options selected that are shown above in Figure 11-38.

7. Click the **FILTER** button and change the Date Range to 9/19/2012 to 9/22/2012.

8. Clear the **SHOW CLEARED** option.

    You should have the options selected that are shown in Figure 11-39.

    Click OK.

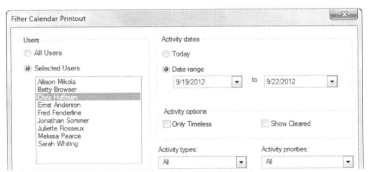

Figure 11-39 Filter Calendar Printout dialog box

Using The Task List And Calendar

9. Click OK to close the Options dialog box.

   If you want to print the calendar, click the Print button on the Print dialog box.

   The calendar will look like the one shown in Figure 11-40.

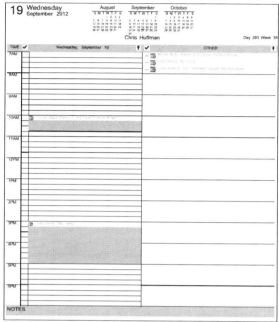

Figure 11-40 ACT! daily calendar

Calendar View Related Tasks

The options shown in Figure 11-41 are for the Calendar view.

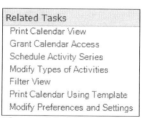

Figure 11-41 Calendar view related tasks

PRINT CALENDAR VIEW [See Chapter 8, Exercise 8.9]

GRANT CALENDAR ACCESS [See Exercise 11.4, earlier in this chapter]

SCHEDULE ACTIVITY SERIES [See Chapter 7, Activity Series]

MODIFY TYPES OF ACTIVITIES [See Chapter 15, Exercise 15.11]

FILTER VIEW [See Calendar Tips box - Filter Calendar, earlier in this chapter]

PRINT CALENDAR USING TEMPLATE [See Exercise 11.5 earlier in this chapter]

MODIFY PREFERENCES AND SETTINGS Opens the Calendar & Scheduling tab on the Preferences dialog box. [See Chapter 2, Calendar & Scheduling Tab Preferences]

DASHBOARDS

In this chapter you will learn how to use dashboards and how to modify them by exploring the following topics:

- ☑ What is a dashboard?
- ☑ Dashboard toolbar
- ☑ Dashboard views
- ☑ Components
- ☑ Filtering data in a dashboard
- ☑ Modifying dashboard layouts
- ☑ Modifying dashboard components
- ☑ Data Chart component

 Shameless Book Plug #2
If your dashboard needs are more than ACT! can handle, you may find my book, SAP Crystal Dashboard Design (ISBN 978-1-935208-11-2) helpful because this software is designed to take dashboards to the next level.

Because you purchased this book on ACT!, you can order the Dashboard Design book for 50% off of the list price. For more information go to www.tolana.com/books/act.html.

Dashboards

What Is A Dashboard?

A dashboard displays a snapshot of data in a graphical format. So far in this book you have created, viewed and edited different types of data, including contacts, activities and opportunities. While it is easy to switch between views to see all of these types of data, you cannot view more than one of these types of data at the same time. You also cannot get a feel for the big picture of your data, as they say.

This is where dashboards come into play. Like other features in ACT!, the data that is displayed in a dashboard can be filtered. You can create, view and edit data from a dashboard. You can edit the default dashboard layouts by adding, modifying and removing components in a dashboard. To create a dashboard from scratch involves selecting the components that are needed, adding them to the layout, then selecting the options on the Component Configuration Wizard.

Dashboard Layouts

ACT! comes with five layouts as shown in Figures 12-1 to 12-5. Each layout can be customized. The layouts contain components that have preset filters. Later you will learn how to customize the layouts and how to change the preset defaults and filters.

The **ACTIVITIES DASHBOARD** displays the contacts schedule and activities. The Activities by User component was replaced with the Activities by Type component in ACT! Pro 2011.

The **ADMINISTRATIVE DASHBOARD** displays user status and remote database information.

The **CONTACTS DASHBOARD** displays contact records that you have created or edited and a count of history records.

The **DEFAULT DASHBOARD** displays your schedule, activities, history and opportunity information.

The **OPPORTUNITY DASHBOARD** displays opportunity sales information in several formats.

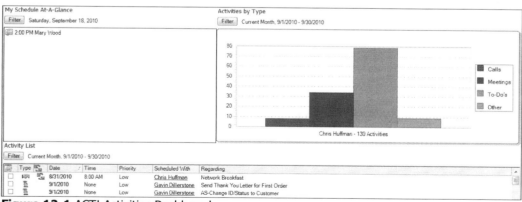

Figure 12-1 ACT! Activities Dashboard

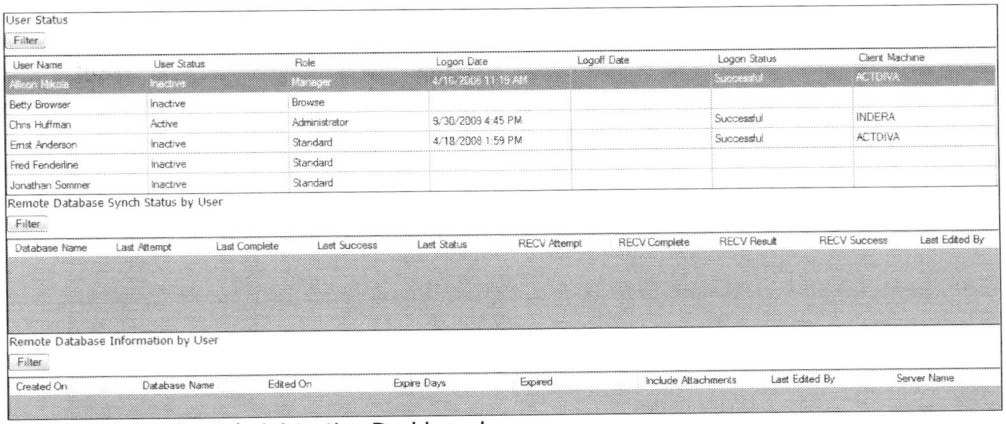

Chapter 12

Figure 12-2 ACT! Administrative Dashboard

Figure 12-3 ACT! Contacts Dashboard

12-3

Dashboards

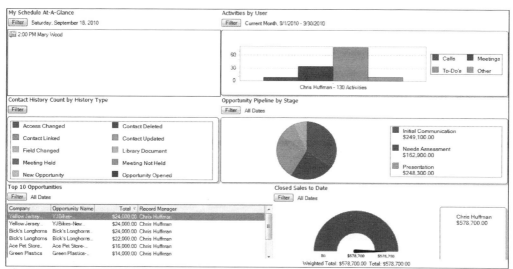

Figure 12-4 ACT! Default Dashboard

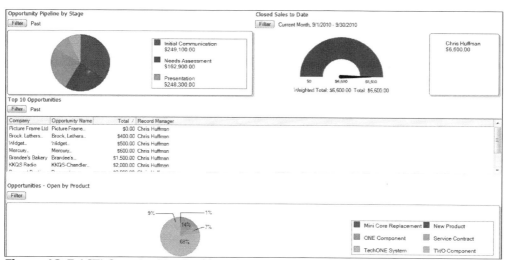

Figure 12-5 ACT! Opportunities Dashboard

Dashboard Toolbar

Figure 12-6 shows the Dashboard toolbar. Table 12-1 explains the buttons on the toolbar.

Figure 12-6 Dashboard toolbar

Chapter 12

Button	Description
1	Is used to edit the dashboard that is displayed.
2	Prints the dashboard that is displayed.
3	Copies the dashboard that is displayed to the clipboard.
4	Refreshes the data in the dashboard.
5	Is used to select a different dashboard layout.

Table 12-1 Dashboard toolbar buttons explained

Exercise 12.1: Selecting A Dashboard Layout

The steps below show you how to select a dashboard.

1. Click the **DASHBOARD** icon on the Navigation Pane.

2. To select a different dashboard, open the Dashboard drop-down list and select one of the options shown in Figure 12-7.

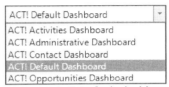

Figure 12-7 Default dashboard layouts

Dashboard Components

Components display different types of data from the database. There are six components in two categories that can be added to a layout, as explained below. The options shown are the defaults for the component, which can be modified. For example, the Closed sales to date component displays opportunities in the CHT1 Sales process. If you created a process, you can modify this component to display your process by default, instead of the CHT1 Sales process.

Activity Components

The two activity components that come with ACT! are explained below.

① **MY ACTIVITIES** Displays a chart with your activities for the current month.
② **MY SCHEDULE AT-A-GLANCE** Displays your scheduled activities for today.

Opportunity Components

The four opportunity components that come with ACT! are explained below. The opportunity data that each component displays is from the CHT1 Sales process.

① **CLOSED SALES TO DATE** Displays opportunities that have the Closed-Won status for the current month.
② **MY OPPORTUNITIES** Displays a bar chart that has open opportunities for the current month.
③ **OPPORTUNITY PIPELINE BY STAGE** Displays a pie chart with open opportunities for the current month.
④ **TOP OPPORTUNITIES** Displays a list of your top 10 opportunities for the current month that have the Closed-Won status.

12-5

Dashboards

Getting Things Done From A Dashboard

Yes, the dashboard provides a great way to view a lot of data in a graphical format, but you still need to be able to get work done. Many of the components have a shortcut menu. This is in addition to the menu and toolbar options on the dashboard.

Activity Component Shortcut Menu Options

The activity shortcut menu options explained in this section are available, regardless of the dashboard that they are on.

1. Open the ACT! Activities Dashboard.

2. Right-click in the My Schedule At-A-Glance component.

   You should see the shortcut menu shown in Figure 12-8.

   These are the activity options that you can use.

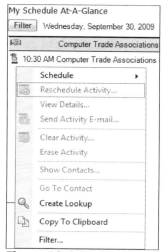

Figure 12-8 My Schedule At-A-Glance shortcut menu

3. If you right-click in the Activity List component, you will see the shortcut menu shown above in Figure 12-8. The Activity List shortcut menu also has the **CUSTOMIZE COLUMNS** option on the menu.

4. If you right-click in the Activities by Type component on the Default Dashboard, you will see that the options shown in Figure 12-9 are the only ones available.

Figure 12-9 Activities by Type shortcut menu

The **COPY TO CLIPBOARD** option creates an image of the component. This image can be pasted into a document.

The **VIEW ALL DATA IN LIST** displays the Task List view.

Opportunity Component Shortcut Menu Options

The opportunity shortcut menu options explained in this section are available in dashboards that have an opportunity component.

1. Open the ACT! Opportunities Dashboard.

2. Right-click in the grid in the Top 10 Opportunities component. You should see the shortcut menu shown in Figure 12-10. These are the opportunity options that you can use.

The majority of the other opportunity components only have the shortcut menu options shown above in Figure 12-9. The Opportunities - Open by Product component has the shortcut menu options shown in Figure 12-11.

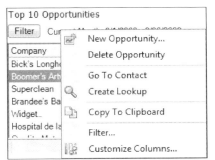

Figure 12-10 Opportunity shortcut menu

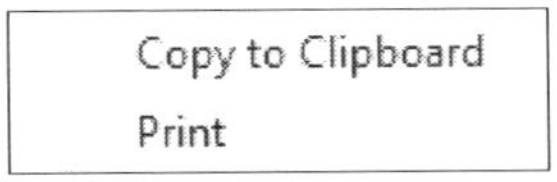

Figure 12-11 Opportunities - Open by Product component shortcut menu

Filtering Data In A Dashboard

As you have seen, each activity component has a filter button. The filter button is used to change the data that is displayed in the component. The options that you will see on the Filter dialog boxes are the default options that were set for the component.

If you select different options on a filter dialog box, the next time that you open a dashboard, those options will still be selected. The exception to this is if you or another administrator or manager of the database modifies the default filter options for the component.

Exercise 12.2: Filtering Activity Component Data

In this exercise you will learn how to filter the activity component data.

My Schedule At-A-Glance Filter Component Options

1. Open the ACT! Activities Dashboard.

2. Click the **FILTER** button for the My Schedule At-A-Glance component. You will see the dialog box shown in Figure 12-12.

   The filter options on this dialog box are a subset of the filter options that are on the Activities tab.

   If the My Schedule At-A-Glance component displays a lot of activities, you can clear some of the options on this dialog box to reduce the number of activities that appear in the component.

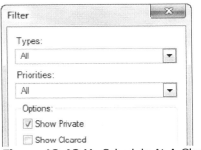

Figure 12-12 My Schedule At-A-Glance component filter options

Dashboards

Activities By Type Filter Component Options

1. Click the **FILTER** button in the Activities By Type component.

    You will see the dialog box shown in Figure 12-13.

    The filter options on this dialog box are the same filter options that are on the Activities tab of the Contact detail view.

    The **SHOW TASKS FROM OTHER APPLICATIONS** option is helpful if you want to display tasks that were created in Outlook or Google.

Figure 12-13 Activities By Type component filter options

Activity List Filter Options

The Activity List filter is the list view display type of the My Activities component.

1. Click the **FILTER** button in the Activity List component. As you see, the Filter dialog box has the same options as the one shown above in Figure 12-13.

2. Clear the Call and To-Do **TYPES**, then click OK. You will see less activities in this component on the dashboard.

Exercise 12.3: Filtering Opportunity Component Data

In this exercise you will learn how to filter the opportunity component data.

1. Open the ACT! Default Dashboard.

2. Click the **FILTER** button in any of the Opportunity components.

    You will see the dialog box shown in Figure 12-14.

    The options on this dialog box are the same filter options that are on all of the Opportunity components.

    They are the same options that are on the Opportunity list view. [See Chapter 10, Using The Opportunity List Filters]

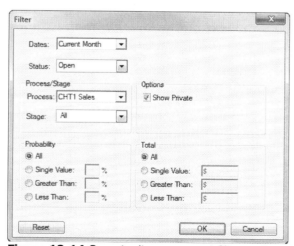

Figure 12-14 Opportunity component filter options

3. Select the options that you want to filter the opportunity records by, then click OK.

Administrative Dashboard

The components on this dashboard display users of the database. The filter buttons in both remote database sections open the dialog box shown in Figure 12-15.

This dialog box is used to enter the name of the remote database that you want to view the status of, as shown in Figure 12-16.

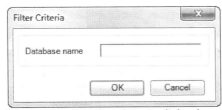

Figure 12-15 Filter Criteria dialog box

User Status

Filter

User Name	User Status	Role	Logon Date	Logoff Date	Logon Status	Client Machine
Alison Mikola	Inactive	Manager	4/16/2008 11:19 AM		Successful	ACTDIVA
Betty Browser	Inactive	Browse				
Chris Huffman	Active	Administrator	10/4/2009 2:34 PM		Successful	INDERA
Ernst Anderson	Inactive	Standard	4/18/2008 1:59 PM		Successful	ACTDIVA
Fred Fenderline	Inactive	Standard				
Jonathan Sommer	Inactive	Standard				

Remote Database Synch Status by User

Filter

Database Name	Last Attempt	Last Complete	Last Success	Last Status	RECV Attempt	RECV Complete	RECV Result	RECV Success	Last Edited By
MyRemoteDB_1	10/4/2009 2:03 PM		10/4/2009 2:03 PM	0					
MyRemoteDB_2	10/4/2009 2:04 PM		10/4/2009 2:04 PM	0					
MyRemoteDB_3	10/4/2009 2:05 PM		10/4/2009 2:05 PM	0					
MyRemoteDB_4	10/4/2009 2:06 PM		10/4/2009 2:06 PM	0					
MyRemoteDB_5	10/4/2009 2:10 PM		10/4/2009 2:09 PM	0					

Remote Database Information by User

Filter

Created On	Database Name	Edited On	Expire Days	Expired	Include Attachments	Last Edited By	Server Name
10/4/2009 1:22 PM	My_ACTDemo		30	No	Yes		INDERA\ACT7
10/4/2009 2:03 PM	MyRemoteDB_1		30	No	No		INDERA\ACT7
10/4/2009 2:04 PM	MyRemoteDB_2		30	No	No		INDERA\ACT7
10/4/2009 2:05 PM	MyRemoteDB_3		30	No	No		INDERA\ACT7

Figure 12-16 Remote database dashboard information

Dashboard Designer

The Dashboard Designer is used to create new dashboards and modify the dashboards that come with ACT!. The Dashboard Designer has the two functions explained below.

① **CREATE OR MODIFY THE LAYOUT** Select this option when you want to create a new dashboard layout or modify an existing layout.

② **MODIFY A DASHBOARD COMPONENT** Select this option when you want to modify a component, like changing the default filter options.

Dashboard Designer Window

When you open the Dashboard Designer in Edit mode, you will see the window shown in Figure 12-17.

Dashboards

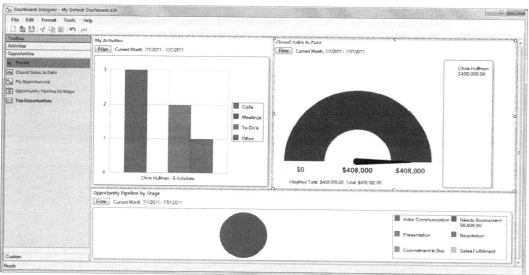

Figure 12-17 Dashboard Designer window

Dashboard Designer Toolbar

Not to be out done, the Dashboard Designer has its own toolbar, as shown in Figure 12-18. Table 12-2 explains the buttons on the toolbar.

Figure 12-18 Dashboard Designer toolbar

Button	Description
1	Creates a new dashboard.
2	Opens an existing dashboard.
3	Saves the changes.
4	Deletes the selected component.
5	Copies the selected component.
6	Pastes the selected component.
7	Undoes the last action.
8	Redoes the previous action.

Table 12-2 Dashboard Designer toolbar buttons explained

Dashboard Designer Menu Options

The Dashboard Designer has some menu options that are unique. They are explained in Table 12-3.

Menu	Option	Description
File	Layout Settings	Opens the dialog box shown in Figure 12-19. These options are used to change the size of the dashboard.
Format	Insert/Delete	Both options have the submenu shown in Figure 12-20. The options are explained below.

Table 12-3 Dashboard Designer menu options explained

Chapter 12

Menu	Option	Description
Tools	Add Component	This option is only available when a dashboard layout has an empty section. It opens the submenu shown in Figure 12-21. This is one way to add a component to the dashboard. The components are divided into the activity, opportunity and custom categories that you read about earlier in this chapter.
Tools	Component Configuration	Opens the **COMPONENT CONFIGURATION WIZARD**, which is covered later in this chapter.

Table 12-3 Dashboard Designer menu options explained (Continued)

The dimensions shown in the **TARGET SIZE** drop-down list are the same size as computer screen resolutions.

This means that if you are creating or modifying a dashboard and all of the people that will use it have the same screen size resolution, you can select that size instead of using the smaller default size.

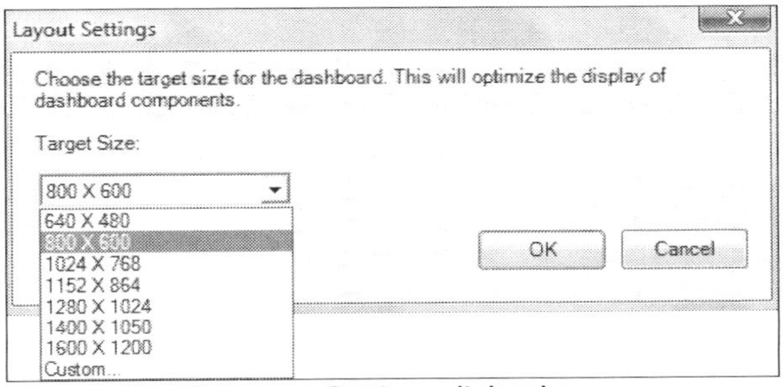

Figure 12-19 Layout Settings dialog box

The **COLUMN ON THE FAR RIGHT** option will add/delete a column on the right side of the dashboard.

Figure 12-20 Insert and Delete layout options

The **ROW AT THE BOTTOM** option will add/delete a row at the bottom of the dashboard.

The **CELL AT END OF THE ROW** option will add/delete a cell at the end of the row that is selected.

Figure 12-21 Add Component options

Dashboard Designer Toolbox

The Dashboard Designer toolbox options are shown in Figures 12-22 to 12-24. Each component was explained earlier in the Dashboard Components section. These are the components that you can add to the dashboard.

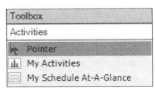

Figure 12-22 Activity components

Figure 12-23 Opportunity components

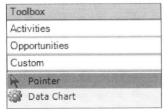

Figure 12-24 Custom component

Dashboards

Dashboard Layout Overview

By default, a new layout has six sections that you can add a component to. It is not a requirement that all six sections be used in a layout. Each section can be resized. I think the Dashboard Designer is a good first step in being able to modify dashboards. It has some quirks that I hope will be worked out in the next release. It is not as user friendly as the other designers in ACT!. For example, in the exercise below, the goal is to move the component that is at the bottom of the dashboard to the top of the dashboard. Sounds easy right? As you will see, it requires several steps.

Exercise 12.4: Modify The ACT! Activities Dashboard Layout

In this exercise you will modify the Activities dashboard layout to put the Activity List component at the top of the layout.

1. Open the ACT! Activities Dashboard, then click the **EDIT CURRENT DASHBOARD** button on the Dashboard toolbar. You will see the Dashboard Designer window.

2. File ⇒ Save As.

    You will see the dialog box shown in Figure 12-25.

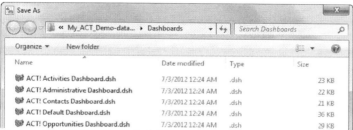

Figure 12-25 Dashboards folder

The folder shown at the top of the figure is where the dashboard layouts are stored that appear in the drop-down list at the top of the dashboard. If you want the dashboard layouts that you create to appear in the drop-down list, you have to save them in this folder.

3. Type `My Activities Dashboard` in the File name field, then press Enter.

4. The My Schedule component should be selected in the layout.

    Format ⇒ Insert ⇒ Row at the bottom.

    You should see a new row at the bottom of the window, as illustrated in Figure 12-26.

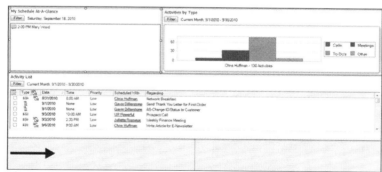

Figure 12-26 New row added to the dashboard layout

5. Drag the Activity List component in the layout to the bottom row.

6. Right-click in the middle row and select Insert ⇒ Cell at End of the row.

Chapter 12

7. Place the mouse pointer on the line between the two cells in the middle row, as shown in Figure 12-27, then drag the line to the left so that it lines up with the one at the end of the My Schedule component.

Figure 12-27 Mouse pointer in position to resize a cell

8. One by one, move the two components in the first row to the cells in the middle row.

9. Right-click in the first row and select Delete ⇒ Cell at End of the row.

10. Move the Activity List component in the third row to the first row.

11. Format ⇒ Delete ⇒ Row at the bottom.

12. File ⇒ Exit. Click Yes, when prompted to save the changes to the dashboard. Wasn't that a lot of steps to rearrange the components on the layout? <smile>

View The Changes

1. On the Dashboard view, open the Dashboard drop-down list.

    You should see your dashboard at the bottom of the list, as shown in Figure 12-28.

Figure 12-28 Dashboard added to the list

2. Select your dashboard.

    It should look like the one shown in Figure 12-29.

    Compare it to the one shown earlier in Figure 12-1.

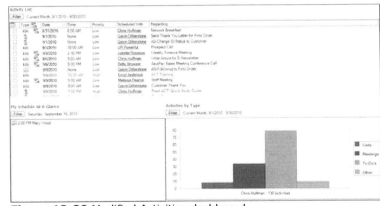

Figure 12-29 Modified Activities dashboard

Exercise 12.5: Modify The ACT! Default Dashboard Layout

In this exercise you will modify the Default Dashboard by removing some of the components and rearranging the remaining components.

1. Open the ACT! Default Dashboard, then click the **EDIT CURRENT DASHBOARD** button on the Dashboard toolbar.

2. File ⇒ Save As. Type `My Default Dashboard` as the file name, then press Enter.

12-13

Dashboards

3. Delete the following components by clicking on them and then pressing the Delete key:
My Schedule At-A-Glance, Contact History Count by History Type and Top 10 Opportunities.

4. Move the My Activities component to the cell on the left of the same row.

5. Move the Closed Sales to Date component up to the first row.

6. Move the Opportunity Pipeline by Stage component to the first cell in the same row.

7. Click in the middle row, then delete the cell on the right in the middle row. Delete the bottom row.

8. Make the first row longer so that it takes up more than 50% of the space in the dashboard.

9. File ⇒ Exit. Save the changes.

10. Select the My Default Dashboard from the drop-down list.

    Change the dates for the Opportunity Pipeline component to display all dates.

    The dashboard should look like the one shown in Figure 12-30.

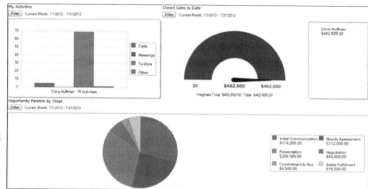

Figure 12-30 My Default Dashboard

Component Configuration Wizard

This wizard is used to add components to a dashboard. It is accessed from the Tools menu in the Dashboard Designer. Once you select an option on a component wizard screen, you can preview the change by clicking the **PREVIEW** button. The following seven steps are available on the Component Configuration Wizard for components once they have been added to a dashboard. All steps are not available for each component. The options available for some steps vary depending on the component that is being added to the dashboard.

Step 1: Select Display Type

This step is used to select the chart type, as shown in Figure 12-31. All chart types are not available for all components. You can also select where to place the filter bar (button), as illustrated at the bottom of Figure 12-31.

Step 2: Edit Default Filters

This step displays the current default filter options for the component and is used to select new default filter options. The filter options change, depending on the display type (chart) that is selected.

Figure 12-32 shows the filter options for the My Activities component.
Figure 12-33 shows the filter options for the Opportunity Pipeline by Stage component.

Chapter 12

Figure 12-31 Display type options for the Closed Sales to Date component

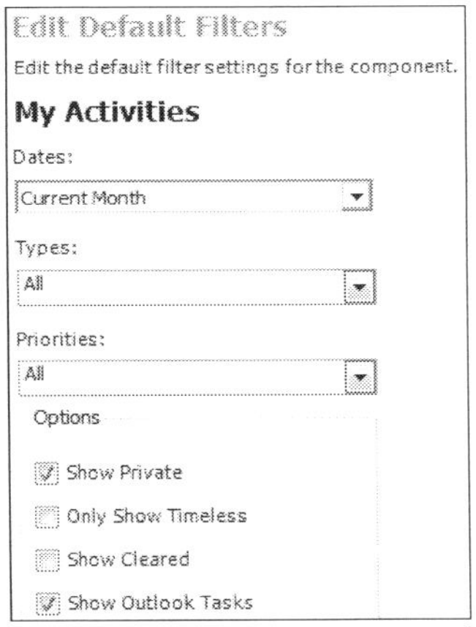

Figure 12-32 Filter options for the My Activities component

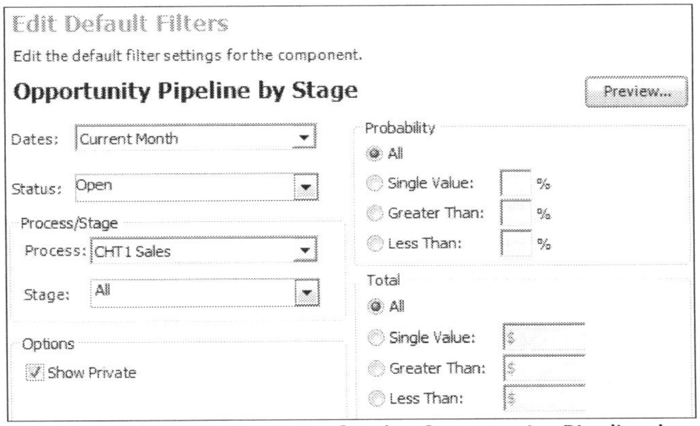

Figure 12-33 Filter options for the Opportunity Pipeline by Stage component

Step 3: Edit Header/Footer

This step is used to add or edit the header and footer information for the component, as shown in Figure 12-34.

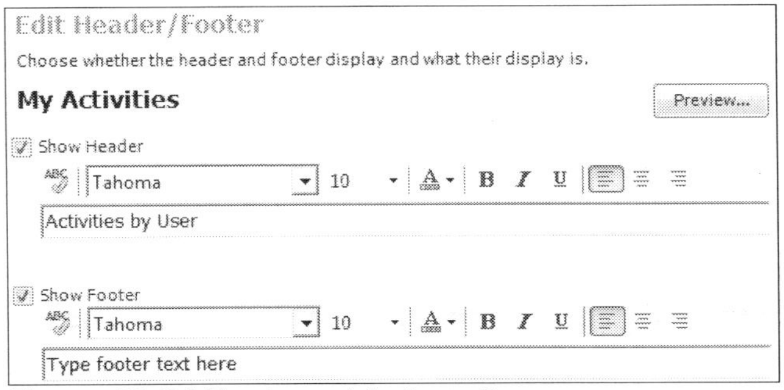

Figure 12-34 Header and footer options

12-15

Dashboards

Step 4: Change Legend

This step is used to select whether or not the component displays a legend and where the legend should be placed, as shown in Figure 12-35.

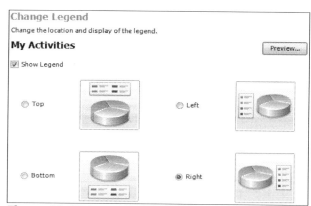

Figure 12-35 Legend options

Step 5: Change Totals

This step is used to select whether or not the component displays totals. The totals for each component type are pre-determined, which means that you can only select whether or not to display totals. Figure 12-36 shows the totals for the Closed Sales to Date component. Figure 12-37 shows the totals for the My Activities component.

Figure 12-36 Total options for the Closed Sales to Date component

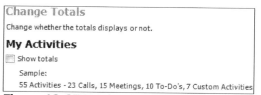

Figure 12-37 Total options for the My Activities component

Step 6: Specify Targets

This step is used to select whether or not the component displays the minimum acceptable amount or value that will reach the expected goal. Figure 12-38 shows the target options. Figure 12-39 illustrates the target option applied to a chart. The line illustrated in Figure 12-39 across the chart, represents the target. This allows the user to see which items meet the goal and which ones do not.

As illustrated in Figure 12-40, the target is $30,000. The target is indicated by a triangle pointer on the chart. In this example, the target has not been met. In Figure 12-41, the target is $17,500, which means that the target has been exceeded.

Figure 12-38 Target options

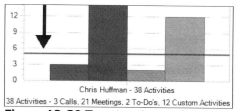

Figure 12-39 Target option on the chart

Chapter 12

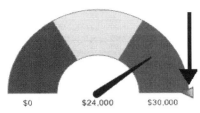

Figure 12-40 Target has not been met

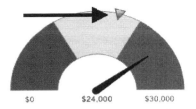

Figure 12-41 Target has been met

Step 7: Scale/Limits

This step is used to select the range that numeric data should be displayed on the chart. The scale and limits change depending on the display type that is selected. Figures 12-42 to 12-44 show different types of scale/limits. The **BREAKPOINT** options are used to measure progress.

Figure 12-42 Top Opportunities component Scale/Limits options

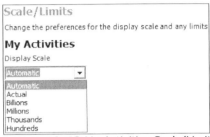

Figure 12-43 My Activities Scale/Limits component options

Figure 12-44 Closed Sales to Date Scale/Limits component options

Dashboards

Top Opportunities Component

This component has an additional step, as shown in Figure 12-45. The options shown are used to change the columns that are displayed in the grid and how the opportunity records are sorted.

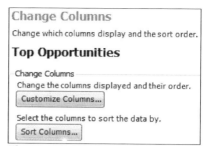

Figure 12-45 Change Columns options for the Top Opportunities component

Exercise 12.6: Modify The Components Of The My Default Dashboard

In this exercise you will modify the default filter options for the My Default Dashboard. Currently, all of the filters are using the current month as the date range.

1. Open the My Default Dashboard, if it is not already open, then click the **EDIT CURRENT DASHBOARD** button on the Dashboard toolbar.

2. File ⇒ Save As. Type `My New Filter Dashboard` as the file name, then press Enter.

Modify The My Activities Component Filter Options

 In ACT! 2009 and earlier, by default, the My Activities component (formerly called **ACTIVITIES BY USER**) displayed totals of the activities for the user by category, at the bottom of the component. In this part of the exercise you will learn how to add these totals to this component.

1. Right-click on the My Activities component and select **COMPONENT CONFIGURATION**.

2. Click on the Select Display Type link, then select the **HORIZONTAL BAR CHART** display type.

3. Open the **FILTER BAR PLACEMENT** drop-down list and select Below Display.

4. On the Edit Default Filters screen, open the Dates drop-down list and select Today and Future.

5. On the Change Legend screen, select Top.

6. On the Change Totals screen, select the Show totals option, then click Finish.

7. Click Yes, when prompted that the changes will affect all users.

    As shown in Figure 12-46, the Details section on the Configuration Wizard screen shows the options that have been selected for the component.

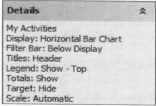

Figure 12-46 Details section

12-18

Chapter 12

8. Click Close to close the Component Configuration dialog box.

Modify The Closed Sales To Date Component Filter Options

1. Right-click on the Closed Sales to Date component and select Component Configuration.

2. On the Edit Default Filters screen, open the Dates drop-down list and select Today and Future.

3. On the Edit Header/Footer screen, type `Pending Sales` in the Header field, then change the font size to 14. Change the color to red.

4. On the Specify Targets screen, display the target and change the Target value to `$100,000.00`.

5. On the Scale/Limits screen, make the changes below. You should have the options shown earlier in Figure 12-44.

   - Breakpoint 1 25000
   - Breakpoint 2 75000
   - Maximum 250000

6. Click Finish. Click Yes to continue with changes, then click Close.

7. File ⇒ Exit, then click Yes to save the changes.

8. Select the My New Filter Dashboard, then make the changes below.
   - Change the Opportunity Pipeline date filter to Past.
   - Change the Pending Sales date filter to Past and the Status to Open.

   The dashboard should look similar to the one shown in Figure 12-47. Compare this to the dashboard shown earlier in Figure 12-30.

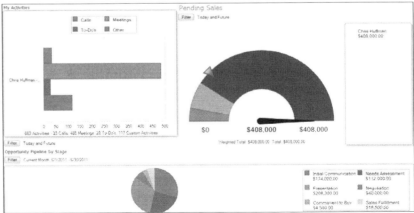

Figure 12-47 Modified dashboard components

Dashboards

Create A New Dashboard

If you need to create a dashboard from scratch, you can follow the steps below.

1. Click the **NEW DASHBOARD** link in the Related Tasks section on the Navigation Pane. You will see an empty layout in the Dashboard Designer.

2. Drag a component from the Toolbox to the layout. The Component Configuration Wizard will automatically open. Select the default options that you need, for the component.

3. Repeat step 2 for each component that you want to add to the dashboard layout.

4. Remove any sections from the layout that are not needed.

5. Save the dashboard and give it a descriptive name.

Data Chart Component

This component is used to create a custom component, as shown earlier in Figure 12-24. When you add the Custom Data Chart component to a section of the layout, you will see the dialog box shown in Figure 12-48. The options on this dialog box are used to configure the component. The options are explained below.

CHOOSE A TEMPLATE The options shown in Figure 12-49 are the layouts that you can select from to create your custom component. You have seen many of these layouts earlier in this chapter.

Some of these templates will disable other options on the dialog box.

SHOW DATA AS CHART If checked, the data will be displayed as a chart in the component instead of in grid format.

CHART TYPE The options shown in Figure 12-50 are the chart types that can be created.

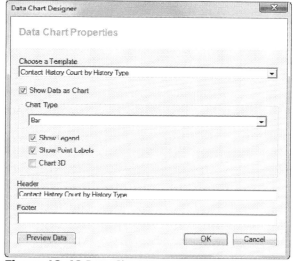

Figure 12-48 Data Chart Designer dialog box

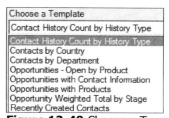

Figure 12-49 Choose a Template drop-down list options

Figure 12-50 Chart Type options

SHOW LEGEND If checked, a legend for the charts data will be displayed on the component.

SHOW POINT LABELS If checked, the value that each part of the chart represents will be displayed on the component, as shown in Figure 12-51.

Depending on the size of the chart, the lines may not be displayed. The lines are displayed when the chart size is small.

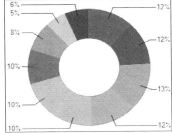

Figure 12-51 Show Point Labels option

CHART 3D If checked, the chart will be displayed in 3D format, as shown in Figure 12-52.

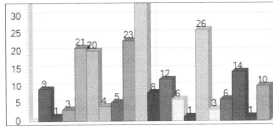

Figure 12-52 Chart in 3D format

HEADER Is used to type in information that you want to appear at the top of the component. By default, the template name is added to this field.

FOOTER Is used to type in information that you want to appear at the bottom of the component.

PREVIEW DATA BUTTON Depending on the template type that is selected, a different dialog box will appear. The options are used to set up the default filter criteria and to view the data.

Figure 12-53 shows the filter criteria options for the Contact History Count By History component.
Figure 12-54 shows the filter criteria options for the Contacts By Department component.
Figure 12-55 shows the filter criteria options for the Opportunities with Products component.

Figure 12-53 Contact History Count By History component Filter Criteria dialog box

Dashboards

Figure 12-55 Opportunities with Products component Filter Criteria dialog box

Figure 12-54 Contacts By Department component Filter Criteria dialog box

Dashboard View Related Tasks

The options shown in Figure 12-56 are for the Dashboard view. The options are explained below.

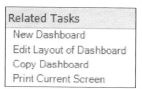

Figure 12-56 Dashboard view related tasks

NEW DASHBOARD Opens the Dashboard Designer to create a new dashboard.

EDIT LAYOUT OF DASHBOARD Opens the current dashboard layout in the Dashboard Designer so that it can be modified.

COPY DASHBOARD Is used to make an image of the entire dashboard that can be pasted into a document.

For example, if you click on this link, then open Microsoft Word, right-click and select Paste, you will see an image of the dashboard in the document, as shown in Figure 12-57.

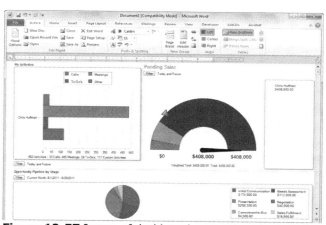

Figure 12-57 Image of dashboard pasted in a document

PRINT CURRENT SCREEN Opens the Quick Print Options dialog box so that you can select options for how the screen, in this case the dashboard, will be printed. The options are similar to those shown in Chapter 8, Exercise 8.9: Using The Quick Print Options.

CREATING QUERIES

In this chapter you will learn the following query techniques:

- ☑ Create queries using the Lookup By Example tool
- ☑ Query operators
- ☑ Running and saving queries
- ☑ Advanced queries
- ☑ Creating dynamic groups
- ☑ Sorting records retrieved from a query

Creating Queries

Queries Overview

Queries and lookups for that matter, are used to get answers to questions like "Which contacts are in a particular state and were referred by Agency 1 or Agency 2?". Another question a query could answer would be "Which customers have not been contacted in the last 60 days?". You have learned how to use the Lookup command to find contacts. Depending on the types of contacts that you are trying to find, you will have to perform several lookups. If you needed to find contacts in two cities, you would have to perform two lookups and add the results of the second lookup to the results of the first lookup.

The Lookup By Example dialog box resembles the Contact detail view. It contains all of the fields that are on the layout. If you add a field to the top of a layout or to a tab, it will also appear on the Lookup By Example dialog box.

Queries have several advantages over lookups. Queries are used to find contacts based on multiple values in the same field or find contacts that match criteria in more than one field at the same time. Another advantage of using queries is that you can save them and use them again. You can create contact, company, group and opportunity lookups on the Lookup By Example dialog box. If you need to lookup data in a range of values, you have to use the Advanced Query tool.

Like other features in ACT!, there is more than one way to create a query. You can use the Lookup By Example dialog box or the Advanced Query tool. In this chapter you will learn how to create queries using both options.

Saved Query File Extensions
Saved queries have one of the file extensions listed below.
.QRY are contact queries.
.CRY are company queries.
.GRY are group queries.
.ORY are opportunity queries.

Exercise 13.1: Creating Queries Using The Lookup By Example Tool

The primary reason to use the Lookup By Example tool is to save a query without having to create all of the syntax that is required when using the Advanced Query tool. The other reason to use the Lookup By Example tool instead of the Lookup technique is if you need to perform the lookup on more than one field. In this exercise you will create a query to find all customers in Arizona.

1. Make sure that all of the contacts are displayed. Lookup ⇒ By Example. You should see the Lookup By Example dialog box.

2. Select AZ in the State field.

3. Check the Customer option in the **ID/STATUS** field drop-down list. You should have the options selected that are shown in Figure 13-1.

Some of the tabs like Personal Info, Contact Access, and User Fields, display fields and some do not, like the History and Notes tabs. The tabs that have fields displayed can be used in the lookup.

Chapter 13

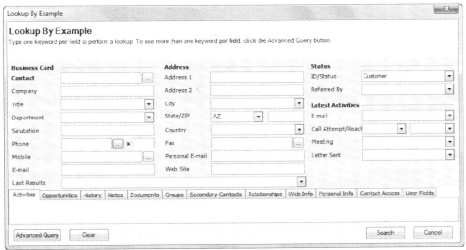

Figure 13-1 Lookup By Example search criteria

Saving Lookup By Example Queries

If you create a query that you will want to run again, you should save it. If you save the query you can also edit and use it as the basis for another query. Actually, you should save the query before you run it. If you do not save the query before it is run and discover that you did not select the correct options, you will have to start over. You cannot save the query on the Lookup By Example dialog box. You have to save it using the Advanced Query tool.

1. Click the Advanced Query button, then click the **SAVE** button (last button at the top) on the Contact Criteria dialog box. The default folder for saving queries that ACT! uses is automatically displayed.

2. Navigate to your folder and type `Customers in AZ` as the query name, then press Enter.

3. You should see the query name in the Title bar at the top of the Contact Criteria dialog box.

   Click the Preview button. The contact records that meet the criteria of the query will be displayed at the bottom of the dialog box, as shown in Figure 13-2.

   There should be nine customers in AZ.

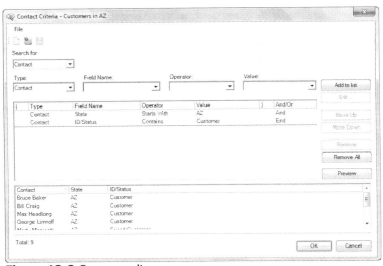

Figure 13-2 Query results

13-3

Creating Queries

The **ADD TO LIST** button adds the criteria from the Type, Field Name, Operator and Value fields to the grid in the middle of the dialog box.

The **EDIT** button opens the Edit dialog box, which is used to modify the selected row of criteria in the grid.

The **MOVE UP** and **MOVE DOWN** buttons are used to change the order of the criteria in the grid.

The **REMOVE** button will delete the criteria on the row that is selected.

The **REMOVE ALL** button deletes all of the criteria.

The **PREVIEW** button runs the query and displays the results at the bottom of the dialog box.

4. Click OK. You will see the dialog box shown in Figure 13-3.

   Click OK.

   If you scroll through the records in the Contact detail view, you will see that each record has **CUSTOMER** in the ID/Status field and **AZ** in the State field.

Figure 13-3 ACT! Run Query Options dialog box

Wildcards

The Lookup By Example tool has two wildcard characters that are used to search for characters in a field. They are discussed below. The default search method will only search for the characters that you enter.

① The **%** (percent sign). This wildcard character is used to find characters any place in the field. If you wanted to find all companies that had a specific word or character, you would type the percent sign followed by the characters that you want to search for like this, %Toys. If you entered this in the Company field, all of the records with "Toys" any place in the Company field would be retrieved.

② The **_** (underscore). Use this wildcard character to replace one character in the string of characters that you are searching for. If you entered t_n as the search criteria, the search would return records that have ten, tan and ton in the field, but not toon.

 If you used a version prior to ACT! 2007 and used the asterisk (*) in a lookup or query and tried it in ACT! 2009 or higher, you saw that it did not work. I do not know why, but the functionality of the asterisk has been changed to the percent sign (%).

Exercise 13.2: How To Run A Saved Query

There are two ways that you can run a saved query, as discussed below.

① From the Advanced Query window (Lookup ⇒ Advanced ⇒ Advanced Query).
② Add it to the Lookup menu and run it from there.

Chapter 13

How To Run A Query From The Advanced Query Window

1. Lookup ⇒ Advanced ⇒ Advanced Query.

2. Click the Open button, then double-click on the query, Customers in AZ, in your folder.

3. Click OK, then select **REPLACE LOOKUP** and click OK. You will see the same nine contacts. If more records were added to the database that met the criteria, they would appear at the bottom of the dialog box. Lookup ⇒ All Contacts.

Advanced Queries

You will need to create an advanced query when the Lookup command and Lookup By Example query options will not retrieve the records that you need. This is usually the case when you need to search for two or more values in the same field. An example of when you would need to create an advanced query is if you need to find all customers and prospects in AZ. Advanced queries are a little harder to create then Lookup By Example queries because syntax is required, but it is not as difficult as you may think. Some conditions must be enclosed in parentheses as shown below.

(ID/STATUS = CUSTOMER OR ID/STATUS = PROSPECT) AND STATE = AZ

The equation above will find all contacts that have "Customer" or "Prospect" in the ID/Status field and AZ in the State field. There is a syntax checker to help you fix syntax errors. You can convert a Lookup By Example query to an advanced query. This may save you some time when creating an advanced query.

Earlier you created a query to find all customers that are in AZ. You can recreate this query on the Lookup By Example dialog box and then open the **ADVANCED QUERY** dialog box to add the prospect criteria to the query.

Even though you can create the entire query in the Advanced Query dialog box, some people feel more comfortable creating as much of an advanced query in the Lookup By Example dialog box as possible and then open the Advanced Query dialog box to finish creating the query.

Query Options

There are four options (drop-down lists) on the Advanced Query dialog box that are used to create the criteria for a query, as explained below.

① **Type** Is used to select the record type (Contact, Company, Opportunity, etc) for the field that you need to create criteria for. The option selected in this field controls the fields that are displayed in the Field Name drop-down list. For example, if you select Company in the Type field, the fields in the Field Name drop-down list will be Company fields.

② **Field Name** Is used to select the field that you will create the criteria for.

③ **Operator** They are used to describe the relationship between the criteria in the query. This relationship is a comparison of the data in the database to the value selected in the query. "Starts With" is the default operator. Table 13-1 explains the query operators. You will only see operators that the selected field can use.

④ **Value** This field contains the data that you want to use in the comparison. If the field selected has a drop-down list, the options in the Value drop-down list come from the data in the field in the database. If the field does not have a drop-down list, you have to type in the value.

Creating Queries

Query Operators

This Operator	Will Find Records That . . .
After Next [days]	Have a date in the future that is at least the number of days from today that you enter in the Value field. (1) (2)
Contains	Have the criteria that you enter any place in the field.
Contains Data	Have data in the field, meaning the field is not empty. (3) (4)
Day Equals [number]	Have the day of the month that you enter. (1)
Does Not Contain	Do not have the value entered in the Value field.
Does Not Contain Data	Do not have any data in the field, meaning that the field is empty. (3) (4)
Ends With	Have data in the field that ends with the criteria that you enter. (3)
Equal To (=)	Are equal to the criteria that you enter. (3)
Greater Than	Have an amount higher than the amount that you specify in the Value field. If you want to see all orders with an order amount over $500, enter $500 in the Value field and the query will display records with an order amount of $500.01 or more. (5)
Greater Than or Equal To	(Works similar to "Greater than"). The difference is that this operator will also select records that have the amount that you specify. In the greater than example above, the query would not retrieve records with an order amount of exactly $500. The greater than or equal to operator will. (5)
Less Than	Have an amount less than the amount that you specify in the Value field. If you want to see products that have a reorder level of less than 10 items in stock, enter 10 in the Value field and the query will display products with a reorder level of nine or less. (5)
Less Than or Equal To	(Works similar to "Less than"). The difference is that this operator will also select records that have the amount that you specify. In the less than example above, the query would not retrieve records with a reorder level of 10 items. The less than or equal to operator will. (5)
Month Equals [number]	Have the month that you enter. (1)
Not Equal To (!=)	Do not have data that matches the criteria that you enter. (3)
Starts With	Have data in the field that starts with the criteria that you enter. (3)
Older Than [days]	Have a date that is more than the number (of days) that you enter. (1) (2)
On or After	Have a date that is greater than or equal to the date that you enter. (1)
On or Before	Have a date that is equal to or less than the date that you enter. (1)
Within Last [days]	Have a date that is within the previous number of days that you specify. (1)
Within Next [days]	Have a date that is within the next number of days that you specify. (1)
Year Equals [number]	Have the year that you enter. (1)

Table 13-1 Query operators explained

(1) This operator is only for date fields.
(2) This operator is not available for the Birth date field in the Contact table.
(3) This operator is for text fields.
(4) The Value field is not enabled when this operator is selected.
(5) This operator is only for numeric fields.

Exercise 13.3: How To Create An Advanced Query

1. Lookup ⇒ Advanced ⇒ Advanced Query, then open the Customers in AZ query.

2. Select the criteria in the Field Name, Operator and Value fields shown at the top of Figure 13-4. The criteria shown at the bottom of the figure is from the Customers in AZ query.

Figure 13-4 Criteria options to select

Contact Type
In ACT! 2012, this type was called **CONTACTS**. It was renamed back to Contact in ACT! 2013. Why they developers keep changing it is beyond my comprehension.

If you look in the **AND/OR** column in the grid, you will see that contacts must meet the criteria of the State starting with AZ and the ID/Status field starting with Customer. Changing the value of the And/Or field in the first ID/Status criteria row to **OR** will retrieve contacts if the value in the ID/Status field is Customer or Prospect, which is what you want in this exercise.

If you previewed the contacts now, based on the criteria shown in Figure 13-5, the query would not retrieve any records. That is because the query criteria needs to enclose the two ID/Status rows of criteria in parentheses so that if a contact has the status of Customer or Prospect, the state still has to be equal to AZ.

Figure 13-5 Incomplete criteria

Using **AND** means that you want both conditions to be met: The condition on the first row with the And condition (in the And/Or column) and the condition on the row below it.

For example, if you want to find all customer and prospect records in AZ that were edited between 1/1/2010 and 5/21/2011, you would create the criteria shown in Figure 13-6.

Figure 13-6 Status, State and Date range criteria

Creating Queries

 I am not sure why "Starts With" is used as the default operator on the Lookup By Example and Lookup Opportunities dialog boxes when most people really want to use **EQUAL TO**. The "Starts With" operator does just that. The operator will look for all records that have the value that you enter at the beginning of the field. Using the Starts With operator can return unexpected results. The problem that I have with using the Starts With operator is that if there are other values that "Start with" the same characters as those in the Value field, those records will also be retrieved when the query is run.

I personally do not use the Starts With operator for this reason. From a programmers perspective, the query criteria shown earlier in Figure 13-5 is not what most users want. The criteria shown in Figure 13-7 is what should be used. You will find out how to correct this query later in the chapter when you learn how to edit a query.

(	Type	Field Name	Operator	Value	)	And/Or
	Contact	State	Equal To (=)	AZ		And
((	Contact	ID/Status	Equal To (=)	Customer		Or
	Contact	ID/Status	Equal To (=)	Prospect	))	And

Figure 13-7 Equal to criteria

3. Click the **ADD TO LIST** button.

4. Click in the **(** column of the first ID/Status criteria row, as shown in Figure 13-8, then select **((**.

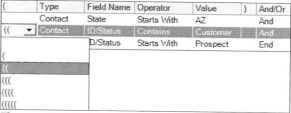

Figure 13-8 Left parenthesis criteria options

5. Open the And/Or drop-down list for the first ID/Status criteria row and select **OR**, as shown in Figure 13-9.

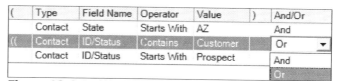

Figure 13-9 And/Or criteria options

Check The Query Syntax

If you preview a query and see a message similar to the one shown in Figure 13-10, it means that there is something wrong with the syntax (code) of the query.

In this example, the message is telling you that there is something wrong with the parentheses.

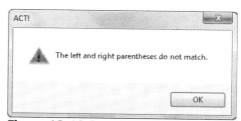

Figure 13-10 Query syntax error message

Look at the parentheses in the query. There should be an equal number of each type of parentheses that you select and the parentheses should be on different lines.

1. If you see the message shown above in Figure 13-10, click OK and fix the query criteria based on the message.

2. Click in the) column on the last criteria row and select)), as shown in Figure 13-11.

Figure 13-11 Right parenthesis criteria options

Save And Run The Query

1. File ⇒ Save As.

2. Type Customers & Prospects in AZ in the File name field, then click the Save button.

3. Click OK. Select Replace Lookup, then click OK. There should be 14 contacts displayed in the Contact list view.

Exercise 13.4: Find Records Created In The Last 30 Days Query

You may have the need to know which contacts you added to the database or modified in the past. An example would be if you wanted to review all of the contacts that you added to the database in the last 30 days. The field that stores when a contact record is added to the database is the **CREATE DATE** field.

1. Lookup ⇒ Advanced ⇒ Advanced Query.

2. Select the Create Date field.

3. Select the **WITHIN LAST [DAYS]** operator, then type 30 in the Value field.

4. Click the Add to list button. You should have the criteria shown in Figure 13-12.

Figure 13-12 Last 30 days criteria

5. Save the query in your folder as New contacts in last 30 days.

6. Preview the results. You will see the contact records that you have added in the last 30 days.

 If you edit the criteria shown above in Figure 13-12 and change the Field Name to **EDIT DATE**, you will see all of the contact records that you have edited in the last 30 days.

Creating Queries

Exercise 13.5: Find Contacts In CA With Open Opportunities

In this exercise you will create a query that finds contacts in California that have opportunities with an open status.

1. If the Contact Criteria dialog box is still open, click the New button, otherwise, Lookup ⇒ Advanced ⇒ Advanced Query.

2. Select the State field, Equal To operator and CA from the Value drop-down list, then click the Add to list button.

3. Open the Type drop-down list and select Opportunity.

4. Select the Status field and Equal To operator, then type 1 in the Value field.

5. Click the Add to list button. You should have the options shown in Figure 13-13.

   Click the Preview button.

(	Type	Field Name	Operator	Value	)	And/Or
	Contact	State	Equal To (=)	CA		And
	Opportunity	Status	Equal To (=)	1		End

   Figure 13-13 Contacts in CA with open opportunities criteria

6. Save the query as Open Opportunities in CA.

7. Run the query. You will see the contacts in CA that have open opportunities. If you double-click on a contact, on the Opportunities tab, you will see at least one open opportunity for the contact.

> **Opening Existing Queries From The Advanced Query Dialog Box**
> Before you open an existing query, you have to select the type of query that you want to open in the Search for drop-down list at the top of the dialog box.

How To Edit A Query

If you need to edit a query you can follow the steps below. For now you can just read this section. If you want to practice editing a query you can change the operator on each criteria row to Equal To (=) in the Customers & Prospects in AZ query.

1. Open the query that you want to edit in the Advanced Query dialog box.

2. Click on the criteria row that needs to be changed, then click the Edit button.

   You will see the dialog box shown in Figure 13-14.

   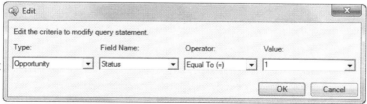

   Figure 13-14 Edit dialog box

3. Make the criteria changes that you need, then click OK. Save the changes.

Exercise 13.6: Sorting Records Retrieved From A Query

You can sort the records that the query retrieves. This will be useful if you will do a bulk mailing and need the records sorted in order by zip code when you print the mailing labels. You can sort the records from the query in the detail or list view by following the steps below.

1. Lookup all contacts. Edit ⇒ Sort.

2. Open the **SORT BY** drop-down list, then select Zip Code.

3. Change the **AND THEN BY** option to <None>.

   You should have the options selected that are shown in Figure 13-15.

   Click OK. The records in the Contact list view will now be sorted by zip code.

Figure 13-15 Sort dialog box options

Dynamically Linking Contacts To Companies

Chapter 5 covered how to manually link contacts to companies. If you want to be able to have contacts automatically linked to a company, you have to create a query.

An example of when this would be useful is when you want to have certain fields filled in for the contact. This is one way to make sure that the data is being maintained. If you needed to make sure that every contact record has a company name, you could create a query that looks for records that do not have data in the Company field.

This works for the Company field, but not for other types of linked fields. For example, if you wanted to put all contact records that do not have a zip code into a company. If the Zip Code field is a linked field, this would not work. You would have to put the records in a group instead of a company.

Exercise 13.7: Find Prospects Query

In this exercise you will create a query to find prospect contacts in the US that do not have an email address. You can use the Lookup By Example and Advanced Query dialog boxes to get the contacts that meet the criteria. Using the Lookup By Example dialog box to create as much of the query as possible and then use the <Type> Criteria dialog box to complete the query is a good idea. (Type is a contact, company, group or opportunity.) This will keep you from having to create the entire query manually.

1. Create a query to display all customers with a prospect ID Status in the United States that do not have an email address.

2. Save the query in your folder as US Prospects with no email address. Figure 13-16 shows the query syntax.

(	Type	Field Name	Operator	Value	)	And/Or
	Contact	Country	Starts With	United States		And
	Contact	ID/Status	Contains	Prospect		And
	Contact	E-mail	Does Not Contain Data	Nothing		End

Figure 13-16 Prospects without an email address query

Creating Queries

Exercise 13.8: How To Create A Dynamic Group

In Exercise 6.6 you created a Sales Reps group and added contacts to it. As time goes on, more contacts will be added to the database and some of them will be sales reps. You could create a lookup to find the new contacts that are sales reps, but you would have to do that on a regular basis so that all of the contacts with this title will be in the group. ACT! has a dynamic option that can be used to create criteria to automatically add records to a group. The dynamic option also causes records to automatically be removed from a group, if they no longer meet the criteria. This is done by creating a query. In this exercise you will modify the Sales Reps group so that it is dynamic. You can add as much criteria as needed to create a dynamic group.

1. On the Group detail view, click on the Sales Reps group in the tree, then click the Add/Remove Contacts button on the Contacts tab.

2. Click the Edit Criteria button on the Add/Remove Contacts dialog box.

3. Open the Field Name drop-down list and select **TITLE**.
   Open the Operator drop-down list and select **EQUAL TO (=)**.
   Open the Value drop-down list and select **SALES REPRESENTATIVE**.

4. Click the Add to list button. You should have the criteria shown in Figure 13-17.

(	Type	Field Name	Operator	Value	)	And/Or
	Contact	Title	Equal To (=)	Sales Representative		End

Figure 13-17 Sales rep group criteria

 If you make a mistake, click on the criteria under the drop-down lists that needs to be changed, then click the **EDIT** button to correct the mistake.

5. Click the **PREVIEW** button. You should see five contacts at the bottom of the dialog box. Click OK to close the Group Criteria dialog box.

6. You should see the criteria in the **DYNAMIC MEMBERS** section of the Add/Remove Contacts dialog box, as shown in Figure 13-18.

   Click OK.

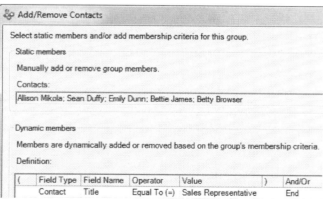

Figure 13-18 Dynamic criteria

Chapter 13

 Contacts that are added to the group via a query will stay in the group as long as they meet the criteria. In the exercise that you just completed, if any of the contacts that were added dynamically has a change in title, they will automatically be removed from the Sales Reps group. If you add a contact to this group manually, they will stay in the group whether or not they meet the criteria.

It is probably best to link contacts to a company on more than the Company name field. It is possible that there is more than one company with the same name in the database, meaning one company could end with "Inc" and the other one doesn't. If you also linked on the street address, the chances of linking to the wrong company is greatly reduced.

 Creating Dynamic Companies
To create a dynamic company, start from the Company detail view in step 1 above instead of the group detail view.

Test The Dynamic Group Criteria

1. Create new records for the contacts in Table 13-2.

   The last two records in the table should automatically be added to the Sales Reps group.

Contact	Title
Tim Dynamic	Sales Manager
Tina Dynamic	Sales Representative
Tom Dynamic	Sales Representative

Table 13-2 Test records for the dynamic group criteria

2. Click the Groups button, then click on the Sales Reps group. You should see the records for Tina and Tom Dynamic, as illustrated in Figure 13-19.

   The Groups/Companies tab on the Contact detail view does not automatically show dynamic groups that the contact is a member of.

You have to click the **SHOW DYNAMIC MEMBERSHIP** button, illustrated in Figure 13-20, to see if the contact is a member of a dynamic group. When you click this button you will see the dialog box shown in Figure 13-21. This dialog box lets you know which dynamic groups the contact is a member of.

Figure 13-19 Result of the dynamic group criteria

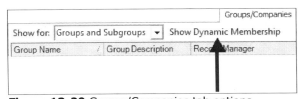

Figure 13-20 Groups/Companies tab options

13-13

Creating Queries

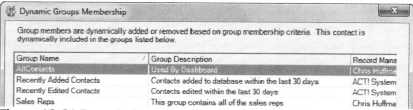

Figure 13-21 Dynamic Groups Membership dialog box

The query for the dynamic group that you just created will automatically run each time either of the following actions occur:

① The Group detail view is opened.
② The Groups/Companies tab is displayed.

USING SMART TASKS

In this chapter you will learn the following Smart Tasks features:

- ☑ Workflow
- ☑ Available steps
- ☑ Duplicating and editing a template
- ☑ Creating a new Smart Task template
- ☑ Running Smart Tasks
- ☑ Manage pending Smart Tasks

Using Smart Tasks

Smart Tasks Overview

Smart Tasks are similar to an activity series because they are a series of related tasks. The difference is that Smart Tasks are automatic and cause an action like scheduling an activity as a follow up or automatically sending an email to contacts based on a condition, to be run without your intervention. Smart Tasks can be created for contact or opportunity records.

Smart Task templates can have more than one step. You can use the Smart Task templates that come with ACT! as they are, modify them or you can create your own template. There are several ways to access Smart Tasks, as listed below.

① Schedule ⇒ Manage Smart Tasks, as shown in Figure 14-1. The menu options are explained in Table 14-1.
② In either contact view, click on the Manage Smart Tasks link in the Related Tasks list.
③ In either opportunity view, click on the Manage Smart Tasks link in the Related Tasks list.

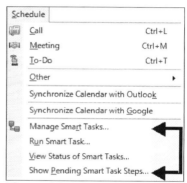

Figure 14-1 Smart Task menu options

Option	Description
Manage Smart Tasks	Opens the dialog box shown in Figure 14-2.
Run Smart Task	Is used to manually run a Smart Task.
View Status of Smart Tasks	Displays the Status tab on the Manage Smart Tasks dialog box.
Show Pending Smart Task Steps	Opens the Pending Smart Tasks Steps dialog box, which is used to view or edit the steps of a Smart Task.

Table 14-1 Smart Task menu options explained

Managing Smart Tasks

The left column in Figure 14-2 shows the Smart Task templates that come with ACT!. On this dialog box you can create, edit, duplicate and delete Smart Task templates.

Workflow

The workflow (is below the Auto-Run option shown in Figure 14-2) displays all of the steps in the selected Smart Task. The workflow for a Smart Task is created in a template. Templates can also use queries to select the records that will be used for the Smart Task.

The first box (known as the top level) in the workflow, shows the details of the Smart Task. The remaining boxes are the steps in the Smart Task. Notice that each step can be edited.

Clicking the **EDIT** button displays the criteria for that step in the Smart Task. A trigger is used to select when the Smart Task should run.

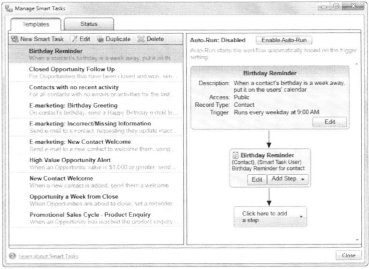

Figure 14-2 Manage Smart Tasks dialog box

Available Steps

As shown in Figure 14-3, there are several types of steps that can be created.

Figure 14-4 shows the options for the Time Delay step. This step is used to select when the next step should start, after the previous step is completed.

Figure 14-5 shows the options for the Send E-mail step.

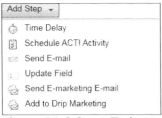

Figure 14-3 Smart Tasks step options

Using Email In A Smart Task
Currently, Outlook is the only email software that Smart Tasks support. You can create an email step without having Outlook installed on your computer, but the step will fail if it is run on a computer that does not have Outlook installed.

The **UPDATE FIELD** step is new in ACT! 2013. It is used to change the value in a field. You can select to have the user prompted before the update takes place. This Smart Task step will remind you of the Replace Data dialog box. [See Chapter 4, Exercise 4.10]

Using Smart Tasks

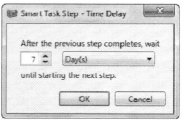

Figure 14-4 Time Delay step options

Figure 14-5 Send E-mail step options

Deleting A Template
If you delete a template, the scheduled tasks associated with the template are not deleted.

Exercise 14.1: Duplicate And Modify A Smart Task Template

Instead of saving changes to a Smart Task template in this exercise, you will learn how to duplicate a template and change it to meet your needs. In this exercise, you will duplicate the Contacts with no recent activity template, change the frequency that the Smart Task runs and enable the Auto-Run feature. There are three required steps and two optional steps for modifying a Smart Task template.

Step 1: Duplicate The Template

Editing And Duplicating Smart Task Templates
If you need to edit or duplicate a template, the **RECORD TYPE** and **TRIGGER** fields cannot be changed.

1. Open the Manage Smart Tasks dialog box.

2. Click on the Contacts with no recent activity template, then click the **DUPLICATE** button.

Step 2: Modify The Template

1. On the New Smart Task dialog box, change the Smart Task Name to `Contacts without activity in 30 days`.

2. Change the Description to 30 days, instead of 90 days.

3. Select the Monthly option, then select the **FIRST** and **WEEKDAY** options.

Chapter 14

Step 3: Modify The Filter Criteria

At the bottom of the New Smart Tasks dialog box you will see the criteria used to select the contact records for this task. Currently, if the data in several fields is greater than 90 days, an activity record is created for the Record Manager (owner of the contact record) to contact them. In this part of the exercise, you will modify the criteria to 30 days.

> **EDIT CONDITIONS BUTTON** In ACT! 2012 and earlier, this button was named Edit Criteria.
> **SMART TASK CONDITIONS DIALOG BOX** In ACT! 2012 and earlier, this dialog box was named Smart Task Criteria.

1. Click the Edit Conditions button. The Smart Task Conditions dialog box should look familiar.

2. Change the value in all four criteria rows to 30, as shown in Figure 14-6, then click OK.

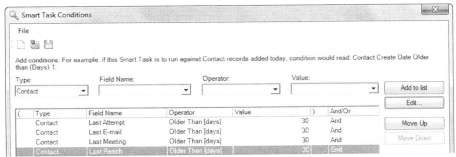

Figure 14-6 Modified Smart Task criteria

3. Clear the Run only once for any record option, at the bottom of the dialog box.

   You should have the options shown in Figure 14-7.

   Click OK.

   You will see your template in the list on the Manage Smart Tasks dialog box.

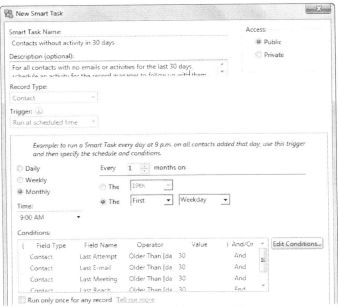

Figure 14-7 New Smart Task dialog box options

Using Smart Tasks

Run Only Once For Any Record Option
This option is at the bottom of the New Smart Task dialog box, shown above in Figure 14-7. If checked, this option prevents a Smart Task from being automatically run (meaning that the Auto-Run feature is already enabled for the Smart Task), against a record more than once by the same user. If the Smart Task is run using records that you select, the Run only option is ignored, even if it is checked.

Step 4: Add, Edit And Delete Steps
This step is optional. It is used to edit steps in the template. For example, the template that you modified in Exercise 14.1 has a step that creates a To-do follow up activity. You could change the Activity Type to Call to edit the step or you could add other contacts to the activity.

Adding A Step
To add a step, click the **ADD STEP** button in the workflow section of the Manage Smart Tasks dialog box. You will see the options shown earlier in Figure 14-3.

Deleting A Step
To delete a step, hold the mouse pointer over the step that you want to delete, as illustrated in Figure 14-8.

When you click on the X in the upper right corner of the step, you will see a message asking if you are sure that you want to delete the step.

Click Yes.

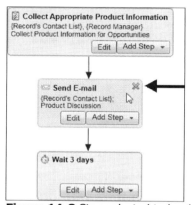

Figure 14-8 Step selected to be deleted

> **Rearranging Steps**
> If you need to change the order of the steps in the template you can, by dragging the step that you want to move, up or down. When you drag the step, you will see a bar in the workflow, in the location that the step will be moved to, as illustrated in Figure 14-9. You will also see the name of the step that you are moving. When you release the mouse button, the step will be moved, as shown in Figure 14-10.

Chapter 14

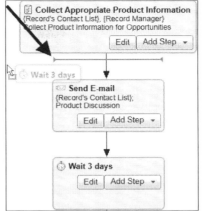

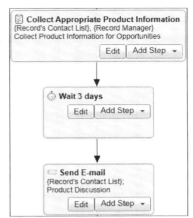

Figure 14-9 Step selected to be moved   **Figure 14-10** Step moved

Step 5: Enable Auto-Run

Using Auto-Run is optional. You can use the Auto-Run feature and still run a Smart Task manually. If this option is enabled, the Smart Task will run automatically, based on a trigger.

1. Click the **ENABLE AUTO-RUN** button on the template that you created. You will see an icon to the left of the template name. This lets you know that the Auto-Run option is enabled for the template.

2. Close the Manage Smart Tasks dialog box. On the first weekday of next month, the Smart Task that you created will automatically run.

Running A Smart Task Manually

 Downside Of Running A Smart Task Manually
While the concept of Smart Tasks is good, the process of manually running a Smart Task is disappointing, at least to me. The reason is because the filter criteria created in the Smart Task is ignored, when the task is run manually. This means that the Smart Task will probably not be run for the records that you intended. There are two ways to get around this, as explained below. Either option has to be completed before opening the Manage Smart Tasks dialog box to retrieve the records for the Smart Task.

① Create a query or run an existing query.
② Create a lookup.

The steps below show you how to run a Smart Task manually.

1. Schedule ⇒ Run Smart Task.

Using Smart Tasks

2. Select the Smart Task that you created, then select the **CURRENT LOOKUP** option, shown in Figure 14-11.

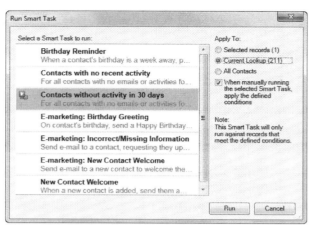

Figure 14-11 Run Smart Task dialog box

3. Click the **RUN** button.

   You will see the dialog box shown in Figure 14-12.

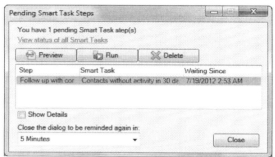

Figure 14-12 Pending Smart Task Steps dialog box

Viewing And Editing Pending Smart Tasks

As shown above in Figure 14-12, you see a list of items that are scheduled to run. Each contact or opportunity record that meets the criteria will have the task in the step created. The options on the Pending Smart Task Steps dialog box are explained in Table 14-2.

Option	Description
View status of all Smart Tasks	Clicking on this link displays the Status tab on the Manage Smart Tasks dialog box, as shown in Figure 14-13. The options are explained in Table 14-3.
Preview	Displays the task for the step. Examples of tasks are emails and activities.
Run	Is used to process the selected item. If the selected item is suppose to create an activity, it will be created. More than one item can be selected and run at the same time. Once the item is processed, it is removed from this dialog box and the status is changed to In Progress. (1)
Delete	Removes the selected item from the dialog box. This will change the status to Cancelled. (1)
Show Details	If checked, the information about the step is displayed.
Close the dialog to be reminded again in	Is used to select when you want this dialog box to open again automatically.

Table 14-2 Pending Smart Task Steps dialog box options explained

14-8

Chapter 14

(1) This status change is on the Status tab on the Manage Smart Tasks dialog box.

It would be nice if there was a way to apply the pause, resume and cancel options to multiple tasks at the same time.

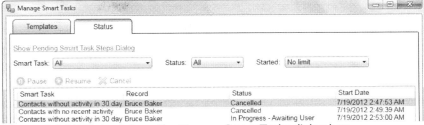

Figure 14-13 Status tab on the Manage Smart Tasks dialog box

Option	Description
Smart Task	This filter is used to select the name of the Smart Task that you want to display. It is very possible that there are items from different templates, displayed on the tab at the same time.
Status	This filter is used to select a specific status of items to display.
Started	This filter is used to select a time frame of items to display based on their start date.
Pause/Resume	Is used to keep the selected items from being processed. The status will change to **PAUSED**, as illustrated in Figure 14-14. When you are ready to allow the item to be processed, click the **RESUME** button.
Cancel	Is used to permanently keep the item from being processed. Once this option is applied, it cannot be undone.

Table 14-3 Status tab options explained

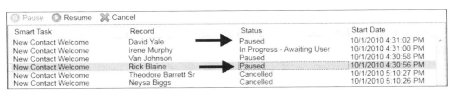

Figure 14-14 Paused items illustrated

4. Close the Pending Smart Task Steps dialog box.

Exercise 14.2: Create A Smart Task Template

In this exercise you will create a new template that has the following five steps.

① Send a postcard to contacts with an opportunity that meets certain criteria.
② 7 day time delay.
③ Send an email with an attachment to the contacts record manager.
④ 3 day time delay.
⑤ Create a follow up activity.

 Step 1 above is for a postcard activity. This activity type has not been created yet. If you want to create it, complete Exercise 15.11 before starting this exercise, otherwise, in Step 1: Create The Postcard Activity on the next page, select a different activity type.

Using Smart Tasks

Create The Template

1. Open the Manage Smart Tasks dialog box, then click the New Smart Task button.

2. In the Smart Task Name field type `Open Opportunities`.

3. In the Description field type `This template is used to follow up with contacts that have an opportunity created since 1/1/2009, that is open and has a total amount greater than or equal to $100.`

4. Open the Record type drop-down list and select Opportunity.

> In ACT! 2012, the Record Type was named Opportunities. In ACT! 2013 it was renamed to Opportunity.

5. Open the Trigger drop-down list and select Run at scheduled time.

   You should have the options shown in Figure 14-15.

Figure 14-15 New Smart Task template options

Select When The Smart Task Will Run

1. Select the Weekly option.

2. Select Tuesday and Friday.

3. Select 8 AM for the (run) Time.

Create The Criteria

1. Click the **EDIT CONDITIONS** button.

2. Create the Opportunity Smart Task criteria in Table 14-4, which should look like the criteria shown in Figure 14-16.

Field Name	Operator	Value
Create Date	On or After	1/1/2009
Total	Greater Than or Equal To	100
Status	Equal to	0 (for the Open status)

Table 14-4 Opportunity criteria

Chapter 14

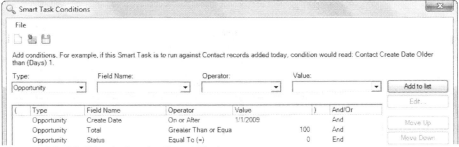

Figure 14-16 Criteria for the Smart Task

3. Click OK.

   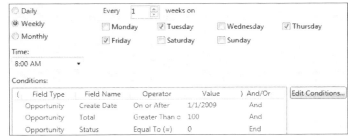

   The schedule and filter options should look like the ones shown in Figure 14-17.

   Click OK to close the New Smart Task dialog box.

Figure 14-17 Schedule and filter options

Step 1: Create The Postcard Activity

1. Select the Open Opportunities template. On the right side of the dialog box, click the Add a Step button, then select the Schedule ACT! Activity option.

2. In the Step Name field, type `Step 1: Send Postcard`.

3. Select the Automatically Schedule activity option, then select the Appointment Activity Type. After you complete Exercise 15.11, come back here and change the activity type to Post Card Mailing.

4. Change the Start Time to 9 AM.

5. In the Regarding field, type `Contact has open opportunity greater than $100`.

14-11

Using Smart Tasks

6. Change the Priority to High.

   The activity should look like the one shown in Figure 14-18.

   Click OK.

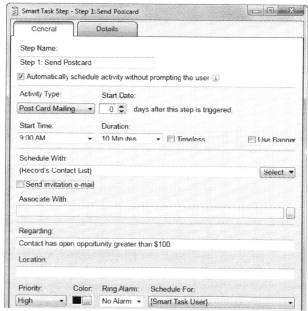

Figure 14-18 Step 1 Postcard activity options

Step 2: Create A 7 Day Time Delay

1. Click the Add Step button, then select the Time Delay option.

2. Select the options shown in Figure 14-19, then click OK.

   This time delay step will prevent the next step (in this exercise, the create an email step) from starting until seven days after the previous step (in this exercise, the create a postcard step) has been marked as completed.

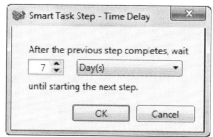

Figure 14-19 7 day time delay options

Step 3: Create An Email For The Contact Record Manager

1. Click the Add Step button on the Time delay step, then select the Send E-mail option.

2. In the Step Name field, type Step 3: Send email to Record Manager.

3. Select the Automatically send email option.

14-12

4. Click the Contacts button at the end of the To field, then select Record Manager, as shown in Figure 14-20.

   The options on the Contacts button are explained in Table 14-5.

Figure 14-20 Contacts button options

Option	Description
Select Contacts	Opens the Select Contacts dialog box so that you can select more contacts to add to the email.
Record's Contact List	Will add the contacts associated with the contact or opportunity that was selected before the Smart Task was selected, to the email.
Record Manager	Adds the user responsible for the contact or opportunity that was selected before the Smart Task was selected, to the email.
Smart Task User	Adds the user that started the Smart Task to the email.

Table 14-5 Contacts button options explained

5. In the Subject field type Opportunity follow-up reminder.

6. Click the Browse button, then double-click on the C3 Attach file.

7. In the Message field type, This is a reminder to follow up with the contact from the post card mailing.

8. Click the **MORE OPTIONS** button, then select the Request Read Receipt option.

9. Open the History Type drop-down list and select the recommended option.

   You should have the options shown in Figure 14-21.

   Click OK.

Figure 14-21 Step 3 Email task options

Step 4: Create A 3 Day Time Delay

1. Click the Add Step button, then select the Time Delay option.

2. Select the options for a 3 day delay, then click OK.

Using Smart Tasks

Step 5: Create The Follow Up Activity

1. Click the Add Step button, then select the Schedule ACT! Activity option.

2. In the Step Name field type, Step 5: Follow up on postcard mailing.

3. Select the Automatically schedule activity option.

4. Select the following options:
   - To-do Activity Type
   - 8 AM Start time
   - Use Banner option

   You should have the options shown in Figure 14-22. Click OK. Your Smart Task template should look like the one shown in Figure 14-23.

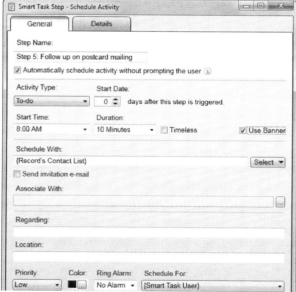

Figure 14-22 Step 5 Follow up activity options

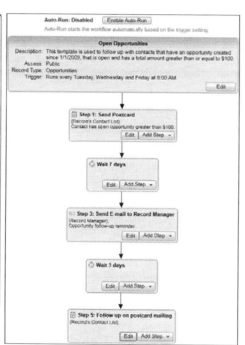

Figure 14-23 Smart Task template

14-14

CUSTOMIZING ACT!

In this chapter you will learn several ways to customize ACT!, including how to:

- ☑ Modify preferences
- ☑ Create and edit drop-down list fields
- ☑ Modify fields
- ☑ Customize columns
- ☑ Create new fields
- ☑ Create an annual event

CHAPTER 15

Customizing ACT!

Why Waiting To Customize ACT! Is A Good Idea

I suspect that this may be the chapter that many readers are very interested in. There was a time when I wanted to customize (aka tweak) software as soon as I installed it, even if I did not know how to use the software. When you think about it, how could one customize software that they really do not know? I call it "Click Fever". We really like clicking on options to see what will happen. Depending on how well you already know the software, that may not be a problem.

If you are not very familiar with the software, waiting until you have used it for a while before customizing it is probably a good idea. If you have a question or something does not work as expected, you will not know if it is a problem with the software or if the cause is from a change that you made and were not aware of all of the ways that a certain customization effects the software.

Modifying Preferences

There are several options in ACT! that you can modify. Chapter 2 covered how to modify the General preferences. In this chapter you will learn how to modify other options on the Preferences dialog box.

Name And Salutation Preferences

You learned how ACT! displays the contact names that you enter. [See Chapter 3, Exercise 3.1] If the default prefix and suffix options do not meet your needs, the options shown in Figures 15-1 to 15-4 should help. The options that are selected in the figures are the defaults.

Tools ⇒ Preferences ⇒ General tab ⇒ Salutation Preferences button, opens this dialog box.

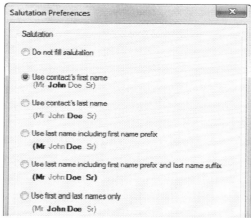

Figure 15-1 Salutation Preferences dialog box

The options shown in the list on the right of Figure 15-2 are the prefixes that ACT! will ignore as being the contacts first name. You can add or delete items in these lists.

Tools ⇒ Preferences ⇒ Admin tab ⇒ Name Preferences button, opens this dialog box.

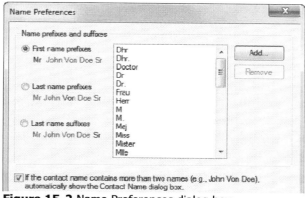

Figure 15-2 Name Preferences dialog box

Chapter 15

The **LAST NAME PREFIXES** options shown in Figure 15-3 are the first part of a last name that has two words.

An example would be Dr. Van Ost. "Van" is the type of prefix that you would add to this list if it was not already there.

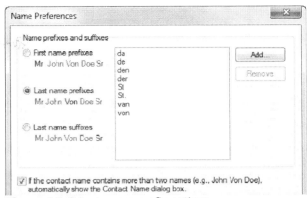

Figure 15-3 Last name prefix options

The **LAST NAME SUFFIXES** options shown in Figure 15-4 are a list of abbreviations that people use after their last name.

If they are the last word entered in the Contact field, they are ignored based on the default options that ACT! uses.

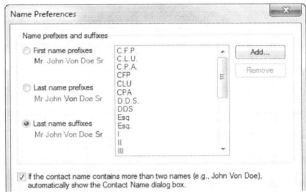

Figure 15-4 Last name suffix options

Exercise 15.1: Calendar Preferences

You can change some of the default calendar settings. The ones that you can change are the day that the calendar week starts on, the time slot increments on the daily and weekly calendars and whether or not you want to only show the current month in the mini-calendar.

1. Tools ⇒ Preferences ⇒ Calendar & Scheduling tab ⇒ **CALENDAR PREFERENCES** button.

Customizing ACT!

2. Change the options in Table 15-1.

Option	Change To
Start Time	9 AM
Daily Calendar	60 minutes

Table 15-1 Calendar options to change

Changing these options will cause the daily calendar to display the time slots in one hour increments.

The dialog box should have the options shown in Figure 15-5.

The default starting time of the calendar will now be 9 AM.

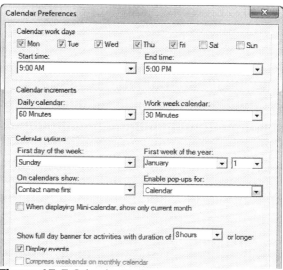

Figure 15-5 Calendar Preferences dialog box

Pop-Up Options

This option is on the Calendar Preferences dialog box shown above in Figure 15-5. ACT! has pop-ups that you may find useful. They will not slow down your computer like the pop-ups that you may see when surfing the Internet. Figure 15-6 shows the parts of ACT! that you can enable pop-ups for. By default, the calendar pop-ups are enabled. Check the options that you want and clear the check mark for the options that you do not want pop-ups for.

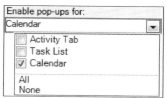

Figure 15-6 Pop-up options

3. Click OK to close the Calendar Preferences dialog box.

Exercise 15.2: Scheduling Preferences

Chapter 7 covered creating a variety of activities. ACT! has scheduling options that you can modify as needed. You can modify the following scheduling preferences:

① Activity type (Call, Meeting, To-Do).
② Priority levels.
③ Alarm options.
④ Have certain types of activities automatically roll over to the next day if they are not completed.
⑤ Designate how cleared activities should appear.

1. On the Calendar & Scheduling tab, click the Scheduling Preferences button.

To change the settings, click on the activity type that you want to change (call, meeting etc.), then select the options that you want to change. If modified, the options in the **DEFAULT ACTIVITY SETTINGS TO** section will change the default values that you see when you create an activity.

Chapter 15

2. Change the options in Table 15-2 for the To-Do activity type. Your dialog box should have the options selected that are shown in Figure 15-7.

Option	Change To
Ring alarm	15 minutes
Duration	1 Hour

Table 15-2 To-do activity options to change

If set, the alarm will start warning you 15 minutes prior to the start time of the activity.

If checked, the **AUTOMATICALLY ROLL OVER TO TODAY** option moves activities that have not been completed to the next day. This can be used to ensure that activities do not fall through the cracks, as they say. This option is only applied to activities that have a single user.

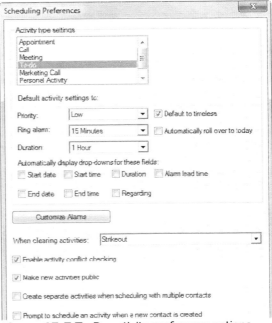

Figure 15-7 To-Do activity preference options

Depending on how many activities you schedule, you may want to check this option. I find this option most useful for phone calls that I did not complete. Take caution when using the roll over option because it is cumulative, meaning that all past activities that were not completed will also be rolled over.

If there were 500 activities that were not completed, all of them will be rolled over. The roll over is not automatic though.

When you open the database, you will be asked if you want to roll over the activities. You will see how many activities would be rolled over, as shown in Figure 15-8.

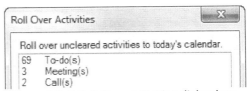

Figure 15-8 Roll Over Activities dialog box

If you create a lot of activities that need to be assigned to multiple contacts and want each contact to have an activity record created automatically, check the option **CREATE SEPARATE ACTIVITIES WHEN SCHEDULING WITH MULTIPLE CONTACTS**.

 If you want to set or remove the same options for all of the activity types, select all of the activity types in the **ACTIVITY TYPE SETTINGS** list and then make the changes to all of them at the same time.

Alarm Preferences

1. On the Scheduling Preferences dialog box, click the **CUSTOMIZE ALARMS** button.

   The options shown in Figure 15-9 are used to customize the sound that the alarm will make.

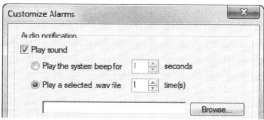

Figure 15-9 Customize Alarms dialog box

2. Click OK to close all of the dialog boxes.

Exercise 15.3: How To Customize The Contact List View

The Contact list view, as well as the Task List view, which you will learn about later, can be customized to sort records according to your needs. You can rearrange the order of the columns. You can make a column smaller or wider. You can also add and remove columns.

Rearrange The Order Of Columns

1. In the Contact list view, click on the Title column heading and drag it to the left, so that it is before the Contact column. The Contact list view should look like the one shown in Figure 15-10.

Figure 15-10 Title column moved

Resize A Column

1. Place the mouse pointer on the line between the Company and Title column headings. The mouse pointer is in the right place when you see a double-headed arrow, as shown in Figure 15-11.

Figure 15-11 Mouse pointer in position to resize a column

2. Hold down the left mouse button and drag the line to the right, as shown in Figure 15-12.

   Release the mouse button. The Company column should be wider.

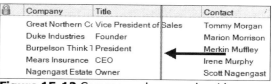

Figure 15-12 Company column made wider

Add A Column

1. Right-click in the list and select **CUSTOMIZE COLUMNS**.

   You should see the dialog box shown in Figure 15-13.

   The **AVAILABLE FIELDS** list contains all of the fields that have not already been added to the view.

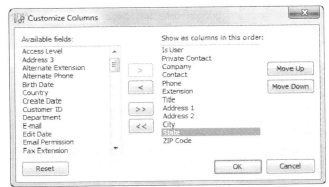

Figure 15-13 Customize Columns dialog box

The fields in the **SHOW AS COLUMNS IN THIS ORDER** list are the order that the columns will be displayed in, on the tab, from left to right.

The **MOVE UP** and **MOVE DOWN** buttons are used to rearrange the order of the columns in the view. Click on the field that you want to move, then click on the appropriate button.

The **RESET** button will restore the columns back to the order they were when ACT! was first installed.

 Tools ⇒ Customize ⇒ Columns, will also open the Customize Columns dialog box.

2. Click on the Department field in the **AVAILABLE FIELDS** list. Press and hold down the Ctrl key. Scroll down the list and select the Last Meeting and Last Results fields.

3. Click the Add button (the top arrow button), then click OK.

4. Scroll to the right in the Contact list view so that you can see the three fields that you just added to the view.

 Another Way To Add Or Remove Columns
If you double-click on a field in the Available Fields section on the Customize Columns dialog box you will add the field to the view. If you double-click on a field in the Show as columns in this order section, you will remove the field from the view. When you remove a column from a view, the data is still in the database. If you need to view the data from a field that you removed, you can add the field back.

Delete A Column

1. Open the Customize Columns dialog box.

2. Click on the Last Meeting field in the list on the right, then click the Remove button (the second arrow button from the top) and click OK. The column will be removed from the Contact list view. Click OK.

Customizing ACT!

Customizing The Columns On The Notes Tab
There are two ways to customize the columns on the Notes tab, as explained below.

① **Resize the columns** by placing the mouse pointer on the line to the right of the column, as shown earlier in Figure 15-11, that you want to resize. Drag the mouse pointer to the right to make the column wider or to the left to make the column smaller.

② **Add or remove columns** You can change which columns are displayed on the tab by using the Customize Columns dialog box shown above in Figure 15-13.

Exercise 15.4: How To Customize Columns On A Tab
Customizing columns on a tab is very similar to adding a column to a view.

1. Click the arrow on the Options button and select **CUSTOMIZE COLUMNS**, as shown in Figure 15-14.

   You will see the Customize Columns dialog box that you saw earlier in Figure 15-13.

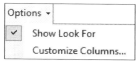

Figure 15-14 Options drop-down list

 All tabs on a view, like the Documents and Personal Info tabs, do not have the Options button. Some tabs only have the Customize Columns option on the drop-down list and other tabs have additional options.

2. Add the fields that you want to see on the tab, then remove the fields from the list on the right that you do not want to see on the tab.

3. Rearrange the order of the fields if necessary, then click OK.

Creating Fields
If you have the need to customize a layout, fields are probably the item that you will customize the most. Depending on your needs, the fields that come with ACT! may not be sufficient. You may have to create additional fields to store data. You have to have administrator or manager rights to create fields. Users cannot be logged into the database while you are creating new fields or editing existing fields. If anyone else is logged in, you will see a message that contains a list of who is logged in.

While the process of creating fields is easy, you should have a plan for the fields that you need to create. If the database has been in use for a while or has a lot of contacts, you can still add fields. You may have to go through all of the records that were in the database before the field was added and fill in the data for the new field. This could be very time consuming. At a minimum, you should have the following items in your plan for each field that you want to add:

① What type of field (drop-down, date, free form, etc.) is best suited for the data that the field needs to store.
② Which views should the field be placed on.
③ Will the field be used as a lookup field or in a report? If so, determine if the field would be more useful if it was a drop-down list.

Chapter 15

Field Data Type Options

If you are creating a new field you can use the data types that are explained in Table 15-3. When editing a field, not all of the data types in the table are available. Each field can only have one data type.

Data Type	Description
Address	When you select this field type, seven fields are automatically created: Address 1, 2 and 3, City, State, Zip Code and Country. (1)
Annual Event	Creates a date field for events that only happen once a year. (2) (3)
Character	Creates a free form data field, which means that any combination of data (text and numbers) can be entered in the field. While it is tempting to use this data type for all fields, it should really only be used when none of the other data types discussed in this table are a better option.
Currency	Only accepts monetary values. By default, a dollar sign, commas and decimal point (for cents) are automatically filled in. If the user entered 123456 in a currency field, the number would be displayed as $1,234.56. (2)
Date	Allows a date to be entered in the field. (2) (3)
Date/Time	Allows a date and time to be entered in the same field. (2) (3)
Decimal	Only allows numbers and decimal points to be entered. (2)
Email	Used to enter an email address. (1)
Initial-Caps	This data type forces the first character of each word entered in the field to be a capital letter and the remaining letters in each word to be lower case.
Lowercase	Converts all upper case characters to lower case.
Memo	Similar to the Character data type because it is free form. The difference is that a memo field allows a lot more data to be entered in the field.
Number	Only accepts numeric values.
Phone	Used to enter telephone numbers. By default, a dash is automatically filled in after the area code and after the first three digits of the phone number. (1)
Picture	Used to store graphic files, images or photos. (1)
Time	Allows a time to be entered in the field. The drop-down list shown in Figure 15-16 is added to this field type when the field is added to a view. A time can be selected from the drop-down list or the time can be typed in. (2)
Uppercase	Converts all lower case characters to capital letters.
URL Address	Enter a web site address.
Yes/No	Creates a check box field. ACT! queries do not use Yes and No values, instead they use True and False. If this field is used in a query, keep in mind that Yes equals True and No equals False. (1)

Table 15-3 Field data types explained

(1) This field type is only available if you are creating a new field.
(2) The format for this field comes from the Region and Language dialog box shown in Figure 15-15. The currency field formats on the Opportunities view also come from this dialog box, which is part of the Windows operating system.
(3) A calendar object is automatically added to this field type so that all dates will be entered in the same format.

 To view the dialog box shown in Figure 15-15, open the Control Panel in Windows, then double-click on the **REGION AND LANGUAGE** option.

Customizing ACT!

Figure 15-15 Region and Language dialog box

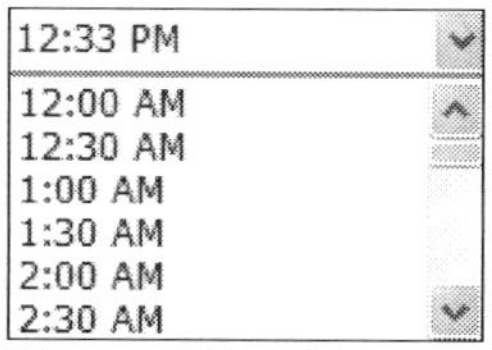

Figure 15-16 Time data type drop-down list

Field Behavior Options

The field behavior options discussed below are used to customize the fields that you create or modify. All of the attributes are not available for each data type.

① **ALLOW BLANK** If checked, this option will not require data to be entered into in the field.
② **GENERATE HISTORY** Automatically creates a history record each time the value in the field is changed. By default, several fields in the database have this option enabled.
③ **PRIMARY FIELD** Designates the field as a primary field. Fields that have this option checked will be duplicated. This is useful when you duplicate a contact record.
④ **USE DROP-DOWN LIST** Is used to select an existing drop-down list or create a new drop-down list.

Customize Field Behavior

The options discussed below are some of the options on the Customize Field Behavior screen.

They allow for more functionality to be added to fields.

The options on the Customize Field Behavior screen shown in Figure 15-17 change depending on the data type that is selected.

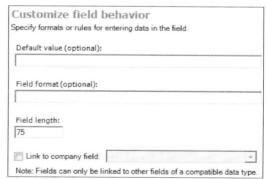

Figure 15-17 Customize field behavior options

① **DEFAULT VALUE** The value that you enter in this field will automatically be filled in the field for each new record added to the database. This is useful if the majority of records need to have the same value in the field.
② **FIELD FORMAT** Is used to enter symbols that will automatically appear in the field. This formatting is used to help the user enter the correct type of numeric data.

Chapter 15

③ **FIELD LENGTH** The number entered in this field is the maximum number of characters that can be entered in the field. Try not to make the field length too long because that will waste space in the database and make the database larger than it needs to be. This will cause the database to run slower then it should.

④ **LINK TO COMPANY FIELD** Is used to link a contact field to a field in the company record. When the company field is updated, the linked field in the contact record is automatically updated. This option is only available when you edit an existing field. [See Chapter 5, Linking and Unlinking Contact And Company Fields]

Triggers

Triggers allow an action to take place on a field in one of three ways, as shown in Figure 15-18.

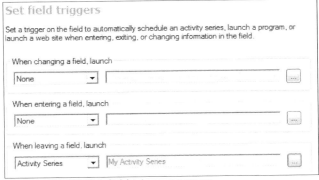

Figure 15-18 Set field triggers screen

Types Of Triggers

There are three types of triggers that can be set, as explained below.

① **NONE** This is the default trigger type. It means that the trigger will not have an event occur.
② **PROGRAMS** Is used to select a program (software package), file or web site to open.
③ **ACTIVITY SERIES** Is used to select a list of activities that you want to schedule.

Trigger Options

There are three triggers that can be set for a field, as explained below.

① **WHEN CHANGING A FIELD**, an event will happen when the value in the field changes.
② **WHEN ENTERING A FIELD**, an event will happen when the cursor first enters the field.
③ **WHEN LEAVING A FIELD**, an event will happen when the cursor leaves the field.

An example of when to use the **WHEN CHANGING A FIELD** trigger would be when the data in a field changes, you want a document to automatically open. You would select the programs option from the drop-down list and add the file name in the field to the right. You could also use this trigger to open a file that provides helpful information about what type of data should be entered in the field.

An example of when to use the **WHEN ENTERING A FIELD** trigger would be when the cursor leaves a field, a web site will open to display information about the field.

An example of when to use the **WHEN LEAVING A FIELD** trigger would be to set up an activity series automatically when the cursor leaves the field, like the activity series that you created in Chapter 7.

Customizing ACT!

Exercise 15.5: Create A Trigger

In this exercise you will create the **WHEN LEAVING THE FIELD** trigger shown above in Figure 15-18. You will add the trigger to the User 7 field.

1. Tools ⇒ Define Fields. Scroll down the list of field names and click on the User 7 field.

2. Click the **EDIT FIELD** link, then click the Next button twice. You will see the Set field triggers screen.

3. Open the **WHEN LEAVING A FIELD** drop-down list and select Activity Series.

4. Click the button at the end of the field and select the Activity Series that you created, as illustrated in Figure 15-19.

    Click OK. You will see the Activity Series name across from the trigger, as shown above in Figure 15-18.

    Click Finish, then close the Define Fields dialog box.

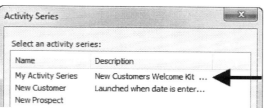

Figure 15-19 Activity Series dialog box

Test The Trigger And Submit An Activity Series

1. Display the record for Tom Dynamic.

2. On the User Fields tab, type `Test trigger` in the User 7 field, then press the Tab key.

    You should see the Schedule Activity Series dialog box shown in Figure 15-20.

    If you needed to add more contacts for the activities you can.

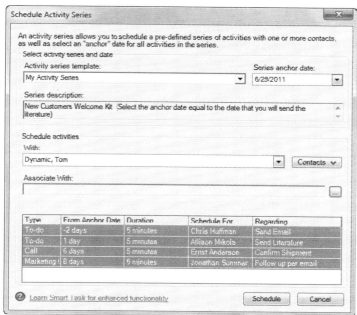

Figure 15-20 Schedule Activity Series dialog box

3. Click the Cancel button to close the Schedule Activity Series dialog box.

Chapter 15

Creating And Editing Drop-Down List Fields

You have already seen and used many of the default drop-down lists that come with ACT!. You can create drop-down lists for a field that you need. You may have a database that has all types of doctors and may want to list their specialty. You could modify a user defined field and add a drop-down list to it, that contains specialties. A list can be used by more than one field.

Exercise 15.6: How To Create A Drop-Down List Field

In this exercise you will create a drop-down list field for doctor specialties.

1. Tools ⇒ Define Fields. If the **DEFINE FIELD** option is not enabled, you are not logged in as an administrator or manager and cannot complete this exercise until you are.

2. Click the **MANAGE DROP-DOWN LISTS** link, then click the **CREATE DROP-DOWN LIST** link.

3. In the **DROP-DOWN LIST NAME** field type `Specializes In`.
   In the Description field type `What the doctor specializes in`.
   The options in the **TYPE** drop-down list were explained earlier in Table 15-3.

 You should avoid using special characters in field names because they can create problems in reports and queries.

4. Clear the **AUTOMATICALLY ADD NEW ITEMS USERS ENTER TO THE LIST** option.

If checked, the Automatically add new items users enter to the list option is used to allow users to type in a value that is not already in the list. When this happens, the value will automatically be added to the list. This could be a problem because typos will not be caught and the lists can get out of hand and hard to manage.

5. You should have the options shown in Figure 15-21.

   The **ALLOW USERS TO EDIT ITEMS IN THIS LIST** option has to be checked for each field that you want to let users add, delete or edit the values in the drop-down list.

   Click Next.

Figure 15-21 Drop-down list name and type options

 The following options cannot be accessed when the **ALLOW USERS TO EDIT ITEMS IN THIS LIST** option is selected: **ALLOW MULTI-SELECT, SHOW DESCRIPTIONS** and **TYPE-AHEAD**. These options can only be enabled from the Define Fields dialog box.

15-13

Customizing ACT!

6. Click the Add button, then type `Brain Surgery` in the Value column.
   Click the Add button, then type `OB-GYN` in the Value column.

   You should have the options shown in Figure 15-22.

   Figure 15-22 Drop-down list values

7. Click Finish. You should see the drop-down list that you just created on the screen shown in Figure 15-23. If you look in the **DETAILS** section illustrated on the left, you will see information about the drop-down list that is selected.

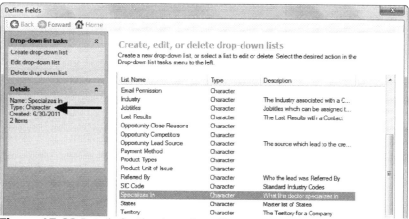

Figure 15-23 Details for the drop-down list

8. Click the Back button in the upper left corner of the dialog box. Leave the Define Fields dialog box open to complete the next exercise.

Managing Drop-Down List Options

If the field has a drop-down list you can decide whether users can add or delete entries in the list. If you need to change the contents of a field like the address field, click in the field and back space out what you do not want and type in the new information. ACT! is in **INSERT** mode by default. In the next exercise you will learn several drop-down list editing techniques.

You can modify drop-down lists on the Define Fields dialog box or as you learned earlier, you can select the Edit List Values option at the bottom of a drop-down list. System fields can be modified on the Define Fields dialog box. Other fields are modified in a view. To use the Define Fields dialog box, other users cannot have the database open.

Exercise 15.7: How To Add Items To A Drop-Down List

In this exercise you will add a value to the Contact ID/Status field.

1. Open the Define Fields dialog box if it is not already open, then click the Manage drop-down lists link in the List Tasks section.

2. Select the Contact ID/Status list name, then click the **EDIT DROP-DOWN LIST** link.

Chapter 15

3. Click Next on the Enter drop-down list name and type screen.

4. Click the Add button, then type `Purchased Book` in the Value field.

   Press the Tab key, then type `Purchased the ACT! Book` in the Description field.

   The entry should look like the one shown at the bottom of Figure 15-24.

Figure 15-24 Drop-down list values

5. Click Finish. The item will be added to the drop-down list. Close the Define Fields dialog box.

View The New Entry

1. Switch to the Contact detail view, then open the ID/Status drop-down list on any contact record.

2. Scroll down the list. You will see the item that you created, as illustrated in Figure 15-25.

Figure 15-25 ID/Status drop-down list options

Exercise 15.8: How To Edit The Values In A Drop-Down List (From A View)

Many of the fields in the contact and company detail views have drop-down lists. You can add, modify or delete the entries in these lists.

How To Add An Item To A Drop-Down List

In this part of the exercise you will learn how to add an item to a drop-down list.

1. Select the 1024x768 contact layout, if it is not already selected.

2. Click on the arrow at the end of the Department field on the Contact detail view, then click the **EDIT LIST VALUES** option. You should see the Edit List dialog box. This is a list of the items that can currently be selected for the Department field.

3. Click the Add button. Type `Computer` in the Value field. If you wanted, you could type in a description to help clarify the item that you are adding.

Customizing ACT!

4. Click OK to close the Edit List dialog box. The item that you just added will be available in the Department drop-down list.

How To Modify Or Delete An Item In A Drop-Down List
The steps below explain how to modify or delete an item in a drop-down list. Read through the steps now, but do not modify or delete anything.

How To Modify An Item In The Drop-Down List
1. Open the Edit List dialog box for the drop-down list that you want to modify.

2. Select the value that you want to modify, then change the item to what you want it to be, as illustrated in Figure 15-26.

   Click OK.

   Notice in Figure 15-24 shown earlier, that the value below the Manufacturer value was Prospect.

   In Figure 15-26, the value was changed to Brand Marketing.

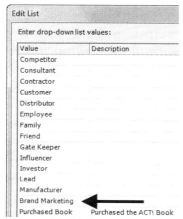

Figure 15-26 Prospect value changed to Brand Marketing

How To Delete An Item In The Drop-Down List
I do not advise deleting items from a drop-down list unless you know that the value is not being used for any contact. If you delete a value and it is being used, the records that are using it will retain the value, but the value will not be available for any other records. If the value that you want to delete for example, is "Computer", I would change it to "Not in use - Computer" or something similar. That way, it is still available and if at some point in the future you need to reclassify contacts that have the value, you will be able to easily find the records.

1. To delete an item in a drop-down list, open the Edit List dialog box shown above in Figure 15-26.

2. Select the value that you want to delete, then click the **DELETE** button. Click Yes, when prompted to delete the list value, then click OK.

 You can also delete an item using the Define Fields dialog box.

Exercise 15.9: How To Modify A User Field
There are 10 contact user fields that you can customize to store data that does not exist in the fields that come with ACT!. If you customize these fields, the name changes on the Define Fields dialog box, but not on the User Fields tab. This is because the "User 1" label on the layout has to be modified. You will not see the label change on the User Fields tab until you edit the layout, which is covered in Chapter 18. In this exercise you will modify the User 1 field.

Chapter 15

1. Tools ⇒ Define Fields.

2. Select the **CONTACTS** field from the drop-down list, if it is not already selected.

3. Scroll down the list and click on the User 1 field, then click the **EDIT FIELD** link.

4. In the Field Name field, type `Specializes In`.

5. Open the Select a field drop-down list and select **INITIAL-CAPS**. This will cause the first letter of each word that is typed in this field to automatically be capitalized. Click Yes when prompted that data may be lost. You will see a dialog box that lets you know that your changes are being saved.

6. Check all of the options in the **CUSTOMIZE FIELD BEHAVIOR** section, as illustrated in Figure 15-27, then click Next.

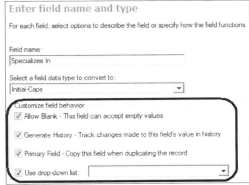

Figure 15-27 Customize field behavior options illustrated

7. In the **DEFAULT VALUE** field type `General Practitioner`, as illustrated in Figure 15-28.

    None of the triggers need to be set.

    Click Finish.

    The User 1 field will be renamed.

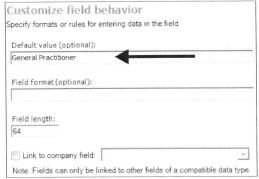

Figure 15-28 Default value for the user field

Exercise 15.10: How To Create A Field

So far in this chapter you have learned how to create and manage drop-down list fields and modify user fields. These are probably the types of fields that you will need to create and modify the most. It is possible though that you may need to create a field that is not a drop-down list. You can create fields and link them to an existing drop-down list. The steps below show you how to create a field that will be linked to an existing drop-down list.

1. Open the Define Fields dialog box if it is not already open, then click the **CREATE NEW FIELD** link.

Customizing ACT!

2. Type `Specialty` in the Field name field.

3. Check the **USE DROP-DOWN LIST** option shown in Figure 15-29, then select Specializes In from the drop-down list.

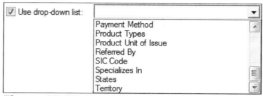

Figure 15-29 Drop-down list options

 The options shown above in Figure 15-29 are the default fields in ACT! that have data for a drop-down list. If one of them is appropriate for the field that you are creating, you can use it.

4. Click Next, then select the **LIMIT TO LIST** option shown in Figure 15-30.

   This will prevent a value from being entered that is not already in the list.

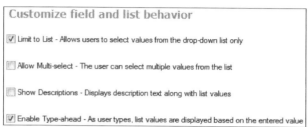

Figure 15-30 Customize field and list behavior options

5. Click Finish. The field will be created. In Chapter 18 you will add this field to the Basic Contact layout.

6. Close the Define Fields dialog box. When prompted to modify the layout, click No.

As shown above in Figure 15-30, the **SHOW DESCRIPTIONS** option is not enabled by default. This description refers to the one that you created in Exercise 15.7.

If the Show Descriptions option is checked, the drop-down list will also display the description, as shown in Figure 15-31. Notice that some options do not have a description.

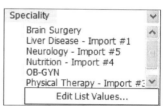

Figure 15-31 Show Descriptions option enabled

Deleting Fields

As a programmer, I do not delete fields from a database that have data when I first come to the conclusion that the data is no longer needed. Instead, I will modify the layouts that display the field, so that the field is not visible on the layout. I will also remove the field from the queries and reports, but not from the database. If you want to delete a field right away, make a backup copy of the database, then delete the field. While deleting the field from the database is easy to do, you should also remove it from the layouts, queries and reports that it is used in. The steps below show you how to delete a field.

1. Tools ⇒ Define Fields.

2. Open the **VIEW FIELDS FOR** drop-down list and select the record type of the field that you want to delete.

3. Click on the field that you want to delete in the list, then click the Delete Field link on the left.

4. Click Yes, when prompted if you are sure that you want to delete the field. Once the field is deleted, close the Define Fields dialog box.

Managing Priority Types

Schedule ⇒ Manage ⇒ Priorities, will open the dialog box shown in Figure 15-32.

Chapter 7 covered how to schedule activities and set the priority for the activity. Renaming or disabling a priority does not effect activities that already have a priority. They will still display with the priority they had when the activity was created.

The changes that you make on this dialog box only effect new activities. There are five priority options that come with ACT!.

Figure 15-32 Manage Priorities dialog box

You cannot create new entries, but you can modify the names of the existing entries to better meet your needs or to be more descriptive. If you need to rename a priority, click on it, then click the **EDIT** button and type in the new name.

If you do not need a priority, clear the check mark for it in the **ACTIVE** column. This prevents users from selecting the priority on the Schedule Activities dialog box.

The **RESTORE DEFAULTS** button will reset the priorities back to what they were when ACT! was first installed.

Exercise 15.11: Creating Activity Types

Chapter 7 covered the activity types that come with ACT!. Only users with administrator or manager level security rights can create new activity types. In this exercise you will learn how to create activity types.

1. Schedule ⇒ Manage ⇒ Activity Types, then click the Add button.

2. Type `Post Card Mailing` in the **NAME** field.

3. If you want the activity type to have an icon, click the **BROWSE** button. Navigate to and double-click on the icon file that you want to use.

4. Click the Add button on the Add Activity Type dialog box. Type `Post Card Mailing Completed` in the **RESULT NAME** field, then click OK.

Customizing ACT!

5. Check the option that you just created on the Add Activity Type dialog box to make it the default. You should have the options shown in Figure 15-33.

   The options on the bottom half of this dialog box are the values that will appear in the Results drop-down list field on the Schedule Activities dialog box. These options are also used to clear an activity on the Clear Activity dialog box. You can enter as many options as you need. When a new activity type is created, the **COMPLETED** and **NOT COMPLETED** result types shown in the figure are added automatically.

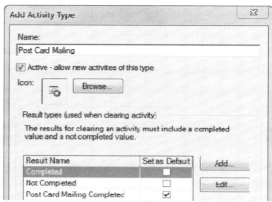

Figure 15-33 Add Activity Type dialog box

6. Click OK. The dialog box should have the Post Card Mailing activity shown in Figure 15-34.

   The activity types that come with ACT! cannot be deleted.

   Click the Close button.

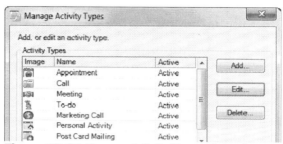

Figure 15-34 Manage Activity Types dialog box

> **Reminder**
> Go back to the Step 1 section in Exercise 14.2 and change the activity type, as specified in step 2.

Annual Events

Annual Events are activities that can be displayed on your calendar, but not on the Task List. Events can be recurring like birthdays or one-time events like a business trip. A good use of the events option is to set up holidays on your calendar. Events do not cause scheduling conflicts and do not appear on reports. Only users with an administrator or manager level account can create events.

Exercise 15.12: Create An Annual Event Activity

In this exercise you will create an event for July 4th.

1. Schedule ⇒ Manage ⇒ Events.

2. Click the **ADD** button, then type `4th of July` in the **EVENT NAME** field.

3. Select July 4th of next year in the Date field, then change the **DURATION** to 1 day, if necessary.

Chapter 15

4. Change the **OCCURS** option to yearly.

    You should have the options shown in Figure 15-35.

Figure 15-35 Add Event dialog box

5. Click OK. You will see the event on the dialog box shown in Figure 15-36.

    Click the Close button.

Figure 15-36 Manage Events dialog box

Add The Event To Your Calendar

In this part of the exercise you will add the event that you just created to your calendar.

1. Tools ⇒ Preferences.

2. On the Calendar and Scheduling tab, click the Calendar Preferences button.

3. Check the **DISPLAY EVENTS** option, illustrated in Figure 15-37, if it is not already checked, then click OK twice to close both dialog boxes.

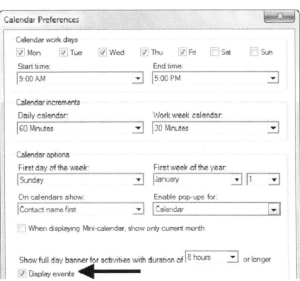
Figure 15-37 Display events option illustrated

15-21

Customizing ACT!

4. Open a calendar view and display July 4th of next year. You will see the entry illustrated in Figure 15-38. If you do not see the entry, make sure that all of the filter options are set to show all.

Figure 15-38 Event added to the calendar

CUSTOMIZING REPORT TEMPLATES

In this chapter you will learn the following report template customization techniques:

- ☑ Resizing fields
- ☑ Adding fields to a report
- ☑ Saving templates
- ☑ Hiding report sections
- ☑ Creating subreports

CHAPTER 16

Customizing Report Templates

Report Design Overview

As you have seen, ACT! comes with over 50 reports. Many of the reports may be exactly what you need and others you may wish were slightly different. For example, you may need an existing report to have totals. ACT! has a tool called the **REPORT DESIGNER**. It is used for the following:

① To modify existing reports.
② Creating a new report based off of an existing report.
③ If you need a report that is not similar to any of the reports that come with ACT!, you can create a report from scratch.

Many of the report design techniques that you will learn about are similar to the techniques that the Layout Designer has to modify the layouts (data entry screens and tabs). The Layout Designer is covered in Chapter 18.

Having modified and designed reports for over two decades, I can tell you that it is much easier to modify and create reports when you are familiar with the data that the report needs and the structure of the database. By structure, I mean knowing which table each field is in that you need for the report. The other thing that will be helpful is to have a draft of what the new or modified report should look like.

Report Creation Options

There are two ways that you can create a report: From an existing report and from scratch. Each option has pros and cons. Once you understand all of the options, you can select the report creation option that best meets the need for each report that you need to create.

Create A Report Based Off Of An Existing Report

If a report exists that is similar to the report that you need to create, select this report creation option. Save the existing report with a new file name and make the necessary changes to the new report. An example of when to create a report based off of an existing report would be when two groups of users need to see the majority of the same fields, but one of the groups needs additional information that the other group does not need. Another example is when one group of users needs the same fields but in a different layout then the other group. You can use one of the templates that come with ACT! and modify the report as needed.

Reports ⇒ Edit Template ⇒ Select report, are the menu options to select when you want to modify an existing report.

Create A Report From Scratch

This option gives you the most flexibility to create a report. You start with a blank canvas so to speak and add the fields and other objects to the layout. For many, this can be intimidating, especially in the beginning. But being the fearless person that you are, I am sure that when you get to the exercise that has you create a report from scratch, that you will do just fine.

Reports ⇒ New Template, opens the dialog box shown in Figure 16-1.

The **REPORT TYPES** list shown in Figure 16-1 is how you select the type of report that you want to create. The report types are based on the type of data. Select the type for the new report, then select the **EMPTY REPORT** option in the Templates list on the right.

Chapter 16

Figure 16-1 Options to create a report from scratch

Report Designer

The Report Designer window shown in Figure 16-2 is used to create new reports and modify existing reports.

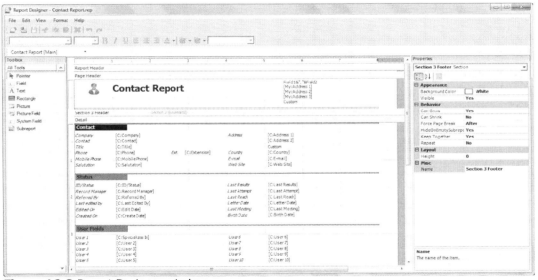

Figure 16-2 Report Designer window

Report Designer Toolbars

The Report Designer has two toolbars that you can use to create and modify reports. Many of the options are the same as options in most word processors. Figure 16-3 shows the Editing toolbar. Table 16-1 explains the buttons on the Editing toolbar. The first eight buttons on the Formatting toolbar shown in Figure 16-4 are the same buttons that are on the Formatting toolbar in most word processors. The remaining buttons on the Formatting toolbar are explained in Table 16-2. The buttons on this toolbar are used to change the look of objects, like fields or labels on the report.

Customizing Report Templates

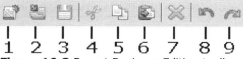

Figure 16-3 Report Designer Editing toolbar

Button	Description
1	Creates a new report.
2	Opens an existing report.
3	Saves the changes.
4	Cuts the selected objects. (1)
5	Copies the selected objects.
6	Pastes the selected objects.
7	Deletes the selected objects. (1)
8	Undoes the last change.
9	Redoes the last change.

Table 16-1 Report Designer Editing toolbar buttons explained

(1) The difference between these options is that the Delete option does not allow the selected objects to be pasted back into the report.

Figure 16-4 Report Designer Formatting toolbar

Button	Is Used To Change The . . .
1	Color of the font.
2	Background color of the object.
3	Border color.
4	Border style.

Table 16-2 Report Designer Formatting toolbar buttons explained

Sections Of A Report

There are five sections of a report that you can modify and place fields and other objects in, as shown in Figure 16-5.

The sections are the Report Header, Page Header, Detail, Page Footer and Report Footer.

You cannot change the order of or delete these sections. If you place the same calculated field in different sections of the report, it could produce different results.

It is important that you understand how each section of the report functions, because they function independently of each other.

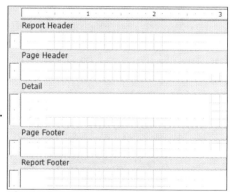

Figure 16-5 Report layout

Keep the following in mind when deciding where to place fields and objects on the report.

① Not all sections are needed for every report.

② If a report does not need a section, the section can be suppressed so that it does not display blank space on the report.

③ Sections can be resized as needed.

Section 1: Report Header
By default, data fields and other objects placed in this section will only print at the top of the first page of the report. It is quite possible that many of the reports that you create will not have anything in this section. Something that you may want to include in this section of the report is the query criteria that was used to create the report. If the report needs a cover page, the report header section can be used for the cover page. If this is what you need to do, add a page break after this section so that the actual report data starts on a new page.

Section 2: Page Header
Data fields and other objects placed in this section will appear at the top of every page in the report. This is where the report title and headings for the fields in the detail section of the report are usually placed. Other objects that are commonly placed in this section include the date and page number.

Section 3: Detail
Data fields and other objects placed in this section will print for each record in the database that meets the criteria. This section is automatically repeated once for each record that will be printed on the report. The data fields in this section usually have field headings in the page header section.

Section 4: Page Footer
Data fields and other objects placed in this section will print at the bottom of each page of the report. The page footer section is similar to the page header section. Items like page numbers and footnotes can be placed in this section.

Section 5: Report Footer
Data fields and other objects placed in this section will print once at the end of the report. This is usually where grand totals and other types of report summary information is placed.

Customizing Report Templates
In Chapter 8 you learned how to run several reports. Now you will learn how to customize report templates. By customizing report templates, you can add fields to a template and delete fields that you do not need. ACT! also allows you to create your own envelope and label templates from scratch.

Exercise 16.1: Customizing The Report Templates
In this exercise you will learn how to add fields to a report. You will also learn about the tools in the Report Designer window.

Saving Report Templates
If you modify a report template that comes with ACT!, it is a good idea to save it with a different name before making any changes. That way, the existing template is not changed. The **UNDO** option does not work in the Report Designer as you may expect.

 Unless instructed otherwise, save the reports that you create or modify in your folder.

1. Lookup all contacts.

Customizing Report Templates

2. Reports ⇒ Edit Template.

   You will see the dialog box shown in Figure 16-6.

   Double-click on the file **CONTACT STATUS.REP**.

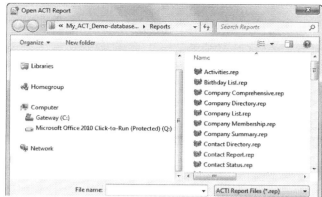

Figure 16-6 Report templates that come with ACT!

3. File ⇒ Save As. Type `My Missing Email Address` as the file name, then press Enter or click the Save button.

Field vs Label

Figure 16-7 shows the fields and labels. The **LABEL** for a field is on the left by default. It is not a requirement to keep the label on the report, nor does the label have to have the same name as the field name. If you do not need the label you can delete it by right-clicking on it and selecting **CUT**, as shown in Figure 16-8.

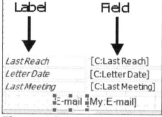

Figure 16-7 Label and field illustrated

Figure 16-8 Label and field shortcut menu

The **FIELD**, which is in brackets, will display data from the database on the report. You can modify the field by right-clicking on it and selecting an option on the shortcut menu shown above in Figure 16-8.

Table 16-3 contains the table names and field codes. The field codes are the letters before the colon in the field name. The Table column below indicates the table that the field is stored in. The abbreviations in the middle of the table are the codes.

For example, the code GA is a group activity. This is how you know if the field is a contact, company, group or opportunity field. System fields do not have an abbreviation in front of them.

Table	Contact	Notes	History	Activity	Secondary Contact	Opportunity
Contact	C	CN	CH	CA	SC	CO
Company		COMN	COMH	COMA		COMO
Group		GN	GH	GA		GO
Opportunity						O

Table 16-3 Field codes

Chapter 16

How To Manually Resize A Field

Often when you add a field to a report, you will probably have to resize it. Just be careful not to make the field so small that all of the data in the field does not print.

1. Click on the field, **C:LAST RESULTS** in the Status section of the report. You should now see squares around the field.

2. Place the mouse pointer on the middle square on the right side of the field. You may have to scroll to the right to see the end of the field.

3. When the pointer changes to a double headed arrow, press and hold down the left mouse button, then drag the mouse to the left until the pointer is near the end of the field, as illustrated in Figure 16-9.

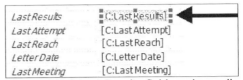

Figure 16-9 Last Results field made smaller

 To **MOVE A FIELD OR LABEL**, click on it. Press and hold down the left mouse button. The mouse pointer will change to a hand icon when you start to move the field, as shown in Figure 16-10.

Figure 16-10 Mouse pointer in position to move the field or label

Report Designer Toolbox

A report can have different types of objects. Earlier you learned about fields, which is one type of object.

The options in the toolbox shown in Figure 16-11 are used to add fields and other types of objects to the report.

Table 16-4 explains the options in the toolbox.

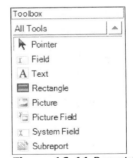

Figure 16-11 Report Designer Toolbox

Option	Description
Pointer	You have to click this button before clicking on an object on the report to select it.
Field	Adds a field from the database to the report.
Text	Free form field for adding text to the report.
Rectangle	Adds a rectangle or box to the report. This object is often used to visually group fields together.
Picture	Adds a graphic or image file to the report.

Table 16-4 Report Designer Toolbox options explained

16-7

Customizing Report Templates

Option	Description
Picture Field	Adds an image to the report. A different image will be displayed for each record on the report. This field is often used for photos.
System Field	Adds a field shown in Figure 16-12 to the report.
Subreport	Adds a report to an existing report. This feature is often used when you want to add multiple rows of the same type of data to a report. Subreports allow fields to be repeated an unlimited number of times on the report. A popular use for a subreport is to add data stored on any of the System tabs. [See Chapter 18, Tabs Overview]

Table 16-4 Report Designer Toolbox options explained (Continued)

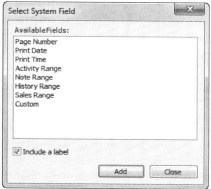

Figure 16-12 Select System Field dialog box

How To Add A Field To A Report

In this part of the exercise you will learn how to add different types of fields to a report. You will also learn basic report editing techniques.

1. Click the **FIELD** button in the Toolbox. The mouse pointer will change to a cross hair (+) when it is on the report.

2. Place the mouse pointer under the C:Last Meeting field. Press the left mouse button and draw a rectangle the same size as the C:Last Meeting field.

   You will see the dialog box shown in Figure 16-13, when you release the mouse button.

   The options in the **SELECT A RECORD TYPE** drop-down list are tables in the database. Each table contains different fields.

   Some of the tables correspond to a tab on a detail view.

Figure 16-13 Select Field dialog box

3. Open the drop-down list and select MyRecord, then click on the E-mail field.

4. Check the **INCLUDE A LABEL** option at the bottom of the Select Field dialog box, if it is not already checked, then click the Add button.

5. Click the Close button.

How To Align Fields On A Report

As you can see, the field that you just added to the template is not lined up with the field above it. The steps below show you how to align and resize fields using menu options.

When aligning fields, select the fields that need to be aligned first, then select the field that you want those fields to line up with. Figure 16-14 shows several fields selected. The one that has the dark handles (the Com:Address 3 field) is the one that the other selected objects will be aligned to.

Figure 16-14 Fields selected to be aligned

1. Click on the E-mail label, then press and hold down the Shift key.

2. Click on the Last Meeting label. Format ⇒ Align ⇒ Left. The E-mail label should now be lined up with the Last Meeting label.

3. Click on a blank space in the report, then click on the E-mail label. Change the font and size to match the Last Meeting label. (For me that is the Tahoma font, size 8, italic.)

4. Click on the E-mail field. Change the font and size to match the Last Meeting field. (For me that is the Tahoma font, size 8, no italic.)

5. Click on the My:Email field, if it is not already selected. Press and hold down the Shift key, then click on the C:Last Meeting field. Format ⇒ Make Same Size ⇒ Height.

6. With the two fields still selected, Format ⇒ Align ⇒ Left, then save the changes.

How To Add Text To A Report

You may have the need to add text to a report to help explain something about the report. For example, the report may need a sub title.

In ACT! 2012 and earlier, the Properties window was displayed by default. If you do not see the Properties window on the right, View ⇒ Properties Window.

1. Click the **TEXT** button in the Toolbox. Place the mouse pointer below the Contact Status report title in the Page Header section and draw a box.

Customizing Report Templates

2. In the **TEXT** field on the Properties window type `Missing E-mail Addresses`, as illustrated in Figure 16-15. Make the field smaller so that the frame is closer to the text on the right.

Properties Window

Earlier you learned that the options on the toolbox are used to add a variety of fields and objects to a report. You also learned that each field or object on the report can be modified.

The Properties window shown in Figure 16-15 is used to customize the fields and objects, which are sometimes called **ELEMENTS**.

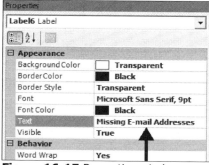

Figure 16-15 Properties window

 The **F4** key opens and closes the Properties window. The options on this window will change depending on the type of object that is selected. If you want to apply the same change to several objects on the report at the same time, select the objects first, then make the changes in the Properties window.

 How To Resize A Section Of The Report
If you are creating a new report or making a lot of changes to an existing report, you may find it easier to work if a section of the report was longer. To make a section longer, place the mouse pointer on the top edge of the section bar below the section that you want to resize. Drag the section down. When you are finished making the changes, drag the section bar back up so that a lot of blank space does not appear at the bottom of the section when you preview or print the report.

 If you need to have more than one text field have the same formatting, create the first field and format it as needed. To duplicate the field, right-click on it and select **COPY**, then right-click on the report and select **PASTE**.

How To Add A Summary Field

Summary fields are used for calculations. You can use summary fields to get totals and averages, as well as, minimums, maximums and counts. Summary fields are usually placed in the report and page header or footer sections.

The purpose of the report in this exercise is to provide a list of contacts to call, to either verify the email address that you have or get an email address from contacts that do not have one listed in the database. The report already prints the total number of contacts. You will add a summary field to count the number of contacts that have an e-mail address.

1. Click the **FIELD** button in the Toolbox, then draw a rectangle to the right of the **NUMBER OF CONTACTS** field in the Page Header section.

2. Select the E-mail field on the Select Field dialog box. Click Add, then click Close.

Chapter 16

3. Right-click on the C:Email field and select Properties.

   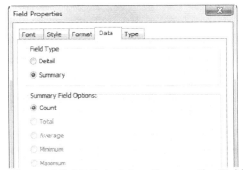

   On the Data tab, select the **SUMMARY** Field Type option. The **COUNT** option should be selected, as shown in Figure 16-16.

   Options that are not enabled cannot be used on the field that is currently selected.

   Click Apply, then click OK.

   Figure 16-16 Data tab options on the Field Properties dialog box

4. Change the label of the field to `Contacts with E-mail Addresses:`, then move and resize the field and label as needed. Left align the field, then save the changes.

Test The Report

You should test the report before you close the Report Designer window.

1. File ⇒ Print Preview.

   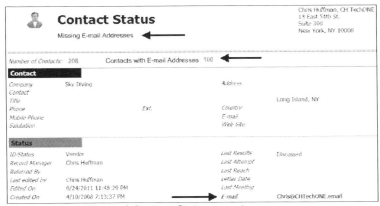

   The top of the report should look like the one shown in Figure 16-17.

   The arrows indicate the items that you added. You may have different totals then the ones shown in the figure.

   Figure 16-17 Revised Contact Status report

2. Close the Print Preview window. Make any changes that are needed, then save the changes.

   How To Align Text In A Label And Field
   If you are having trouble aligning the text in the label and field, follow the steps below.

   1. Select the label and field.
   2. On the Properties window, open the **ALIGNMENT** drop-down list shown in Figure 16-18, then select the option that will best line up the text in both fields.

Customizing Report Templates

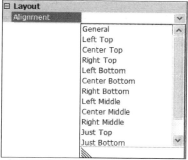

Figure 16-18 Alignment options

Custom Fields

Custom fields are not stored in the database. Many of the reports that come with ACT! have custom fields. The custom field in the upper right corner of the Contact Status report is an example. This custom field contains the City, State and Zip Code fields combined into one field.

One of the more popular custom fields that is created is to combine two or more fields into one. Combining the city, state and zip code fields is probably the most popular custom field. If you added these three fields to a report individually, they would be printed as shown in Figure 16-19.

Figure 16-19 City, state and zip code fields added to the report

This is probably not the way that you want the fields to print. You probably want these fields to look the way that they do at the top of the Contact Status report shown earlier in Figure 16-17. You can create custom fields in one of two ways, as explained below:

① Use fields that are already on the report.
② Add fields to the report and then hide them.

The benefit of using option 1 is that it is less work. To get the name of the fields that you want to use, click on the fields in the report.

Figure 16-20 shows that the Email count field is selected. If you look at the top of the Properties window on the right of the figure, you will see the field name E-mail2. If you wanted to use this field in a custom field, you would reference it as E-mail2.

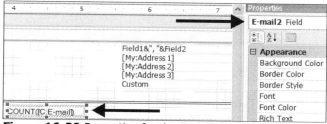

Figure 16-20 Properties for the E-mail count field

Select the second option listed above when the fields that you need are not already on the report. If you look closely below the custom field in the Contact Status report, in the design view, you will see light gray lines.

Chapter 16

If you click on the first gray line and then look at the top of the Properties window, you should see Field6, as illustrated in Figure 16-21.

If you see Field7 or 8, you are in the right place. Field6 is the City field. Field7 is the State field and Field8 is the Zip Code field.

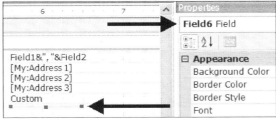

Figure 16-21 Hidden field selected

Exercise 16.2: How To Create A Custom Field

In this exercise you will create a custom field for fields that are not on the report. You will create a custom field that combines the city, state and zip code fields into one field.

1. Save the Birthday List report as `My Custom Field Report`.

2. Delete the three fields below the Custom field shown above in Figure 16-21. If you cannot see them, click in the area below the Custom field. Delete the Custom field shown above in Figure 16-21.

Hiding Fields On A Report

When you have to use fields that are not already on the report to create a custom field, you have to add them to the report and then hide them. The reason that you hide the fields is because they should not be printed in their current format. When you draw the box for a field that you have to hide, you should make it as small as possible and place it in a location that is not in the way of the other fields on the report. In step 2 above, you deleted three fields. You do not have to make the fields as small as the ones that you deleted, if you do not want to.

 Once you double-click on the first field that you need to add to the report, you do not have to close the Select Field dialog box. Double-click on the next field in the dialog box that you need to add.

3. Add the My Record type City, State and Zip Code fields, but not the labels, to the Page Header section.

4. Select the three fields that you just added, then change the **VISIBLE** option on the Properties window to False.

Figure 16-22 shows the hidden fields. I don't know about you, but I find these fields easier to work with and know what they are, then the three fields that you deleted under the custom field earlier in this exercise, that you can't see.

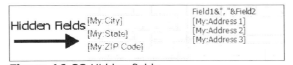

Figure 16-22 Hidden fields

5. Click the System Field button in the Toolbox, then draw a box under the My:Address 3 field in the Page Header section.

6. Select the Custom field option, then clear the **INCLUDE A LABEL** option. Click Add, then click Close.

Customizing Report Templates

7. Select the Custom field. Type the following in the **EXPRESSION** field on the Properties window, as shown in Figure 16-23. `City1&", "&State1&" "&ZipCode1`. The only place that there should be a space is between each set of quotes and after the comma.

Figure 16-23 Expression for the custom field

 If you look at the fields above the Custom field that you created, you will see that there is no space between them. This is done to make the report look better. It is not mandatory though.

8. Align the custom field on the left with the Address 3 field.

9. Make the font and size of the custom field the same as the My:Address 3 field, if it is not already.

10. Save the changes and preview the report. The name and address section should look like the one shown in Figure 16-24.

    The blank line is because the record does not have any data in the Address 3 field.

```
Chris Huffman, CH TechONE
13 East 54th St.
Suite 300

New York, NY 10008
```
Figure 16-24 Result of the custom field

Modifying Report Sections

There will be times when an existing report has the layout and many of the fields that you need for a new report. Instead of creating a report from scratch, you can save an existing report with a different file name and modify it. You can hide or delete the fields in sections of a report that are not needed. You can also force a section to start on a new page.

Exercise 16.3: Hiding A Report Section

As you learned earlier, sections of the report cannot be removed. If a report does not need a section, you can hide it by following the steps below.

1. Lookup all contacts.

2. Save the Contact Status report as `My Contact Report - Hidden Section`.

3. Click on the Page Footer section bar, then press the F4 key if the Properties window is not open.

 If the Properties window is already open, you can open the drop-down list at the top and select the section of the report that you want to change the properties of.

4. Click in the **VISIBLE** property to open the drop-down list, then select No.

5. Save the changes. If you preview the report you will not see the fields in the Page Footer section.

Chapter 16

Exercise 16.4: Adding A Section To A Report

Sections are added to a report to group and sort the detail records. Once you add a section to the report, you can add fields and other objects to it. You will group the report by company name, sorted in ascending order.

1. Save the My Contact Report - Hidden Section report as `My Contact Report - Added Section`.

2. Edit ⇒ Define Sections. Click the Add button.

3. Select Company in the Fields list on the dialog box shown in Figure 16-25, then click OK.

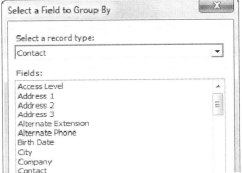

Figure 16-25 Select a Field to Group By dialog box

4. Click on the **SECTION 2** option on the left. At the bottom of Figure 16-26 you will see that the section will be sorted in ascending order, which is what you want. Leave the dialog box open to complete the next part of the exercise.

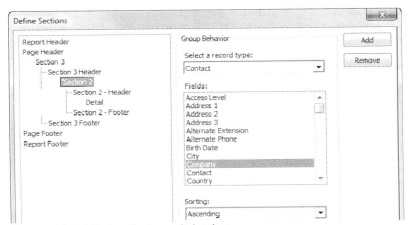

Figure 16-26 Define Sections dialog box

 Double-clicking on any section header in the Report Designer window will open the Define Sections dialog box.

16-15

Customizing Report Templates

Define Sections Dialog Box Options

The options on the right shown in Figure 16-27 are used to customize the sections of the report. They are explained below.

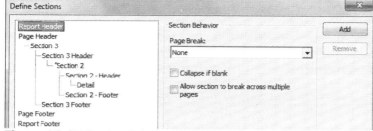

Figure 16-27 Section Behavior options

① The **PAGE BREAK** options shown in Figure 16-28 are used to determine whether or not a section will start on a new page. I often use the **AFTER** option on the Report Header section as the way to make that section print on a page by itself, so that it can be used as a cover page for the report.

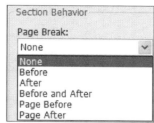

Figure 16-28 Page Break options

② If checked, the **COLLAPSE IF BLANK** option shown on the right of Figure 16-27 above will hide the section when the report is printed if it does not have any fields or objects in it.

③ If checked, the **ALLOW SECTION TO BREAK ACROSS MULTIPLE PAGES** option allows a report section to print on more than one page.

How To Remove A Section Of The Report

If you slide the dialog box out of the way, you will see that the report is also grouped on the Contact field. (See Section 3 Header.) This group is not needed. The steps below show you how to remove a section.

1. Click on the section that you want to remove on the Define Sections dialog box. In this exercise click on the Section 3 option, then click the **REMOVE** button.

2. Click Yes when prompted to delete the report section, then click OK to close the Define Sections dialog box.

3. Save the changes and preview the report.

You should see that the contacts on the first few pages do not have a company name, which is why the records are at the beginning of the report. When you get past the contacts without a company name, you should see that the report is now in order by company name.

Resize A Section Of The Report

You can manually resize a report section to make it smaller or you can hide a section by dragging the section bar above or below the section that you want to resize. In Exercise 16.3 you used the **VISIBLE** option on the Properties window to hide a section of the report.

Report Margins
File ⇒ Page Setup, is used to change the margins for the report. The options on this dialog box work the same way that they do in word processing software.

Exercise 16.5: How To Create A Section Break
In this exercise you will create a section break. You will use the Report Header section to create a cover page for the report. You will also add a system field to the Report Header section.

Create The Cover Page
The Contact Status report already has the Print Date, Print Time and Page Number system fields in the Page Footer section. In this part of the exercise you will add the Print Date system field to the Report Header section of the report. Yes, I know that the report already has this field, but I did not want to select a field that would not make sense on a cover page.

1. Save the Contact Status report as `My Cover Page Report`.

2. Make the Report Header section longer, then add a Text field to the section and type `Report Cover Page` in the Text field in the Properties window.

3. Change the Border Style to **DASH DOT DOT**, then change the font to Comic Sans MS, bold, size 18.

4. Center the text across the top of the Report Header section.

Add A System Field
1. Click the System Field button in the Toolbox and draw a box below the text that you just added. Select the Print Date field. Click Add, then click Close.

2. Change the label of the field to `This report was printed on`. Resize the label so that you can see all of the text.

Add A Page Break
In this part of the exercise you will add a page break after the Report Header section so that it is the only content that prints on the first page of the report.

1. Double-click on the Report Header bar.

2. Open the Page Break drop-down list and select **AFTER**, then click OK.

Selecting the Page Header section and the **BEFORE** Page option will produce the same result as the steps above.

3. Save the changes, then preview the report.

The top of the first page should look like the one shown in Figure 16-29.

Figure 16-29 Report cover page

Customizing Report Templates

At the bottom of the page you should see the Page Footer information. I could not find a way to keep this from printing on the first page. The second page of the report contains the data.

Exercise 16.6: Using The Picture Field

Picture Field Not Working
This field did not work as intended when testing it in ACT! 2013. It did work in ACT! 2012. I left this exercise in the book in case there is a fix for it after this book is published.

The Picture Field displays a different image or photo for each detail record on the report. In this exercise you will modify the Birthday List report to print the contacts photo on the report.

1. Save the Birthday List report as My Photo Birthday List.

2. Make the Detail section a little longer. Click the Picture Field button on the Toolbox, then draw a box to the right of the Birth Date field.

3. Select the Photo field, then clear the Include a label option. Click Add, then click Close.

4. Save the changes, then preview the report. It should look like the one shown in Figure 16-30. If you scroll through the report, you will see some photos that are a lot larger than the one shown in Figure 16-30. The best way to handle this is to make all of the photos the same size before adding them to the database.

Figure 16-30 Report with photo added

Exercise 16.7: Create A New Report

So far you have modified existing reports. At some point you may need a report that is completely different then the ones that come with ACT!. If so, you will have to create a report from scratch. What many people do is create their own template to use as the basis for new reports. The template that you will create in this exercise will include fields and objects that you want to include on every new report. That way, you do not have to spend time adding page numbers, print dates and logos to every report that you create from scratch.

Create A Custom Report Template

In this part of the exercise you will use an existing report as the basis for the template for new reports that you will create.

1. Save the Contact Status report as My Report Template.

2. Change the Contact Status title to Report Title goes here. Display the entire title.

3. Leave the logo and blue line in the Page Header section. Delete all of the other fields in this section including the three hidden fields below the Custom field.

4. Delete everything in the Detail and Report Header sections.

5. Save the changes. Minimize the Report Designer window.

Look Up The Records

In this part of the exercise, you will use an existing query as the basis for the records that will appear on the report. This report will display all records that were created in the last 30 days.

1. Lookup ⇒ Advanced ⇒ Advanced Query.

2. File ⇒ Open. Double-click on the New contacts in last 30 days query file in your folder.

3. Click the Preview button. You should see the query and results shown in Figure 16-31.

    The records at the bottom of the dialog box are the ones that you created in the last 30 days.

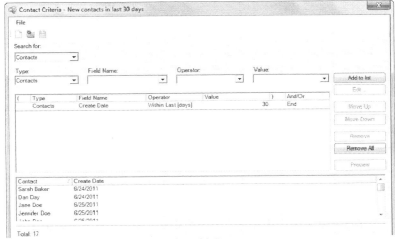

Figure 16-31 New contacts in last 30 Days query

4. Click OK. Click OK again to replace the current lookup.

Create A Report From Scratch

Before creating a new report, it is a good idea to look up all of the contacts so that you will have some data to test the report with. In this part of the exercise you will create a new report. You will use the template that you created earlier in this exercise.

1. Save the My Report Template report that you created as My Custom Contact Report.

2. Change the report title to the file name.

3. Click the Field button in the Toolbox and draw a box in the Detail section. Add the following fields with labels: Contact, Company, Create Date and Record Creator.

 To select the field and label, hold down the left mouse button and draw a box around the label and field. This allows you to move both objects at the same time. This is sometimes referred to as the **LASSO** technique.

Customizing Report Templates

4. Drag the labels to the bottom of the Page Header section.

   Rearrange the fields and labels so that your report looks like the one shown in Figure 16-32.

Figure 16-32 Layout for a new report

5. Save the changes, then preview the report. You should see the same records that were retrieved from the query.

Subreports

A subreport is a report inside of another report. Subreports have many uses. Often a subreport contains data from a tab on a detail view, but you are not limited to only using data from a tab on a subreport. For example, if you are a realtor, you could add three image fields to the top of the Contact detail view to display three photos for each house that they have listed for sale. Subreports can be used to display an unlimited amount of the same type of information, like all of the opportunities for a contact. The opportunities would be added to the subreport.

Another example is you may have the need to display all of the notes for each contact.

The Notes field would be added to the subreport.

If you look at the bottom of the Detail section of the layout shown in Figure 16-33, you will see five subreports.

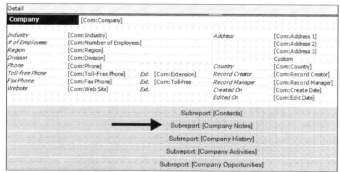

Figure 16-33 Subreports illustrated

Exercise 16.8: Create A Subreport

In this exercise you will create a subreport and add it to the report that you created in the previous exercise. The subreport will contain data from each contacts History tab.

1. Open the My Custom Contact report, if it is not already open. Save it as `My First Subreport`.

2. Make the Detail section a little longer, then click the Subreport button in the Toolbox and draw a box below the fields in the Detail section. The box should start at the one inch mark go to the 7.5 inch mark on the ruler.

3. Type `My History Subreport` in the Subreport name field, as shown in Figure 16-34.

   Double-click on the Contact1 field.

Figure 16-34 Subreports dialog box

4. Save the changes, then double-click on the Subreport field in the Detail section.

5. Make the Header and Detail sections longer, then change the Visible option to Yes for both sections.

6. Add a text field to the Header section. Type `History Records`. Make the field bold and underlined.

7. Add a field to the Detail section. On the Select Field dialog box, open the Record Type drop-down list field and select Contact History.

8. Add the following fields with labels to the Detail section of the subreport: Date, Result, Regarding & Details, Record Manager. Leave the Select Field dialog box open.

Add The Subreport To The Main Report

In this part of the exercise you will add the subreport that you just created to the Detail section of the My Custom Contact report. Adding the Subreport is not sufficient. The subreport must also be linked to the Custom Contact report by a field that is unique and in both tables. This is usually an **ID** field. ID fields hold unique values like a social security number. The ID field that both tables have that is unique is the Contact ID field. This is how the correct records are retrieved for the subreport.

1. Open the Record Type drop-down list field and select Contact. Add the Contact ID field without a label. Change the Visible option to False for this field.

2. When you move the labels to the Header section below the History Records text field, make them bold and underlined.

3. Add a rectangle above the labels in the Header section. Make it narrow so that it looks like two lines.

4. Rearrange and align the fields and labels to match the layout shown in Figure 16-35. You can make the Date field smaller and the Regarding & Details field wider.

Figure 16-35 Subreport layout

Customizing Report Templates

5. Change the **RICH TEXT** property of the Regarding & Details field to Yes.

6. Save the changes. Open the drop-down list above the Toolbox shown in Figure 16-36, then select My First Subreport Report [Main].

Figure 16-36 Subreports drop-down list

Finish The Main Report

1. Change the Can Shrink option to Yes and the Hide on empty subreports option to No for the detail section and the subreport.

2. Edit ⇒ Define Sections. Delete the Section 3 option, then click OK.

3. Save the changes.

4. File ⇒ Run. Select the All contacts option. Clear the Exclude My Record option.

5. The History tab was automatically added to the Define Filters dialog box when you created the subreport for history records.

    On the History tab, check all three history type options, then change the Date Range to All.

    Click OK.

    The report should look like the one shown in Figure 16-37.

    Close the Report Designer.

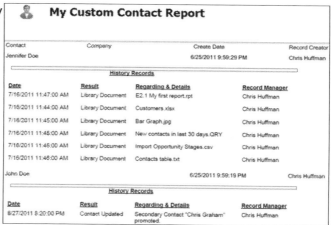

Figure 16-37 My Custom Contact report

Modifying Labels And Envelopes

In previous exercises in this chapter you learned how to modify reports. Modifying labels and envelopes is very similar. The main difference is that there are less options. The steps to modify labels are the same as envelopes. In the next exercise you will learn how to modify an envelope. If you want to modify a label, in step 2 below, select "Labels" instead of "Envelopes" on the Print dialog box. Like reports, the first thing that you should do when you open a label or envelope template is to save it with a new name if you are going to modify it.

Exercise 16.9: Modify An Envelope (Or Label) Template

In this exercise you will add text to an envelope. If you were sending out letters to invite people to an event, you could add a line of text to the envelope that lets the recipient know that they have been invited.

1. Look up the records in the Potential Book Customer group.

Chapter 16

2. File ⇒ Print. Select **ENVELOPES**, then select the size. In this exercise select size 10.

3. Click the **EDIT TEMPLATE** button.

4. File ⇒ Save As. Save the file as `My Custom Envelope`.

5. Add a Text field above the first custom field in the center of the envelope. Type `You are invited to our Spring Gala` in the Text field. Change the font size to 10 and make the text italic. Save the changes.

6. File ⇒ Run. Select the Current Lookup option, then click OK.

   When you preview the envelope it should look like the one shown in Figure 16-38.

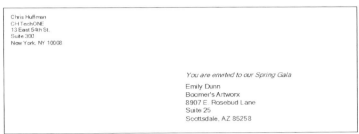

Figure 16-38 Custom envelope

Creating Label And Envelope Templates

If the label or envelope size that you need is not in ACT! you can create your own. The majority of the steps are the same as creating a report. The steps below are for envelopes. If you need to create labels, in step 2, select a label template.

1. File ⇒ New, from the Report Designer window or Reports ⇒ New Template, from an ACT! view. You will see the New Report dialog box.

2. Select the Contact Reports type, then double-click on the Contact Envelopes option.

3. Open the Select an envelope size drop-down list and select Custom. Accept the default height and width options, then click OK. The rest of the process is the same as creating a report.

CUSTOMIZING THE MENU AND TOOLBARS

In this chapter you will learn several ways to customize the menu and toolbars, including how to:

- ☑ Modify menus
- ☑ Create custom menus
- ☑ Create custom commands
- ☑ Modify toolbars
- ☑ Create keyboard shortcuts
- ☑ Modify the Navigation Pane

Check The ACT! Forum For An Update Before Doing The Exercises In This Chapter

In prior versions of ACT!, creating custom toolbars did not cause any problems. At the time this book went to print, creating custom toolbars caused ACT! not to open anymore. I decided to leave this chapter in the book in case there is an update to ACT! 2013 that fixes this.

CHAPTER 17

Customizing The Menu And Toolbars

Modifying Menus

You can modify menus by adding more commands to them. You can also create custom submenus. If you created several of your own reports, you could create a submenu off of the Reports menu and add your reports there. The commands that are on the menus that come with ACT! can also be modified. If you run the same queries all the time you can add them to a menu or a toolbar.

Modifications to menus and toolbars are not saved in the database. If you make changes to the menus and toolbars and want other users to have the same changes, the changes have to be added to each computer.

Exercise 17.1: Using The Customize Dialog Box To Modify Menus

In this exercise you will learn how to perform the following tasks to modify menus.

① Add a command to a menu.
② Create a custom menu.
③ Create a custom submenu.
④ Rearrange commands on menus.
⑤ Delete commands on a menu.

How To Add A Command To A Menu

In ACT!, a command is a series of instructions that perform a task like open a dialog box. Usually, commands are created for repetitive tasks. In this part of the exercise you will add a command to the Contacts menu.

1. Open the Contact detail view.

   Tools ⇒ Customize ⇒ Menus and Toolbars.

   You will see the dialog box shown in Figure 17-1.

   These are the toolbars that come with ACT!.

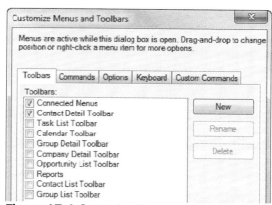

Figure 17-1 Customize Menus and Toolbars dialog box

2. On the Commands tab, click on the Opportunities option in the **CATEGORIES** list.

3. Click on the **CREATE QUOTE** command in the Commands list, as shown in Figure 17-2.

Chapter 17

Figure 17-2 Commands tab options

4. Drag the Create Quote command to the Contacts menu, as illustrated below in Figure 17-3. The Contacts menu will open.

5. Drag the mouse down past the **EDIT CONTACT ACCESS** option, as illustrated below in Figure 17-4, then release the mouse button.

6. Close the Customize Menus and Toolbars dialog box. The Contacts menu should look like the one shown in Figure 17-5.

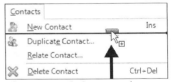

Figure 17-3 Command dragged to the Contacts menu

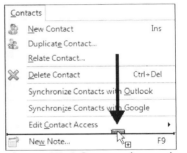

Figure 17-4 Command moved on the menu

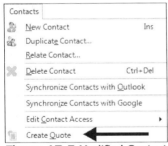

Figure 17-5 Modified Contacts menu

How To Create A Custom Menu

If you have the need to add several commands to menus, it may be easier to find the commands by creating your own menu and placing all of your commands there. The steps below show you how to create a custom menu. You can add commands to menus that you create, just like you did in the previous part of this exercise.

1. Tools ⇒ Customize ⇒ Menus and Toolbars ⇒ Custom Commands tab, then click the **NEW** button.

Customizing The Menu And Toolbars

2. Type `MyMenu` in the Command name field, then click the **ADD COMMAND** button.

   Your dialog box should look like the one shown in Figure 17-6.

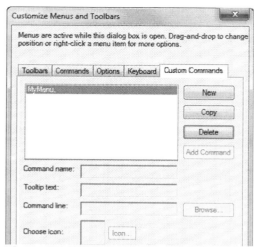

Figure 17-6 Command name added

3. On the Commands tab, click on the Custom Commands category.

   You should see the menu that you created on the Custom Commands tab, as shown in Figure 17-7.

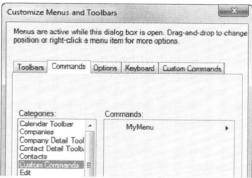

Figure 17-7 Customized menu created

4. Drag the MyMenu command to the menu bar in ACT!. Place it to the right of the Help menu, as shown in Figure 17-8. Leave the dialog box open.

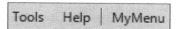

Figure 17-8 Custom menu added to the menu bar

 You can add menus that you create between existing menu options, meaning you could add your menu after the Reports menu for example.

How To Create A Custom Submenu

Submenus are menus that open from an option on a menu. You can add as many commands to a submenu as you need. Commands that have a triangle, as shown earlier in Figure 17-5, have submenus.

In this part of the exercise you will add a submenu to the custom menu that you just created. Adding submenus is the same process as adding other commands.

1. On the Commands tab, select the Reports category.

2. Drag the Company Reports command to the menu that you just created and added to the workspace. You will see a white box below the menu that you created, as shown in Figure 17-9.

Figure 17-9 Menu command in position

3. Drag the submenu to the white box and release the mouse button.

4. Close the Customize Menus and Toolbars dialog box. Your menu should look like the one shown in Figure 17-10.

Figure 17-10 Submenu added to the menu

Rearrange Commands On A Menu

If you decide that you do not like the order of the commands on a menu, you can change the order by following the steps below. In this part of the exercise you will move the Create Quote option on the Contacts menu.

1. Open the Customize Menus and Toolbars dialog box.

2. Open the Contacts menu on the workspace and drag the Create Quote command up and place it below the **DUPLICATE CONTACT** command, as illustrated in Figure 17-11.

   In addition to being able to add commands to a menu from the dialog box, you can drag items from one menu to another.

Figure 17-11 Command moved on the menu

How To Delete Commands From A Menu

You can delete a command from a menu by following the steps below. In this part of the exercise you will delete the Create Quote command from the Contacts menu.

1. Open the Customize Menus and Toolbars dialog box.

2. Open the Contacts menu, then right-click on the **CREATE QUOTE** command and select Delete.

Exercise 17.2: Creating Custom Commands

If you use documents like a template or another software application on a regular basis in conjunction with ACT! and do not want to keep opening the file from outside of ACT!, you can create a custom command to open the template or software package from inside of ACT!.

In this exercise you will create two custom commands. One to open a document and one to open an application. You will then add the commands to the custom menu that you created earlier in this chapter.

Customizing The Menu And Toolbars

Create A Custom Command For A Document

1. Tools ⇒ Customize ⇒ Menus and Toolbars ⇒ Custom Commands tab, then click the New button.

2. In the Command name field type `My Document Command`.

3. In the **TOOLTIP TEXT** field type `Opens the Specialties document`.

4. Click the Browse button at the end of the **COMMAND LINE** field, then double-click on the Specialties.txt file in your folder.

   You should have the options shown in Figure 17-12.

Figure 17-12 Options to open a document

 If you know the full path to the file or application that you are creating the command for, you can type it in the **COMMAND LINE** field instead of clicking the Browse button. If you wanted to use a different icon then the one in the **CHOOSE ICON** section, click the **ICON** button to select the icon file that you want to use.

5. Click the Add Command button. Leave the dialog box open to complete the next part of the exercise.

Create A Custom Command For An Application

1. On the Custom Commands tab, click New.

2. In the Command name field, type `My Application Command`.

3. In the Tooltip text field, type `Opens Notepad`.

Chapter 17

4. Click the Browse button at the end of the Command line field, then double-click on the **NOTEPAD.EXE** file in the C:\Windows folder.

   You should have the options shown in Figure 17-13.

   Click the Add Command button.

   Leave the dialog box open to complete the next part of the exercise.

Figure 17-13 Options to open an application

Add The Commands To The Menu

Earlier you added a command to the custom menu that you created. Follow the same steps to add the two commands that you just created to your custom menu.

Place the commands below the Company Reports option. Your custom menu should look like the one shown in Figure 17-14.

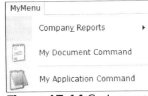

Figure 17-14 Custom menu with commands added

Close the Customize Menus and Toolbars dialog box. Notice that the icons that are at the bottom of the dialog boxes shown earlier in Figures 17-12 and 17-13 are displayed on the menu.

Test The Commands

1. My Menu ⇒ My Document Command. The Specialties document will open.

2. My Menu ⇒ My Application Command. The Notepad application will open.

Deleting Custom Menus

If you have created a custom menu that you no longer need, you can delete it by following the steps below.

1. Open the Customize Menus and Toolbars dialog box, then click on the Custom Commands tab. You should see the menu that you created, as shown earlier in Figure 17-13.

2. Select the command that you want to delete, then click the Delete button. Click OK when you see the Delete Custom Command message.

3. Close the dialog box. The custom menu that you created should no longer be on the menu bar.

Customizing The Menu And Toolbars

Modifying Toolbars

You can modify the toolbars by adding or removing commands. You can also rearrange the order of the buttons on the toolbar. Each view has its own toolbar. That means that if you add a button to the Groups toolbar you will not see it on the Contacts toolbar. You can also add custom commands to a toolbar like you can to a menu. The difference between customizing a menu and a toolbar is that the changes to menus are visible throughout ACT! regardless of the view that is open. Changes to toolbars are only visible on the views that have the toolbar that you change.

One reason people customize toolbars is to place the commands, files and applications that they use the most out in the open where they can be seen. This allows you to be more efficient because you do not have to remember which menu has the option that you are looking for.

Exercise 17.3: Customizing Toolbars

In this exercise you will learn how to perform the following tasks to customize toolbars.

① Add a command to a toolbar.
② Add a custom command to a toolbar.
③ Rearrange commands on a toolbar.
④ Customize toolbar buttons.

How To Add A Command To A Toolbar

In this part of the exercise you will add a command to the Contacts toolbar.

1. Open the Contact list view.

2. Right-click on the Contact list toolbar (not a button) and select Customize, as shown in Figure 17-15.

   Move the dialog box off of the toolbar if necessary.

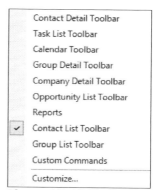

Figure 17-15 Toolbar shortcut menu

3. On the Commands tab, click on the **REPORTS** category, then drag the Contact Report command to the Contact list toolbar and place it after the **EXPORT TO EXCEL** button.

4. Close the dialog box. The Contact list toolbar should look like the one shown in Figure 17-16.

Figure 17-16 Command added to the Contacts toolbar

How To Add A Custom Command To A Toolbar

Just like you added a custom command to a menu, you can add a custom command to a toolbar. In this part of the exercise you will add a custom command that you created earlier in this chapter to the Groups toolbar.

1. Open the Group detail view.

2. Right-click on the Group detail toolbar and select Customize.

3. On the Commands tab, click on the Custom Commands category.

4. Drag the **MY APPLICATION COMMAND** to the toolbar and place it after the Save Changes button.

5. Close the dialog box. The Group detail toolbar should look like the one shown in Figure 17-17. If you click on the button that you just added, the Notepad application will open.

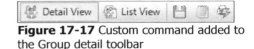

Figure 17-17 Custom command added to the Group detail toolbar

How To Rearrange Commands On A Toolbar

If you do not like the order that the commands (buttons) are in on the toolbar, you can change the order, just like you rearranged the order of the commands on a menu in Exercise 17.1. In this exercise you will move the report command to the left of the Export to Excel command on the Contact list view toolbar.

1. Open the Contact list view, then open the Customize Menus and Toolbars dialog box.

2. Drag the Contact Report command to the left of the Export to Excel command and release the mouse button.

How To Customize Toolbar Buttons

You can customize each button on a toolbar. Figure 17-18 shows the toolbar button customization options.

Table 17-1 explains the customization options.

To open this shortcut menu right-click on a button on the toolbar when the Customize Menus and Toolbars dialog box is open.

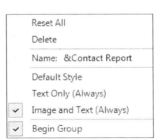

Figure 17-18 Toolbar button shortcut menu

Customizing The Menu And Toolbars

Option	Description
Reset All	Resets all toolbars and menus to the way they were when ACT! was first installed. I don't know why the menus are reset with this option when all of the other options on this shortcut menu are only for toolbar buttons. The only thing that I can think of is because the Reset All command shares code with the Reset Menus and Toolbars command.
Delete	Deletes the command that you right-click on.
Name	Is used to change the name of the button.
Default Style	Only displays the icon for the command without any text. This is how many of the toolbar buttons are, by default.
Text Only (Always)	Only displays text with no icon, as shown earlier in Figure 17-16.
Image and Text (Always)	Displays the icon and name of the button, as illustrated in Figure 17-19.
Begin Group	Creates a group of buttons by inserting a vertical line on the toolbar, as illustrated in Figure 17-20. The buttons in the group do not have to have anything in common. One use for this may be if you need to add a few buttons to the toolbar that open the applications that you use often. You could add vertical lines to the toolbar to group them together.

Table 17-1 Toolbar button shortcut menu options explained

Figure 17-19 Image and Name button illustrated

Figure 17-20 Vertical line added to the toolbar

 If you right-click on a blank space at the end of the toolbar and select **CUSTOM COMMANDS** on the shortcut menu shown earlier in Figure 17-15, you will see all of the commands that you have created on their own row of the toolbar, as illustrated in Figure 17-21.

Figure 17-21 Custom commands on the toolbar

How To Distribute Custom Menus And Toolbars To Other Users

Earlier in this chapter you learned how to customize menus and toolbars. If you want other people that use the database to have the same customized menus and toolbars that you created, follow the steps below. For now you can just read the steps.

1. File ⇒ Back Up ⇒ Personal Files.

2. Click the **BROWSE** button. Select a folder on a server or external hard drive that you want to store the files with the custom menus and toolbars on, that will be copied to other computers.

Chapter 17

3. You can rename the zip file or accept the default zip file name that is shown in Figure 17-22.

   Clear all of the options except the Menus and Toolbars option, then click OK. The files will be backed up.

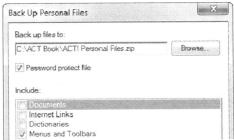

Figure 17-22 Back Up Personal Files dialog box

How To Install The Custom Menu And Toolbar On Another Computer

Before installing the customized menus on another computer, you should confirm that the computer does not already have a custom ACT! menu or toolbar. If it does, you will overwrite it when you copy your custom menu or toolbar to the hard drive.

1. Go to the computer that you want to install the custom menu and toolbar on, then open ACT!.

2. File ⇒ Restore ⇒ Personal Files.

3. Click the Browse button shown in Figure 17-23, then navigate to the folder that has the zip file with the customizations that you created and double-click on the zip file.

Figure 17-23 Restore Personal Files dialog box

4. Click OK on the Restore Personal Files dialog box. The custom menus and toolbars will be installed on the computer. Repeat this process on each computer that you want to have the custom menus and toolbars.

How To Delete A Command From A Toolbar

Deleting a command from a toolbar is the same as deleting a command from a menu. In this part of the exercise you will delete the Open NotePad command that you created from the toolbar.

1. Open the view that has the toolbar that you want to delete a command from. In this exercise open the Group detail view.

2. Open the Customize Menus and Toolbars dialog box.

3. Right-click on the command on the toolbar that you want to delete and select Delete.

4. Close the Customize Menus and Toolbars dialog box.

Customizing The Menu And Toolbars

How To Reset Menus And Toolbars

If you have made changes to a menu or toolbar and no longer want or need the changes, you can manually remove the changes one by one or you can reset the menus and toolbars back to the way that they were when ACT! was first installed. Any keyboard shortcuts that you created will also be reset. If you need to reset these tools, follow the steps below. The commands that you create are not deleted, just removed from the menus and toolbars.

1. Tools ⇒ Customize ⇒ Reset Menus and Toolbars.

    You will see the message shown in Figure 17-24.

Figure 17-24 Reset Menus and Toolbars message

2. Click OK and the menus and toolbars will be reset.

Exercise 17.4: Creating Keyboard Shortcuts

In addition to being able to customize menus and toolbars, you can create keyboard shortcuts. Keyboard shortcuts are the keystrokes shown at the end of some options on a menu, as shown earlier in Figure 17-11. The steps below show you how to create a keyboard shortcut.

1. Tools ⇒ Customize ⇒ Menus and Toolbars.

2. On the Keyboard tab, click on the Custom Command category at the bottom of the list.

3. Click on the My Document command, as shown in Figure 17-25, then click the **ASSIGN SHORTCUT** button.

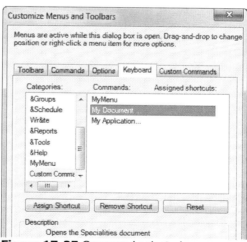

Figure 17-25 Command selected

4. Press and hold down the Alt key, then press the letter D. You should see OK in the bottom field on the dialog box shown in Figure 17-26.

5. Click OK, then click Close. If you open the menu that you created, you will see the keyboard shortcut next to the My Document command, as shown in Figure 17-27.

17-12

Chapter 17

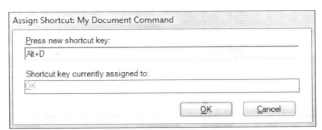

Figure 17-26 Assign Shortcut dialog box

Figure 17-27 Keyboard shortcut added to a command

Keyboard Shortcuts

ACT!, like other software has keyboard shortcuts. Many of them use the Control (CTRL) key.
Table 17-2 contains some of the keyboard shortcuts. If you want to know whether or not a specific command has a shortcut, open the menu that the command is on to find out.

Shortcut	What It Does . . .
CTRL + C	Copies the selected text.
CTRL + D	Clears an activity.
CTRL + H	Creates a history record.
CTRL + I	Attaches a file.
CTRL + L	Schedules a telephone call activity.
CTRL + M	Schedules a meeting activity.
CTRL + P	Prints an address book, calendar, envelope, label and reports.
CTRL + T	Schedules a To-Do activity.
CTRL + V	Pastes the contents of the clipboard into a field in ACT!.
CTRL + X	Cuts (deletes) the selected text.
CTRL + Z	Undoes the last action.
CTRL + F5	Refreshes the window.
CTRL + F11	Opens a new sales opportunity.
F1	Opens the Help system.
F3	Opens the weekly calendar.
F5	Opens the monthly calendar.
F7	Opens the Task List view.
F8	Opens the Contact list view.
F9	Inserts a note.
F10	Opens the Group list view.
F11	Opens the Contact detail view.

Table 17-2 ACT! keyboard shortcuts explained

Navigation Pane Customization Options

The default buttons on the Navigation Pane provide links to the screens in ACT!. This section explains the customization options.

 If you used ACT! 2009 or earlier, you will see that ACT! Pro 2011 and higher has fewer customization options for the Navigation Pane.

Customizing The Menu And Toolbars

When you click on the arrow on the last button on the Navigation Pane. You will see the menu shown in Figure 17-28. The options are explained below.

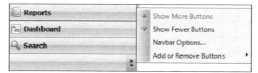

Figure 17-28 Navigation Pane shortcut menu

The **SHOW MORE BUTTONS** option restores the first option on the empty button to the Navigation Pane.

The **SHOW FEWER BUTTONS** option removes the last visible button on the Navigation Pane and places it on the empty button at the bottom of the Navigation Pane.

The **NAVBAR OPTIONS** option opens the dialog box shown in Figure 17-29.

This dialog box is used to display or hide buttons and change the order of the buttons on the Navigation Pane.

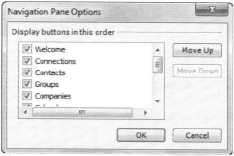

Figure 17-29 Navigation Pane Options dialog box

The **ADD OR REMOVE BUTTONS** option displays the options shown on the right side of Figure 17-30.

Options without a border like the Welcome and Groups options means that they will not appear on the Navigation Pane.

To restore a button to the Navigation Pane, select it here or on the Navigation Pane Options dialog box shown above in Figure 17-29.

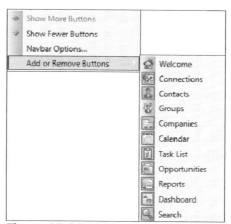

Figure 17-30 Add or Remove Buttons menu options

USING THE LAYOUT DESIGNER

In this chapter you will learn how to use the Layout Designer to modify the views. To modify the views, you will learn about the following:

- ☑ Layout Designer options
- ☑ Formatting toolbar
- ☑ Layout Designer ToolBox
- ☑ Customizing tabs on a view
- ☑ Adding fields to a tab
- ☑ Adding graphics to a layout
- ☑ Changing the background color of a tab
- ☑ Using the Properties window
- ☑ Changing the label for a field on a layout
- ☑ Aligning fields on a layout
- ☑ Changing the tab stop order

Using The Layout Designer

What Is A Layout?

A layout is how the fields and tabs are arranged on the view.

ACT! Layouts

ACT! comes with the layouts shown in Figure 18-1. Each layout can have different fields. An example of this is the Photo field shown in Figure 18-2 from the ACTDemo layout. The Personal Info tab on the two basic layouts do not have the Photo field by default.

Figure 18-2 Photo field on the Personal Info tab of the ACTDemo layout

Figure 18-1 ACT! Layouts

Layout File Extensions

As shown above in Figure 18-1, layout files have one of the file extensions explained below.

.ALY is for company layouts.
.CLY is for contact layouts.
.GLY is for group layouts.
.OLY is for opportunity layouts.

> The numbers after the Basic Layouts shown above in Figure 18-1, refer to the screen resolution. If your monitor or LCD has a resolution of 1024x768, that is the layout that would look best on your computer screen. What I noticed between these two layout resolutions is that some fields are in different places. This was probably done to accommodate the different screen resolutions.

Layout Designer

The Layout Designer (Tools ⇒ Design Layouts) shown in Figure 18-3 is used to change what the views, including the tabs, look like. You can change the background color, add fields, remove fields, rearrange the order of fields and much more.

Chapter 15 covered how to create new fields. Fields can only be used when they are on a layout. If an existing layout meets most of your needs, you can add the new fields to it or you can save an existing layout with a new file name and add the fields to the layout with the new file name. You can also create a new layout from scratch. Creating and modifying layouts require administrator or manager rights. While the layout modification exercises in this chapter are for the contact view and tabs, you can modify the opportunity, company and group layouts also.

Chapter 18

Figure 18-3 Layout Designer window

Layout Design Tips

There are some things to take into consideration when creating or modifying a layout, as discussed below.

① Many new layout designers are often more concerned with how a layout looks, instead of how functional it is. A primary goal of a layout is to make the data entry as easy as possible.
② If you find that you are constantly going from tab to tab to enter basic information, the layout may need to be modified. If there are fields on a layout that are not being used, consider deleting them from the layout.
③ Layouts that you modify or create can be used by other databases. If you plan to use a layout created or modified in one database in a different database, make sure that the second database has the same fields.

Layout Designer Options

There are a lot of options that you can use to design or modify the layout for a view. Many of them are similar to the options used to modify a report.

Edit Menu The options on this menu are the same as the editing options in word processing software. The exception to this is the **TABS** option. The tabs option opens the Edit Tabs dialog box. You can create new tabs, delete tabs and rearrange the order of tabs on a view.

Using The Layout Designer

View Menu The first option on this menu opens the Properties window shown in Figure 18-4.

Different options are available on the Properties window depending on the object that is selected in the layout before the Properties window is opened.

If the Properties window is too small, you can resize it by putting the mouse pointer on the edge of the window and dragging the edge to the size that you want.

As shown at the bottom of Figure 18-4, the tabs can be placed at the top or bottom of the tab section.

Figure 18-4 Properties window

The default is to display the tabs at the top. Figure 18-5 shows the tabs displayed at the bottom of the layout.

Figure 18-5 Tabs displayed at the bottom of the layout

The **Toolbox** option opens and closes the ToolBox that is on the left side of the Designer window.

The **View ⇒ Tab Stops ⇒ Show Tab Stops** option displays the order (in red numbers) that the Tab key will move through the fields on the layout, as shown in Figure 18-6.

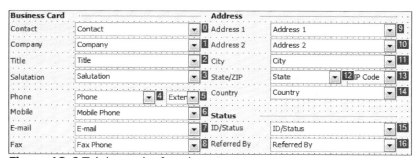

Figure 18-6 Tab key order for a layout

The **View ⇒ Enter Stops ⇒ Show Enter Stops** option will display the order (in green numbers) that the Enter key will move through the fields on the layout. It looks like the one for Tab stops.

Format Menu The options on this menu are used to align, size and space the fields on the layout.

18-4

Chapter 18

Layout Designer Formatting Toolbar

The first nine buttons on the toolbar shown in Figure 18-7 are the same buttons that are on the Formatting toolbar in most word processors. The remaining buttons are explained in Table 18-1. The buttons on this toolbar are used to change the look of objects like fields or labels on the layout.

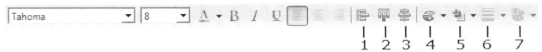

Figure 18-7 Layout Designer Formatting toolbar

Button	Description
1	Aligns the selected objects on the left side of the object. (1)
2	Aligns the selected objects on the top of the object. (1)
3	Aligns the selected objects on the center of the object. (1)
4	Select the background color of the object. If you want to match the color of an existing background on the layout, view the **BACKGROUND COLOR** option on the Properties window in the top portion of the view or the tab that has the color that you want to match.
5	The options shown in Figure 18-9 are used to add a border around the object.
6	Change the thickness of a line. (2)
7	Change the color of a line. (2)

Table 18-1 Layout Designer Formatting toolbar buttons explained

(1) This option is only available if two or more objects are selected. The align options are also available on the shortcut menu shown in Figure 18-8.
(2) The border is created by using a Drawing Object. This option is not used for fields.

Figure 18-9 Border Style options

Figure 18-8 Object shortcut menu

18-5

Using The Layout Designer

Layout Designer ToolBox

Figures 18-10 and 18-11 show the tabs on the ToolBox.

The **FIELD** tab has all of the field types that can be added to a layout.

The **DRAWING** tab contains other objects that can be added to a layout.

Figure 18-10 Field tab options

Figure 18-11 Drawing tab options

Field Tab Options

The **MEMO FIELD** is a free form field that is used as a comments field. It is similar to the fields on the User Fields tab. The difference is that you can allow more text to be entered into a memo field.

The **YES/NO FIELD** is a check box field. The Yes/No fields that you have seen on the layout are some of the fields used to filter records.

Tabs Overview

The detail views in ACT! come with tabs. If you need to add more fields to an existing tab or if you want to put certain fields on a tab by themselves, you can. The only limitation is that you cannot add a field to a tab that is already on a tab. The tabs in ACT! have features that you need to be aware of before you modify them. The following tabs are **SYSTEM TABS**: Notes, History, Activities, Opportunities, Groups/Companies, Secondary Contacts and Documents. If you do not need these tabs you can hide them. Each of these tabs has its own table in the database and because of this, you cannot customize these tabs like you can the other tabs that come with ACT! or tabs that you create. This is the reason that you can enter an unlimited number of records on each of these tabs for the same contact. This is known as **RELATIONAL** data.

Customizing Tabs

Tabs are used to organize fields. If there are fields that are only used for a season or promotion, it may be a good idea to put them on their own tab or create a layout for them. If the order of the tabs on a layout does not meet your needs or your users needs, you can change the order that the tabs are in. An example would be if you rarely use the History tab. Moving it to the last position in the row of tabs may be a good idea.

Exercise 18.1: Create A Tab On A Layout

In this exercise you will create a new tab on the Basic Contact Layout and add the Specializes In field that you created in Exercise 15.6 to the layout.

1. Switch to the Basic Contact Layout - 800x600.

2. Tools ⇒ Design Layouts ⇒ Contact. You should see the words **BASIC CONTACT LAYOUT - 800x600** in the Title bar of the Layout Designer window.

3. Edit ⇒ Tabs, then click the **ADD TAB** button on the Edit Tabs dialog box.

Chapter 18

4. Type My Tab in the Tab name field, as shown in Figure 18-12, then click OK.

Figure 18-12 Add Tab dialog box

5. On the Edit Tabs dialog box, click on the tab that you just created, then click the Move Up button once.

Hiding A Tab

To keep a tab from being displayed on the layout, click on the Tab name in the **SHOW TABS IN THIS ORDER** list, shown in Figure 18-13, then click the < button.

The tab will now be in the **HIDDEN TABS** list.

Figure 18-13 Edit Tabs dialog box

6. Your tab should be the second one from the bottom in the list, as shown above in Figure 18-13. Click the Close button.

Edit Tab Options

In addition to being able to add and hide tabs on the Edit Tabs dialog box you can also rename and delete tabs, as explained below.

① The **EDIT TAB** button is used to rename any tab except the System tabs.

② The **DELETE TAB** button is used to delete any tab except the System tabs. When deleting a tab, the fields on the tab are not deleted from the database. If you are not comfortable deleting a tab or are not 100% sure that the tab should be deleted, you should hide it instead.

Changing The Order Of The Tabs

The **MOVE UP** and **MOVE DOWN** buttons shown above in Figure 18-13 are used to change the order that the tabs are displayed in, from left to right on the layout.

Fields On A Layout

Like fields on a report, fields on a layout have two parts and work the same way that they do on a report. [See Chapter 16, Field vs Label]

Using The Layout Designer

Exercise 18.2: Adding Fields To A Tab

1. Click on the tab that you created at the bottom of the layout.

2. Click the **FIELD** button in the ToolBox.

3. Place the mouse pointer in the position where you want the upper left corner of the field to be placed on the layout.

   Draw a rectangle in the grid below the tabs, starting about a half an inch from the left border of the layout. When you release the mouse button you will see the dialog box shown in Figure 18-14.

   The fields on this dialog box are fields that have not already been added to the layout. You may be wondering why you do not see the Specializes In field that you created. The reason that you do not see the field in the list is because it was created as a drop-down list, not a field.

   The **NEW FIELD** button is used to create a new field.

Figure 18-14 Select Field dialog box with multiple fields selected

4. Click on the Specialty field at the bottom of the list, then click the Add button.

5. Click on a blank space on the layout so that the field is not selected. If necessary, click on the label and drag it to the left so that it is not touching the field.

> You can add more than one field to the layout at the same time. Click on the first field that you want to add in the Select Field dialog box. Press and hold down the **CTRL** key, then click on the other fields that you want to add, as shown above in Figure 18-14. Once you have selected all of the fields, click the Add button.

Text Boxes

Text boxes serve the same purpose that text fields serve in reports. They are used to add free form text to the layout. The one thing that text boxes are useful for in a layout is to provide helpful information or a reminder for the type of information that should be entered in a field. The other reason that I have added a text box to a layout is to add a name to a group or section of fields.

For example, there is no requirement that the fields have to be in a two column layout like you see on the Contact detail view. I have had the need to create a custom layout. The majority of contacts did not have street addresses (don't ask), so I put the address fields all the way on the right side of the layout to make room for new fields that were needed.

To save space, I used a text box to indicate that the fields on the right side of the layout were address fields. Another use for a text box is to indicate that a field is required. If you need to add a text box to a layout, follow the steps below. For now you can just read the steps to become familiar with the process.

1. Click on the **DRAWING** button on the ToolBox, then click the Text button.

2. Draw a box on the layout where you need it. To add the text, double-click on the text box, then type in the text.

3. If you need to change an attribute of the text box like the font, you can change it on the Properties window.

Resizing Fields On A Layout

When you select a field or object, you will see **RESIZE HANDLES** around the object, as shown in Figure 18-15.

Figure 18-15 Resize handles

If you need to resize several objects, select all of them first and then resize the objects. When you place the mouse pointer on a handle, you can drag the border of the objects to change the size. When you add fields to a layout, it is very possible that the fields are not the exact size that you need them to be. There are two ways to resize fields as explained below.

① **Use the anchor** This option is used to resize fields to match the size of an existing field in the layout. To use this method, select the fields that need to be resized. Press and hold down the **CTRL** key, then click on the field that has the dimensions that you want the other fields to be the size of. The handles on the field that you want to use to resize the other fields to should be white, as shown above in Figure 18-15. Format ⇒ Make Same Size ⇒ Select the option that you need (width, height or both).

② **Resize a field manually** Use this option when none of the fields on the layout is the size that you want. Select the fields that you want to resize. Place the mouse pointer on the side of the field that you want to resize and drag the handle to the size that you want all of the selected fields to be.

 If you want to move a field and label, you have to select both of them because they are separate objects.

Exercise 18.3: Adding Graphics To A Layout

If your company has a logo, you may want to add it to a layout. The steps below show you how to add a graphic file to a layout. You will add the ACT! icon to the tab that you created. If there are fields where you want to put the graphic in the layout, move the fields out of the way. In this exercise, no fields need to be moved.

1. Click the Drawing button in the ToolBox, then click the Image button. Draw a small box to the left of the drop-down field that you added to the tab.

2. Right-click on the image field and select Edit Properties. Navigate to the location of the graphic file that you want to add, then double-click on the image file name. To complete this exercise, use the ACT! icon, which is in this location: C:\Program Files\ACT\Act for Windows\act.ico or C:\Program Files (x86)\ACT\Act for Windows\act.ico.

3. Make the frame of the image smaller.

Using The Layout Designer

Exercise 18.4: Changing The Background Color Of A Tab

While this exercise will change the background color of a tab, the steps are the same to change the background color of the top portion of a layout.

1. Click on a blank space on the tab that you created, then click on the arrow on the **BACKGROUND COLOR** button on the toolbar, as shown at the top of Figure 18-16.

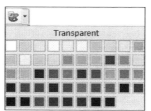

Figure 18-16 Background color options

2. Click on the first yellow square in the second row. The background color of the tab that you created should now be yellow.

> **How To Use An Image For The Background**
> If you wanted to use an image for the background instead of a color, follow the steps below.
>
> 1. Click the button at the end of the Background Image option, in the **APPEARANCE** section of the Properties window illustrated in Figure 18-17.
> 2. Select the image file for the background.

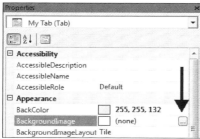

Figure 18-17 Background options

Saving The Layout Changes

You have two options for saving changes to a layout. You can save the changes to the existing layout or save the changes as a new layout. In this exercise you will save the changes to a new layout.

1. File ⇒ Save As. You should see the Layouts folder. Type `My Basic Contact Layout` as the file name, then press Enter or click the Save button.

2. Close the Layout Designer window. (File ⇒ Exit.)

View The Layout

1. Open the Select Layout drop-down list on the toolbar, then select the layout that you just created, from the list shown in Figure 18-18.

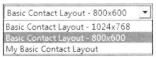
Figure 18-18 Layout options

2. Click on the tab that you created, then open the Specialty drop-down list, as shown in Figure 18-19.

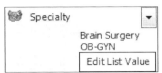

Figure 18-19 Drop-down list field added to a tab

Using The Properties Window To Change The Appearance Of A Field Or Label

Earlier in this chapter you used the Properties window to change the behavior of a tab. You can also use the options on this window to modify the appearance of a field. When you click on the field that you want to modify, you can change the border style and font.

If you click on the label that you want to modify, you can change the label text. The differences between the Properties window and the Edit Properties dialog box is that the Properties window has more options and you can modify more than one field or label at the same time.

Edit Properties Dialog Box

The options shown in Figure 18-20 are used to modify the font properties. The tab shown in Figure 18-21 has options to modify the borders. To change any of these properties, right-click on the field or label that you want to modify in the Layout Designer and select **EDIT PROPERTIES**.

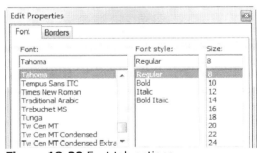

Figure 18-20 Font tab options

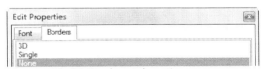

Figure 18-21 Borders tab options

Exercise 18.5: How To Change The Label For A Field On A Layout

In Chapter 15 you modified the User 1 field. When you viewed the field on the User Fields tab, the label was still User 1. In this exercise you will change the text that is displayed on the label for the User 1 field.

1. Open the Basic Contact Layout 800x600 in the Layout Designer.

2. On the User Fields tab, double-click on the User 1 label. The background color should have changed to white.

3. Highlight the text in the label and type MD Type. Press Enter, then click on a blank space on the layout. The label for the field should look like the one shown in Figure 18-22.

Using The Layout Designer

Figure 18-22 Label changed

4. Save the changes to the layout and close the Layout Designer.

5. Display the Basic Contact Layout - 800x600 in the Contacts detail view. Click on the User Fields tab. The label for the first user field should have "MD Type", as shown above in Figure 18-22.

Annual Event Fields

This type of field is used to track dates of events that happen once a year. To create an annual event field you need administrator or manager level rights. You can create a reminder of the annual event by creating a yearly recurring To-do activity.

Exercise 18.6: Create An Annual Event Field

In this exercise you will create a renewal date annual field.

1. Display the My Basic Contact Layout that you created earlier in this chapter.

2. Tools ⇒ Define Fields. Click the Create new field link.

3. Type `Renewal Date` in the Field name field.

4. Open the Field data type drop-down list and select Annual Event.

5. Check the **GENERATE HISTORY** option, then click Finish. This may take 10-20 seconds to finish.

6. Close the Define Fields dialog box. When prompted to modify the layout, click Yes.

7. Add the Renewal Date (Annual Event) field below the Specialty field on the tab that you created.

8. Add a 3D border to the Renewal Date field, then save the changes.

   When you view the layout, it should look like the one shown in Figure 18-23.

Figure 18-23 Annual Event field added to the layout

Annual Event Field Tips
These tips are for the options on the Define Fields dialog box.

① A text field cannot be converted to an Annual Date field.
② A date field can be converted to an Annual Event field by changing the **SELECT A FIELD DATA TYPE TO CONVERT TO** option to Annual Event, as shown in Figure 18-24.

Chapter 18

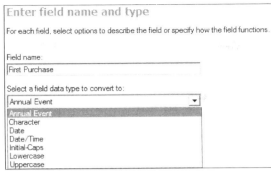

Figure 18-24 Data Type options

Exercise 18.7: Aligning Fields

Chapter 16 covered how to align fields on a report. Aligning fields on a layout is similar. I don't know for sure, but I get the feeling that aligning fields is not something that most people like to do, even though it makes the layout or report look more professional. Table 18-2 explains the align options. When you have to align fields, follow the steps below.

Option	How It Aligns . . .
Lefts	On the left side of the object.
Center	On the center of the object.
Rights	On the right side of the object.
Tops	On the top of the object.
Middles	On the middle of the object.
Bottoms	On the bottom of the object.
To Grid	To the closest grid point (the dots on the layout) of the object that you right-click on. You need to have the **GRID** option enabled to see how this works.

Table 18-2 Alignment options explained

1. Open the layout that you created in the Layout Designer. Currently, there are no fields that need to be aligned on the layout.

2. On the User Fields tab, drag the User 2 field to the right, as shown in Figure 18-25.

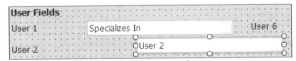

Figure 18-25 User 2 field moved

3. Click on the field that needs to be aligned. In this exercise click on the User 2 field, then press and hold down the Shift key.

4. Click on the field that you want to align the field with. In this exercise click on the Specializes In field.

 The boxes around the field that you just selected should be white. The second field is known as the **ANCHOR** field because it is the field that the other fields will be aligned to.

18-13

Using The Layout Designer

5. Right-click on the Specializes In field, then select the align option that corresponds to how you need to align the field. In this exercise select **ALIGN LEFTS**. The User 2 field should now be aligned with the Specializes In field.

6. Close the layout, but do not save the changes.

Exercise 18.8: How To Change The Tab Stop Order

Chapter 3 covered Tab key functionality. Earlier in this chapter you learned that the tab order can be changed. In this exercise you will learn how to change the tab stop order on the Basic Contact layout.

1. In the Layout Designer window, save the Basic Contact Layout - 1024x768 as `My Revised Tab Order Layout` in the Layouts folder.

2. View ⇒ Tab Stops ⇒ Show Tab Stops, then View ⇒ Tab Stops ⇒ Clear.

I find it easier to remove all of the existing tab stops and start from scratch, but you can change the order without clearing all of the tab stops. The way to include a field in the tab stop order is to click in the fields in the order that you want the Tab key to follow. When you click in a field without a tab stop number, the next available tab stop number is assigned.

3. Click in the following fields in this order: Company, Contact, Address 1, Address 2, Title and Department. The fields should have the order shown in Figure 18-26.

Figure 18-26 Tab stop order

4. Right-click in the City field and type a 3 in the **ENTER THE NEW INDEX** field shown in Figure 18-27, then click OK.

   You should see the tab order shown in Figure 18-28. If you do not see a number by the City field, click in the field.

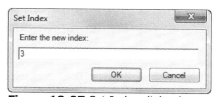

Figure 18-27 Set Index dialog box

Figure 18-28 Modified tab stop order

Notice that the City field is the fourth field that the Tab key will go to instead of the Address 2 field shown earlier in Figure 18-26. The City field is the fourth field because the Tab key stops in the Company field first.

Chapter 18

Modified Tab Stop Order
While testing ACT! 2013, I noticed that the tab stop number did not consistently appear for the modified field like it does in Figure 18-28, shown above. The modified tab stop number would not appear, but all of the other tab stop numbers would change as expected.

The **SET INDEX** dialog box is used to insert a field into the existing tab order, but there is no way to remove a field from the tab order without clearing all of the tab stops in the index and starting over.

5. View ⇒ Tab Stops ⇒ Show Tab Stops.

6. Save the changes and close the layout. You can test the new tab order. When you finish, switch back to the Basic Contact 800x600 layout.

DATABASE MAINTENANCE AND SECURITY

Overview

In this chapter you will learn how to use the following database maintenance tools and techniques:

- ☑ Delete database tool
- ☑ Backup tool
- ☑ Check and Repair tool
- ☑ Restoring databases
- ☑ Removing old data
- ☑ The Copy/Move Contact Data dialog box
- ☑ ACT! Scheduler
- ☑ ACT! Diagnostics

You will also learn the following security features:

- ☑ Creating, editing and deleting user accounts
- ☑ Password protecting a database
- ☑ Security roles and permissions
- ☑ Record access data security
- ☑ Password security and policies

CHAPTER 19

Database Maintenance

There are several things that you should do to keep a database working properly. If you are constantly adding and editing records in a database, you should back up the database frequently. Databases can become corrupt, which means that the database will not function properly and eventually may not open. It may run very slow or will not let you login. If you have a backup copy of the database you can restore it. You will have to re-enter any additions or changes that were made after the database was last backed up, but that is better than having to try to recreate the entire database. If you do not have a very recent backup, or worse, no backup at all, you will no longer have a database.

Many people say that they do not have time for maintenance. My thought is that it takes less time for maintenance then it does to type in all of the data again. More than likely, all of the notes and history records at the very least, cannot be recreated because you and anyone else that uses the database, probably cannot remember every note and activity that they created.

Most companies create a backup of all files that are on servers every night. If your database is on a server, you may not have to do the database maintenance tasks discussed in this chapter because they will be handled by the computer department in your company. The majority of the ACT! maintenance tasks require administrator rights and that no other user has the database open when these tasks are being performed. The easy way to tell if you have administrator rights is if the options on the Database Maintenance submenu are enabled.

ACT! has several database maintenance tools that you can use to keep the database running smoothly. These tools are listed below.

① Backup
② Check and repair
③ Removing old data

Tools ⇒ Database Maintenance, will display the options shown in Figure 19-1.

I do not consider all of the options on this menu a maintenance tool, but all of the options on the menu are covered in this chapter.

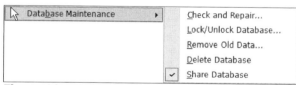

Figure 19-1 Database Maintenance tools

Locking A Database

If you need to perform any type of maintenance like deleting, restoring, repairing or updating a database other than creating a back up, you must lock the database first. Locking a database means that you are the only person that can have the database open.

How To Lock A Database

1. Tools ⇒ Database Maintenance ⇒ Lock/Unlock Database.

If no users have the database open, it is locked automatically. When locked, you will see the word **(LOCKED)** in the Title bar after the database name.

If users have the database open, you will see the Lock Database dialog box, which will list all of the users that have the database open. On this dialog box you can specify how long they can keep the database open before they are locked out. A warning message will then be sent to each user telling them to close the database.

Using The Delete Database Tool

This tool is used to delete a database and all of the files associated with the database. The steps below show you how to delete a database. You can just read these steps now, because you do not have a database to delete.

1. Open the database that you want to delete.

2. Tools ⇒ Database Maintenance ⇒ Delete Database.

    You will see the message shown in Figure 19-2.

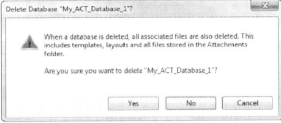

Figure 19-2 Delete Database message

3. Click Yes. You will see the message shown in Figure 19-3.

    Click Yes to delete the database. The database will now be deleted.

Figure 19-3 Proceed With Delete message

 Once you delete a database, you cannot restore or retrieve it.

The Backup Tool

There are three ways that you can create a back up copy of a database:

① Use Windows Explorer.
② Use the Save Copy As command.
③ Use the Back Up command.

Windows Explorer allows you to create a copy of the database. The **Save Copy As** command in ACT! also allows you to create a copy of the database, which was covered in Chapter 1. Each database has additional files that it needs and uses. Unless you select these files when using Windows Explorer, you will not make a complete back up of the database using this option. The Save Copy As command will automatically make a back up copy of the additional files.

The **Back Up** command has the same features as the Save Copy As command, plus it allows you to back up a database to disk, even if the database needs more than one disk. The back up files are saved in .zip format. The zip file format compacts files by removing the empty space in the file.

Database Maintenance And Security

The default file folder location for saving backups is:

Vista and Windows 7   C:\Users\YourUserName\My Documents\ACT\ACT Data\Backup

Windows XP   C:\Documents and Settings\YourUserName\My Documents\ACT\ACT Data\Backup

In addition to being able to back up databases, **PERSONAL FILES** can also be backed up.
[See Chapter 9, What Are Supplemental Files?]

> When ACT! is installed, a backup folder is created on the same hard drive as the database. Please do not store your backups in this folder. There is nothing wrong with the folder, just hear me out. The goal of creating a backup is to have a copy of the database should something go wrong with the original one. If the "thing" that goes wrong is that the hard drive that the original database is on, dies or gets a virus, not only is the original database destroyed, so is the backup copy of the database if you store it on the same hard drive as the original database.
>
> This is why I do not understand the purpose of the Backup folder that is automatically created. The backup file **SHOULD NOT** be stored on the same hard drive as the original database. It should be stored on a different hard drive. This is also true for databases that are stored on a server.
>
> If your database is being backed up to the same server as the original database, do yourself a favor and start pricing an external hard drive if you do not already have one. Look for one that has the most space for $99 or less. You should be able to find a 1 TB drive for this price. There is an article on the web site for creating an image of the entire hard drive. www.tolana.com/tips/image.html

Exercise 19.1: How To Back Up A Database Using The Back Up Command

> Users with administrator or manager rights can back up a database, but only someone with administrator rights can restore a database.

In this exercise you will back up the new database that you created. You will save the backup file in the folder that you created. The reason that I am doing this is because I cannot guarantee that everyone that reads this book has an external device like an external hard drive. The problem with CD's and DVD's in my opinion, is that for a reason that I do not understand, files that are copied to them are sometimes automatically set to **READ-ONLY**, which makes it difficult, if not impossible to use the file. CD-RW and DVD-RW formats work much better for me.

1. Open the My_ACT_Database database.

2. File ⇒ Back Up ⇒ Database, then click the Browse button.

3. Navigate to and double-click on your folder, then click the Save button. You should see the folder that you selected in the field on the dialog box, as shown in Figure 19-4. Selecting the **INCLUDE ATTACHMENTS** option will back up the files in the Attachments folder.

4. Click OK. You will see the dialog box shown in Figure 19-5.

Chapter 19

Figure 19-4 Back Up Database dialog box

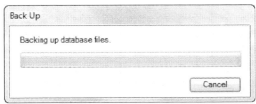

Figure 19-5 Back Up in progress dialog box

5. Click OK when you see the message that the backup completed successfully.

6. Open the My_ACT_Demo database.

Password Protecting The Backup File

If checked, the password option shown earlier in Figure 19-4 is used to create a password for the backup file that will be created. Figure 19-6 shows the Backup Password dialog box.

Figure 19-6 Enter Backup Password dialog box

Exercise 19.2: How To Back Up Personal Files

Unlike backing up databases which requires administrator rights, anyone can back up personal files. You should give the personal backup file a different name then the file that it is being created from. This will prevent the original file from being overwritten by mistake if you have to restore it.

Tools ⇒ Preferences ⇒ General tab, will let you know where your personal files are stored. Look in the **PERSONAL FILE LOCATIONS** section and select the file type that you want to back up. The location of the files will be displayed. To complete this exercise, the location for personal files is your folder. The steps below show you how to back up personal files.

1. File ⇒ Back Up ⇒ Personal Files.

2. If your folder is not at the beginning of the **BACK UP FILES TO** field, click the Browse button, then select your folder.

3. Change the file name to
   `ACT Dictionary Backup.zip`
   on the Save As dialog box, then click the Save button.

   You will see the dialog box shown in Figure 19-7.

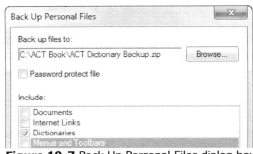

Figure 19-7 Back Up Personal Files dialog box

19-5

Database Maintenance And Security

The reason that I had you change the file name is because you already created a backup of the custom menus and toolbars in Chapter 16 and used the default filename. Using the default file name now would overwrite the custom menu backup file.

If you have to restore a file, it will be easier to find the right backup file if your backup files have meaningful names. If you want to password protect the back up file, check the **PASSWORD PROTECT FILE** option. The Backup personal zip file is stored in the folder that you selected in step 2 above.

4. At the bottom of the dialog box shown above in Figure 19-7, select the types of files that you want to back up and clear the options for the file types that you do not want to back up. For this exercise check the **DICTIONARIES** option and clear the other options, then click OK to back up your dictionary files.

Check And Repair Tools

This maintenance tool is used to improve database performance. Checking and repairing a database is a two step process as discussed below.

① **Integrity Check** Looks for errors in the database and repairs them when possible.
② **Re-Index** Reorganizes the records in the database. This allows the database to perform better. This step removes spaces from the database and defrags the database. This can take a long time to complete, especially the first time that it is run on the database. During the defrag process, the database is rewritten to the hard drive. Doing this makes the size of the database smaller, which allows it to perform tasks like retrieve, sort and save records faster.

One way that performance is improved is by removing fragmentation. Fragmentation is caused when records are added or deleted in the database. It also occurs when other types of records like notes, history and opportunity records are deleted.

Reindexing Databases

Reindexing databases is another feature that the Check and Repair tool handles. Reindexing will make the queries, lookups and database run faster. Only deleting records does not give back disk space. Compressing a database will give back the disk space that deleted records and references to them take up in the index. Reindexing and compressing a database will take more time if the database is large. You should reindex and compress databases on a regular basis.

Figure 19-8 shows the current size of the database.

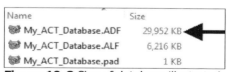

Figure 19-8 Size of database illustrated

Check And Repair A Database

Before using this tool you should back up the database. It can take 30 minutes for the check and repair process to run.

1. Back up the database that you want to check and repair.

2. Lock the database if you are not the only user.

Chapter 19

3. Tools ⇒ Database Maintenance ⇒ Check and Repair.

   You will see the dialog box shown in Figure 19-9.

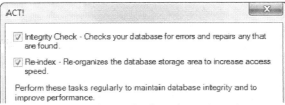

Figure 19-9 Database check and repair options

4. Both options shown above in Figure 19-9 should be checked to have the database perform at its best.

   Click OK.

   You will see the dialog box shown in Figure 19-10.

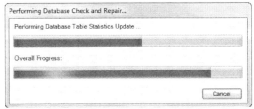

Figure 19-10 Check and Repair status dialog box

5. When the utility is finished click OK, then unlock the database.

Restoring Databases

The backup database files are usually restored when the current version of the database has been corrupted or is not working properly. Only administrators can restore databases. It is best to restore databases back to their original location, especially if it is a database that is part of a synchronization process. Not restoring a synchronized database back to its original location will break the synchronization between the two databases.

Restore Options

There are three ways that a database can be restored, as explained below.

① **Restore** Restores all of the files to their original location. Select this option if the original database is corrupt or was deleted.
② **Restore As** Is used to restore the database to a location other then the original location and to rename the database if necessary.
③ **Unpack And Restore Remote Database** Is used to restore a remote database that has been synced back to the main database.

How To Restore A Database

The steps below show you how to restore a database.

1. File ⇒ Restore ⇒ Database.

2. Select the Restore option, then click OK.

3. Click the Browse button, then double-click on the zip file that contains the database that you want to restore.

Database Maintenance And Security

4. Click OK on the dialog box shown in Figure 19-11.

   If prompted, enter your username and password, then click OK.

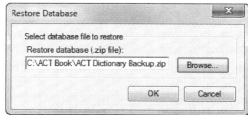

Figure 19-11 Restore Database (zip file) dialog box

5. Click Yes when prompted that files that were modified after the backup was created will be overwritten.

6. When the restore process is complete, open the database that was restored to make sure that it is working properly.

Removing Old Data

There may be data in the database that is no longer needed. If that is the case you can remove the data that is not needed. The following types of data can be removed: notes, attachments and activities. This is also known as **PURGING A DATABASE**. The main benefit of removing data that is not needed is that it will make the database smaller, which will allow the database to run more efficiently. Only administrators can remove data. You should back up the database before deleting records and attachments.

 If you are using a Microsoft SQL Server 2005 Express database, from time to time you should check the file size of the .ADF file (shown earlier in Figure 19-8) to make sure that it is not close to the 4GB limit. If it is, you should remove old data. Microsoft SQL Server 2008 Express databases have a 10GB limit.

Exercise 19.3: How To Remove Old Data

In this exercise you will create criteria that will be used to remove old data from the My_ACT_Demo database.

1. Tools ⇒ Database Maintenance ⇒ Remove Old Data.

2. Check the options and number of days in Table 19-1.

   Your dialog box should have the options selected that are shown in Figure 19-12.

Option	# Of Days
Notes older than	90
Cleared activities older than	50
Document tab entries older than	100

Table 19-1 Criteria for selecting old data

Chapter 19

The options shown are used to select the type of data that you want to remove and select how far back to search for data that you want to remove.

Figure 19-12 Remove Old Data dialog box

3. Click OK. You will see the message shown in Figure 19-13. You will see a different number of records to be removed because you are not running the utility on the same day that I did.

   Click Yes.

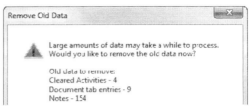
Figure 19-13 Remove Old Data message

4. When you see the purge message shown in Figure 19-14, you can click No.

   If this were a live database, you should reindex the database.

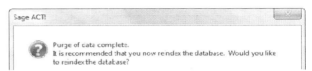
Figure 19-14 Purge message

Finding And Deleting Duplicate Records

Deleting duplicate records will help keep the size of the database as small as possible. It will also keep the data accurate. You can delete duplicate contact and group records. By default, Contact records are considered duplicate if they have the same Company, Contact and Phone number. You can select other fields on the dialog box shown in Figure 19-15 to use as criteria to determine duplicate contact records. Group records are considered duplicate if they have the same Record Creator (the person that created the group) and group name.

1. Open the database that you want to check for duplicates.

2. Tools ⇒ Scan for Duplicates.

   The options on the Scan for Duplicate Contacts dialog box are used to select the fields that you want to use to determine what makes a contact record a duplicate.

   Often, duplicate contact records are caught when they are being created.

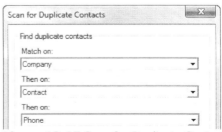
Figure 19-15 Scan for Duplicate Contacts dialog box

19-9

Database Maintenance And Security

If you wanted to use different fields to determine if there are duplicate records, you would select them on this dialog box.

3. Click OK. If there are duplicate records you will see a message that says that there are duplicate contacts. Click Yes.

Using The Copy/Move Contact Data Wizard

If the scan for duplicate records process explained above finds duplicate contacts, this wizard will open automatically. This wizard can also be opened from the Tools menu.

1. Click Next on the first wizard screen.

The options on the dialog box shown in Figure 19-16 are used to select what to do with the duplicate records.

The following options are available.

① Copy or move data from one record to another.
② Combine business and personal records for the same contact.
③ Merge the duplicate records for the same contact into one record.

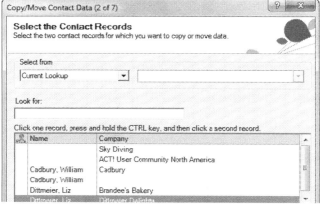

Figure 19-16 Select the Contact Records screen

 Tools ⇒ Copy/Move Contact Data, will also open the dialog box shown above in Figure 19-16.

 Take your time and be careful when merging records. Once they are merged, the merge cannot be undone. The good thing is that the merge process has to be completed for each set of duplicate records, so the worse case is that you would only have to restore a few records and not all of the duplicate records in the database.

2. Click on the first record that is a duplicate, then press and hold down the **CTRL** key and click on the second record for the same contact. Click Next.

On the screen shown in Figure 19-17, you have to decide which record you want to keep. It seems to me that this would be a great place to be able to delete a record from the main database, because enough information about each contact record is displayed.

You should scroll down and view the data in both records to determine which one you want to keep. Two contact information fields that I find helpful are the **EDIT DATE** and **IS IMPORTED** fields.

I tend to select the record that has more of the data that I want to keep as the target record.

The **SOURCE** record contains the data that will be copied.

The **TARGET** record is where the data from the source record will be copied to.

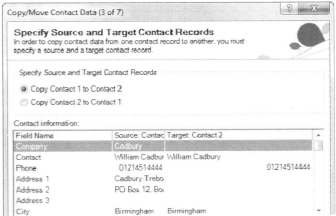

Figure 19-17 Specify Source and Target Contact Records screen

The **COPY/MOVE DATA** options are used to copy or move data on a field by field basis, as shown below in Figure 19-18.

The **KEEP/DELETE DATA** options are used to keep or delete the source record. If you copy or move data from the source record, I think that the source record should be deleted. If you have a reason to keep it, then you should.

 You can resize the columns on the wizard screens so that you can see the data better.

3. Select the **COPY CONTACT** option that represents how you want to copy the records, then click Next.

   The options on the screen shown in Figure 19-18 are helpful if the source record has data in fields that the target record does not.

Figure 19-18 Copy Data from Source to Target Record screen

4. Click Next on screen 4 of 7. The options shown in Figure 19-19 are optional types of data that can be copied to the target record. Check the items that you want to move to the target record, then click Next.

Database Maintenance And Security

You would probably select all of the items on this screen so that you would have a complete history of the contact.

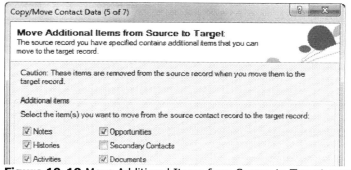

Figure 19-19 Move Additional Items from Source to Target screen

The options shown in Figure 19-20 are used to select whether or not to delete the record that you designated as the source record.

More than likely, you would want to delete the source record.

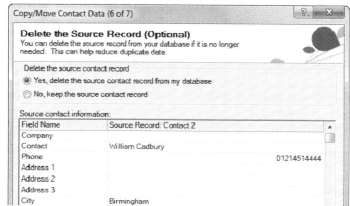

Figure 19-20 Delete the Source Record screen

5. Select the option Yes, delete the source record from my database, then click Next.

6. Click Yes when you see the message that says deleting a contact cannot be undone.

7. Click Finish to close the wizard. The changes to the record that you are keeping will be made. You have to repeat this process for all of the potential duplicate records displayed in the list at the bottom of the screen shown earlier in Figure 19-16.

Deleting Duplicate Records From The Contact List View

After using the Copy/Move Contact Data wizard, the database can still have duplicate records because the scan for duplicates process only checks for records that have identical information in up to three fields. If the contact name is spelled differently in two or more records, it would be skipped when the check for duplicate scan was run. Therefore, it is a good idea to visually view the records in the Contact List to see if there are other duplicate records.

When I do this, I first sort by the contact name, which is often the field that has duplicates due to typos. Then I sort the list by company to see if there are any company names that are spelled wrong. As you can imagine, as more records are added to the database the longer this can take, especially if it is not done on a regular basis.

If you do not want to merge data from one contact record to another, like you just learned how to do, you can manually delete the duplicate records that you do not want to keep. Keep in mind that deleting the duplicate records from a view means that if you want to keep any data from the record that you will delete, you will have to type the information in the record that you want to keep.

View The Deleted Records

ACT! keeps a log of all records that are deleted on the History tab of the My Record.

1. Lookup ⇒ My Record.

2. Click on the History tab. The records that you deleted are at the top of the list, if the list is sorted in descending date order, as shown in Figure 19-21. You will see today's date and time instead of the one shown in the figure.

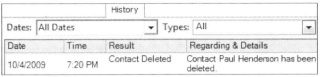

Figure 19-21 Deleted records on the History tab

ACT! Scheduler

So far in this chapter you have learned about a variety of maintenance tasks. If you are thinking that you will not remember to do them on a regular basis, you can set them up in the ACT! Scheduler, because this tool will run the tasks for you at the time that you select, even if ACT! is not open.

In addition to being able to run maintenance tasks, the scheduler can also be used to automatically run a synchronization process, including the process to sync ACT! and Outlook calendars.

Exercise 19.4: Schedule A Maintenance Task

In this exercise you will schedule the database maintenance utility to check and re-index the demo database that you created, once a week.

1. Tools ⇒ ACT! Scheduler.

2. Click on the **CREATE A TASK** link.

3. Click the **BROWSE** button on the Select a Database screen, then double-click on the My_ACT_Database.pad file.

4. You should see the database name, as shown in Figure 19-22.

   Click Next.

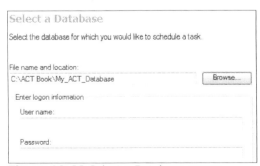

Figure 19-22 Select a Database screen

Database Maintenance And Security

5. Open the **TASK** drop-down list and select Database Maintenance, as shown in Figure 19-23.

   Click Next.

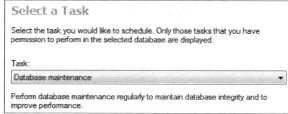

Figure 19-23 Select a Task screen

6. Check both options shown in Figure 19-24 if they are not already selected, then click Next.

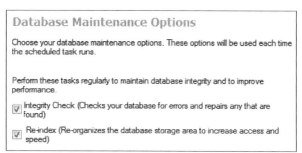

Figure 19-24 Database Maintenance Options screen

7. Select the weekly option, then select Thursday from the drop-down list on the right.

8. Change the **START TIME** to 10 PM, as shown in Figure 19-25, then click Finish.

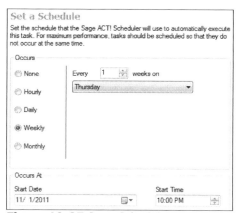

Figure 19-25 Set a Schedule screen

9. If you click on the task that you just created, you will see the details for it in the lower left corner, as shown in Figure 19-26. Click Exit. You should see the Scheduler icon in the Windows task bar. If not, open the ACT! Scheduler, then click on the **START SERVICE** link, shown in Figure 19-26.

Chapter 19

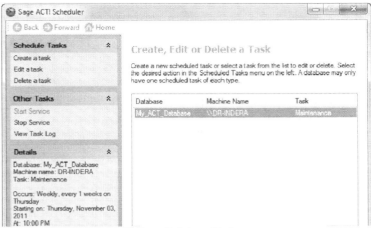

Figure 19-26 Create, Edit or Delete a Task screen

Security

ACT! comes with several security options. With so many companies having their data stolen, it may be a good idea to implement as much security as possible, without going overboard.

 If you add a password to a user account or database, select one that you will remember. Using the word **PASSWORD** for a password is not a good idea, as this is the default password for some software packages. It is best to select passwords that have a combination of letters and numbers.

User Security

User security allows the administrator to create accounts so that other people can use the database. ACT! provides the following types of user level security.

① User accounts
② Security roles
③ Logon status
④ Permissions

Exercise 19.5: Creating User Accounts

In this exercise you will create a user account with your name.

1. Open the My_ACT_Demo database. Tools ⇒ Manage Users. You will see a list of the users, their security role and log on status.

2. Click on the **CREATE NEW USER** link.

    The Create New User option will create a new contact record. You should make sure that the person that you are creating the account for does not already have a contact record in the database, so that you do not create a duplicate record.

19-15

Database Maintenance And Security

There are two ways that you can create a new user account, as shown in Figure 19-27. If you see a message in the **DETAILS** section that says that there is only one license, it means that only one person at a time can use the database. This is usually the case for home users. It does not mean that additional user accounts cannot be created.

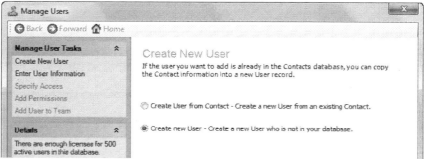

Figure 19-27 Create New User screen

 The links in the **MANAGE USER TASKS** section are used to display the screen that you want, instead of clicking the Next and Back buttons to get to another screen.

If you select the **CREATE USER FROM CONTACT** option, then click Next, you will see the screen shown in Figure 19-28.

The options are used to select a name from the database to use for the user account that you want to create.

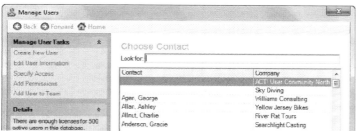

Figure 19-28 Choose Contact screen

When you click the Next button you will see the screen shown in Figure 19-29 with the Contact and User name fields filled in. From this point on, the screens are the same to finish creating the user account.

If you select the **CREATE NEW USER** option shown earlier in Figure 19-27, you will see the screen shown in Figure 19-29. It is used to enter the information for the new user. A contact record will be created for this user.

Figure 19-29 Enter User Information screen

Chapter 19

User Account Creation Tips
① User names and passwords are not case sensitive.
② Passwords for user accounts are optional. If you leave the password field empty, the user will not have to enter a password unless the password policy option requires one.

3. Select the **CREATE NEW USER** option for this exercise, then click Next.

4. Type your first and last name in the Contact Name field, then press the Tab key. Your name should automatically be filled in the User Name field.

5. Select the **ADMINISTRATOR** Security Role, then check the **PASSWORD NEVER EXPIRES** option. Security Roles are explained at the end of this exercise.

6. If you want to add a password, type your first name and the year in the **NEW PASSWORD** and **CONFIRM PASSWORD** fields (for example, Indera2011), then click Next.

If you do not enter the same password in the New Password and Confirm Password fields, the **NEXT** and **FINISH** buttons will not be enabled.

If any of the password options discussed below are selected, they override the database password policy options that are discussed later in this chapter.

① If you check the **USER MUST CHANGE PASSWORD AT NEXT LOG ON** option, you do not have to enter a password when setting up the account. This will cause the user to be prompted to create a password the first time that they log on.
② The **USER CANNOT CHANGE PASSWORD** option if checked, will disable the File ⇒ Set Password option, which is how users change their password.
③ If checked, the **PASSWORD NEVER EXPIRES** option will not require the user to ever change their password.

7. Select the **INACTIVE** option, then click Next.

    The options shown in Figure 19-30 are used to select the logon access options.

Figure 19-30 Specify Access screen

The options shown in Figure 19-31 are used to select the permissions for the user account.

The permissions available are based on the security role that is selected for the account.

Some security roles come with some of the permissions selected by default.

Figure 19-31 Add Permissions screen

19-17

Database Maintenance And Security

Because you selected the Administrator security role, all of the permissions are available by default. They will appear in the ADDED PERMISSIONS column. These permissions are only available for Manager and Standard roles and are explained at the end of this exercise.

8. Click Finish.

   If you see a message asking if you want to share the database, click No.

   The new user account and contact record will be created.

   Once the account is created you will see it on the screen shown in Figure 19-32.

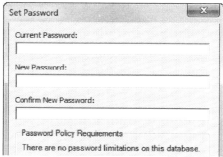

Figure 19-32 Select A User screen

Reset Passwords

The **RESET PASSWORD** button shown earlier in Figure 19-29 will let the administrator reset the password. This is helpful when a user forgets their password. Once the password has been reset, you can tell the user to set up a new password on the dialog box shown in Figure 19-33.

File ⇒ Set Password, will open this dialog box.

Figure 19-33 Set Password dialog box

 Earlier I stated that I believe that there should be at least two administrator accounts per database. Resetting passwords is one reason. An administrator account cannot reset its own password because the account being reset cannot be logged on. If you do not know or remember the administrator account password and the database only has one administrator account set up, the only way that I know of to retrieve the password is to send a copy of the database to Sage.

Security Roles

As you saw earlier, there are five security roles (levels) that can be given to a user. The security roles determine what data a user has access to and what they can and cannot do to the records that they have access to. The goal of setting up security is to only give enough rights so that a user can get their job done. The five security levels that you can assign a user are explained below.

Browse This level allows the user to view records and calendars of other users that they have access to. Users at this security level cannot edit or add any data, which includes sending an email or writing a letter from inside of ACT!. This is the most limited security level.

Restricted This level can only access public areas of the database. Users at this security level can create and edit contacts and opportunities, but cannot delete any data, even data that they create. This level cannot create groups or companies.

Standard This security level allows the user to view, edit, add and delete contacts and groups, as well as, synchronize databases. This is the most common security level. Users cannot delete other users data, create backups, import and export data, schedule activities for other users without being granted access to their calendar, modify layouts or perform database maintenance.

Manager This security level has access to the entire database, except for private records, but does not have administrator rights, which means users cannot create user accounts or perform database maintenance tasks.

Administrator This security level has full rights to the database. If the database is used by several people, there should be two administrator accounts, in my opinion, in case one account becomes corrupt or one person does something wrong. If there are other users and they mark records as private, people with administrator rights cannot view the records.

Permissions

These permissions give Standard and Manager level accounts additional rights. The available permissions are explained below.

① **Accounting Link Tasks** The user can work on accounting tasks if an accounting software package like QuickBooks has been configured to work with ACT!.
② **Handheld Device Sync** Allows the user to synchronize ACT! data with a handheld device like a PDA (Personal Digital Assistant).
③ **Remote Administration** Allows the user to repair, back up, restore and check remote databases that they have rights to. This permission is primarily useful for remote users.
④ **Manage Sync Subscription List** Allows the user to make changes to the subscription (contact) list for a remote database.

How To Edit User Account Information

In the previous exercise you created a new user account that had administrator rights and was inactive. The steps below show you how to edit a user account and set up the permissions.

1. Open the Manage Users Utility.

2. Click on the user account with your name, then click the **EDIT USER INFORMATION** link.

3. Change the Security Role to Standard, then click on the **ADD PERMISSIONS** link.

4. Add the Remote Administration permission to the account, then click the Back button.

Database Maintenance And Security

5. Change the logon access to Active, then click Finish.

   You will see that your account is active, as shown in Figure 19-34.

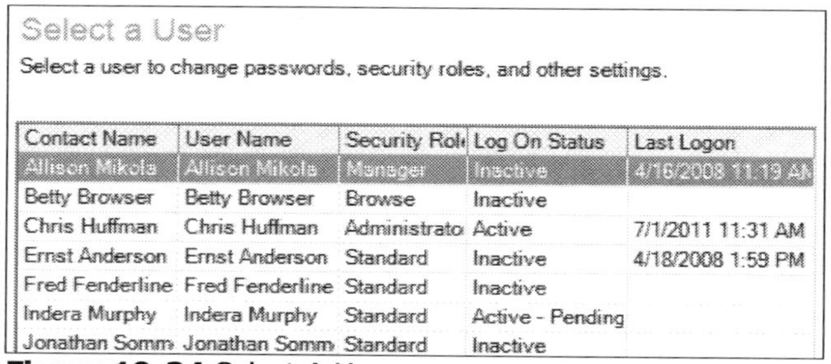

Figure 19-34 Select A User screen

How To Delete A User Account

Usually an account is deleted because the person will no longer use the database. There was a time that if you deleted a user account, all traces of the account would also be deleted. In an ACT! database, that would have meant that the attachments or notes that were added to the database under the user account, would also be deleted. The good news is that ACT! databases have evolved and now you can delete a user account and keep the work that was created under the account. You do not have to delete a user account. You can make the account inactive. The steps below show you how to delete a user account.

1. Click on the user account that you want to delete on the screen shown above in Figure 19-34. For this example, you can click on the account with your name.

2. Click the **DELETE USER** link. You will see the message shown in Figure 19-35. This message is letting you know that any private data will be deleted. Click Yes. When prompted if you are sure, click Yes.

   Figure 19-35 Delete User Account message

3. If you see the message shown in Figure 19-36, clicking Yes, will keep the records that the user created, linked to the user. Clicking No will let you reassign the records to another user. For now, click No. You will see the dialog box shown in Figure 19-37 if the user added or modified any data.

Figure 19-36 Retain as Contact message

Figure 19-37 Delete User dialog box

Chapter 19

The **DELETE RECORDS BELONGING TO THIS USER** option will do just that, delete the contact records that the user created, as well as, any notes for the contact, regardless of who created the note or activity.

The **REASSIGN RECORDS TO ANOTHER USER** option moves the records that were created under the account that you are in the process of deleting, to another user. This prevents the records from being deleted. In my opinion, this is the best option to select.

4. Select the appropriate options on the Delete User dialog box. When finished, the user account will be removed from the Select a User screen.

5. Close the Manage Users dialog box.

Data Security

Some of the data security options like security roles and permissions, are handled under user security. ACT! has the following types of data security.

① Record access
② Record Manager
③ Password policy

Record Access

This option determines which users can view the record. Access to records occur on two levels, as discussed below.

① Parent or Extended access
② Public or Private access

Parent Or Extended Access

Parent records are the contact, company and group records. Extended records are the notes, history, activity, opportunity and secondary contacts for the parent record. If a user does not have access to the parent record, they also do not have access to the extended records associated with the parent record. For example, if a user does not have access to the Jane Doe contact record, they will not have access to the records on the tabs (on the views) for the contact Jane Doe.

Public Or Private Access

Records that are marked as public can be viewed by anyone that has access to the database. Records that are marked as private can only be viewed by the Record Manager (record owner). If you have the need for more functionality to limit access, you will have to upgrade to ACT! Premium. Company and group records can be marked as private. Like many features in ACT!, there is more than one way to mark a record as public or private, as explained below.

① On the Contact detail view, click on the Contact Access tab and select Public or Private. [See Chapter 3, Contact Access Tab]
② On a Contact view (with all contacts displayed), Contacts ⇒ Edit Contact Access, as shown in Figure 19-38.
③ On the Contact list view, right-click on the records that you want to change the access of and select Edit Contact Access. You will see the submenu options shown in Figure 19-38.

Database Maintenance And Security

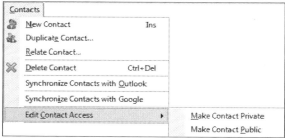

Figure 19-38 Edit Contact Access menu options

 There was a time when there was no option to make company or group records private. They were always public.

Record Manager

The Record Manager is the user that creates the record. Anyone that adds or edits data should have their own login account that has Record Manager rights. The reason is so that ACT! can fill in certain system fields with the name of the person that made a change to the record. An example of this is who created an activity for a contact. If you created an activity, but are logged into the database as me, ACT! would enter my name as the person that created the activity. Record Managers and Administrators can change who the Record Manager is.

Field Security

In addition to being able to add security to specific records, you can add security to individual fields. The security on system fields cannot be changed. The two types of field security are explained below. The next section shows you how to change the field security.

① **Read Only** Users can view, select and copy the data in the field, but cannot edit or delete the data.
② **Full Access** This is the default security option for all fields. Users have all of the rights that Read Only users have, plus they can edit, add and delete data in the field.

Assigning Field Security

The steps below show you how to assign security to a field.

1. Tools ⇒ Define Fields.

2. Open the **VIEW FIELDS FOR** drop-down list and select the Record type that you need to secure.

3. Select the field, then click on the **FIELD SECURITY** link in the Field Tasks section of the screen.

4. Select the permission that you want, as shown in Figure 19-39, then click Finish.

Figure 19-39 Field security options

With all of the attacks on data these days, you may be tempted to protect the database as much as possible. When applying field level security, there are some things to keep in mind when limiting access, as explained below.

① Even with administrator or manager rights, if your rights to a field are read-only you cannot import or export data for the field.
② You cannot sync fields that you do not have full access to.
③ The data in the field with read-only access cannot be used for queries and will not appear in a report.

Password Security

User accounts have the option of having password security. Earlier in Exercise 19.5 when you created a user account, you saw the password options. These user options are managed by an administrator through a password policy for the database.

How Users Change A Password

One of the policies that you can set is when user passwords expire. If that option is enabled, users have to change their password. Later in this chapter you will learn how to set a password policy. The steps below show users how to change a password.

1. File ⇒ Set Password. You will see the dialog box shown earlier in Figure 19-33.

2. Type the existing password in the **CURRENT PASSWORD** field. If the account did not have a password, this field has to be left blank.

3. Type the new password in the **NEW PASSWORD** and **CONFIRM NEW PASSWORD** fields, then click OK.

Password Policy

Password policies are created to provide more security for a database. Whenever you change the password policy, users are prompted to enter a password the next time that they log in if their current password does not meet the new password policy. The options discussed below are the password policy options that can be set. The X in the option name represents the number that you select.

① **User cannot reuse last X passwords** Is used to select how many of the previously used passwords cannot be reused. The maximum number that can be entered in this field is nine. For example, if this option is set to three, the last three passwords that were used, could not be used when the user creates the fourth password.
② **Password must change every X days** Is used to select in days how often users must change their password. If this option is set to zero, users do not have to change the password. (1)
③ **Minimum duration between password changes is X days** Is used to select the least number of days that a password has to be in use before the user can change it. (1)
④ **Password must be at least X characters in length** Is used to select the minimum number of characters that a password must have. Setting this option to one is the same as requiring a password. A zero means that the user can enter a password up to 25 characters, which is the maximum number of characters.

Database Maintenance And Security

⑤ **Password must contain X of 4 character groups** Is used to select the types of characters that the password has to have. The character groups are lower case, upper case, numbers and special characters. If the numbers option is selected, users must create a password that has at least one number in it.

(1) The maximum number for this field is 365 days.

How To Create A Password Policy

The steps below show you how to create a password policy.

1. Tools ⇒ Password Policy.

2. Select the options in Figure 19-40 that you want to use, then click OK.

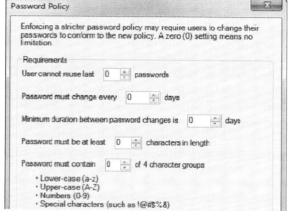

Figure 19-40 Password Policy dialog box

ACT! Diagnostics

This is a utility that comes with ACT! that is used to display databases that are stored locally. You can use it to maintain and repair databases, as well as, manage the local ACT! SQL server. Follow the steps below to run this utility.

1. Close ACT!.

2. Windows Start button ⇒ Run.

3. Type `actdiag` in the field, then press Enter. If you see the ACT! Diagnostics Disclaimer message, click OK.

4. Databases ⇒ Database List. You will see the dialog box shown in Figure 19-41. The menu options shown in Figure 19-42 are the database actions that you can use.

Chapter 19

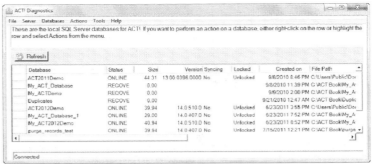

Figure 19-41 ACT! Diagnostics dialog box

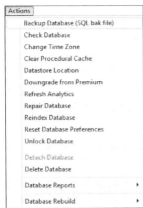

Figure 19-42 Database actions menu

19-25

USING CRYSTAL REPORTS WITH ACT! DATABASES

In this bonus chapter you will learn some of the basics of using Crystal Reports with ACT! databases. Hopefully, this chapter peeks your curiosity about creating reports outside of ACT!.

This chapter comes from my book, Using Crystal Reports 2008 With ACT! 2010 Databases. For more information, go to www.tolana.com/books/act.html.

About Crystal Reports

Crystal Reports is a software package that allows you to create reports. It is the report writing software that many companies use. Almost all businesses today that maintain data, have a need for reports to help them get their job done and to make business decisions. Reports allow one to be able to read and make sense of large amounts of information that is most often stored in a database. Most databases have limited reporting capabilities and only allow reports to be created in that "type" of database. Database types include Sybase, Microsoft SQL Server and Oracle, to name a few. These are often called SQL databases and are usually stored on a database server. Some of them do provide a desktop version that is used for learning purposes. If you need to create a report that has data (information) in both Oracle and Sybase databases for example, you would have to use Crystal Reports because neither database allows you to create reports that have data in other types of databases.

Crystal Reports provides the ability to use data from a variety of database types and combine the data in one report. Crystal Reports can use databases of any size. In addition to the SQL databases mentioned above, you can also use mainframe databases and what I call desktop or PC databases like Microsoft Access and Visual FoxPro. This type of database usually contains a lot less data than the SQL databases and do not have the capacity to support hundreds or thousands of end-users like SQL databases do. Crystal Reports also comes bundled with a lot of software development tools including Visual Studio. It also comes bundled with several leading software packages like PeopleSoft and JD Edwards. In addition to creating paper reports, reports can be exported to Word, Excel and PDF formats from Crystal Reports. You can create almost any type of report that you can dream up.

Normally, Crystal Reports is a read-only program, meaning that when you create or modify reports the data in the database is not changed. You can however, include SQL commands in the report, which will allow the report to edit, delete and add records to a database.

The primary goal of Crystal Reports is to allow a wide range of users to have the ability to work with the raw data in databases to be able to create reports that allow data to be interpreted and analyzed. Crystal Reports makes creating basic reports easier through the use of report wizards, which are similar to wizards that you may have used in other software packages. You can also create complex reports that include subreports, formulas, charts and much more.

Bonus Chapter Assumptions

Yes, I know one should never assume anything, but the following assumptions have been made. It is assumed that . . . .

- ☑ In addition to having ACT! installed, you have Crystal Reports 2008 or higher installed on your computer. If you are not sure what version of Crystal Reports you have, open Crystal Reports, then select Help ⇒ About Crystal Reports. At the top of the dialog box shown in Figure 20-1 you will see the version that you have.

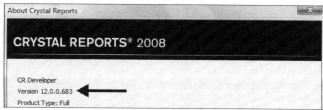

Figure 20-1 About Crystal Reports dialog box

Chapter 20

☑ If you do not have Crystal Reports installed, you can download a trial copy from http://www.sap.com/solutions/sme/freetrials.epx
☑ You know that the operating system used to write this chapter is Windows 7. If you are using a different version of Windows, some of the screen shots may have a slightly different look.

Crystal Reports Toolbars

There are five main toolbars in Crystal Reports: Standard, Formatting, Insert Tools, Navigation Tools and Expert Tools, as discussed below. They are right below the menu that you read about earlier in this lesson. Like toolbars in other applications, you can rearrange the toolbars by clicking on the dots at the beginning of the toolbar with the left mouse button and dragging the toolbar to a new location in the workspace. You cannot add or delete buttons on the toolbars, but you can turn off (remove) toolbars that you do not need or use. If you have used other Windows based applications, you are already familiar with many of the menu options. You will probably find that you will use the toolbar buttons more frequently then the options on the menu.

 Keep in mind that the buttons on the toolbars are available based on what you are doing and the object that is selected. There are some differences between the toolbar buttons and their menu counterparts. These differences will be pointed out.

Standard Toolbar

The Standard toolbar shown in Figure 20-2 contains options from the File, Edit, Format, View, Report and Help menus. Table 20-1 explains the purpose of each button on the Standard toolbar.

Figure 20-2 Standard toolbar

Button	Purpose
1	Creates a new report.
2	Opens an existing report. If you click on the arrow at the end of the button, you will see the last nine reports that you opened.
3	Saves the active report.
4	Opens the Print dialog box.
5	Displays the active report in the Preview window. This is the same as clicking on the Preview tab. You can click this button if the Preview tab is not visible.
6	Displays the active report as a web page in the HTML Preview window.
7	Opens the Export dialog box which is used to export the report to one of several popular formats.
8	Removes the selected object(s) from the report and places it on the clipboard.
9	Copies the selected object(s) to the clipboard.
10	Pastes object(s) from the clipboard into the report.
11	Copies (absolute or conditional) formatting properties from one object to one or more other objects. This is a shortcut to the Format Painter command.
12	Undoes an action. (1)

Table 20-1 Standard toolbar buttons explained

Using Crystal Reports With ACT! Databases

Button	Purpose
13	Redoes the last action that was undone. (1)
14	Toggles the Preview Panel on and off on the Preview window.
15	Opens the Field Explorer so that you can add fields and other objects to the report. (2)
16	Opens the Report Explorer so that you can see the objects on the report in tree view. (2)
17	Opens the Repository Explorer so that you can see the contents of the repository. (2)
18	Opens the Dependency Checker so that you can check reports for errors.
19	Displays or hides the Workbench.
20	Opens the Find dialog box, which lets you search for information in the report.

Table 20-1 Standard toolbar buttons explained (Continued)

(1) You can select how many changes that you want to undo and redo from the drop-down list. This capability is not available from the Edit menu.
(2) Clicking this button a second time does not close the Explorer window.

Formatting Toolbar

The Formatting toolbar shown in Figure 20-3 contains options to format objects. Table 20-2 explains the purpose of each button on the Formatting toolbar.

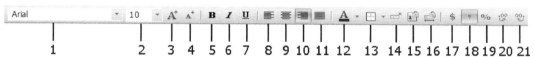

Figure 20-3 Formatting toolbar

Button	Purpose
1	Select a font.
2	Change the size for the font that is currently selected.
3	Increases the font size of the selected object one point each time this button is clicked. (3)
4	Decreases the font size of the selected object one point each time this button is clicked. (3)
5	Makes the selected object bold.
6	Makes the selected object italic.
7	Underlines the selected object.
8	Aligns the selected object flush left.
9	Centers the data of the selected object in the frame.
10	Aligns the data in the selected object flush right.
11	Justifies the data in the selected object between the length of the frame that the object is in.
12	This button is used to select or define colors in the Color dialog box. If you click on this button, the font color will change to the color that is on the line at the bottom of the button. Click on the arrow to change the color.
13	Applies the selected border to the object. You can select from several border style options. Click on the arrow to change the border style.

Table 20-2 Formatting toolbar buttons explained

Chapter 20

Button	Purpose
14	Suppresses the selected object. This means that the object will not print on the report.
15	Locks or unlocks the formatting of an object so that it can't be changed accidentally.
16	Locks the size and position of an object in relation to the object to its right.
17	Adds or removes the currency symbol in the selected numeric field.
18	Adds or removes the comma in the selected numeric field.
19	Adds or removes the percent sign in the selected numeric field.
20	Moves the decimal point in the selected numeric field one place to the right each time this button is clicked. (4)
21	Moves the decimal point in the selected numeric field one place to the left each time this button is clicked. (4)

Table 20-2 Formatting toolbar buttons explained (Continued)

(3) There is no menu option that has this functionality.
(4) Rounding is set to the number of decimal places in the field.

Font Size Tip
If the font size that you want is not in the drop-down list, highlight whatever size is showing in the font size drop-down list and type in the size that you want. You can also type in half sizes like 9.5.

Insert Tools Toolbar

The Insert Tools toolbar shown in Figure 20-4 contains additional report options. Table 20-3 explains the object type that each button will add to a report. These options are also available on the Insert menu.

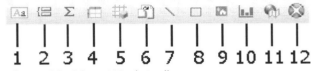

Figure 20-4 Insert Tools toolbar

Button	Is Used To Insert A ...
1	text object
2	group
3	summary field
4	Cross-Tab object
5	OLAP grid object
6	subreport
7	line
8	box
9	picture
10	chart
11	map
12	Flash object

Table 20-3 Insert Tools toolbar buttons explained

Using Crystal Reports With ACT! Databases

Navigation Tools Toolbar

The Navigation Tools toolbar show in Figure 20-5 contains options to navigate in a report and refresh data. This toolbar is activated once you preview a report. Table 20-4 explains the purpose of each button on the Navigation Tools toolbar.

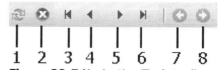

Figure 20-5 Navigation Tools toolbar

Button	Purpose
1	Refreshes the report data.
2	Stops the processing of data and only displays the report with the data that has been processed prior to clicking this button.
3	Displays the first page of the report.
4	Displays the previous page of the report.
5	Displays the next page of the report.
6	Displays the last page of the report.
7	Displays the previous page of the report. (5)
8	Displays the next page of the report. (5)

Table 20-4 Navigation Tools toolbar buttons explained

(5) This button is only available when you are using the HTML Preview option.

Expert Tools Toolbar

The Expert Tools toolbar shown in Figure 20-6 provides access to the experts, including the database, group and template experts. The buttons on this toolbar open dialog boxes that provide options to complete a task. Table 20-5 explains the purpose of each button on the Expert Tools toolbar. These options are also available on the Report menu.

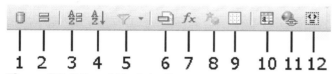

Figure 20-6 Expert Tools toolbar

Button	Purpose
1	Opens the Database Expert. It is used to add (or remove) data sources for the report.
2	Opens the Group Expert. It is used to create, modify and delete groups.
3	Opens the Group Sort Expert. It is used to find the Top or Bottom N records or sort the report on summary fields.
4	Opens the Record Sort Expert. It is used to select the order that the detail records will be sorted in.
5	Opens the Select Expert. It is used to create report selection criteria. (6)
6	Opens the Section Expert. It is used to format any section of the report.
7	Opens the Formula Workshop. It is used to create formulas and add functions to the report.
8	Opens the OLAP Cube Wizard. It is used to create a report that uses an OLAP Cube or .CAR FILE as the data source.

Table 20-5 Expert Tools toolbar buttons explained

Chapter 20

Button	Purpose
9	Opens the Template Expert. It is used to apply a template to a report.
10	Opens the appropriate Format Editor. It is used to modify formatting properties of the selected object.
11	Opens the Hyperlink tab on the Format Editor. It is used to add a hyperlink to a report.
12	Opens the Highlighting Expert. It is used to apply conditional formatting to an object.

Table 20-5 Expert Tools toolbar buttons explained (Continued)

(6) The Select Expert button has a menu, as shown in Figure 20-7.

Table 20-6 explains the Select Expert menu options.

Figure 20-7 Select Expert menu

Select Expert Button Menu

Option	Description
Record	Creates selection criteria based on a field.
Group	Creates selection criteria based on a group name or summary field. Group processing is done after the record processing.
Saved Data	Filters data that has already been saved with the report. This option reduces the number of times a database has to be refreshed. This is helpful for reports that have parameter fields. When selected, this option only uses data that has already been saved with the report instead of retrieving data from the database.

Table 20-6 Select Expert button menu options explained

Sections Of A Report

There are seven sections of a report that you can place data and other objects in. If you place the same calculated field in different sections of the report, it can produce different results (numbers, totals or amounts). It is important that you understand how each section of the report functions because they function independently of each other. Keep the following items in mind when deciding where to place fields and objects on the report.

① Not all sections are needed for every report.
② If you create a report using a wizard, the majority of fields are automatically placed in an appropriate section of the report.
③ All of the report sections discussed below except the group header and footer, will automatically appear in all reports, whether you use them or not. Grouping is optional.
④ The order of the default sections cannot be changed.
⑤ If a report does not need a section, it can be suppressed so that it does not display blank space on the report.
⑥ Sections can be resized vertically as needed.

Section 1: Report Header

Data fields and other objects placed in this section will only print at the top of the first page of the report. It is quite possible that many of the reports that you create will not have anything in this section. Something that you may want to include in this section of the report is the criteria and parameters of the report. If the report needs a cover page, the report header section can be used for the cover page. If this is what you need to do, add a page break after this section so that the actual report starts on a new page.

Section 2: Page Header

Data fields and other objects placed in this section will appear at the top of every page in the report except the report header page if it prints on a page by itself. This is where most people put the report title. Other objects that are commonly placed in this section include the date, page number and headings for the fields in the details section of the report. Report wizards will automatically place field headings and the system generated "print date" field in this section.

Section 3: Group Header

This section is only used if the data is grouped. Data fields and other objects placed in this section will print at the beginning of each group section of the report. Each time the data in the field the group is based on changes, another group header and footer section is dynamically created. This section is always right above the details section. If a report is grouped on two or more fields, a new group header and footer section will automatically be created for each field that the report is grouped on.

Section 4: Details

Data fields and other objects placed in this section will print for each record that meets the selection criteria. The data fields and other objects in this section usually have field headings in the page header section. This section is automatically repeated once for each record that will be printed on the report.

Section 5: Group Footer

This section is only used if the data is grouped. Data fields and other objects placed in this section will print at the end of each group. The group footer section often includes subtotals and other summary data for the group. This section is always right below the details section.

Section 6: Report Footer

Data fields and other objects placed in this section will print once at the end of the report. This is usually where grand totals and other types of report summary information is placed.

Section 7: Page Footer

Data fields and other objects placed in this section will print at the bottom of each page of the report. The page footer section is similar to the page header section. Page numbers are often placed in this section. Report wizards will automatically place the page number in this section.

ACT! Demo Database

This is the database that you will use as the basis for the reports that you will create in this chapter. The database has tables that store the following types of information: Contact, Company, Opportunity and Activities.

While the ACT! demo database has a lot of tables, many of them are used to link to other tables.

The main tables, as I call them, like Activity, Contact and Opportunity, do not have a large variety of data, which made is somewhat difficult to use a wider variety of fields in the exercises.

Figure 20-8 shows the data model for some of the tables in the database. The fields with the arrows are the **PRIMARY KEY** fields.

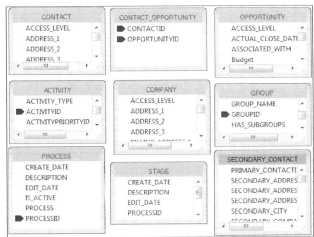

Figure 20-8 ACT! database data model

Why Do I Have To Connect To A Data Source?

First, I should explain what a data source is. A data source contains the underlying data for the report that you will create or modify. The most common data source is a database. In addition to there being several types of data sources that you can connect to, there are multiple ways to connect to some data sources. You connect to an ACT! database via the ACT! OLE DB Provider for Reporting 2.0 connection type that comes with ACT!. (This is why you need to have ACT! installed.) There are two reasons that you would need to connect to a data source, as discussed below.

① To view reports that do not have the data saved with it.
② If you want to create a new report or modify an existing report that does not have the data saved with it.

Exercise 20.1: Create Your First Report

I suspect that this is the moment that you have been waiting for - to create your first report. The first report that you will create is a report that only uses data from one table. The report layout is basic, but you will use almost every screen on the wizard dialog box so that you can become familiar with all of the options.

Using Crystal Reports With ACT! Databases

Step 1: Create A Connection To The Data Source

There are several types of data sources that you can use in Crystal Reports.

Figure 20-9 shows the categories of connection options that are available.

Even though you see an option for ACT!, you will not use it in this chapter.

Figure 20-9 Available connection options illustrated

 You may see different data source options depending on the data components that were selected when you installed Crystal Reports. You will also see data source options that you have added.

If you haven't created a connection to any ACT! 2010 or higher database, follow the steps below to create a connection. You can go to the section, Step 2: Select The Tables, if you already have a connection to the ACT! demo database.

How To Create A Connection To An ACT! 2010 Or Higher Database

1. Open Crystal Reports, then click on the **REPORT WIZARD** link on the Start Page.

2. Click on the plus sign in front of the **CREATE NEW CONNECTION** folder, then click on the plus sign in front of the OLE DB (ADO) option.

3. Select the **ACT! OLE DB PROVIDER FOR REPORTING 2.0** option illustrated in Figure 20-10, then click Next.

   Depending on your computers operating system, the demo database may be in a different location.

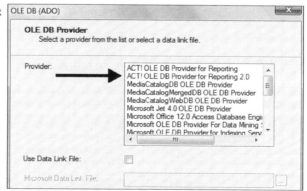

Figure 20-10 OLE DB (ADO) dialog box

On the Connection Information screen you have to enter the full path to the database. It would be really great if the developers would add a Browse button to the **DATA SOURCE** field.

Chapter 20

4. Type in the path to the database in the Data Source field. For example based on my installation, I would type C:\Users\MyUserName\My Documents\ACT\ACT Data\ACT2013demo.pad.

 OLE DB (ADO) connections are used to select a data source that has the connection information saved in a file. That is why you selected the ACT! .pad file in the Data Source option instead of the actual database (.dbf) file. The connection information is stored in this file.

5. Type Chris Huffman in the User ID field, as shown in Figure 20-11, then click Finish.

   You have completed creating your first connection to an ACT! database in Crystal Reports. That wasn't so bad, was it?

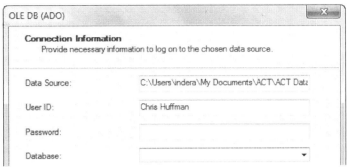

Figure 20-11 Connection Information screen

Step 2: Select The Tables

Under the OLE DB (ADO) connection option, you should see a connection to the demo database, as shown in Figure 20-12. The **DBO** and **SYS** nodes contain the tables in the database. The tables in the dbo node, shown in Figure 20-13, contain the data that you use in the ACT! demo database.

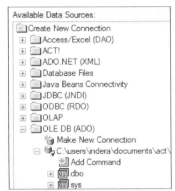

Figure 20-12 Connection to the ACT! demo database

Figure 20-13 Tables in the ACT! demo database

 The tables whose names start with ACT_ are similar to system tables, meaning that you probably will not have a need to use them for any of the reports that you create.

1. Click on the plus sign in front of the dbo node.

20-11

Using Crystal Reports With ACT! Databases

2. Click on the **PICKLIST** table, then click the **>** button.

    The Picklist table should now be in the **SELECTED TABLES** list, as shown in Figure 20-14.

    Click Next.

Figure 20-14 Picklist table selected

View The Data In A Field

The **BROWSE DATA** button on the Fields screen is used to view data in a field. This is helpful if you are not familiar with the data. This button is on several dialog boxes in Crystal Reports.

1. Click on the **DESCRIPTION** field, then click the **BROWSE DATA** button. You will see the dialog box shown in Figure 20-15. What you see is the data in the Description field.

    Click the Close button when you are finished viewing the data.

    If the dialog box does not display data, it means that no records in the table have any data in the field.

Figure 20-15 Data in the Description field

 Notice that the field **TYPE** and **LENGTH** are displayed at the top of the dialog box. This information is helpful because it tells you the type of field and the length of the field.

You can also view the data on the design tab. By default, the first 500 distinct values in a field are displayed. The actual values that you see can be changed by clearing the **SELECT DISTINCT DATA FOR BROWSING** option on the Database tab on the Options dialog box or on the Report Options dialog box, if you only want the change applied the current report. OK, that's the way that it is suppose to work, but it doesn't. If this actually worked, it probably is not a good idea to turn this option off because you could see duplicate data in the Browse Data dialog box shown above in Figure 20-15. But since it doesn't work, turning it off has no effect. If you want to view a different number of records, you have to modify this registry entry: HKEY_CURRENT_USER\Software\Business Objects\Suite #\Crystal Reports\DatabaseServer. Change the **MAXNBROWSEVALUES** decimal key to the maximum number of records that you want to see.

How To Find A Field

The **FIND FIELD** button is used to search for a field in the table. You will see this button on a few dialog boxes in Crystal Reports. I'm not sure that I understand the purpose of this button because all of the fields in a table are displayed on this dialog box. It could be helpful if you don't know which table a field is in.

Chapter 20

The Find Field button will only find the first field that matches the text that you enter in the dialog box shown in Figure 20-16. The first matching field that it finds depends on what field is currently selected in the Available Fields list. The search starts from the field that is selected and goes down the list. You can also enter a partial field name.

Figure 20-16 Enter Search Name dialog box

If the same field name is in more than one table, the search does not continue. If you were creating a report on your own, in the report design process you would have already written down a list of fields and where they are located because you learned to do this in the previous lesson <smile>.

Step 3: Select The Fields

1. Click on the Create Date field, then click the **>** button. You should see the field in the **FIELDS TO DISPLAY** list.

2. Add the following fields to the Fields To Display list: Name, Description and Picklist Type.

All of the items in the **AVAILABLE FIELDS** list are the fields in the Picklist table.

Figure 20-17 shows the fields that should have been added.

Click Next.

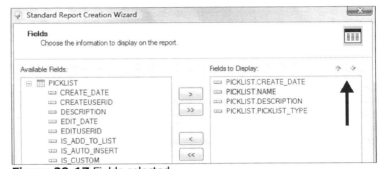

Figure 20-17 Fields selected

To add all of the fields in the table at one time, click the **>>** button. You do not have to select any fields before clicking this button.

To remove a field that you do not need on the report, click on the field in the Fields To Display list, then click the **<** button.

To remove all of the fields from the Fields to Display list, click the **<<** button.

 You can add several fields at the same time by clicking on the first field that you want to add, then press and hold down the **CTRL** key and click on the other fields, one by one that you want to add. When you have all of the fields selected that you want to add, click the **>** button.

The order that you add the fields to the Fields to Display list is the order that they will appear on the report in the details section from left to right. If you discover that the fields are not in the order that you want them to appear on the report, click on the field in the Fields To Display section and click the **UP** or **DOWN** arrow buttons illustrated above in Figure 20-17 to move the field to where it should be.

20-13

Using Crystal Reports With ACT! Databases

 When using a wizard to create a report, the order that the fields are in will change automatically if at least one field is selected to group on. Fields that are grouped on are moved to the beginning of the details section. You can rearrange the fields after the wizard has created the report. This does not happen when you create a report from scratch that has groups.

Notice in Figure 20-17 above that fields in the Fields To Display list have the table name in front of the field name. This is done to let you know which table the field is located in. This is helpful when you are using more than one table to create the report. Primary key fields in tables often have the same field name when the tables have related information. Without adding the table name, you would not know which table a field is in.

 Primary key fields are fields that are used to link one table to another table.

Step 4: Select The Grouping Options

Grouping is used to organize and sort the data. Grouping data forces all records that have the same value in the field that is being grouped on, to print together. Grouping data makes reports that have a lot of data easier to read. Grouping the data in a report is optional. You can group on more than one field. You can group on fields that have already been selected to print on the report, or you can select fields to group on that will not print on the report. The Accessibility report that you saw in the previous lesson uses the grouping option. That report is grouped on customer name and contact name.

1. Add the Picklist Type field to the Group By list. The default grouping option **IN ASCENDING ORDER** is correct. Figure 20-18 shows the grouping options that you should have selected. Click Next.

There are two options that you can select from to group the records by, as discussed below. This is how you sort the values that are in the field that is being grouped on.

IN ASCENDING ORDER This is the default grouping option. The values in the field being grouped on will be sorted in A to Z order if the field is a string field. If the field is numeric, the values will be sorted in 0 to 9 order.

IN DESCENDING ORDER The values in the field being grouped on will be sorted in Z to A order if the field is a string field. If the field is numeric, the values will be sorted in 9 to 0 order.

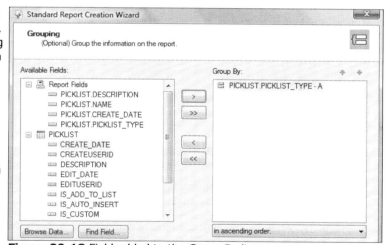

Figure 20-18 Field added to the Group By list

Chapter 20

 The only reason that I can think of to click the **CANCEL** button on a screen in the wizard is if you decide that you no longer want to create the report. You will lose all of the options that you have selected if you click the Cancel button. It is better to use the **BACK** button to go back and make changes because you cannot reopen the wizard to make changes or pick up where you left off.

Step 5: Select The Summary Options

1. Add the Name field to the **SUMMARIZED FIELDS** list.

Creating summary fields is optional. Summary options usually involve calculated fields.

By default, the wizard will create a summary field for all numeric fields that were selected to print on the report. You can remove the ones that are not needed.

There are built-in summary functions that you can use. Some of them are shown at the bottom of Figure 20-19.

The number of summary functions that are in the list depends on the data type of the field that you are summarizing on. Not all data types can use all of the summary functions. Many of the summary functions are only for numeric fields.

Figure 20-19 Summary function options

2. Open the drop-down list shown above in Figure 20-19 and select **DISTINCT COUNT**.

    Figure 20-20 shows the summary options that should be selected.

    Click Next.

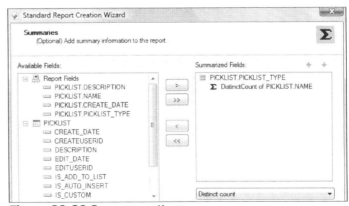
Figure 20-20 Summary options

20-15

Using Crystal Reports With ACT! Databases

3. Select the **TOP 5 GROUPS** option.

   Figure 20-21 shows the Group Sorting options that should be selected.

   Click Next.

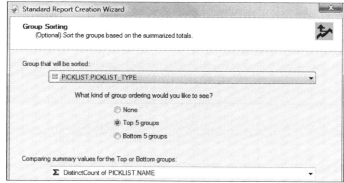

Figure 20-21 Group Sorting options

 The Top 5 Groups option will only display data for the five groups that have the highest value in the field selected in the **SUMMARY VALUES** field. Selecting **NONE**, which is the default, will display all groups. It is possible that you will not get the five groups that you think should appear on the report. This is because of the way that Crystal Reports processes data.

Step 6: Select The Chart Type

Adding a chart to a report is optional. Once you select a chart type, the wizard will fill in information for the other fields on the dialog box. If you are not sure what options to select, accept the defaults, preview the report and then decide which chart options need to be modified.

1. Select the **PIE CHART** option. Figure 20-22 shows the chart options that should be selected.

   Click Next.

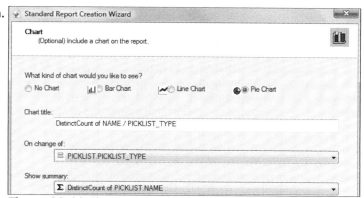

Figure 20-22 Chart options

Step 7: Select The Fields To Filter On

Creating filters is optional. Filters are another way that you can narrow down the number of records that will appear on the report. You can create more than one filter. In this step you will create a filter for the Is Add To List field to only display records that have True in the field.

1. Add the Is Add To List field to the **FILTER FIELDS** list. Open the drop-down list and select **IS TRUE**.

Chapter 20

2. Figure 20-23 shows the filter options that should be selected. Click Next.

   The filter that you just created will only display pick list items that have the value True in the Is Add To List field.

   Click Next.

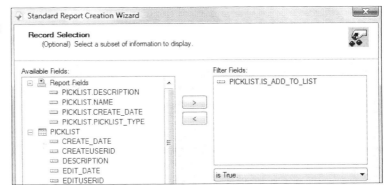

Figure 20-23 Filter options

Step 8: Select A Template

Selecting a template on the screen shown in Figure 20-24 is optional. If you do not want to use a template, select the **NO TEMPLATE** option. You can preview what the other template options look like by clicking on them.

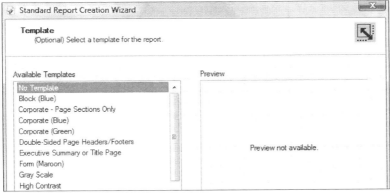

Figure 20-24 Template screen

1. Select the **CORPORATE (BLUE)** template, then click Finish. The first page of the report should look like the one shown in Figure 20-25. The top of the second page of the report should look like the one shown in Figure 20-26. As you scroll through the report, you may see things that you would like to change on the report.

In Step 4, because grouping options were selected, the **GROUP TREE** shown down the left side of the report in Figure 20-25, is displayed. Clicking on the options in the group tree will display that section of the report. If for some reason the group tree is not visible or you do not want to see it, you can click the **TOGGLE PREVIEW PANEL** button on the Standard toolbar to turn it on or off.

20-17

Using Crystal Reports With ACT! Databases

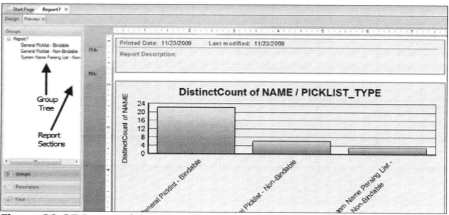

Figure 20-25 Page 1 of the report

PICKLIST_TYPE	CREATE_DATE	NAME	DESCRIPTION
General Picklist - Bindable	5/24/2006 2:37:46	Access Level	Security Access Level of a record
General Picklist - Bindable	5/24/2006 2:37:47	Activity Location	Available Locations for Activities
General Picklist - Bindable	5/24/2006 2:37:46	Cities	Master list of Cities
General Picklist - Bindable	5/24/2006 2:37:46	Company ID/Status	The categorization of a Company
General Picklist - Bindable	5/24/2006 2:37:46	Contact ID/Status	The categorization of a Contact
General Picklist - Bindable	4/24/2007 12:20:14	Contact Relations	Contact Relationship Roles
General Picklist - Bindable	5/24/2006 2:37:46	Countries	Master list of Countries
General Picklist - Bindable	4/28/2009 2:45:00	FDecision	

General Picklist - Bindable
Printed Date: 11/23/2009   Last modified: 11/23/2009

Figure 20-26 Page 2 of the report

Step 9: Save The Report

As shown earlier in Figure 20-25, the report was given a default name of **REPORT 1** which you can use. You should save the report with a name that is more meaningful. In addition to giving the report a meaningful name, you have to decide whether or not you want to save the data with the report, which is discussed below.

Save The Report

 The default file extension for reports is **.RPT** in Crystal Reports. Report file names can have up to 255 characters and can include spaces and special characters. Reports can be stored in almost any folder on your hard drive or server. You should not store reports in operating system folders.

1. File ⇒ Save As. Open the **SAVE AS** drop-down list on the Save As dialog box and navigate to the folder that you created.

 You can also click the **SAVE** button on the Standard toolbar when saving a report for the first time.

20-18

Chapter 20

2. Type My first report as the file name, as shown at the bottom of Figure 20-27, then press Enter or click the Save button.

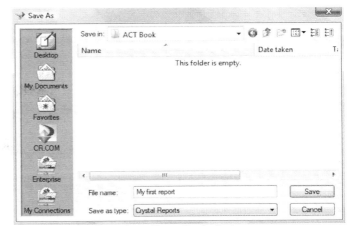

Figure 20-27 Save As options illustrated

Exercise 20.2: Create A Contact List Report

The fields that are needed to create this report are stored in two tables. This report will be grouped by the State field.

1. Open the Report Wizard, then select the ACT demo database connection.

2. Add the Contact and Contact Contact tables, then click Next.

Linking Tables

You will see the screen shown in Figure 20-28. The options on this screen are used to select the appropriate links for the tables that you have selected. Most of the time, the link that is automatically selected is the one that you need. Fields are automatically linked if they have the same name and compatible data type.

In other types of databases that I have used with Crystal Reports, the links that are automatically created do not have to be changed. I have noticed with ACT! databases, that I have to clear all of the links that are automatically created and create the links manually because too many links are created.

In this exercise, the tables should be linked by the Contact ID field.

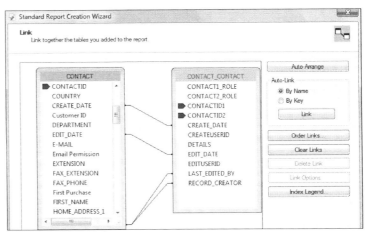

Figure 20-28 Link screen

20-19

Using Crystal Reports With ACT! Databases

 You may need to make the dialog box wider to see both tables. To make the dialog box wider, place the mouse pointer on the right side of the dialog box and drag the border of the dialog box to the right. You can also make the tables longer if you want to see all of the fields in the table.

 If you right-click on a field and select **BROWSE FIELD**, you will be able to see the first 500 unique values for the field that you selected. If you see more than one occurrence of the same value, it means that you have turned off the Select Distinct Data For Browsing option on the Database tab on the Options dialog box or on the Report Options dialog box.

Index Legend

As you saw earlier in Figure 20-28, there are colored arrows next to some fields. If you click the **INDEX LEGEND** button, you will see the index that each colored arrow represents.

Change The Links

1. Click the Clear Links button, then click Yes when prompted to remove all links.

2. Drag the Contact ID field in the Contact table to the Contact ID1 field in the Contact Contact table. You will see blue line connecting the fields.

Add The Fields To The Report

1. Click Next on the dialog box shown earlier in Figure 20-28, then add the fields in Table 20-7 to the Fields to Display list. Figure 20-29 shows the order that the fields should be in. Click Next.

Contact	Contact Contact
State	Contact 1 Role
Contact ID	
First Name	
Last Name	
Home Phone	

Table 20-7 Fields to add to the report

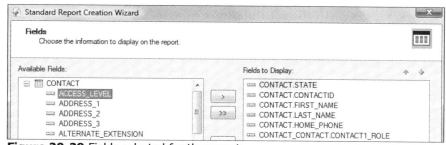

Figure 20-29 Fields selected for the report

Select The Grouping Options

This report would look better if it was grouped on the State field and within each State group, the contact names were sorted by last and first name. It would also be helpful if there was a count of contacts per state.

1. Add the State field to the **GROUP BY** list, then click Next.

Chapter 20

2. Add the Contact ID field to the **SUMMARIZED FIELDS** list.

3. Open the drop-down list and select **COUNT**. Figure 20-30 shows the summary options that should be selected.

    This option will count the number of Contact ID's in each state. When you want a count of records, you should select a field that has unique values. Each contact is assigned a unique ID. Think of ID's as being the equivalent of social security numbers, where each persons social security number is unique.

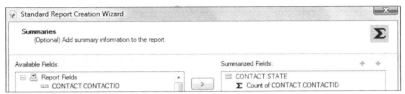

Figure 20-30 Summary options

4. Click Next. Click Next again on the Group Sorting screen because you do not need to change any of the options.

Select The Chart Options

1. Select the **BAR CHART** option.

2. Type `Count of contacts per state` in the **CHART TITLE** field.

Figure 20-31 shows the chart options that should be selected.

Figure 20-31 Chart options

20-21

Finish The Report

1. Click Finish because you do not need to select any other options.

   Your report should look like the one shown in Figure 20-32.

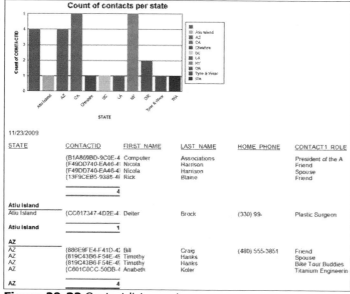

Figure 20-32 Contact list report

2. Close the report and save it as Contact list by state.

Exercise 20.3: Create The State = OH Or FL List Report

List reports are one of the easiest types of reports to create. The report that you will create in this exercise is a list report that selects certain records. In this exercise you will select options on the wizard that will filter the data in the Contacts table to retrieve contacts that are in OH or FL.

1. Open the Report Wizard and add the Contact table, then click Next.

2. Add the following fields: Company, Address1, State, Zip Code and Country, then click Next.

3. Click Next on the Grouping screen because this report does not have any grouping requirements. Add the State field to the **FILTER FIELDS** list on the Record Selection screen.

4. Open the drop-down list and select **IS ONE OF**, then open the next drop-down list and select **OH** or you can type it in.

Chapter 20

5. Open the same drop-down list that you just used and select **FL** or you can type it in.

   Figure 20-33 shows the filter options that should be selected.

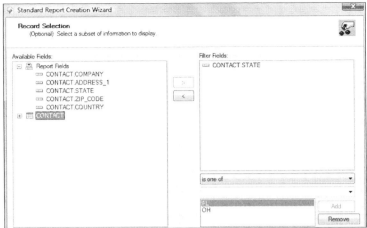

Figure 20-33 Record Selection screen options

6. The report does not require a template. Click **FINISH**. Your report should look like the one shown in Figure 20-34. Notice that a date field was automatically added to the report. Save the report as `State = OH or FL list`, then close the report.

12/1/2009				
COMPANY	ADDRESS 1	STATE	ZIP CODE	COUNTRY
Modern Electric Supply	1919 Tecoma Dr.	FL	34655	United States
Golf Greens Extraordina	1800 Boca Club Drive	FL	33487	United States
MRP Enterprises	6161 Busch Blvd.	OH	43229-2508	United States
Dylan Inc.	1881 Easton Dr	OH	44325	
Golf Greens Extraordina	1800 Boca Club Drive	FL	33487	United States

Figure 20-34 State = OH or FL list report

20-23

INDEX

.adf file, 1-14, 9-7
.alf file, 1-14
.aly layout file, 18-2
.cly layout file, 18-2
.cry query file, 13-2
.csv file, 10-28
.gly layout file, 18-2
.gry query file, 13-2
.oly layout file, 18-2
.ory query file, 13-2
.pad file, 1-14
.qry query file, 13-2

A

access level options, 3-15
ACT! demo database, 1-7
ACT! diagnostics, 19-24
ACT! e-mail editor tab preferences, 2-16
ACT! layouts, 18-2
ACT! Scheduler, 19-13
ACT! workspace, 2-2
act. close date option, 10-8
activities by user component, 12-18
activities dashboard, 12-2
activities list, 11-8
activities report, 8-8
activities tab, 2-10
Activity Component Filter dialog box, 12-7
activity components, 12-5
activity conflicts, 7-13
activity details tab options, 7-8
activity recurrence tab options, 7-8
activity series, 7-22
Activity Series dialog box, 15-12
Activity Series Template Creation wizard, 7-23
activity types, 7-5
Add Activity Type dialog box, 15-20
add column to a view, 15-7
add command to a menu, 17-2
add contacts to a group, 6-4
add contacts to an existing group, 6-7
add contacts to divisions, 5-16
add event to your calendar, 15-21
add field to a report, 16-8
add graphics to a layout, 18-9
add graphics to notes, 9-18
add page break, 16-17

add sections to a report, 16-15
Add Selected Contacts To Group dialog box, 6-7, 6-16
add summary field to a report, 16-10
Add Tab dialog box, 18-7
add to lookup option, 4-3, 4-7
Add/Edit Product dialog box, 10-10
Add/Remove Contacts dialog box, 5-7
Add/Remove dialog box, 3-8
address book, 8-15
address data type, 15-9
addresses tab, 5-14
adjusted for probability report, 10-21
admin tab preferences, 2-20
administrative dashboard, 12-2, 12-3, 12-9
advanced queries, 13-5
alarm, 7-10
Alarms dialog box, 7-11
align fields on a layout, 18-13
align fields on a report, 16-9
allow section to break across multiple pages option, 16-16
anchor date, 7-23
annual event data type, 15-9
annual event field, 18-12
annual events, 15-20
annual events lookup, 4-9
annual events report, 4-11
Annual Events Search dialog box, 4-10
appointment activity, 7-5
associate an opportunity to a company, 10-13
associate notes, 6-12
associate vs linking, 5-10
associating contacts to companies and divisions, 5-6
attach a file to a group, 6-9
attach button options, 3-9
attach document to a note, 9-10
attach file to a contact record, 3-9
attach files on the documents tab, 3-11
automatically link new contacts option, 5-9
automatically record history when contacts are linked or unlinked, 5-9, 10-13
automatically roll over to today option, 15-5
Auto-Run (smart task), 14-7

B

back button options, 2-5
back up command, 19-3
Back Up Database dialog box, 19-5
backing up personal files, 19-5
backup location, 2-13
backup tool, 19-3
banner option, 11-9
bar graph, 10-22
billing and shipping tab, 2-10, 5-14

C

calendar & scheduling tab preferences, 2-14
Calendar Access dialog box, 11-13
calendar filter options, 11-12
calendar pop-ups, 11-10, 15-4
calendar preferences, 2-14, 15-3
Calendar Preferences dialog box, 15-4
calendar status bar, 11-12
calendar toolbar, 11-7
calendar view related tasks, 11-16
calendar views, 11-7
call activity, 7-10
cell at end of the row option, 12-11
change color scheme of ACT! option, 1-7
change to be subgroup of option, 6-20
change user password, 19-23
changing the background color of
    a tab, 18-10
check and repair tools, 19-6
check for updates, 1-9, 2-20
check spelling before saving option, 2-19
check spelling before sending e-mail
    option, 2-16
clear activities, 7-20
Clear Activity dialog box, 7-19
clear future recurring activities, 7-19
clear group activity, 7-21
clear tasks from task list, 11-4
close an opportunity, 10-15
collapse if blank option, 16-16
colors & fonts tab preferences, 2-13
column on the far right option, 12-11
communication tab preferences, 2-17
companies tree, 5-4
company access tab, 2-10, 5-16
company comprehensive report, 8-10
company detail view related tasks, 5-20
company detail view toolbar, 5-3
company info tab, 5-16
company list view, 5-21
company list view related tasks, 5-21

Company Preferences dialog box, 5-9
company profile tab, 2-10, 5-15
Component Configuration wizard, 12-14
Component Filter dialog box, 12-7
Conflict Alert dialog box, 7-14
contact access tab, 2-10, 3-14
Contact Activity dialog box, 4-12
contact activity lookup, 4-11
Contact Criteria dialog box, 13-3
contact detail view related tasks, 3-17
contact detail view toolbar, 3-2
contact directory report, 8-7
contact info tab, 3-14
contact list view, 4-14
contact list view related tasks, 3-19
contact list view toolbar, 3-3
Contact Name dialog box, 3-4
contact report, 8-3
contacts dashboard, 12-2, 12-3
contacts tab, 2-10
control menu, 2-3
Convert Groups To Companies wizard, 6-18
copy a database, 1-15
copy calendar information option, 2-15
copy dashboard, 12-22
Copy Data dialog box, 9-5
copy note to another contact, 9-10
Copy/Move Contact Data Wizard, 19-10
copying data, 9-5
country codes, 3-5
create a database, 1-11
create a field, 15-17
create a report, 16-18
Create a Smart Task template, 14-9
create activity types, 15-19
create advanced query, 13-7
create annual event field, 18-12
create company record from contact
    record, 5-8
create company record, 5-5
create contact record, 3-3
create custom commands, 17-5
create custom menu, 17-3
create dashboard, 12-20
create divisions for a company, 5-5
create drop-down list field, 15-13
create dynamic group, 13-12
create envelopes, 16-23
create fields, 15-8
create graphs, 10-22
create group record, 6-4
create history record, 9-13
create labels, 16-23

create opportunities, 10-7
create password policy, 19-24
create process lists and stages, 10-27
create product list in Excel, 10-29
create quote, 10-19
create report section break, 16-17
create separate activity for each contact, 7-3, 7-8
create tab on a layout, 18-6
create user account, 19-15
created on/by fields, 3-15
Crystal Reports, 20-2
current lookup options, 4-3
custom date range, 8-8
custom menu, 17-3
custom menu and toolbar distribution, 17-10
custom report fields, 16-12
customize ACT!, 15-2
Customize Alarms dialog box, 15-6
Customize Columns dialog box, 15-7
customize columns on a tab, 15-8
customize field behavior, 15-10
Customize Menus and Toolbars dialog box, 17-2
customize products and processes, 10-26
customize report templates, 16-5
customize tabs, 18-6
customize task list view, 11-6
customize toolbar buttons, 17-9

D

daily calendar, 11-9
dashboard components, 12-5
dashboard designer, 12-9
dashboard designer menu, 12-10
dashboard designer toolbar, 12-10
dashboard designer toolbox, 12-11
dashboard layouts, 12-2, 12-5, 12-12
dashboard shortcut menu, 12-6
dashboard toolbar, 12-4
dashboard view related tasks, 12-22
data chart component, 12-20
Data Chart Designer dialog box, 12-20
data security, 19-21
data type options, 15-9
database defined, 1-6
database maintenance, 19-2
database naming conventions, 1-11
date data type, 15-9
date field calendar, 3-14
date/time data type, 15-9
dates field, 9-12

days open option, 10-8
default dashboard, 12-2, 12-4
Define Filters dialog box, 8-2
Define Sections dialog box, 16-15
delete a field, 15-18
delete activities, 7-22
delete attachments on notes tab, 3-11
delete column from a view, 15-7
delete contact records, 4-17
delete custom menus, 17-7
delete database tool, 19-3
delete duplicate records, 19-9, 19-12
delete groups, 6-17
delete multiple records, 4-17
delete recurring activities, 7-19
delete secondary contacts, 9-9
delete subgroups, 6-17
Delete User dialog box, 19-20
demo database, 1-7
detail view tabs, 2-10
details tab options, 7-8
distribute custom menus and toolbars, 17-10
division field, 5-21
divisions, 5-2, 5-5
divisions tab, 2-10
documents tab, 2-10, 9-14
Duplicate Checking dialog box, 2-21
duplicate company and division records, 5-17
Duplicate Contact dialog box, 3-16
duplicate contact information, 3-16
Duplicate Opportunity dialog box, 10-30
duplicate records, 19-9
Duplicate Subgroup dialog box, 6-21
dynamic group, 6-4, 13-12
Dynamic Group Membership dialog box, 13-14
dynamic link, 5-6
dynamic linking queries, 13-11

E

edit a shared note, 6-12
Edit Access dialog box, 11-13
edit activity series, 7-26
edit attachments, 9-18
edit conditions button, 14-5
edit history records, 9-13
Edit List dialog box, 15-16
edit list values option, 3-5, 15-15
edit mode option, 5-21, 9-4
edit notes, 9-10
Edit Phone Formats dialog box, 3-5
Edit Properties dialog box (layouts), 18-11
Edit Properties dialog box (reports), 8-12

edit queries, 13-10
Edit Shared History dialog box, 9-14
Edit Shared Note dialog box, 6-12
edit tab options, 18-7
Edit Tabs dialog box, 18-7
edited on/by fields, 3-15, 5-16
ellipsis button, 3-4
e-mail & outlook sync tab preferences, 2-15
e-mail button options, 2-5
e-mail report format, 8-3
E-mail Setup wizard, 2-15
enable preview option, 8-14
enter key, 3-3
Enter Phone Number dialog box, 3-5
envelope printing, 8-14
est. close date option, 10-8
exclude 'my record' option, 8-3
export data to Excel, 9-17
export opportunities to Excel, 10-16
export products, 10-30
export stages, 10-28

F

F4 key, 16-10
favorite reports option, 8-11
feature tours, 1-8
field behavior options, 15-10
field codes, 16-6
field data type options, 15-9
field defined, 1-6
Field Properties dialog box, 16-11
field security, 19-22
filter activities, 7-22
filter activities (calendar), 11-12
Filter Activities dialog box (task list), 11-4
Filter Calendar dialog box, 11-8
Filter Calendar Printout dialog box, 11-15
Filter Criteria dialog box, 12-21, 12-22
filter dashboard data, 12-7
Filter Notes dialog box, 9-10
Filter Opportunities dialog box, 10-7, 10-20
filter options (task list), 11-3
Footer Options dialog box, 2-18

G

general tab preferences, 2-12
generate history option, 3-16
generate quotes, 10-18
getting help, 1-8
global toolbar, 2-4
grant calendar access, 11-13
group access tab, 2-10, 6-20

group activities, 7-15
group address tab, 2-10, 6-20
group detail view related tasks, 6-22
group detail view toolbar, 6-2
group info tab, 6-20
group list view, 6-21
group list view related tasks, 6-22
group membership report, 8-9
groups, 6-2
groups tree, 6-3
groups/companies tab, 2-10

H

has divisions field, 5-21
hiding a tab, 18-7
hiding fields on a report, 16-13
hiding sections on a report, 16-14
hierarchy level field, 5-21
history record types, 9-12
history tab, 2-10, 9-11
home address tab, 3-13
HTML report format, 8-3

I

ID/Status field, 9-2
import products, 10-28
Import Products dialog box, 10-29
import stages, 10-27
include a label option, 16-9
include divisions option, 5-21
include private option, 4-4
include subgroups option, 6-22
include users option, 4-4
initial-caps data type, 15-9
Insert Note dialog box, 6-10
Insert Note dialog box toolbar, 3-6

K

keyboard shortcuts, 17-12
keyword search lookups, 4-4

L

label printing, 8-12
last workday of the month activity, 7-18
latest activities tab, 2-10, 3-15
layout designer, 18-2
layout designer formatting toolbar, 18-5
layout designer toolbox, 18-6
Layout Settings dialog box, 12-11
layouts, 18-2

limit to list option, 9-3
line graph, 10-24
Link To Company dialog box, 5-10, 5-20
linking and unlinking contact and
   company fields, 5-12
linking company and contact records, 5-9
locking a database, 19-2
Log On dialog box (share a database), 1-15
Log On dialog box (use a database), 1-13
look for option, 9-4
Lookup By Example dialog box, 13-3
lookup command, 4-2
lookup companies, 5-18
Lookup Contacts dialog box, 4-3
lookup groups, 6-6
lookup opportunities, 10-13
lookup records for a report, 16-19
lookup selected option, 9-4

M

mail merge contacts option, 3-19
Mail Merge Wizard dialog box, 5-22
Manage Activity Types dialog box, 15-20
manage drop-down list options, 15-14
manage group notes and attachments, 6-9
Manage Priorities dialog box, 15-19
Manage Product List dialog box, 10-12
Manage Smart Tasks dialog box, 14-2
marketing call activity, 7-5
marketing results tab, 2-10, 9-17
memo data type, 15-9
menu bar, 2-3
menu modification, 17-2
mini-calendar, 11-7
modify dashboard layout, 12-12
Modify Dictionary File dialog box, 2-19
modify envelopes, 16-22
modify labels, 16-22
modify menus, 17-2
modify report sections, 16-14
modify user field, 15-16
monthly calendar, 11-11
move companies and divisions, 5-19
move contact records between
   groups & subgroups, 6-15
Move Group Option dialog box, 6-19
multiple field lookup, 4-6
my activities component, 12-18
my record, 1-10

N

Name Preferences dialog box, 15-2
narrow lookup option, 4-3, 4-6
navigation pane, 2-4
navigation pane customizations, 17-13
navigation pane lookup options, 4-2
new button options, 2-5
New Contact dialog box, 3-8
New Database dialog box, 1-13
New History dialog box, 9-11
New Report dialog box, 16-3
New Smart Task dialog box, 14-5
notes tab, 2-11, 3-6, 9-9
notes/history report, 8-11

O

omit selected option, 9-4, 9-5
online manuals, 1-8
open date option, 10-8
Open/Share Database dialog box, 1-15
operators, 13-6
opportunities, 10-2
opportunities tab, 2-11, 10-20
opportunity access tab, 2-10, 10-2
Opportunity Component Filter dialog
   box, 12-8
opportunity components, 12-5
opportunity dashboard, 12-2, 12-4
opportunity detail view, 10-2
opportunity detail view related tasks, 10-30
opportunity detail view tabs, 10-2
opportunity detail view toolbar, 10-4
opportunity details tab, 10-11
opportunity graphs, 10-22
opportunity info tab, 2-10, 10-2
opportunity list filters, 10-5
opportunity list report, 10-7
opportunity list view, 10-4
opportunity list view related tasks, 10-31
opportunity list view shortcut menu, 10-6
opportunity list view toolbar, 10-4
opportunity pipelines, 10-25
opportunity reports, 10-20
opportunity status bar, 10-6
opportunity status options, 10-8
options button drop-down list, 6-13
Options dialog box, 8-16
outlook synchronization preferences, 2-16

P

page break options, 16-16
parent or extended access, 19-21
password policy, 19-23
password protected databases, 1-13
password security, 19-23
PDF report format, 8-3
Pending Smart Task Steps dialog box, 14-8
permissions, 19-19
personal activity, 7-5
personal file back up process, 19-5
personal files, 9-7
personal files locations, 2-12
personal info tab, 2-11, 3-13
phone list report, 8-7
phone number formatting, 3-5
picture field on a report, 16-18
pipelines, 10-25
pivot table data, 10-17
pop-ups, 11-10, 15-4
position tab, 8-13
preferences, 2-12
Preferences dialog box, 2-12
preview area, 6-13
primary contact fields, 3-16
print address book, 8-15
print calendars, 11-14
Print dialog box, 8-14
print envelopes, 8-14
print labels, 8-12
print opportunity list option, 10-7
print task list, 11-5
printer report format, 8-3
printing, 8-12
private access option, 3-15
private activities, 7-5
private option, 3-10
private status, 2-11
probability field, 10-8
process list, 10-9
product list, 10-12
products/services tab, 2-10, 10-2
Promote Secondary Contact dialog box, 9-9
promote subgroup to group option, 6-20
properties window (layouts), 18-4, 18-10
properties window (reports), 16-10
public access option, 3-15
public activities, 7-5
public or private access, 19-21
public status, 2-11
purging a database, 19-8

Q

queries, 13-2
query operators, 13-6
query syntax, 13-8
quick print current window option, 8-17
Quick Print Options dialog box, 8-17
quick print preferences, 2-17
quote preferences, 10-18
quote.adt file, 10-19
quote.xlt file, 10-19

R

random activities, 7-17
rearranging column order, 15-6
recap list, 11-9
recap list calendar, 11-8
record access, 19-21
Record Creation Options dialog box, 9-16
record defined, 1-6
Record History dialog box, 9-11
record manager, 19-22
record manager field, 3-15
recurrence tab options, 7-8
recurring activity types, 7-15
referred by field, 9-2
refreshing linked data, 5-9
Region and Language dialog box, 15-10
reindex databases, 19-6
Relate Contact dialog box, 3-12
related tasks, 2-8
relationships, 3-11
relationships tab, 2-11, 3-11
remove a report section, 16-16
remove contacts from companies or groups, 6-17
remove old data, 19-8
rename a group, 6-6
Replace Data dialog box, 4-13
replace field command, 4-13
replace lookup option, 4-3
report creation options, 16-2
report custom date range, 8-8
report designer, 16-3
report designer editing toolbar, 16-4
report designer formatting toolbar, 16-4
report designer toolbox, 16-7
report print preview toolbar, 8-5
reports menu, 8-2
reports view, 8-11
reports view related tasks, 8-17
reports view toolbar, 8-12
reschedule activity, 7-12

rescheduling a conflicting activity, 7-14
reset menus and toolbars, 17-12
reset passwords, 19-18
resize columns in a view, 15-6
resize fields on a layout, 18-9
resize fields on a report, 16-7
resize handles, 18-9
resize report section, 16-10, 16-17
resize workspace, 2-9
restore databases, 19-7
restore options, 19-7
rich-text report format, 8-3
Roll Over Activities dialog box, 15-5
row at the bottom option, 12-11
run as administrator, 1-12, 1-16
Run Query Options dialog box, 13-4

S

Sage connection services, 2-8
sales analysis by record manager
  report, 10-21
Salutation Preferences dialog box, 15-2
Save Copy As dialog box, 1-16
save font in my list view option, 8-17
save lookup as a group or company, 6-13
saved queries, 13-4
Scan For Duplicate Contacts dialog box, 19-9
schedule a call, 7-10
schedule a to-do, 7-6
schedule activities for other users, 7-10
schedule activities on the calendar, 11-12
Schedule Activity dialog box, 7-2
Schedule Activity Series
  dialog box, 7-26, 15-12
Schedule for dialog box, 7-4
schedule opportunity activities, 10-12
scheduled by field, 11-6
scheduled for field, 11-6
scheduling preferences, 2-14
Scheduling Preferences dialog box, 15-5
scratchpad, 9-18
Search on Keywords dialog box, 4-5
secondary contacts, 9-7
secondary contacts tab, 2-11
sections of a report, 16-4
security, 19-15
security roles, 19-18
Select A Field To Group By dialog box, 16-15
Select Contacts dialog box, 3-7, 6-5
Select Date Range dialog box, 8-8
Select Field dialog box, 16-8, 18-8
Select System Field dialog box, 16-8

Select Users dialog box, 9-13
send invitation email option, 7-3, 7-9
Set Index dialog box, 18-14
setup assistant wizard, 1-9
share this database with other
  users option, 1-12, 1-16
show data as chart option, 12-20
show dynamic membership option, 13-13
show for drop-down list, 6-13
show grid lines options, 2-14
show legend, 12-21
show navigation bar button, 8-6
show point labels, 12-21
Smart Task Conditions dialog box, 14-5
smart tasks, 14-2
Snooze Alarm dialog box, 7-12
social updates tab, 2-10
sort activities, 7-22
sort contact list view by columns, 4-15
Sort dialog box, 4-17
sort records, 4-16
sort records from a query, 13-11
source of referrals report, 8-11
Spelling Preferences dialog box, 2-18
startup database button, 2-19
Startup Database dialog box, 2-20
startup tab preferences, 2-19
startup view options, 2-19
static group, 6-4
static link, 5-6
static members, 6-6
status bar (calendar), 11-12
status bar (opportunity), 10-6
status bar (task list), 11-2
status field lookup 10-14
subdivisions, 5-3
subgroups, 6-14
subgroups tab, 2-11
submenus, 17-4
subreports, 16-20
Subreports dialog box, 16-21
supplemental files, 9-7
swapping data, 9-6
system tabs, 18-6

T

tab key, 3-3
tab stop order, 18-14
tab stops, 18-4
table name in lookup, 10-15
tag all option, 9-4
tag mode options, 9-4

tagging contacts, 9-3
target size option, 12-11
task list filter options, 11-3
task list lookup, 11-3
task list options button, 11-3
task list status bar, 11-2
task list toolbar, 11-2
task list view, 11-2
task list view related tasks, 11-6
text boxes, 18-8
text report format, 8-3
themes, 2-14
timeless activities, 7-5
today (calendar) button, 3-14, 11-10
toolbar button customization, 17-9
toolbar modification, 17-8
toolbox (dashboard designer), 12-11
toolbox (layout designer), 18-6
toolbox (report designer), 16-7
triggers, 15-11

U

universal search, 4-8
unlink company record field, 5-16
Unlink From Company dialog box, 5-19
untag all option, 9-4
URL address data type, 15-9
use banner option, 7-3, 7-8
user account creation, 19-15
user account deletion, 19-20
user account editing, 19-19
user dictionary, 2-18
user field modifications, 15-16
user fields tab, 2-11, 3-15, 5-15, 10-2

V

vacation activity, 7-5
view activity with multiple contacts, 7-9
view attachments on notes tab, 3-11
view contacts in a group, 6-8
View Groups/Companies dialog box, 3-18
view layouts, 2-22
View Linked Fields dialog box, 5-13
view menu, 2-22
view other users calendars, 11-14

W

web info tab, 2-11, 9-16
weekly calendar, 11-10
welcome view, 1-6
wildcards, 13-4

work week calendar, 11-10
workspace, 2-2
write e-mail using template, 5-20, 6-21
write letter option, 3-18

Y

yes/no data type, 15-9

No Stress Tech Guides

ISBN: 978-1-935208-23-5

ISBN: 978-1-935208-22-8

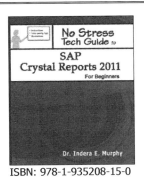
ISBN: 978-1-935208-15-0

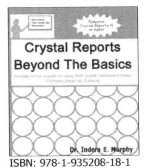
ISBN: 978-1-935208-18-1

ISBN: 978-1-935208-16-7

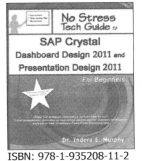
ISBN: 978-1-935208-11-2

ISBN: 978-1-935208-14-3

ISBN: 978-1-935208-00-6

ISBN: 978-0-9773912-7-1

ISBN: 978-1-935208-12-9

ISBN: 1-935208-01-2

ISBN: 978-1-935208-05-1

ISBN: 978-0-9773912-9-5

ISBN: 978-1-935208-17-4

ISBN: 978-1-935208-10-5

ISBN: 978-1-935208-08-2

Visit us online to see the entire series www.tolanapublishing.com

Made in the USA
Lexington, KY
07 September 2016